Praise for *System Architecture with XML*

In a fast-moving, dynamic environment like XML and system design, it is hard to keep up and understand the principles underlying the technologies. In *System Architecture with XML,* Daum and Merten capture the fundamentals of three fields that are shaping XML in a way that provides insight critical to building effective and persistent XML-based system architectures.

> —Dave Hollander, CTO of Contivo, Inc. and cochair
> of the W3C XML Schema Work Group

This inspiring and lively book is a solid and practical guide for IT architects.

> —Efstratios Koutiris, IT Architect

System Architecture with XML covers today's most important issues in XML specifications and technology. It is a "must read" for architects who need to integrate XML into their enterprise systems.

> —Tom Marrs, Senior J2EE/XML Architect,
> Distributed Computing Solutions, Inc.

A well-researched book from a solid real world perspective. It gives a broad overview of XML systems architecture on top of a strong foundation.

> —Daniel Krech, Semantic Web Developer/Architect,
> Redfoot.net

System Architecture with XML brings together object-oriented and relational theory with XML best practice, and it introduces a wide-ranging survey of current techniques and cutting-edge tools for XML application developers. I recommend it to anyone wanting to learn the basics and beyond about the design of XML systems.

> —Jeni Tennison, Director, Jeni Tennison Consulting, Ltd.

System Architecture with XML

About the Authors

Berthold Daum holds a Ph.D. in mathematics and was a codeveloper of NATURAL 4GL at Software AG. He has lectured in database design at the University of Karlsruhe and has practical experience in the design and implementation of large distributed online systems. In the 1980s, he became involved in artificial intelligence and was a member of the ISO standardization committee for PROLOG. Currently, Daum runs a consulting agency for industrial communication. He has published various articles in trade magazines and scientific publications, and he is coauthor of the recent book *Success with Electronic Business* (Addison-Wesley).

Udo Merten holds a Ph.D. in economics. He is cofounder of *Dr. Merten + Steinke Information Management GmbH,* a consultancy firm specializing in the development of interactive electronic business applications and the automation of business processes. Merten has authored and coauthored various articles in scientific publications and contributions to conferences.

System Architecture
with XML

Berthold Daum

Udo Merten

MORGAN KAUFMANN PUBLISHERS

AN IMPRINT OF ELSEVIER SCIENCE

AMSTERDAM   BOSTON   LONDON   NEW YORK
OXFORD   PARIS   SAN DIEGO   SAN FRANCISCO
SINGAPORE   SYDNEY   TOKYO

Acquisitions Editor	Tim Cox
Assistant Publishing Services Manager	Edward Wade
Production Editor	Howard Severson
Editorial Coordinator	Stacie Pierce
Cover Design	Yvo Riezebos
Text Design	Mark Ong
Illustration	Dartmouth Publishing Industries
Composition	TBH Typecast, Inc.
Copyeditor	Ken DellaPenta
Proofreader	Mary Roybal
Indexer	Ty Koontz
Printer	Edwards Brothers

Cover Credits: Marrakech, Morocco, Africa/Guido Alberto Rossi/Imagebank

Designations used by companies to distinguish their products are often claimed as trademarks or registered trademarks. In all instances in which Morgan Kaufmann Publishers is aware of a claim, the product names appear in initial capital or all capital letters. Readers, however, should contact the appropriate companies for more complete information regarding trademarks and registration.

Morgan Kaufmann Publishers
An Imprint of Elsevier Science
340 Pine Street, Sixth Floor
San Francisco, CA 94104-3205, USA
www.mkp.com

07 06 05 04 03   5 4 3 2 1

Library of Congress Control Number: **2002107238**
ISBN: 1-55860-745-5

This book is printed on acid-free paper.

Foreword

Peter Mossack
Vice President of Research and Development
Software AG

What's all the fuss about a markup language? Read this book and you'll find out!

XML represents a movement. It is similar in nature to the "open" movement. Open source, open interfaces, open (operating) systems. In fact, XML is the next pillar in this movement. It can be viewed as the open movement extended to the Internet. It is because of this that, as a set of pure standards, XML is looked after by the World Wide Web Consortium.

However, the whole world is talking XML, and the ramifications of its universal adoption are only beginning to surface. Whole business models will be affected by it; whole new business interests are being pursued because of it. The software industry itself will be rocked by it more than it cares to admit. This is so because XML brings us into the promised land of componentware. Take XML-based componentware, add the Internet, and you get Web services. A very explosive mixture indeed!

By adhering to open standards, smaller companies with strong vertical knowledge will be able to deliver components and services that can be integrated with those of other suppliers, and so be able to compete effectively in their area of expertise.

Besides the purely technical merit of this, what lies at the bottom of the movement is an unwillingness on the part of the consumer of technology, especially the corporate consumer, to be continually locked in by megavendors of proprietary technology and application software.

Since a technology lock-in also implies economic dependency, there are real business reasons behind the open movement. It is therefore very important that people involved in making technology decisions, as well as business decisions based on technology, understand the basis of it.

This book should not only help with this, but also provide the reader with food for thought in conceiving and conceptualizing new strategic applications based on XML technology.

Contents

Preface

XML is an explosive mix. It is set in a triangle made up of document processing, traditional data processing, and the Internet (see Figure P. 1). Its language roots are in well-established document processing technologies (SGML), its technology moves massively into the area of databases and enterprise IT technology, and its application is mainly to establish communication between collaborating parties on the Internet, extranet, and intranet.

The same three ingredients also define electronic business:

Electronic Business = Internet + Enterprise IT + Documents

XML is thus well positioned as a core technology for the rapidly growing area of electronic business (see Figure P. 2). Its adoption by the industry has consequently been quick. Although the initial hype has faded away, XML has now achieved mainstream status in the corporate IT world. The question of today for XML is not *if* but *how*.

A recent study done by the Giga Information Group (2001) among companies that use XML shows

- 45% use XML for mission-critical applications.
- 13% use XML for non–mission-critical applications.
- 40% use XML for pilot applications.

The study shows also that XML is used in different areas. Not surprisingly most areas are somehow connected to communication and integration:

- 33% use XML for data exchange and messaging.
- 27% use XML for application integration.
- 13% use XML for data integration.
- 12% use XML for content publishing.
- 6% use XML for the construction of portals.
- 6% use XML for other purposes.

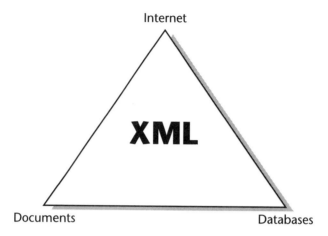

Figure P.1 Set between three technologies: XML.

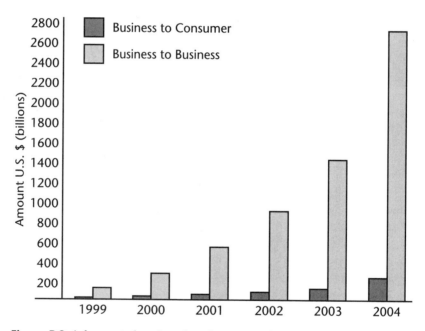

Figure P.2 A forecast showing the phenomenal growth of U.S. electronic business, especially in the area of business-to-business (B2B). (Source: Forrester Research.)

Given these fairly disparate application areas and the triangle of documents, databases, and Internet, we witness an extraordinary culture clash: document people trying to understand what a transaction is, database analysts getting upset because the relational model doesn't fit anymore, and Web designers having to deal with schemata and rule-based transformations.

Finally, when they have sorted out their differences, they start to realize that agreement about "where to put the brackets" is only the first step in mastering what is probably the most difficult thing on earth: human communication. What lurks behind the standardization of communication *structures* are the semantic aspects of communications, the vocabularies, thesauri, ontologies, and contexts—a topic that has been placed onto the agenda of the W3C under the name "Semantic Web," and optimistically scheduled for 2003!

ABOUT THIS BOOK

It was this situation that made us write this book. The first step when different technologies meet is to do an inventory of what is there. The second step is a critical review in the light of the new requirements. Finally a synthesis can be tried and a new technology begins to emerge.

So, if you are expecting a description of the final tried-and-tested XML architecture, this book isn't for you. Such a thing does not exist, not yet. (Maybe it never will.) But if you have an inquiring mind and want to look over the fence, this book is definitely for you. But be warned: you may end up more curious about XML and related technologies than you were before. At least, that is what happened to us . . .

People with a background in document processing will find it interesting how they can use conceptual modeling to model business scenarios consisting of business objects, relationships, processes, and transactions in a document-centric way. They might also discover that XML can be used for some things that are very different from "library style" documents—standards such as SMIL and SVG allow the definition of rich multimedia presentations.

Database people might wonder if XML is subject to relational normalization and how this meshes with the hierarchical structure of XML documents. We will therefore revisit tried and tested modeling techniques such as entity relationship modeling, but we will also introduce asset-oriented modeling—a new technique that is better suited to capturing the higher-order relationships between entities and artifacts.

Web designers will discover that XML puts them into a position to automatically generate visually pleasing Web pages and rich multimedia shows from otherwise dry product catalogues by using XSLT and other transformation tools. They will also learn why "hard linked" Web pages are bad, and what the alternatives are to allow for sophisticated navigation by end users.

Business architects will see how XML can help them to define applications that can be quickly adapted to the ever-changing requirements of the market. Hard-coded workflows and business rules in applications are replaced by XML documents that can be changed quickly. Even better: new technologies like ebXML allow business partners to negotiate common business processes in an automatic or semiautomatic fashion.

Chapter 1 sets the *scenario*. We compare the Internet with an unplanned settlement. XML can be the glue that holds it all together to build an infrastructure. We strongly argue that—because XML is really about communication—the current challenge is to build medium-scale well-working applications that can communicate with each other. We present some architectural patterns that have proved to work.

Chapter 2 lays the *groundwork*. It discusses many of the W3C and other basic standards and techniques related to XML: DTDs, XML Schema, XPath, XPointer, Xinclude, XML Base, XLink, XQuery, XSL, SAX, DOM, Schematron, and architectural forms.

Chapter 3 discusses techniques to model the *structure* of information. We revisit good old entity relationship modeling and also introduce asset-oriented modeling—a modeling method that is easy to use and fits well into an XML-oriented architecture. We show how RDF can be utilized to describe conceptual models, and how UML can deal with XML.

Chapter 4 moves from structure to *meaning*. Communication across company borders and company mergers demonstrates that it is not sufficient to agree about the structure of information. We discuss ways to model semantics, such as ontologies and topic maps. If you want to know what the Semantic Web is about, here it is!

Chapter 5 takes a close look at modeling *processes* such as workflows or business processes. We show how process can be described by means of XML.

Chapter 6 introduces a layered approach to *communication*. We discuss channels, ports, messages, transactions, and scenarios in the context of open communication across company borders.

Chapter 7 illustrates ways of *navigation* that go beyond links in Web pages. With WebML we discuss an integrated approach from conceptual model to finished Web site. We revisit topic maps as a powerful means for an independent navigation layer. We also discuss the navigational possibilities that exist with peer-to-peer communication.

The topic of Chapter 8 is *presentation*. XML isn't just about data representation and communication; it is also the basis for powerful multimedia standards such as SMIL, SVG, and XSL formatting objects.

Chapter 9 deals with document *transformation,* in particular with XSLT, with its advantages and shortcomings. We take a look at alternatives, too.

Chapter 10 introduces recent standards that define an *infrastructure* for electronic business. In particular we discuss SOAP, WSDL, UDDI, and most importantly, ebXML.

Chapter 11 acts as a showcase for existing *solutions*. We look into (the still rare) XML-related design tools, discuss XML-enabled database management systems and middleware solutions such as RosettaNet and BizTalk (even the non-XML technology e-speak), and finally some XML-related authoring tools.

The glossary explains relevant terms in the context of XML and electronic business.

ACKNOWLEDGMENTS

This book incorporates many research and development results from a number of XML-oriented communities. Our first debt of gratitude is to our colleagues in and the members of those communities. Without their work, this book would have never happened. We also render our deepest appreciation to all the people that helped us in so many different ways at the various stages in the writing of this book.

First we would like to thank Morgan Kaufmann Publishers and dpunkt.verlag for giving us the opportunity to publish our work. It has been a great pleasure, indeed, to work with the people at MKP and dpunkt. Thanks go especially to Tim Cox and Stacie Pierce from Morgan Kaufmann, who patiently helped us through the materialization and publication of the book and had to put up with our slightly Teutonic English, and to Rene Schönfeldt from dpunkt, who guided us from the very beginning of the project.

We also deeply acknowledge the work of our reviewers: Tom Jell, Kevin Jones, Jeff Jurvis, Janne Kalliola, Eve Maler, Tom Marrs, and David

Orchard. Their enthusiasm, expertise, and wisdom have helped us in bringing this project to success. Their invaluable advice has significantly improved the book in detail and overall structure.

Our rough manuscript was brought into shape and was transformed into a real book by the production staff at MKP. Howard Severson was the production editor, Ken DellaPenta was the copyeditor, Mary Roybal did the proofreading, and Ty Koontz did the indexing. After seeing the marked-up manuscript, we know how much we owe these four.

Thanks go also to our friends at Software AG, especially to Nigel O. Hutchinson, Michael Kay, Peter Mosack, Jonathan Robie, and Walter Waterfeld for providing valuable insight into the world of XML Schema, XQuery, XSLT, and native XML databases. Thanks go, too, to Tina Eisinger from altova GmbH for helping us with the production of XML Schema diagrams.

And finally, none of this could have been realized without the help of our families and friends. Family members and partners, friends and colleagues suffered a lot—not only with us but sometimes also because of us—in countless situations. When the going gets tough. . . . Our thanks and love goes to all of you for helping us and patiently supporting our work throughout the entire authoring process.

Scenario

X ML would not exist if there were no Internet. Without the requirements of the open and diverse Internet community, the extensibility and standardization of XML would be wasted. Therefore, XML architecture must take the Internet into account: its topology, its philosophy, and its history.

In this chapter, we first take a look at the topology of so-called nonplanned settlements, which applies to the Internet. We argue that architects must, above all, be good communicators who facilitate mutual learning between the Net squatters.

Aside from that, there are a few common concepts that become more important in such an environment. Applications increasingly consist of collaborating but separate units, instead of being implemented as monolithic blocks. Soft logic, such as the formulation of business rules with XML, allows reconfiguring applications rapidly, and techniques derived from artificial intelligence allow the configuration in a more declarative way.

Finally, we look at some of the more common architectural patterns currently found on the Internet such as catalogues, workflow orchestration, repositories, and more.

A list of top-level best practices for XML architecture closes this chapter.

1.1 MEGAPOLIS INTERNET

This section first reports on the outcome of a trip to the Bauhaus but then moves quickly from African villages to communities on the Internet.

1.1.1 The Nonplanned Settlement

During a visit to the Bauhaus Institute in Dessau, Germany, one book in the institute's bookshop caught my attention. It was titled *Non-planned Settlements*. My first thought was the Internet. My second thought was to buy the book. On closer examination it turned out that it did not deal with the Internet at all but with the topology of African villages and some of the world's megacities. One result of the author's research was the discovery that the network of roads, streets, and paths in these settlements was arranged in such a way that the effort to travel between A and B plus the effort to maintain this network is close to minimal (Schaur 1991). Similar networks were found in nature (leaves, insect wings). The author was also able to obtain these structures by simulation: because the equations proved to be too complex for silicon-based computers, more traditional means like soap water, wet threads, and sand were used.

Well, she got me hooked. I did a bit more research on unplanned settlements and discovered that most unplanned settlements serve the requirements of their residents better than formally planned settlements (Portela 1992). Although unplanned settlements usually start with low-quality housing, the housing and the infrastructure continually improve and result in many cases in higher-quality housing than obtained with formal planning because the inhabitants are in control (Figure 1.1).

The Internet's architecture

What made me buy this book without further hesitation was the fact that the Internet is nothing but a nonplanned settlement. That does not mean, however, that the creation of Internet technology was unplanned; in fact, Internet technology was created as the result of a careful planning process by the U.S. Department of Defense. What I mean is that the current topology of the Internet is not the result of a single planned process. Nor was the speed with which the Internet and especially the World Wide Web grew in any way anticipated. The computer and software industry, for example, was completely taken by surprise.

Figure 1.1 Architecture that works. Structural patterns of a Mediterranean megapolis.

Also the way the Internet would be used was not anticipated. First planned as a computer network for military use, it was soon taken over by scientists and became a major communication device between scientific institutions worldwide. Then, beginning in 1995 the Internet became commercial and—by now—electronic business is the main driving force in the development of the Internet (Daum and Scheller 2000).

Five years later we are a bit wiser. We have witnessed tremendous success stories on the Web, but we have also seen many dot.coms and some other Internet squatters vanishing. Many ideas that looked good on paper did not succeed in the field. Even a technically brilliant company like Sun Microsystems ("The network is the computer") had to retarget a major development (Java moved from the browser to the server).

While the reasons for these "failure stories" are manifold—and not all are of a technical nature—we feel that in many cases the problem was that the Internet introduces a new set of challenges into software engineering. Traditional software engineering concepts are certainly valid within an enterprise context, but for the macro level of the settlement Internet they are simply inappropriate.

Not required are architects who try to superimpose the tried-and-tested constructs of the past—such as three- or four-tier client-server architectures—onto the Internet world. Not that there is anything wrong with these models (they have served well within the enterprise world), but what is really required in the global village are architects who act as communicators and multipliers, architects who enable the inhabitants of the Internet to learn from each other and to improve their levels of skill and self-organization. The architects of systems become architects of communication. Let's see how.

1.1.2 Topology—Transactional, Relational, Navigational

The first time two users were connected to the same computer, the computer ceased to be a plain but expensive calculator and became a communication device. Data that was entered by one user could be read and modified by another user.

Transactional topology

The first of these systems evolved at a time when computer hardware needed huge halls, air-conditioning, and specialist operators. Embedding computers into end user devices was unthinkable. End users communicated with the computer through teletypes and later through cathode ray tubes (CRTs) and keyboards. In terms of software, a major paradigm evolved at this time: the transactional multiuser database was developed. These databases guaranteed that a user could safely process a certain work unit (a transaction); the system guaranteed that a work unit was completely processed (or not at all) and that other users could not interfere. Neither a system crash nor concurrent activities could corrupt the data. The transactional approach is still a core paradigm of today's enterprise computing.

The situation changed when microelectronics made computers small enough to fit on a desktop. When cheap workstations and PCs arrived on the market, departments would simply buy these devices without asking the computer center or corporate controllers for permission. They had done this before with typewriters. In the view of the enterprises' computer centers this was just another case of unplanned settlement. It evolved because it served the requirements of the users better than the centralized IT departments could. New functionality in shrink-wrapped packages could be bought in the computer shop around the corner. The traditional way of sending a request to the IT department and waiting for months for its realization had become too slow for a faster-moving business world.

But, with the now ubiquitous desktop machines, users had acquired a problem. Their computer had regressed from being a communication machine to being a simple typewriter or calculator. Data was exchanged on floppies, resulting in chaos and a data jungle.

To establish communication again, it was necessary to connect the desktop machines to a network. Local area networks (LANs) were introduced, and the former computer center now operated the enterprise's servers, where the critical data of the enterprise was held. This was the beginning of the client-server era. The client on the desktop would be responsible for the (mostly graphic) user interface and for application logic, while the server in the computer center would run the big databases and care for database backup and security. The role of the computer center had changed: instead of caring for individual "housing," it cared for the public infrastructure.

This had consequences for the database software, too. The old CODA-SYL databases were too inflexible for this job. Because many different clients with different requirements could hook up to the same server, it was necessary that the same data could be interpreted in different "views" (different combinations of data elements) depending on the application of the client. Relational databases were able to solve this problem. Because these databases store the data in the form of very simple, basic tables, they allow the arbitrary recombination of this data at will. While relational technology had already developed alongside transactional systems, it had its breakthrough with client-server technology.

Relational topology

The Internet, and especially the World Wide Web, have changed this landscape once again. In the classic client-server scenario the relation is "many clients, one server," and usually both client and server work in the same enterprise environment. In the World Wide Web it is, in contrast, not one server but millions of servers in millions of enterprises. Each client can access any server on the Web and any Web service. In a few years, it will be billions of servers: any device connected to the Internet and able to hold data—a PC, a PDA, or an embedded device—can act as a Web server.

What does this mean for the user? It means that a vast array of new services are (or soon will be) available on the desktop, in the car, or in the palm of the hand—services that were previously unthinkable, or services that can be better performed by a third party than in-house. While in the beginning of the Internet only a few basic services were offered (email, home pages, search engines, file transfer), the landscape is now getting more and more diverse. The range goes from financial services like credit card validation, to community services such as an ontology server for the knitwear industry or a knowledge base for hazardous chemicals, to generic applications hosted by Internet service providers.

Navigational topology

Navigation and service discovery

The most frequent activity for a Web client thus becomes—besides performing transactions—navigation and service discovery. In real cities we are used to using certain helpful devices to find what we want. There are street and telephone directories. We know that shopping malls host the full spectrum of shops we need for daily life. If we don't know our way around, we can rely (more or less) on the expertise of a taxi driver or of a passerby. And so on.

On the Internet things are similar. Within the short time of its existence the Internet has developed certain patterns that can help us in the task of navigation. There are simple structures like Web rings or Web communities, sophisticated search engines and directory services, and fully serviced marketplaces and portals. More recently, peer-to-peer technology has gained a lot of attention, especially, but not only, for exchanging MP3 records.

1.1.3 Babel

Open standards

The development of the Internet and the World Wide Web was made possible through the definition of open standards. Among those that have shaped the Internet are

- TCP/IP (Transmission Control Protocol for the Internet)
- HTTP (Hypertext Transfer Protocol)
- SMTP (Simple Mail Protocol)
- FTP (File Transfer Protocol)
- HTML (Hypertext Markup Language)

Hardwired semantics

All these standards serve a specific task—they have clearly defined semantics. The HTML specification, for example, not only describes the syntax of Web pages, but also defines how a browser has to process the elements of an HTML Web page. Measured by numbers, these standards have been a tremendous success. Given the decentralized nature of the Internet, it is difficult to get reliable statistics, but it is estimated that by the end of 2000 more than 400 million users were connected to the Internet (Nua Internet Surveys) and that servers stored about 2 billion Web pages, with 7 million new Web pages being created every day.

But the hardwired semantics of these standards (especially those of HTML) have led to a problem: it is difficult to adapt this technology to new application domains. Consequently HTML was subject to a number of proprietary "enhancements" during the period of the "Browser Wars" in the late 1990s. Today, Web pages consist of a wild mixture of HTML, JavaScript, Java, Shockwave, and so on, augmented by server technology to generate dynamic Web pages such as ASP, JSP, Java Servlets, CGI, and so on.

The release of the XML recommendation in 1998 marks a break in this tradition (Bray, Paoli, and Sperberg-McQueen 1998). XML was designed not as a special-purpose language but as a "mother of languages," a generic metalanguage. The goal of its definition was extensibility. However, the initial perception of XML was that of a "successor for HTML," a misconception that needed to be clarified before XML could really take off. The purpose of XML is not to become a better HTML (although one of its applications, XHTML, is the designated successor of HTML) but to allow interested user groups the definition of their own specific languages.

And this is exactly what has happened since then. In the few years of its existence, XML has been the basis for numerous (approximately 500) language definitions, some of which are covered in this book. There is probably not one single human being—except perhaps Robin Cover (*www.oasis-open.org/cover/*)—who has an overview of all XML-based language definitions.

In this context, some commentators have talked of "Babelization." This is, in fact, what this plethora of languages looks like at first sight. To understand what is going on, we have to take a deeper look into human nature in general.

1.1.4 Subcultures and Ontologies

You have probably already guessed it: the Bible is right—Babel belongs to the human condition (Figure 1.2). Although English has become a world language, it is hard to say *which* English is the world language. One word processor lists the following flavors: English (Australia), English (Belize), English (Great Britain), English (Ireland), English (Jamaica), English (Canada), English (Caribbean), English (New Zealand), English (Philippines), English (South Africa), English (Trinidad), English (USA), English (Zimbabwe). This doesn't mean that a reader of English (USA) necessarily understands what a writer of English (USA) has written—not if they belong to different scientific communities or different trades. Medical scientists speak a different language than nuclear scientists, and their vocabulary vastly differs from that used by social scientists, computer programmers, or butchers.

In the world of the Internet, XML can play a similar role as a universal language. It acts as a common substrate on which different special-purpose languages can be developed. Some of the 500 XML-based languages exist because they serve specific purposes—for example, SMIL for

Figure 1.2 Architecture that didn't work—the Tower of Babel.

multimedia presentations and VoiceXML for speech processing. Others came into existence for the simple reason of competition: some manufacturer wanted to stake a claim in the virtual world of e-business.

Is this really so bad? We don't think so. The existence of 500 XML-based languages is not a sign of confusion; it simply shows that XML has made its way into many different application areas.

Later we will see that the definition of an XML-based language can be compared to the definition of a database schema: both define an ontology, a—albeit narrow—concept of the world. As virtually each enterprise and each organization fosters its own database schema, there would be millions of "languages" to learn if we were to try to exchange data on a bilateral basis between two companies using relational technology. This has been more or less the approach of classic EDI (electronic data interchange). EDI worked well in some subcultures of the IT community, such as the automotive industry, however, only on a bilateral basis.

But this approach does not work on the Internet: the number of agreements between partners rises astronomically, and the process of negotiation is too slow. What is needed in electronic business are standards that apply to a whole community of prospective partners. Within the last few years, such standards have been developed by industry associations and interest groups. Horizontal standards (i.e., standards that apply to certain tasks like procurement or product data exchange) have been developed by IT companies and universities. These standards act as unifying forces across the various industries. In contrast, vertical standards, used within an industry, divide the Web into subcultures, such as the automotive industry, the health industry, librarians, museums, and so on. Each of these subcultures nurtures its own ontology; that is, it uses a certain vocabulary and thinks in certain associations and contexts.

So why not use one language for all? The answer is simple:

One language for all?

- *Complexity.* A language able to express any topic in the world would be so complex that nobody could define it, nobody could agree upon it, nobody could implement it, and nobody could learn it.
- *Responsiveness.* The world is moving fast, especially the world of electronic business. Adapting a one-for-all language to ever-changing requirements would require a constant change of this language, making development with such a language almost impossible.

It is, therefore, a misconception to understand XML as *the* language for all. We should rather see XML as a core technology for the implementation of special-purpose languages and document schemata. Within Internet and electronic business, XML can play a similar role as SQL did for relational databases. In contrast to SQL, the scope of XML goes far beyond data storage and also covers domains such as communication, presentation, process control, and navigation.

1.1.5 Challenges

The Internet poses new challenges for software developers and software architects alike—challenges that, if they existed in a closed enterprise scenario, would play only a minor role there.

Communication
The ability to communicate *across* company borders is essential for future enterprise IT systems. This includes communication not only with other businesses but also with consumers and administration. New technologies like mobile computing and embedded systems extend the reach of corporate IT systems. Typical-use cases include supply chain integration, health system integration, remote monitoring (vending machines, home appliances, industrial equipment), traffic control, and others.

Service-Oriented Architecture
The traditional integration of enterprise services via EDI happened to be hardwired and manual. Establishing a new (bilateral) EDI relationship

between partners was a lengthy and expensive process. Within enterprises, however, more advanced IT technologies evolved. Component technologies like CORBA allowed the integration of software components in a flexible and dynamic way. Services offered by components could be published within a network. Other components could discover these services and establish a binding to them.

Loose coupling

On the Internet these techniques proved to be too tightly coupled. Emerging XML-based standards such as SOAP (see Section 6.5.2), WSDL (Section 6.6.3), UDDI (Section 7.3), and ebXML (Section 10.3) were introduced to allow for a loosely coupled, service-oriented architecture. Typical Web services include credit card validation, shipping, fulfillment, marketplaces, mediation, brokerage, and so on.

Knowledge Retrieval

Semantic networks and Semantic Web

XML-based formats like RDF (Resource Description Framework) and XTM (XML Topic Maps) allow the modeling of semantic networks (see Chapters 4 and 7). Topic maps especially have become a core technology for content management solutions, while RDF is seen by the W3C as the basis for the construction of the future Semantic Web (Berners-Lee 1998a).

Navigation

The chaotic nature of the Internet requires powerful navigation tools. Knowledge retrieval technologies will aid end users and software agents in finding the target destination. Similar technologies, based on RDF, topic maps, and directory services (see Section 7.3), will, for example, allow manufacturers to locate possible suppliers for a product or service.

Mediation

The existence of hundreds of different subcultures on the Web, and also the existence of millions of legacy systems, requires powerful mediation services. Already existing are XML processors that are able to hook up with relational databases and to map XML document types to relational schemata. Similar services can mediate between different XML dialects and schemata.

Flexibility and Responsiveness

The Internet changes every day. New sites are connected to the Internet; new technologies and standards are introduced in short order. This requires a software architecture that is flexible enough to incorporate new, and even previously unknown, technologies. The classical development cycles of months and even years are out of the question: it must be possible to make changes to business rules effective almost instantly.

The traditional way to implement business rules—hardwired within program code—will certainly continue to exist in legacy code. For new developments it will give way to "soft-coded" business rules—business rules that are formulated in some description language, possibly an XML-based description language (see Chapter 5). Business rules coded that way are easy to change and to deploy and can even be exchanged between applications.

Soft-coded business rules

Similarly, the navigational structures will cease to be hard-coded (i.e., links in HTML pages) but will give way to soft-coding techniques using RDF (see Section 3.3), topic maps (Section 7.2), or XLink linkbases (Section 7.1).

Process Model

The backbone of classical enterprise applications is the database transaction. Although the transaction model works well in applications that are orchestrated by human operators and with transactions spanning only a short time (milliseconds to a few seconds), it does not work well for automated business processes that span a longer time, from a few hours to even years. These long-running processes are typically found in electronic business applications, enterprise application integration, and workflow systems (see Chapter 5). They must be persistent (i.e., survive a system crash or shutdown), be portable (which rules out proprietary formats), and offer the possibility of compensating actions (e.g., canceling an order). Several proprietary formats to describe business processes have been developed, some of them based on XML. The definition of a common standard is still an issue.

Long-running processes

Autonomy

Applications in electronic business have to organize business processes autonomously. Human operators can be called in for certain tasks or for assistance, but they no longer drive the process. Business processes must be able to modify themselves, for example, when a change in environment conditions is detected, when new services are discovered, when the best option is temporarily not available, or when new intelligence is gained on how a certain goal may be achieved. For example, a sales agent may react intelligently when the market situation changes (e.g., change prices or move to a different marketplace).

Trusted Information Sources and Traceability

Since anybody can publish information on the Internet, the information found there is sometimes not trustworthy. Systems that rely on information found on the Internet, such as agents, knowledge retrieval systems, intelligent search systems, or self-modifying processes, must be able to distinguish between "hard" (trusted) and "soft" information sources. Mediation systems and knowledge processors must be able to trace back and reveal on what basis a certain result was obtained.

1.2 IMPLICATIONS

In the following sections we'll discuss some of the implications of XML technology on the current IT landscape.

1.2.1 The Blurring of the Classical Application

On the Web the classical stand-alone application vanishes. Electronic business applications turn more and more into temporary and changing constellations of Web services. Single instances on the Web provide low-order services such as authentication, credit card validation, directory services, mediation services, logistics, and so on. Higher-order services such as a whole business process invoke these lower-order services—in sequence or simultaneously.

Web services

Web services are currently the catchphrase, most notably since Microsoft announced its .NET initiative. As we have just pointed out, Web services can act as building blocks for business processes, and all major developments in this area, such as BizTalk, RosettaNet, or ebXML, provide a way to express the orchestration of business processes via XML (Chapters 10 and 11).

Using the Web as an infrastructure for interaction will change the nature of the Web itself. We are used to the Web as a huge library of hyperlinked documents. (Try *www.shibumi.org/eoti.htm* for the ultimate link.) Since the beginning of the Web, these documents have become more colorful, more animated, and interactive. However, the essential character of the Web stayed the same: it is a library, consisting of (relatively) few servers and an overwhelming mass of clients. The Web of the future will consist of a huge mass of whatever-the-name-will-bes, combining the functionality of servers and clients. These units will host active and autonomous objects (or agents) that interact with each other in a peer-to-peer (P2P) fashion. Maybe we will still call the Web "the Web" then, but we also might call it "the Brain." We will look into P2P technology in Section 7.4.

1.2.2 Collaboration Instead of Integration

Although at the end of the 1990s "enterprise application integration" became the catchphrase of the IT industry, it now is becoming more and more obvious that *integration* is not what the industry really needs. An enterprise with a tightly integrated IT infrastructure (such as, for example, a huge ERP system) in the e-business world would be about as maneuverable as a big oil tanker in a yacht regatta.

Building ad hoc business relationships or setting up virtual enterprises for specific business models does not require integration but *collaboration* between autonomous partners. More often than not, collaboration with external partners has proved to be more productive than cooperation between internal departments, so much so that the principle of collaborating autonomous work units is now even applied within the enterprise. The traditional hierarchical enterprise structure has given way to a more democratic model.

The consequences for XML architectures are that we don't have to think in terms of megaprojects, but in terms of medium-sized applications and specialized Web services with an open communication structure. XML with its extensibility allows for such loosely coupled, open communication structures.

No megaprojects!

1.2.3 The Return of AI

Many techniques related to XML remind us of techniques developed when artificial intelligence (AI) became an issue in the 1980s. Techniques such as rule-based programming (e.g., in XSLT), semantic networks (e.g., with topic maps), agent technology, and reasoning on the Semantic Web can draw on experiences had during this period when expert systems and programming in logic comprised the latest hype.

This makes sense, indeed. As the Web becomes more complex every day, AI methods become more necessary to successfully navigate the Web, publish and discover business services, negotiate protocols, or mediate between different ontologies.

1.2.4 Soft Logic

Moving around and making business in the megapolis Internet requires—as we pointed out—some intelligence. Other than in the closed world of the enterprises' information systems, we experience on the Internet very diverse environments and conditions. The *context* of operation frequently changes. Software systems must be able to negotiate this change of contexts. We will discuss this in detail in Section 4.4.

It requires, too, that systems have the ability to compromise. In many cases it might not be possible to obtain the best solution. This could have technical reasons, for example, when a server is down. Or it could have business reasons, when for example a supplier is booked up by the competition. In this case, an automated system must be able to go for a good solution instead of the best solution (wait for the server to go up again or search for another supplier).

In other cases, the distinction between "required" and "should" is by design in order to achieve a certain normative behavior without imposing restrictions that are too harsh. Administrations (such as customs or environment control) usually have rules and laws that *must* be enforced and others that *should* be enforced. If we model such behavior into software agents, we end up with systems that can negotiate and find compromises (Raskin and Tan 1996). Then it is time to talk about ethics for computers. Just see John McCarthy's novel *The Robot and the Baby* (McCarthy 2001).

1.3 ARCHITECTURAL PATTERNS

At the time of writing, XML has already made the transition from "if" to "how." It is no longer a question *if* corporations and software manufacturers will employ XML to provide solutions, but it is still very much a question *how* this can be done. Often the methodology to be used is unclear, and the available tools and infrastructure are still scarce and do not have the same maturity as, for example, relational technology.

The biggest problem is the human factor. Today, software engineers in the field of XML come from three directions: from the SGML camp, from the object-oriented camp, and from the relational camp. We can therefore expect—and, indeed, we do experience—that techniques and skills learned in these fields will be employed in the new field of XML. This will occasionally result in frictions and misunderstandings, but it is not really bad. Eventually the technological crossover will breed a new discipline of design and programming, of which we now only see a glimpse.

This requires an attitude of learning mutually from each other and opening the mind to new ideas. Members of the SGML camp, for example, who are used to a more document-centric design style, will have to adapt to the more data-centric style. They will also find that concepts such as entity relationship modeling and referential integrity are exciting new fields where there remains a lot to do. Members of the SQL camp, in contrast, will miss concepts of referential integrity in XML but will find that the rich structuring possibilities that exist in XML open a whole new world of database design. Finally members of the object-oriented camp will sadly miss a behavior model in XML documents. On the other hand, they may find it exciting that XML actually does make remote procedure calls work across company, platform, and language boundaries.

This situation is also the reason why this book goes a bit deeper into theory than usual. In the current situation, where none of the existing design methods exactly fits the new technology, it can be beneficial to take a close look at the science.

But before we do this, let's take a look at some applications and structures that have already been built with XML. In the following two sections we will list a few popular architectural patterns. As our earlier metaphor of the unplanned settlement suggests, we will structure this overview into the sections "Dwellings" and "Community Infrastructure."

What you will not find in this book is a blueprint for a large-scale application based on XML. Another large-scale application would be the last thing we would want to build with XML. We do not need another Tower of Babel, and we do not need another XML-ified ERP technology. What we do need is for ERP manufacturers to open up their packages and make the functions available as Web services—with the help of XML. In fact, this is what they currently do.

1.3.1 Dwellings

In this section we present a few architectural patterns that could be compared with a single dwelling, the typical "family home." They are applications that either operate within an enterprise or organization or somehow showcase the enterprise to the outside world. Usually these applications follow the classical client-server architecture, which typically consists of three tiers: a database tier, a middle tier, and a presentation tier.

Patterns

Catalogues
This pattern is used for catalogues of all kinds, in particular for product catalogues.

The *database tier* consists of a native XML database storing product data in XML format or of a relational database containing product data and an XML wrapping layer.

Three tiers

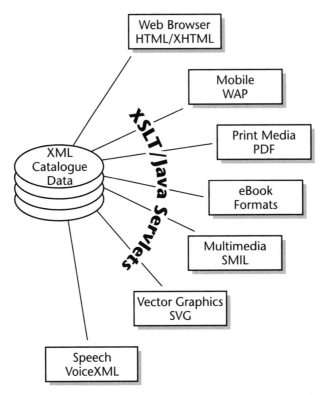

Figure 1.3 A transformation layer converts presentation-neutral catalogue data into a variety of presentation formats.

The *representation tier* consists of client software, typically Web browsers that are equipped with suitable multimedia plug-ins. The formats used here are HTML or XHTML combined with XML-based multimedia formats such as SVG and SMIL. Alternative clients are mobile, WAP-enabled devices, eBook devices, or even plain old telephones that are driven via VoiceXML.

Between these two tiers exists a *transformation tier*, typically implemented in the form of XSLT style sheets, Java servlets, and/or Java Server Pages (JSP) that transform the presentation-neutral product data into the required presentation format (Figure 1.3).

Encyclopedias

This pattern can, as a matter of fact, be used to implement online encyclopedias, but it is also applicable to other forms of knowledge bases, anywhere that navigation structures are required that are independent from

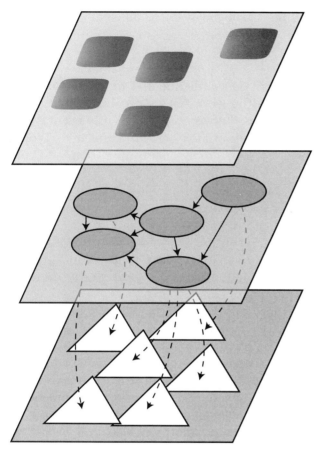

Figure 1.4 The navigation layer separates navigation from presentation and content.

the physical layout of the data. It can be used to apply sophisticated navigation techniques to whole Web sites, product catalogues, Web shops, and so on. It allows the establishment of semantic relationships between Web resources and can provide additional access structures to users such as links, paths, indices, taxonomies, guided tours, and so on.

It adds a separate navigational layer that is independent from the physical structure of the knowledge base (Figure 1.4). The separate navigation tier can be implemented with technologies such as topic maps, RDF, or XLink linkbases. This allows for easy modification of navigation structures without touching the actual resources or the representation logic. It also easily allows the implementation of different navigational structures for different types of users.

Soft-coded navigation tier

In combination with the catalogue pattern, different presentation forms are possible.

Workflow System

Orchestration   While the previous two patterns leave the initiative to the end user, the workflow pattern orchestrates the work tasks for a single end user or multiple end users. However, workflows can react to user events, thus leaving a controlled part of the initiative with the end user. Typical applications are shopping systems, supply chain integration, and content management.

The workflow pattern again consists of an XML database tier (XML repository) storing not only the resources and artifacts of the work process, but also the description of the workflow itself.

The workflow tier (Figure 1.5) consists of a workflow engine interpreting the workflow description, which is typically formulated in XML. Depending on the state of the workflow, certain resources or artifacts are presented to the user for viewing or editing.

In combination with the catalogue pattern, different presentation forms are possible.

A real world example of the application of this pattern is discussed in Ahmed (2001). This content management system was designed for the Society of Automotive Engineers (SAE) to automate their standards development process. The system supports online browsing of documents in HTML or PDF format, online change request authoring, online workflow support for change request approval (including an electronic ballot process), keyword searches, and browsing in archives.

1.3.2 Community Infrastructure

The infrastructure of the online community is constituted of facilities that are provided for public use such as libraries, directories, marketplaces, and other Web services. These facilities are provided by institutions, enterprises, or individuals. They may be free to use, or they may be available for a fee.

Typically such infrastructures are provided on the Internet, but intranets and extranets may also offer such facilities for their respective communities.

Libraries

Libraries are the oldest institutions on the Web. In fact, the Web can be seen as one huge library. This was facilitated by standard protocol formats

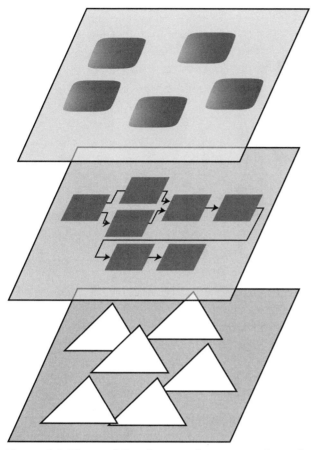

Figure 1.5 The workflow layer orchestrates tasks and services.

such as TCP/IP, HTTP, and HTML and the integration of the necessary access software (TCP/IP stack, Web browsers) into operating systems.

Web Services

The introduction of Web services marks a paradigm shift for the Internet—the conversion from a huge document base into an interconnected network of clients, agents, and applications. A Web service is such an application (usually with a specialized functionality). The service can be invoked from a client or from another Web service (Figure 1.6). The invocation can be of a simple request/response type, or it can have a more complex protocol consisting of several messages exchanged. In Chapter 10 we discuss Web services in more detail.

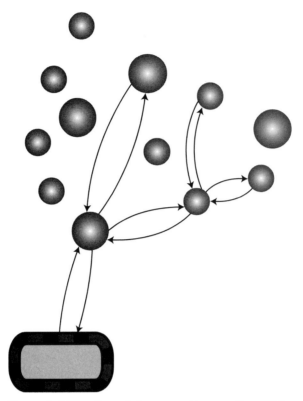

Figure 1.6 Distributed functionality: a call to Web services can cascade through several service providers somewhere on the Internet.

SOAP, WSDL, and UDDI

Web services are based on three technological standards: SOAP, WSDL, and UDDI (see Chapters 6 and 7); all of them are XML applications. SOAP defines the transport format, WSDL is used to describe Web service access points and protocols, and UDDI is used for the registration and discovery of Web services in directories.

In the context of its .NET architecture, Microsoft has included SOAP in their Windows operating system, thus allowing any Windows application to use Web services. To give a simple example: a spreadsheet application could use a Web service for currency conversion, thus always ensuring that the current conversion rate is used.

Marketplaces

Marketplaces bring buyers and sellers together (Figure 1.7). They include functionality such as product catalogue integration, content manage-

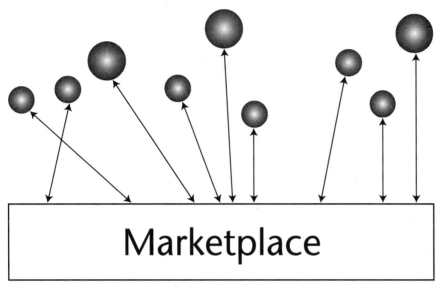

Figure 1.7 The marketplace acts as a single point of access for buyers and sellers.

ment for product catalogues, query routing, vocabulary matching, shared ontologies, communication with other marketplaces, and so on.

Marketplaces can offer additional services such as order acquisition, fulfillment, clearing, settlement, or payment flow. They also attract third-party services such as buyer cooperatives, logistics, financial services, researchers, directory services, and industry associations.

Advanced marketplaces offer support for business processes beyond pure procurement. For example, they may provide services for supply chain management and shared product development.

Portals

A portal serves as an entry point to an Internet community, a large enterprise, an online market, and so on. The portal aggregates information from several sources and personalizes the presentation for each user according to his or her preferences and role.

Portals also attract third-party services such as directory services, industry associations, trade publications, and news feeds.

Repositories

Repositories are used to register Web services, business partners, and other resources. A service provider that wants to offer a particular Web

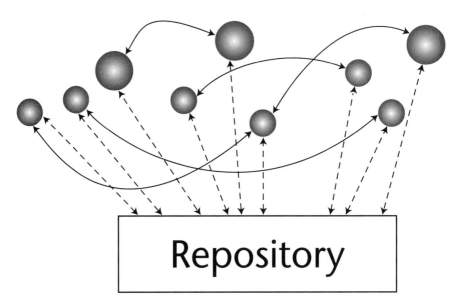

Figure 1.8 Clients use a repository as an "introduction agency," then communicate on a peer-to-peer basis.

service can register the Web service with a UDDI directory (see Chapter 7). Clients that look for a particular Web service can query that directory to find it.

Finding a partner and services   Similarly a company that wants to engage in electronic business can register with an ebXML repository (see Chapter 10) and store its company profile. Another company looking for a partner can query the repository. After finding a prospective partner in the repository it can negotiate the details directly with this partner (Figure 1.8).

Repositories can also act as libraries for shared resources such as common business objects, vocabularies, and other schemata. They may offer extra services for adapting generic resources to local or industry conventions.

1.4 BEST PRACTICES

The following (very general) principles apply when designing systems that are flexible, open, and collaborative.

- *Reification.* Instead of hard-coding relationships between entities and process dynamics (business rules) within your application, model these relationships as entities (see Section 3.2.2) and implement them in the form of XML documents, a process that, in terms of logic, can be seen as reification. (Reification = "to make into a thing.")

  Construct generic software that is able to interpret these documents. That way it will be much easier to adapt your applications when changes become necessary. Hard-coded business rules are at the core of EDI's inflexibility.
- *Context awareness.* Instead of constructing the same software modules (and document schemata) again and again, construct generic software modules and document schemata that are context aware and can adapt to different contexts. An example is the definition of business objects in ebXML (actually this is something learned from EDI).
- *Autonomy.* Instead of constructing huge applications and similarly huge document schemata, construct small specialized units that do what they can do best, but that also can collaborate with others. This also means that the definition of basic units should be fairly complete, specifying not only data structure but also semantics and behavior. While agent technology may not yet be mature enough for production, a lot can already be learned from this technology. We believe that over time XML will move in this direction. XML schemata will allow the definition of self-contained objects that exhibit a behavior and that control their own life cycle.

Groundwork

2

This chapter introduces most of the basic standards for XML. If you are familiar with the syntax and the information model of XML, you can skip Section 2.2. If you are new to XML or need to refresh your memory, you will find this chapter helpful.

Schema definition is the subject of a long (and ongoing) debate in the XML community. We introduce its origins, derived from SGML (DTD), then discuss the now-released W3C recommendation XML Schema. We will pick up the schema thread again in Section 2.9, where we discuss techniques that go beyond XML Schema such as Schematron, architectural forms, and design patterns.

In between we discuss several standards that define access to documents, document composition, and document transformation, including XPath, XPointer, XInclude, XBase,

XQuery, XSL, and the SAX and DOM APIs that allow access to document structures from programming languages. Please note that document transformation (including XSLT) is discussed in more detail in Chapter 9.

XML's history

The XML recommendation (Bray, Paoli, and Sperberg-McQueen 1998) was released in 1998 by the World Wide Web Consortium (the W3C). Initially the adoption of XML by the Internet community was quite slow—because of a misconception. By many XML was seen as a successor to HTML. When it became clear that this was not the case (although XML deals with some of the deficiencies of HTML), but that XML is good for anything else but Web pages, things started to move. The adoption of XML by industry heavyweights such as IBM, Microsoft, Sun, SAP, and Software AG gave massive momentum to XML.

The roots of XML

The initial proposal for XML was based on an already existing standard called the Standard Generalized Markup Language (SGML). SGML had its immediate origins in 1986, but its roots go back well into the 1960s, when at IBM Charles Goldfarb, Edward Mosher, and Raymond Lorie defined the Generalized Markup Language (GML). Is it by accident or by intention that this acronym also matches the initials of its three inventors?

The domain of SGML lies in document processing—for example, book publishing. SGML is incredibly powerful but is also very complex—too complex to be used on the Web. The specification alone has more than 500 pages. The XML working group cut this down to 26 pages while keeping about 95% of the SGML functionality, in the process also depriving Goldfarb of his initial. Goldfarb took revenge and wrote one of the best books about XML (Goldfarb and Prescod 2000). This time he needed only 900 pages.

2.1 XML: A LANGUAGE FACTORY

Special-purpose languages

The main purpose of XML seems to be to spawn other languages. By the end of 2000 there existed about 500 XML-based special-purpose languages. Some of these are domain oriented (vertical) and define exchange formats within an industry sector or another community. Others are task oriented (horizontal) and act as global languages for specific technical or application-oriented tasks, such as service description, procurement, product life cycle management, and so on. For an overview of such industry languages, see Section 10.4.

Although, at first sight, this might look a bit dazzling, this situation has its benefits. There is a special-purpose language for almost any purpose. Because the base technology is the same for all these languages—namely, XML—the learning curve for each of these languages is short: in most cases it's only a few new tags and attributes that must be learned. The other advantage is that these languages can be processed with the same basic tools. Transformations between these different languages can be achieved by simple means such as XSLT style sheets (XSLT is an XML-based language for document transformation). For example, it is possible to query an XML database with an XQuery or XPath search expression for product information. The result would be an XML document that describes the product in a transformation-neutral format. This document can be transformed with an XSLT style sheet into presentation formats such as XHTML, SMIL, WML, or even VoiceXML. Or the data could be packed into a SOAP message and sent to a business partner. Or we could compile sales figures and display them with the help of SVG, an XML-based vector graphics standard.

All of these acronyms denote XML-based special-purpose languages. We will discuss each in more detail in later chapters. At the moment, it is only important to know that all of these languages are based on XML. As in many cases, here, too, the whole is more than the sum of its parts.

2.2 XML BASICS

There are already many books about XML on the market, including the one by Charles Goldfarb and Paul Prescod mentioned earlier (Goldfarb and Prescod 2000). We will therefore explain the basic XML concepts here only briefly.

2.2.1 The Syntax

The XML syntax rules define the "well-formedness" of XML documents. "Well-formed" means that a document is syntactically correct. Any well-formed XML document can be processed with a standard XML parser.

Markup

XML is a *markup* language—a document can be structured with the help of syntactical markup elements, similar to those used in HTML. Identifiable elements within a document are enclosed between start and end tags:

```
<lastName>Goldfarb</lastName>
```
Tags

In contrast to HTML, a start tag must always have a corresponding end tag. (We are talking here of classic HTML. The new XHTML standard is based on XML, so the strict XML syntax rules apply for XHTML as well.)

For empty elements there is a shorthand notation. Instead of writing the canonical form
</br>, we can write <br/>.

Also in contrast to HTML, upper and lower case does matter: <lastName> is different from <lastname>.

Attributes

Elements can be decorated with attributes:

```
<title xml:lang="en-us">The XML-Handbook™</title>
<title xml:lang="de-de">Das XML-Handbuch</title>
```

Attributes consist of a name and a value. Unlike HTML, an attribute must always have a value, and the value must always be enclosed in single or double quotes. The attribute we have used here is one of the few predefined attributes in XML (indicated by the namespace prefix xml:). Consequently, this prefix is forbidden for user-defined attributes (including prefixes such as XML:, xML:, Xml:, etc.).

Multilingual documents

This particular attribute defines the language of an element. The value of the attribute consists of a combination of language code and country code. The language code follows ISO639 (*www.w3.org/WAI/ER/IG/ert/iso639.htm*), while the country code is the same as that used for Web domain addresses. Using this attribute it is easy to create multilingual documents, as shown in the following example.

Using markup, it is possible to create documents of an arbitrarily complex structure:

```
<book>
  <title xml:lang="en-us">The XML-Handbook™</title>
  <title xml:lang="de-de">Das XML-Handbuch</title>
  <authors>
    <author aid="a1">
      <name>
        <firstName>Charles</firstName>
        <middleName>F.</middleName>
        <lastName>Goldfarb</lastName>
      </name>
    </author>
    <author aid="a2">
      <name>
        <firstName>Paul</firstName>
        <lastName>Prescod</lastName>
```

```
      </name>
    </author>
  </authors>
</book>
```

Note that by nesting elements our document is organized as a tree structure. Compare this to the flat relational tables: we would have needed at least three different tables to store such a data structure in a relational database.

Also note that the elements can be variable in layout. The first author has a middle name; the second has only a first and a last name. In a relational table this would have been modeled with the rather artificial construct of a null value for the middle name of the second author.

Elements can contain an arbitrary mixture of subelements and text, a fact that can cause some headache when mapping XML structures onto object-oriented or relational structures. For example:

Mixed elements

```
<title>
  The XML-Handbook™
  <subtitle>Second Edition</subtitle>
</title>
```

XML documents should be introduced by a prolog, at least with an XML declaration in its minimal form:

Prolog

```
<?xml version="1.0" ?>
```

XML's character set is Unicode, which allows XML to contain most of the international characters. The default character encodings are UTF-8 and UTF-16 (Standard ASCII code is a subset of UTF-8), but other code systems can be specified with an XML declaration in the document prolog:

Encoding

```
<?xml version="1.0" encoding="ISO-10646-UCS-2" ?>
```

Comments are inserted into XML documents using the following syntax:

Comments

```
<!-- This is a comment -->
```

That is basically all you need to know to write your first XML document.

Extensibility

The X in "XML" stands for "extensible," which more or less means that you can introduce your own tags and attributes. And this is exactly the strength of XML. In HTML, in contrast, all tags and attributes are predefined. Most of these tags are used for presentation purposes, and some are used for navigation. This is sufficient for displaying nice Web pages but not for processing business data over the Internet. For a search engine, an agent, a partner application, or even a human reader, the markup 415-555-1234 is quite meaningless. That this item will be printed in bold type has no significance in this context. More important would be to know what this number means. Is it a product number, a phone number, or an employee number? Markup like <phone_number>415-555-1234</phone_number> is much more helpful here, and this is exactly what XML was designed for. By using this type of semantic markup, a document can be self-describing. In our earlier <book> document, for example, we can easily identify the title and the authors.

However, it was not the goal of the XML designers that everybody would now start to invent their own tags and attributes as they please. The result would be total chaos, with nobody understanding each other's documents. Instead, it was intended that user groups, industry associations, and communities would get together and agree on certain *document types*. By using a DOCTYPE instruction, an XML file can be tied to a given document type:

```
<!DOCTYPE book SYSTEM "http://www.book.org/book">
```

Document type   The DOCTYPE instruction must be given within the document prolog, after the XML specification. This instruction is not mandatory, but if it is supplied, a validating parser can check the document structure against the specified Document Type Definition (DTD). We will discuss DTDs in more detail shortly. At the moment, it is sufficient to know that a DTD defines the vocabulary (tag and attribute names) and the structure of documents. A document with a DOCTYPE declaration that conforms with the specified document type is called *valid*.

It is important to know that even documents with a specified document type remain extensible. The external DTD defines only the minimal layout of a document. It is always possible to add additional elements (and text) to such a document by extending the external DTD with a local DTD subset (for an example, see Section 2.9.3). This allows users to use standard DTDs but add custom elements for individual purposes. This flexibility makes it easier for users to adopt existing standards.

Namespaces

Extensibility, however, creates some problems. When tag names can be created at will, it is very likely that the same tag names will be used by different people for different purposes. This is normally not a problem as long as documents are kept apart. But when documents are merged, or modularized document types are combined, there can be name clashes. For example, in an XSLT style sheet that transforms document A into document B, we need to decorate the tags used for the XSLT control elements in order to differentiate them from the tags in the processed documents (see Chapter 9).

This is done with namespaces. You could compare a namespace to a city or a township. There may be a Marine Parade in both Sydney and Melbourne. By decorating the street name "Marine Parade" with a city name, you can uniquely identify the street.

In XML, namespaces (Bray, Hollander, and Layman 1999) are represented by a URI (Uniform Resource Identifier)—either a URL (Uniform Resource Locator) or a URN (Uniform Resource Name). Such identifiers are constructed from a registered domain name, owned by the author, and an arbitrary path expression. It is important to use a registered domain name and not some fantasy name, since only registered domain names are globally unique. (However, in the examples in this book we use fantasy names.) The path name is used to differentiate between several namespaces defined by the domain owner. With this technique, anybody who owns a registered domain name can create as many namespaces as he or she likes.

Namespace URI

Namespaces can be used within a document in two ways, default namespaces and prefixes. First we will look at an example of a default namespace:

```
<book xmlns='http://www.books.org/computer/xml'>
  <title>The XML-Handbook™</title>
  <authors>
  ...
  </authors>
</book>
```

In this example all tags in the book element now belong to namespace http://www.books.org/computer/xml. It is also possible to scope namespaces:

```
<book xmlns='http://www.books.org/computer/xml'>
  <title>The XML-Handbook™</title>
  <authors xmlns='http://www.books.org/authors'>
  ...
  </authors>
</book>
```

Now the `<authors>` element and all child elements belong to a different namespace, `http://www.books.org/authors`.

Now let's look at an example of prefixes:

```
<book xmlns='http://www.books.org/computer/xml'>
  <title>The XML-Handbook™</title>
  <a:authors xmlns:a='http://www.books.org/authors'>
  ...
  </a:authors>
</book>
```

Prefixes can be chosen arbitrarily and are used as a shorthand notation for the full namespace specification. By combining the prefix with a tag name we have assigned only the tag `<authors>` to the namespace `http://www.books.org/authors`. The child elements would still belong to the default namespace `http://www.books.org/computer/xml`, unless we prefix them with `a:`, too.

Advanced Topics

CDATA provides a way to denote text as unparsed character data:

```
<![CDATA[
  if(ThisYear < 100) ThisYear+=1900;
]]>
```

CDATA is especially useful when you want to place some program code into an XML element, or if you want an element to contain marked-up text but want the markup to be treated as plain text. CDATA advises XML processors not to parse the included text for subelements.

Processing instructions

XML documents can contain processing instructions, for example, to specify the URI of an attached style sheet:

```
<?xml:stylesheet type="text/xsl" href="mystyle.xsl"?>
```

(This syntax is specified in an extra W3C recommendation; see Clark 1999b.) This processing instruction indicates to a Web browser that the document should not be displayed in its native form but should be transformed with the referenced style sheet and that the result of that transformation should be displayed.

Entities

Document text can contain predefined entity references. These are used to substitute characters that are otherwise used in a special syntactic role (see Table 2.1). For example:

```
<formula> 3&gt;2 </formula>
```

Table 2.1 Character Entities in XML.

Character	Entity
&	&
"	"
'	'
<	<
>	>

Similarly, character references can be used. Characters can be specified as decimal code numbers or as hexadecimal code numbers. For example, both © and © denote the copyright character.

In addition, user-defined entities can be used. These must be declared in a DTD—either inline within the document or in the external DTD (see Section 2.3.1).[1] For example:

&legal; π

2.2.2 The XML Information Model

Before we discuss the standards to access XML structures like XBase, XPath, XPointer, XLink, and DOM, it is necessary to get a better understanding of the XML data model, also called the XML information set. This is described in detail in Cowan and Tobin (2001). The XML information set is independent of the actual format of a document: the document may exist in the form of an XML text file, a DOM tree, and so on.

All XML documents have a tree structure, with the nodes of the tree constituted of *elements* and *attributes* (see Figure 2.1). Attributes are always leaf nodes; they do not have child nodes. Element nodes may have child nodes. All nodes except the root node have one parent node.

Tree structure

The attribute nodes of an element form an unordered list; that is, it is not possible to make statements about the order in which the attributes of an element occur. In contrast the child elements of an element form an ordered list. Consequently there is a positional order relation between the child elements of an element. This means that we can rely on the position of an element when accessing parts of an XML document.

---

[1] We are a bit sloppy here. To be correct, we have to speak of the "external DTD subset," since a DTD can consist of an external subset and an internal subset.

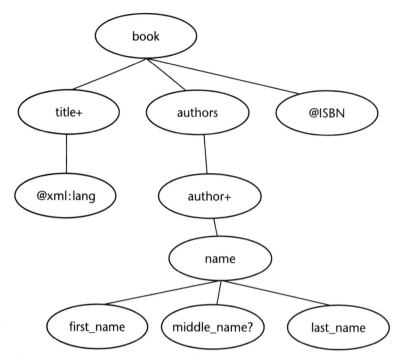

Figure 2.1 Structure of the <book> schema. <title> and <author> are marked with "+" to indicate multiple occurrences. <middleName> is marked with "?" to indicate that this element is optional. The attributes xml:lang and ISBN are prefixed with "@", indicating an attribute. Although this figure shows a tree diagram, schema diagrams can be cyclic (recursive).

Namespace identifier

Each node—element or attribute—has a local name and can have a namespace identifier. The local name (also the combination of local name and namespace identifier) is not required to be unique within a document: elements and attributes may appear with the same name in different contexts (i.e., under different parent elements) in the document.[2]

Repetition

Furthermore, elements can repeat within a context. In contrast, attributes must not repeat within a context.

2.3 SCHEMA DEFINITION—STAGE 1

In this section, we take a look at schema definitions for XML. We begin with the basic DTD, as defined in the XML V1.0 Recommendation.

---

[2] This has consequences for the authoring of XML documents: it makes sense to always qualify elements with a namespace prefix but not to qualify attributes.

2.3.1 The Document Type Definition (DTD)

As we mentioned earlier, it is possible to classify XML documents into document types. This is achieved with a DOCTYPE definition. We have already given an example of an external DOCTYPE definition:

```
<!DOCTYPE book SYSTEM "http://www.book.org/book">
```

However, it is also possible to specify an internal DOCTYPE definition after the document prolog:

```
<!DOCTYPE book [
 . . . .
]>
```

with the whole document type specification contained within the brackets. This form, however, is of only limited use because the so-defined document type applies only to the current document. Normally a DTD is provided as an external file (which may be extended by an internal DOCTYPE definition).

Element Definition

Let's now see what can be specified within a DTD.

```
<!ELEMENT book (title+,authors)>
<!ELEMENT title ANY>
<!ELEMENT authors (author+)>
<!ELEMENT author (firstName,middleName?,lastName)>
<!ATTLIST author
          aid ID #REQUIRED
          role (contributor|editor) "contributor">
<!ELEMENT firstName (#PCDATA)>
<!ELEMENT middleName (#PCDATA)>
<!ELEMENT lastName (#PCDATA)>
```

This could be a complete DTD for the earlier <book> example. We see that each element in the document has a corresponding ELEMENT declaration in the DTD. This declaration specifies how each element is structured. The following element types are possible:

Element structure

ANY | The element can contain mixed content including character data and child elements.

EMPTY | Denotes an empty element.

#PCDATA | The element contains parsed character data. (Parsed character data must not contain characters such as "<" or "&".)

(...) | The element contains a model group (discussed below).

Model groups   Model groups are constructed by child elements used in sequence or as alternatives. Both operations may be nested to obtain complex structures:

`(child)`	Single child element
`(child1,child2,...,childn)`	Sequence of child elements
`(child1|child2|...|childn)`	Alternate child elements
`(child1,(child2|(child3,child4)),` `    child5)`	Complex child structure

Constraints   In addition, each element can be postfixed with a modifier that denotes the number of occurrences (cardinality) of the element and whether the element is mandatory or optional:

No modifier	One occurrence, mandatory (1..1)
?	One occurrence, optional (0..1)
+	Multiple occurrences, mandatory (0..n)
*	Multiple occurrences, optional (1..n)

Earlier we had defined

```
<!ELEMENT authors (author+)>
```

because the element <authors> can contain multiple <author> elements but must contain at least one of them. We had defined

```
<!ELEMENT author (firstName, middleName?, lastName)>
```

because the element <author> must contain the elements <firstName> and <lastName> but may contain the element <middleName>.

Recursion   The element definitions can be recursive, meaning that a child element in a model group can refer to a previously defined parent element.

```
<!ELEMENT chapter (title,abstract?,section+)>
<!ELEMENT section
          (title,(content | (abstract?,section+)))>
```

This defines the structure of book chapters. Each chapter consists of a mandatory title, an optional abstract, and multiple sections. Each section consists of a mandatory title, followed either by content or by an optional abstract and multiple nested sections.

Formal languages   If you have experience in the definition of formal languages, you might have noticed that a DTD very much resembles the production rules of a formal language. To be precise, DTDs form a subclass of forest-regular grammars (FRG).

And, in fact, DTDs are used to define other XML-based languages. So there is an XHTML DTD, an SVG DTD, an SMIL DTD, an XSLT DTD, and so on.

Attribute Definition

In a similar way, attributes can be defined for each element. This is done using ATTLIST, which lists all attributes of an element. Each attribute definition consists of an attribute name, an attribute type, and a default value.

In contrast to XML elements, which are typeless, attributes do have a type:

Attribute types

CDATA	Character data.
NMTOKEN	Name token. (Valid name tokens consist of letters, digits, and the characters ".", "-", "_", or ":".)
NMTOKENS	NMTOKEN list (separated by white space).
(writer|editor|artist)	Enumeration. Each token must be a valid name token.
NOTATION (n1|n2|...)	Enumeration of notation symbols (see below).
ID	Element identifier. This must be a valid name. Element identifiers must be unique in the context of a document. (Names start with a letter or with "_" and can contain letters, digits, ".", "-", or "_". Names must not start with the string "xml" or variations such as "XML", xML, "XmL", etc.)
IDREF	Reference to an element ID.
IDREFS	IDREF list (separated by white space).

The following default value specifications can be used for attribute definitions:

Default values

#IMPLIED	Attribute is not required nor does it have a default value.
#REQUIRED	Attribute must be specified.
"fax","42","yes"	Default values. These apply when the attribute is not specified.
#FIXED "v1"	Fixed content. If specified, instances must match this value.

In our earlier example we defined

```
<!ATTLIST author
        aid ID #REQUIRED
        role (contributor|editor) "contributor">
```

This means that the element `<author>` has a required attribute of type ID and an optional attribute `role`. If the attribute `role` is specified, it can take two valid values, "contributor" and "editor". If it is not specified, the default value "contributor" applies.

2.3.2 Advanced Topics

Identifiers

The ID and IDREF attribute types can be used to establish relations between elements, allowing the establishment of networklike document structures that could not be captured in tree structures. In particular, it is possible to define documents that model relational tables by using the ID and IDREF constructs. ID acts as a primary key, while IDREF acts as a foreign key. Some XML parsers support the location of elements by ID.

NOTATION

The `NOTATION` attribute type is a kind of type extension mechanism for elements. A `NOTATION` attribute advises XML processors that the element to which the attribute is attached should contain content that complies with the specified notation. An XML processor could then check the element for specific content, possibly by using a helper application.

In practical applications the `NOTATION` construct is hardly used, especially now that there are better ways to define datatypes for XML elements with XML Schema. We will discuss this in Section 2.4.2.

Entities

A DTD can declare user-defined entities. These entities can be used within the document text and will be resolved to the entity definition by XML processors. User-defined entities are used to abbreviate frequently used terms and phrases, or to introduce a symbolic notation for commonly needed constants:

```
<!ENTITY legal "All rights preserved">
<!ENTITY pi "3.141593">
```

A DTD can also define external entities—entities that do not specify a literal value within the DTD but refer to an external document. However, this is beyond the scope of this discussion. Especially in the context of message exchange and databases, we do not recommend the use of external entities. In traditional SGML environments, however, external entities are widely used for document composition.

Parameter Entities

Parameter entities are used only within a DTD; they do not appear in XML instances. A parameter entity is just an abbreviation for a string that is frequently used within a DTD and thus allows factoring out frequently used strings.

A parameter entity can be declared through

```
<!ENTITY % entity-name "string-value">
```

All occurrences of %entity-name; within the DTD will be substituted with string-value. It is possible to nest parameter entities.

2.4 SCHEMA DEFINITION—STAGE 2

In the past, DTDs were the standard way to define a schema for an XML document type. However, more than a dozen alternative schema definition languages have been created by several institutions and individuals. The W3C itself has produced a new schema definition language, XML Schema (XSD), which is discussed in Section 2.4.2.

2.4.1 DTD Deficiencies

The reason for the flood of schema definition languages lies in the deficiencies of the DTD:

- *Syntax:* DTDs are not XML documents themselves. This is a problem because the ubiquitous XML tools cannot be used to edit, validate, parse, and transform DTDs.
- *Namespaces:* DTDs do not support namespaces. A DTD doesn't stop you from using prefix:name combinations for element and attribute names, but it interprets these combinations as simple names. This can lead to confusion.
- *Datatypes:* DTDs do not support datatypes in the classical sense. We cannot define, for example, elements and attributes that must be numeric or integer. The content of elements and the value of attributes are always regarded as character data. This can have unpleasant effects when we want to compare two elements that contain numeric

values: "–1" is regarded as smaller than "–2"; the floating point number "3.3e–10" is regarded as larger than "2.2e+16"; and so on.

Except for some datatypes for attributes (such as NMTOKEN, ID, IDREF, etc.), DTDs do not feature built-in datatypes. It is not possible to create user-defined datatypes either.

- *Bags:* DTDs cannot specify unordered sequences of elements (bags). For a given model group (e1,e2,e3) the elements e1 . . . e3 must appear in the document instance in the defined sequence. To simulate an unordered sequence, all possible permutations must be given as alternatives: ((e1,e2,e3) | (e1,e3,e2) | (e2,e1,e3) | . . .).
- *Context:* In DTDs all elements are defined on the document level. This makes it impossible to define context-sensitive elements—elements with the same name but with different structure in different contexts.
- *Cross-references:* The support for cross-references in DTDs is poor. Only attribute values can be used as keys, and it is not possible to combine a key from several attributes. Keys are always defined on the document level, so it is not possible to scope keys.

2.4.2 XML Schema

That was reason enough for the W3C to start with the definition of a new schema language. The XML Schema working draft was first published in May 1999. It could already rely on several other schema languages such as XSchema, DDML, XML-Data, and SOX (Schema for Object-oriented XML). One of the more recent additions was XDR, which was used by the BizTalk community for schema definition. Now, with the XML Schema recommendation (Fallside 2001) released in May 2001, most XML communities—including the BizTalk community—are moving toward XML Schema.

XML Schema is quite a complex standard. To begin to understand XML Schema, it is best to think of it in terms of DTDs + Namespaces + Datatypes and worry about the rest later. Because we have already covered DTDs and namespaces, we will begin with datatypes.

Datatypes

The introduction of a full type system (Biron and Malhotra 2001) for elements and attributes is the most important aspect of XML Schema. It includes the attribute types known from DTDs but also introduces basic datatypes as they are known in SQL or programming languages. User-defined datatypes are possible, too.

Built-in Datatypes   The type system of XML Schema makes a clear distinction between *value space* and *lexical space*. While the value space is constituted of an abstract collection of valid values for a datatype, the lexical space contains the lexical representation of these values—the tokens that can appear in the XML document. Depending on the permitted formats, each value can have several lexical representations (see Figure 2.2).

XML Schema defines datatypes by attributing *facets* to datatypes. Facets define single properties of datatypes; that is, the definition of a datatype is made up of a collection of constituting facets. XML Schema differentiates between fundamental facets and constraining facets.

Fundamental facets define the basic properties of datatypes. Fundamental facets are:

Value space and lexical space

Facets

equal	Defines equality between values of a datatype. For example, two attributes are equal if their values (not necessarily their string representations) are equal.
ordered	Defines order relations between values of a datatype.
bounded	Defines upper and lower bounds for the values of a datatype.
cardinality	Defines whether the value space of a datatype is *finite, countably infinite,* or *uncountably infinite*. For example,

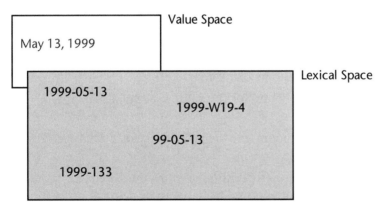

Figure 2.2 Possible lexical representations for a given date value. Transformations between value space and lexical space are bidirectional: parsing operations transform lexical representations into values; formatting operations transform values into lexical representations.

enumerations are finite and integer numbers are
countably infinite.

numeric   Defines whether or not a datatype is numeric.

Constraining facets do not add new properties to a datatype but—as
the name says—constrain existing fundamental facets. Constraining
facets are

length	Defines the length of a datatype value (number of characters for strings, number of octets for binary, etc.). For example, a country code such as us, de, uk, fr, and so on would have a fixed length of 2.
minLength	Lower bound for the length of a datatype value.
maxLength	Upper bound for the length of a datatype value.
pattern	Constrains the values of a datatype by constraining the lexical space of a datatype to match a specified character pattern. A pattern is defined via regular expressions. Example: '[0-9]-[0-9] {3}-[0-9] {5}-[0-9]' constrains the lexical space of a datatype to the format of an ISBN
enumeration	Constrains the value space of a datatype to a specified enumeration of values.
whiteSpace	Constrains the value space of a datatype by imposing a policy for whitespace handling: *preserve* (keep all whitespace characters), *replace* (replace each whitespace character with the blank character), *collapse* (reduce all sequences of whitespace characters with a single blank character).
maxInclusive *maxExclusive*	Upper bound for the value space of a datatype.
minInclusive *minExclusive*	Lower bound for the value space of a datatype.
totalDigits	Maximum total number of decimal digits in values of datatypes derived from datatype *decimal*.
fractionDigits	Maximum number of decimal digits in the fractional part of values of datatypes derived from *decimal*.

Type hierarchy   Using these facets, XML Schema defines a rich set of built-in datatypes (see Figure 2.3). Some of these datatypes are primitives—they do

not rely on the definition of other datatypes. Other datatypes are derived datatypes—datatypes that are derived from primitive datatypes or from other existing derived datatypes.

User-defined datatypes   User-defined datatypes allow schema designers to create custom datatypes. User-defined datatypes are always derived datatypes. They are derived either from built-in datatypes or from other user-defined datatypes. There are three methods for deriving a datatype from another datatype: restriction, list, and union.

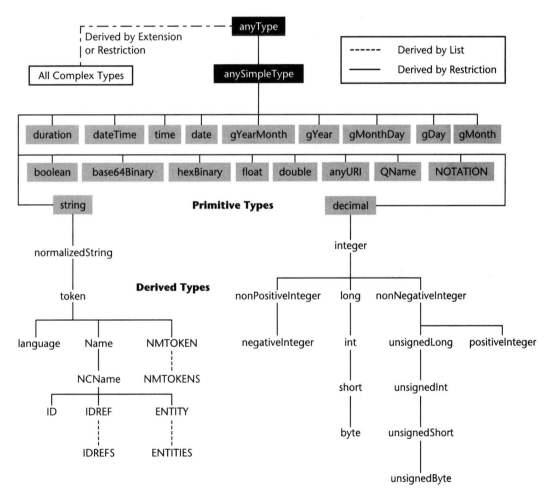

Figure 2.3 The hierarchy of built-in types in XML Schema. Primitive datatypes are presented in reverse style. Derivation by list (extension) is indicated with a dotted line; derivation by restriction, with a solid line.

Restriction is done by adding more constraining facets. Here is an example for constraining the value space of base type string by enumeration:

```
<xsd:simpleType name="gender">
  <xsd:restriction base="xsd:string">
    <xsd:enumeration value="male"/>
    <xsd:enumeration value="female"/>
  </xsd:restriction>
</xsd:simpleType>
```

Any datatype can be extended to a list of this datatype. The following example shows the definition of a list of integer values between 0 and 255 of length 3. As we can see, it is possible to use the facet length to constrain the size of a list.

```
<xsd:simpleType name="byteList">
  <xsd:list itemType="xsd:unsignedByte"/>
</xsd:simpleType>

<xsd:simpleType name="rgbColor">
  <xsd:restriction base="byteList"/>
  <xsd:length value="3"/>
  </xsd:restriction>
</xsd:simpleType>
```

With the union operation, it is possible to combine disparate datatypes into a single datatype. In the following example we combine the rgbColor datatype definition from above with a text-oriented color datatype. This allows us to specify a color either by a triple of integers or by a keyword.

```
<xsd:simpleType name="unitedColor">
  <xsd:union/>
  <xsd:union memberTypes="rgbColor">
    <xsd:simpleType>
      <xsd:restriction base="xsd:string">
        <xsd:enumeration value="red"/>
        <xsd:enumeration value="green"/>
        <xsd:enumeration value="blue"/>
      </xsd:restriction>
    </xsd:simpleType>
  </xsd:union>
</xsd:simpleType>
```

This example also shows that an operator such as union may refer to an existing datatype or may define member datatypes implicitly.

Complex Datatypes It would seem that where there is a simpleType declaration, there must also be a complexType declaration. And, in fact, there is. Complex types are used to combine several XML elements and attributes into one datatype, so they are a central element in schema definition (Thompson et al. 2001).

Here is an example: Simple content

```
<xsd:complexType name="price">
 <xsd:simpleContent>
  <xsd:extension base="xsd:decimal">
   <xsd:attribute name="currency" type="xsd:string" />
  </xsd:extension>
 </xsd:simpleContent>
</xsd:complexType>
```

This definition uses a simple content model (i.e., only character data, no child elements) of type decimal and extends it with an attribute of type string and with the name currency.

As we can see, complex types can constrain the content of an element to a certain model. In particular, complex datatypes can construct aggregations of child elements, as is possible with model groups in a DTD.

The content model can be defined as

- *empty.* The element must not have content but may have attributes.

Or it can be defined as a model group. Model groups consist of a list of   Complex content
particles combined using connectors:

- *sequence.* An ordered sequence of child elements or other model groups.
- *choice.* Alternative child elements or other model groups.
- *all.* An unordered sequence of simple or complex child elements (all groups cannot contain other model groups).
- *group.* This connector allows naming a model group or referring to a named model group. So model group definitions may be reused.

A particle consists of an element, a *wildcard,* or another model group with optional minOccurs and maxOccurs properties that control the number of occurrences of the particle. These replace the "?", "*", "+" modifiers known from DTDs but allow a finer control over the number of occurrences.

Wildcards

Wildcards are declared with the schema elements <xsd:any> and <xsd:anyAttribute> and allow for the inclusion of elements and attributes from foreign namespaces in the schema. For example, sections of XHTML, SVG, RDF, and other content can be included in a document.

Mixed content

By default, a complex type must only contain element data; that is, text cannot be interspersed with elements. To allow for mixed content (i.e., interspersed text between child elements), the attribute mixed="true" must be declared in the definition of the complex type. Unlike DTDs, XML Schema allows control over the number and order of child elements within the mixed content.

Document Structure

To define an XML schema we need only four basic elements. The <xsd:schema> element contains the whole schema definition and defines the XML Schema namespace. As children of the <schema> element we have the following:

- <xsd:element> defines elements. The first definition within <schema> defines the root element of a document. These elements have either a simple or a complex type.
- <xsd:complexType> defines the substructure of elements of that type, that is, which attributes these elements have and which child elements they contain.
- <xsd:simpleType> defines the type of a leaf element or of an attribute.

We demonstrate this in an example:

```
<?xml version="1.0"?>

<bookOrder orderDate="2001-01-27"
  xmlns:xsi="http://www.w3.org/1999/XMLSchema-instance"
  xsi:schemaLocation="http://www.bookdomain.com/bookorder
                      http://www.bookdomain.com/bookorder.xsd"
>

    <shipTo country="US">
        <name>Venus Reader</name>
        <street>585 Chapel Street</street>
        <city>Papermoon</city>
        <state>CA</state>
        <zip>97989</zip>
    </shipTo>
```

```
<billTo country="AU">
    <name>Rick Reader</name>
    <street>18 Marine Parade</street>
    <city>Albany</city>
    <state>WA</state>
    <zip>9832</zip>
</billTo>

<note>Special Valentine's wrapping!</note>

<orderlist>
    <item ISBN="0-3932-5855-9">
        <title>The mint lawn</title>
        <quantity>1</quantity>
        <price currency="USD">19.95</price>
        <note>On stock</note>
    </item>
</orderlist>

</bookOrder>
```

In the root element of this document we declared the namespace for XML Schema instances and the location of the schema definition. The location declaration consists of a pair of values defining the namespace `http://www.bookdomain.com/bookorder` and the schema location `http://www.bookdomain.com/bookorder.xsd`. The namespace identifies the schema definition by its *target namespace* definition, while the schema location gives a hint to the processor about where to find the schema file.

Schema location

Target namespace

The schema definition could look like this:

```
<xsd:schema
        xmlns:xsd="http://www.w3.org/2000/08/XMLSchema"
        targetNamespace="http://www.bookdomain.com/bookorder">

<xsd:element name="bookOrder" type="bookOrderType"/>

<xsd:element name="comment" type="xsd:string"/>

<xsd:complexType name="bookOrderType">
  <xsd:sequence>
    <xsd:element name="shipTo" type="address"/>
    <xsd:element name="billTo" type="address"/>
    <xsd:element ref="comment" minOccurs="0"/>
    <xsd:element name="orderlist" type="items"/>
```

```
      </xsd:sequence>
      <xsd:attribute name="orderDate" type="xsd:date"/>
    </xsd:complexType>

    <xsd:complexType name="address">
      <xsd:sequence>
        <xsd:element name="name" type="xsd:string"/>
        <xsd:element name="street" type="xsd:string"/>
        <xsd:element name="city" type="xsd:string"/>
        <xsd:element name="state" type="xsd:string"/>
        <xsd:element name="zip" type="xsd:decimal"/>
      </xsd:sequence>
      <xsd:attribute name="country" type="xsd:NMTOKEN"/>
    </xsd:complexType>

    <xsd:complexType name="Items">
      <xsd:sequence>
        <xsd:element name="item" minOccurs="1"
                                 maxOccurs="unbounded">
          <xsd:complexType>
            <xsd:sequence>
              <xsd:element name="title" type="xsd:string"/>
              <xsd:element name="quantity">
                <xsd:simpleType>
                  <xsd:restriction base="xsd:positiveInteger">
                    <xsd:maxInclusive value="20"/>
                  </xsd:restriction>
                </xsd:simpleType>
              </xsd:element>
              <xsd:element name="price">
                <xsd:complexType>
                  <xsd:simpleContent>
                    <xsd:extension base="xsd:decimal">
                      <xsd:attribute name="currency"
                                     type="xsd:string"/>
                    </xsd:extension>
                  </xsd:simpleContent>
                </xsd:complexType>
              </xsd:element>
              <xsd:element ref="comment" minOccurs="0"/>
            </xsd:sequence>
```

```
        <xsd:attribute name="ISBN" type="isbnType"/>
      </xsd:complexType>
    </xsd:element>
  </xsd:sequence>
</xsd:complexType>
<xsd:simpleType name="ISBN">
  <xsd:restriction base="xsd:string">
    <xsd:pattern value="\d{1}-d{4}-d{4}-d{1}"/>
  </xsd:restriction>
</xsd:simpleType>

</xsd:schema>
```

Here we see that most elements are defined locally within the `complexType` declaration. Only the root element `<bookOrder>` and the `<note>` element are declared globally on the schema level, the `<note>` element for the reason that it is used in various places. Also interesting is the pattern definition for the ISBN datatype.

Namespaces

XML Schema provides full support for namespaces. Not only element and attribute names can be associated with a target namespace but also type names. The schema can enforce the specification of namespaces for elements and attributes individually or for all elements and attributes defined in the schema. It is good practice to enforce namespace qualification for elements but not for attributes.

Multinamespace documents are supported, too. Document instances can use elements and attributes from multiple namespaces defined in the corresponding schemata. Schema definitions may refer to types from other namespaces by importing external schemata. Finally, the wildcards `any` and `anyAttribute` allow the inclusion of content from foreign namespaces.

Multiple namespaces

Nil Values, Uniqueness, and Keys

DTDs support only the concept of optional elements. An element is either present or absent.

XML Schema also allows the expression of the absence of a value in another manner by introducing the concept of "nillable" elements. Within a schema an element can be defined as `nillable`. In the document instance a nillable element can—via the attribute `xsi:nil`—indicate that its content is indeed *nil*. An element with the attribute `xsi:nil= "true"` may not contain content, but it can have other attributes.

Of course, this concept was not introduced to split hairs about nothingness but to support the exchange of data with relational databases. In SQL databases, field contents can have the value *null*, so supporting a similar concept in XML makes it easier to convert XML to SQL and vice versa (for example, to export/import without a schema definition).

Cross-
references

XML Schema provides the built-in datatypes ID and IDREF for modeling relations between document elements. However, the main purpose of these datatypes is to provide backwards compatibility with existing XML documents:

- Because ID and IDREF are attribute datatypes, it is not possible to declare another datatype for a key. For example, is it not possible to declare a primary key of type date. It is also not possible to use an element as a key.
- ID and IDREF cannot handle composite keys. This is required if we want to be compatible with relational databases.
- ID and IDREF cannot be scoped; that is, they always apply to the whole document.

XML Schema therefore introduces several new constructs. The unique clause defines elements, attributes, or combinations thereof that need to be unique within a defined context:

```
<unique name="uniqueISBN">
  <selector xpath="."/>
  <field xpath="item/@ISBN"/>
</unique>
```

We assume that we have placed the definition of this unique clause into the definition of element bookOrder/orderlist. We declare the attribute ISBN (indicated by "@") as unique within the context of bookOrder /orderlist because we do not want more than one item within element orderlist with the same ISBN. The xpath specification in the field element locates the attribute relative to the context specified in the selector element. (XPath is described in Section 2.5.1.) The <selector> clause could contain several <field> clauses to specify field combinations as unique.

The key clause looks similar. It allows the definition of tuples of elements and attributes as primary keys. These tuples must be unique, and they must exist within the defined context.

```
<key name="primaryKeyISBN">
  <selector xpath="orderlist"/>
  <field xpath="item/@ISBN"/>
</key>
```

Assuming that we have placed the definition of this key clause into the definition of the root element bookOrder, it allows us to access the items in orderlist directly via a key.

Similarly there is a keyref clause to define foreign keys:

```
<keyref name="foreignKeyISBN" refer="primaryKeyISBN">
  <selector xpath="undeliverableItems"/>
  <field xpath="item/@badISBN"/>
</keyref>
```

Assuming that we have placed the definition of this keyref clause into the definition of the root element bookOrder and that bookOrder contains another element undeliverableItems that lists undeliverable items, we have established here a cross-reference between undeliverableItems and orderlist. To this purpose the keyref clause refers to the previously defined key primaryKeyISBN via the refer attribute.

With the support for null values, full support for uniqueness, primary and foreign keys, and the support for classical datatypes, XML Schema improves the compatibility of XML with relational technology.

It is now easier to convert XML schemata into SQL schemata and vice versa, and to import XML into relational databases or to export XML from relational databases. However, whether this always makes sense remains questionable. Relational databases require data structures to be normalized, but XML documents are usually not. On the other hand, normalized relational data structures do not contain all structural information because some of this information is lost during the normalization process—information that has to be added by the applications that process this data. Exporting relational databases into XML results therefore in a poor data model, losing some of the expressive power of XML. We will discuss these modeling aspects in the next chapter.

XML and SQL

Reuse Mechanisms

XML Schema provides a rich set of mechanisms that allow the reuse of schema definitions or parts thereof:

- *Attribute groups*. Attribute groups can combine several attribute definitions into a single named group. The whole group can then be referenced by specifying the group name.
- *Substitution groups*. These work as a kind of alias mechanism for elements, allowing the substitution for occurrences of the so-called *head element* of a substitution group with type-compatible members of the same substitution group.

- *Abstract type definitions.* Type definitions can be classified as abstract. These types can be used only to derive other types and not for element or attribute definition.
- *Inclusion and import.* External schemata and types can be included or imported into a schema definition. While inclusion works within a single namespace, import can compose schemata across several namespaces. This allows the establishment of type libraries, for example, for companywide datatypes.
- *Redefinition.* Redefinition works similarly to inclusion but allows the modification of the included types.
- *Instance subtyping.* XML Schema is flexible enough to allow instance elements to be subtyped; that is, the original type is replaced with a derived type (either a restricted or an extended type). This is achieved via the xsi:type attribute.

Final Remarks about XML Schema

Advantages

XML Schema marks a major step forward in schema definition for XML. With its rich hierarchy of datatypes, support for user-defined datatypes, support for namespaces, improved compatibility with relational databases, and support for schema modularization and reuse, XML Schema elevates XML from a mere document description language to a general data description language.

Restrictions

There are, however, a few restrictions:

- XML Schema does not support XML entities, which can require the use of both DTDs and XML Schema for document type definition. The order of processing is such that first the entities defined in the DTD are resolved (default values for attributes are also inserted into the document) before the document is validated against the XSD schema.
- Modeling constraints are limited under XML Schema. Single-field constraints can be modeled via user-defined datatype definitions and the unique construct. Cross-field constraints, however, such as referential integrity constraints, are limited to the key/keyref construct. We will discuss advanced schema validation techniques in Section 2.9.
- The definition of context-sensitive elements is possible via local element definitions but not for recursive elements. Recursive elements must be defined on the document level.
- XSD schemata can be quite long. In many cases, this will exclude XML Schema from client-side validation because transmission takes too long.

2.5 ACCESS AND COMPOSITION

While XML and XML Schema can be regarded as the core standards for XML, there are several other W3C specifications such as XPath, XPointer, XInclude, XQuery, XSL, and DOM that regulate access to XML documents and their composition and transformation.

2.5.1 XPath

The XPath recommendation (Clark and DeRose 1999) defines how nodes within XML documents can be accessed. XPath expressions are used in many other standards. We have already seen XPath utilized in the `unique`, key, and `keyref` constructs in XML Schema. XPath plays a crucial role in standards such as XSLT (Chapter 9) and XQuery (Section 2.6).

Because the XML information set has a tree structure it should be easy to pinpoint an element or an attribute by specifying all parent nodes, because this is done with path expressions that specify a file within a file directory. Therefore, for our <book> example, the expression

Tree structure

```
/book/@ISBN
```

identifies the ISBN attribute of the <book> element. In XPath's *abbreviated syntax*, attribute names are always prefixed with "@" (in the full syntax the prefix is `attribute::`).

That was easy. Things get a little bit more complicated when we have to deal with recurring elements. What does, for example,

Node sets

```
/book/authors/author/lastName
```

mean? Because the author element is recurring, the expression does not unambiguously identify a single node. Instead it resolves to a node *set*. The expression identifies the <lastName> elements in all <author> elements. In our example this would resolve to Goldfarb and Prescod. When we discuss the features of XPath, it is important to remember that XPath is operating with node sets and not only with single nodes.

To restrict node sets, XPath allows the specification of filters within a path expression. Here is a very simple filter that helps us select a specific author:

Filters

```
/book/authors/author[1]/lastName
```

Filters are always specified in brackets. The filter here selects the first element within the node set obtained by

```
/book/authors/author
```

Using filters we can thus pinpoint a single element within an XML document.

Axis specifiers   In the previous examples we have used only the parent-child relation to specify a node set. In addition, XPath allows the specification of node sets by exploiting other relations such as the ancestor-descendant relation, the positional order relation, or the relation between namespace and nodes. For this purpose, XPath provides *axis specifiers* such as `parent::`, `ancestor::`, `child::`, `descendant::`, `following::`, `namespace::`, and so on. However, what is mostly used is the *abbreviated syntax,* which we use in Table 2.2.

Upper and lower case   Like everything else in XML, string comparisons are also case sensitive. If we want to make case-insensitive comparisons, we have to translate both operands of the comparison into upper case. This can be done with the translate function:

```
translate("Goldfarb","abcdefghijklmnopqrstuvwxyz","ABCDEFGHIJKLMNO
PQRSTUVWXYZ")
```

However, this function, despite the rather extensive notation, does not work well for uppercase-lowercase translations in all languages. XPath 2.0 will address this issue.

Functions   In addition to the translate function, XPath supports other functions to test conditions or to compare contents (see Table 2.3).

2.5.2 XPointer

XPointer (DeRose, Maler, and Daniel 2001) is built on XPath. Its purpose is to augment URI addressing, so that it becomes possible to address fragments of an XML file. A similar feature is known in HTML: a specific anchor within an HTML page can be addressed by complementing a URI with the anchor name, for example,

```
http://www.bookshop.com/book/the_comic_book.html#reviews.
```

However, HTML requires the definition of an anchor element within the target document. XPointer, in contrast, allows access to document elements that are not specifically marked. It does so by exploiting the ability of XPath to pinpoint single elements within an XML document.

The syntax is simple:

document_uri#xpointer(*xpath_expression*)

Table 2.2 Operators in XPath.

Operator	Operation	Example	Result
/N1	document root node	/book	root node <book>
//N1	arbitrary element within document	//author	all <author> nodes in the document
N1/N2	parent-child relation	/book/title	all <title> elements that are direct children of node <book>
N1//N2	ancestor-descendant relation	/authors//lastName	all <lastName> elements that are descendants of node <authors>
*	wild card	/book/*/author	all <author> nodes that are grandchildren of node <book>
:	namespace	a:*	all nodes in namespace a
.	current node	.//@xml:lang	all xml:lang attributes which are descendants of the current node
..	parent node	..//@ISBN	all ISBN attributes which are descendants of the parent node
N1,N2	concatenation	/book//(title,author)	all <title> and <author> nodes that are descendants of node <book>
N1[n]	position	/book//author[1,last()]	first and last author
N1[N2]	existence	/book//author [middleName]/lastName	last names of all authors that have a middle name
N1[C2]	filter	/book/title [@xml:lang='US-EN']	all US-English titles
= !=	equality inequality	/book/author[lastName= 'Goldfarb']/firstName	<firstName>Charles</firstName>
>, >=, <, <=	comparison	/book//author [lastName>='K']	list of all authors from 'K' onward
?, *	wildcards	/book//author [lastName='G*']	list of all authors with last name starting with 'G'
or	Boolean OR	/book//author [lastName='G*' or lastName='P*']	list of all authors with last name starting with 'G' or with 'P'
and	Boolean AND	/book//author [lastName='Goldfarb' and firstName='Charles']	list of all authors with last name Goldfarb and first name Charles
+, -, *, div, mod	arithmetic operators	/bookOrder/orderList/ item/price*0.6	computes wholesale prices of all order items

Table 2.3 Functions in XPath.

Function	Operation	Example	Result
`id('foo')`	selects the element with the ID of `'foo'`	`id('a1')`	the author element with aid=`'a1'`
`last()`	number of last node in current context	`/book//author[1,last()]`	first and last author
`position()`	position of current node in parent context	`/book//author[position () < 3]`	first and second author
`count(node-set)`	number of nodes in node-set	`count(/book//author)`	number of authors
`not(object)`	all nodes of current context without the nodes contained in operand	`/book//author[not (lastName='Goldfarb')]`	all <author> nodes with a last name not equal to `'Goldfarb'`
`true()`, `false()`	Boolean values true and false	`/book/title[false()]`	returns empty node list
`number(object)`	converts to numeric value	`number(price) > 20.00`	true if price is greater than 20.00
`sum(node-set)`	sums up numeric values of a node set	`sum(/item/price) div count(/item/price)`	computes average price over all items
`contains (str,str)`	containment	`/book[contains(title,'XML')]`	all book titles containing `'XML'`
`translate(str, str,str)`	translates a string using a character translation table	`translate('XML','LMX','lmx')`	returns `'xml'`

For example,

```
http://www.bookdomain.com/books/
        the_xml_handbook.xml#xpointer(//author[1])
```

Multiple targets

addresses the first <author> element within our XML book example. If we had omitted the [1], we would have addressed all <author> elements: pointers can point to multiple targets.

XPointer introduces some extensions of its own:

```
#xpointer(string-range(path,substring))
```

addresses all strings matching 'substring' within the element that is specified by path. For example,

http://www.bookdomain.com/books/the_xml_handbook.xml
                #xpointer(string-range(//title,'XML'))

addresses all 'XML' substrings in the <title> elements of our example.

Another feature of XPointer is the ability to address *ranges* within a   Ranges document:

#xpointer(startpoint/range-to(endpoint))

For example, the expression

#xpointer(//author[1]/firstName/range-to(lastName))

addresses the range from the <firstName> element to the <lastName> element of the first <author> element in our book example.

We finish our short discussion of XPointer with two forms of abbreviated syntax that XPointer entertains:

#identifier

is equivalent to

#xpointer(id("identifier"))

meaning that it points to the element with the ID "identifier". Although this notation is similar to a fragment pointer in HTML, there is a difference: in HTML the fragment is identified by an <A> element with a specific name attribute. XPointer, in contrast, can use this syntax to point to any element that has an attribute of type ID.

#/1/3/2/1/2

addresses elements by counting, starting at the root element. When an element is found, the process continues with the next number, counting the child elements of that element, and so on. In the context of our example the above specification would be equivalent to

#xpointer(/book/authors/author[2]/name/lastName)

2.5.3 XInclude

XInclude (currently a working draft) specifies how to include external XML documents (or, by using the XPointer notation, parts thereof) in a target XML document (Marsh and Orchard 2001). As such it is designed to eventually replace external entities.

For example:

```
<?xml version="1.0"?>
<book xmlns:xi="http://www.w3.org/1999/XML/xinclude">
...
  <xi:include href="legaldoc.xml"/>
</book>
```

with `legal.xml` defined as

```
<legaldoc>
  The publishers' view may differ from the authors' expressed
opinion
</legaldoc>
```

This would result in the following document:

```
<?xml version="1.0"?>
<book xmlns:xi="http://www.w3.org/1999/XML/xinclude">
...
  <legaldoc>
    The publishers' view may differ from the authors' expressed
opinion
  </legaldoc>
</book>
```

Namespace support

XInclude can compose documents from different namespaces. The attribute `parse="text"` allows the inclusion of unparsed text. Otherwise, the default value of `parse="xml"` forces the processor to parse the included text and reject non–well-formed XML. If the parsed text contains nested inclusions, these are resolved as well.

2.5.4 XML Base

XML Base is probably the shortest standard the W3C has ever published. It specifies just a single attribute: `xml:base` (Marsh 2001). We will keep this section similarly short. Basically, `xml:base` specifies a *base URI* as the basis for all *relative URIs* that appear in the element where `xml:base` is specified. Typical applications are XLink and XInclude.

2.6 QUERYING XML

XQuery currently has the status of a working draft (Chamberlin, Clark, et al. 2001): "It is inappropriate to use W3C Working Drafts as reference material or to cite them as other than work in progress." Given that, here we will take only a short browse through the major concepts of XQuery. An extensive base of use cases, queries, and expected results is contained in Chamberlin, Fankhauser, et al. (2001).

XQuery is derived from Jonathan Robie's Quilt, which in turn utilizes   Origins
concepts from other query language proposals. There had been quite a few: the definition of a standard query language for XML has a history. Many of the results obtained by this work found their way into the definition of XPath (see Section 2.5.1). XQuery, therefore, addresses topics that are not covered by XPath. XQuery expressions look a bit similar to SQL expressions, and indeed XQuery borrows concepts from SQL and OQL. Figure 2.4 shows XQuery in action.

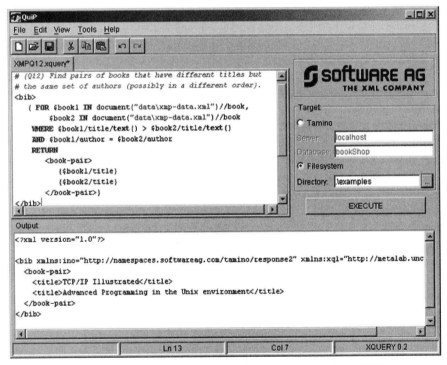

Figure 2.4 XQuery in action: QuiP, an early implementation of XQuery, doing a join over a document base of books.

2.6.1 Expression Types

An XQuery expression can consist of a number of expression types.

Path Expressions

Path expressions are formulated using XPath (see Section 2.5.1), which is currently also under revision (XPath 2.0). XQuery is expected to be a superset of XPath 2.0.

In XQuery, only the abbreviated XPath syntax is used. The result of a path expression is a list of nodes. For XQuery two operators were added: the *dereference operator* and the *range operator.*

- The range operator `RANGE x TO y` specifies a range of nodes.

  For example: `//book/authors/author [RANGE 1 TO 2]/name` results in a list of name elements for two authors.
- The dereference operator `=>` can follow an IDREF-type attribute. It returns the element(s) that are referenced by the attribute. This operator has a similar function as the `id()` function in XPath.

  For example: `//PurchaseOrder/Orderline/@pid=>Description` would extract the product id from a purchase order document, look up the product element identified by this product id, and return the description of the product.

  The XQuery Draft currently specifies the dereference operator only for IDREF-type attributes, not for the more general `keyref` construct of XML Schema.

Variables

XQuery supports the use of variables. Variable names are prefixed with "$". It is possible to assign a value to a variable (see below) and to reuse that value in a later part of the same query. This is an important feature for performing complex joins.

Element Constructors

Element constructors are, as the name says, used to construct new elements. These can constitute the result of the query, or they can be assigned to a variable for later usage. Element constructors allow the output of a query to be freely structured. For example:

```
<book ISBN = $isbn>
   <title> $t </title>
   <author> $a </author>
</book>
```

Using variables in place of tag names is also allowed:

```
<$ProductOrService productID = $pid>
```

FLWR Expressions

"Flower" expressions are constituted from the keywords FOR, LET, WHERE, and RETURN, which are used in this sequence. These keywords make an XQuery expression look almost like an SQL expression.

The first part of a query consists of a FOR or LET clause or a combination. FOR is used where iterations are needed. For example:

```
FOR $a IN //book/authors
```

This iterates over all elements in authors, assigning with each iteration a new author element to $a.

LET assigns the result of an expression to a variable. For example:

```
LET $v := //book/authors
```

This assigns the whole authors element to $v.

The second part is optional and consists of a WHERE clause. WHERE acts as a filter. Only when the WHERE clause is true is the RETURN clause invoked. The condition in the WHERE clause may be a Boolean expression connected by AND, OR, or NOT. For example:

```
WHERE $a/Name/LastName = "Goldfarb"
  AND $a/Name/FirstName = "Charles"
```

The last part of the expression consists of a RETURN clause. RETURN returns the results of the FLWR expression. Its operand is usually a reference to a variable or an element constructor. For example:

```
RETURN $a/@aid
```

This would return the @aid attribute of the author element that was previously assigned to $a.

Expressions Involving Operators and Functions

Expressions can be constructed in XQuery using infix and prefix operators. Parentheses are used for nested expressions. XQuery supports the usual set of arithmetic and logical operators. In addition it supports the collection operators UNION, INTERSECT, and EXCEPT. The operators BEFORE and AFTER can be used to select nodes by relative position.

Conditional Expressions

Conditional expressions are constructed in the usual way with the keywords IF, THEN, ELSE. For example:

```
IF name($e) = "Service"
   THEN $e/Duration
   ELSE <Duration xsi:nil="true"/>
```

Quantified Expressions

The keywords SOME and EVERY, in combination with SATISFIES, allow us to test if some or all elements in a collection meet a specific condition. For example:

```
FOR $b IN //book
WHERE SOME $p IN $b/authors SATISFIES
  $p/Name/LastName = "Goldfarb"
RETURN $b/Title
```

List Constructors

Lists can be constructed with brackets; the list elements are separated by commas. The empty list is represented by []. The function distinct() can be used to remove duplicates from a list. The operator SORTBY can be used to sort a list.

Expressions That Test or Modify Datatypes

XQuery uses the type system defined in XML Schema (see Section 2.4.2). The keyword ELEMENT is used for element types defined with <xsd:any>. LIST(x) is used for lists containing elements of type x.

It is possible to test the type of a node (INSTANCEOF) or to modify the type of a node (CAST). The keyword TREAT allows us to narrow down a type. For example:

```
IF $a INSTANCEOF postalAddress
THEN computePostage(TREAT AS postalAddress($a))
```

Functions

XQuery defines a set of built-in functions. We have already used the function name(), which returns the tag name of an element. Contained in XQuery are the functions known from XPath, all the aggregation functions of SQL (such as avg(), sum(), count(), max(), and min()), and some other useful functions such as distinct() or empty().

In addition, XQuery allows the definition of user-defined functions. For example:

User-defined functions

```
FUNCTION grandchildren(ELEMENT $e)
                    RETURNS LIST(ELEMENT)
{ $e/*/* }
```

Functions can be defined recursively. The following function lists all part and subpart IDs for a product:

```
FUNCTION subpartIDs(ELEMENT $e)
                    RETURNS LIST(ELEMENT)
{
 $e/@pid UNION subpartIDs($e/parts/@pid=>*)
}
```

Joins

Using this functionality, it is possible to construct powerful queries. The use of variables allows the construction of any type of joins (there is no special join operator in XQuery).

For example:

```
<books-with-or-without-reviews>
{
  FOR $s IN document("book.xml")
  RETURN
    <book>
      {
        $s/title, $s/authors
        FOR $r IN document("reviews.xml")
                            [title = $s/title],
        RETURN $r/review, $r/reviewer
      }
    </book>
  SORTBY(authors/author[1]/name/lastName)
}
</books-with-or-without-reviews>
```

This is a left outer join, listing all books. If reviews exist for a specific book, the reviews are merged into the result; if not, the book is listed without reviews. The results are sorted according to the last name of the first author.

Here is another example:

```
<books-with-reviews>
{
  FOR $s IN document("book.xml"),
      $r IN document("reviews.xml")[title = $s/title]
  RETURN
    <book>
      {
        $s/title, $s/authors, $r/review, $r/reviewer
      }
    </book>
  SORTBY(authors/author[1]/name/lastName)
}
</books-with-reviews>
```

This is the classic inner join, listing only the books having reviews. Note that the join is accomplished with a filter expression ([title = $s/title]). This construct allows for a very wide range of joins indeed; the equality join is only a special case.

2.6.2 Discussion

XML is an integrative data format. A large amount of information on the Web is in XML format, relational databases provide XML interfaces, and knowledge bases using RDF (see Section 3.3) or topic maps (Section 7.2) have an XML serialization format. With a language such as XQuery it becomes possible to query and *combine* all these sources of wisdom.

Syntax   While the proposed syntax is well suited for user interfaces and builds on the knowledge of SQL-educated users, an alternate XML-ish syntax is needed as well, to allow the programmatic generation of queries through a DOM API or with the help of an XSLT style sheet. The W3C has published a working draft for such a syntax (Malhotra, Robie, and Rys 2001).

2.7 XSL (EXTENSIBLE STYLESHEET LANGUAGE)

The XSL specifications define how XML documents can be transformed into another format, especially into a presentation format. The specifications come in three parts: XPath, XSLT, and XSLFO.

XPath   XPath (see Section 2.5.1) was originally designed in the context of XSL. Now it has become a separate recommendation that plays an important role both within XSL and within XQuery. Many other specifications, such as XML Schema and XPointer, rely on XPath.

XSLT (XSL Transformations) specifies—as the name says—how XML **XSLT** documents can be transformed into another XML (or non-XML) format. XSLT has both declarative and procedural elements to specify transformations and relies heavily on XPath. Because of its importance as a multipurpose tool for processing XML documents, we discuss XSLT extensively in Chapter 9.

One possible outcome of such transformations is formatting objects **XSLFO** (XSLFO). Formatting objects (see Section 8.2.4) conclude the XSL trilogy. XSLFO can be compared to CSS in the HTML domain. It must be said that the transformation into HTML + CSS is currently a more realistic approach for displaying XML documents than the transformation into formatting objects because few Web browsers support formatting objects. However, formatting objects can be used as an intermediate format when converting an XML document into a PDF document (see also Section 8.6).

2.8 XML APIs

Application program interfaces for XML define how applications can make use of existing parsers and other XML tools. Although applications are free to treat an XML document as a plain character string and do the parsing with custom logic, it is better if they avoid this and use a standard parser such as SAX or DOM.

2.8.1 SAX

SAX (Simple API for XML) is not a W3C standard but a joint development of the members of the XML-DEV mailing list. Various SAX parsers for different programming languages, such as Java, C++, Python, Perl, or Delphi, are publicly available. The SAX specifications are published at *www.megginson.com*.

SAX is an event-based parser—the parser reads an XML input stream. **Event based** In the case of events (such as `startDocument`, `endDocument`, `startElement`, `endElement`, `characters`, `ignorableWhitespace`, and `processingInstruction`), the parser calls back similarly named methods or routines of the host program, which can then take appropriate action. Because XML documents have a tree structure, the host program can analyze a document with relative ease. Encountering a `startElement` event, the program pushes the node onto a stack, while an endElement event removes the top element from the stack. Using such a technique, the host program is always aware of the current context of an element.

SAX is relatively easy on resources. It does not require much memory because it is not necessary to store the whole XML document in memory. Because of its simplicity, SAX is easy to learn, too. On the other hand, SAX is a read-only API: it is not possible to modify an existing XML document via SAX.

SAX2

The new SAX2 API additionally incorporates support for XML namespaces, filter chains, and querying.

SAX parsers are also called push-parsers because the parser pushes recognized tokens toward the client. Recently, so-called pull-parsers have appeared, parsers where the client controls the parsing process. This provides increased flexibility to the client, and consequently newer DOM implementations (see next section) use pull-parsing techniques.

2.8.2 DOM

The Document Object Model (DOM) is a full application programming interface for XML documents. It allows clients not only to navigate within XML documents but also to retrieve, add, modify, or delete elements and content. To provide a language-independent API description, the DOM specification makes use of the OMG IDL (Object Management Group Interface Description Language) as defined in the CORBA 2.2 specification.

Performance issues

In contrast to SAX, DOM stores the complete document structure in memory. The document is first read in and parsed, and then a tree of node objects is built in memory. Because at least one object is needed for each document node, DOM is relatively heavy on resources. More recent DOM implementations, however, such as Enhydra DOM (Java) and pulldom, contained in pyXML (Python), use lazy instantiation to save resources. This technique requires slightly more overhead if you access an element at the very end of a document, but should provide a SAX-like resource utilization when you access an element at the very beginning of a document.

After the complete document has been parsed, control is passed back to the host program. This program can then use the methods of the DOM API to navigate the document tree and to retrieve content, modify nodes, delete nodes, or insert new nodes. After processing, the document tree can be written to an output stream.

Random access

The advantage of DOM for the programmer is that it is not he or she who has to do the bookkeeping. Context information can be readily obtained via the DOM API. For programmers, DOM is the API of choice when random access to document content is required.

Because the DOM API is very rich (the Element interface alone has 27 different methods, and DOM knows 17 different interfaces), for programmers there is some effort involved in mastering DOM programming.

A popular DOM implementation on Windows platforms is Microsoft's MSXML. Since it has a COM interface, it equips any COM-enabled Windows application (including VBScript) with an XML DOM. Another popular DOM implementation is Xerces, from the Apache Software Foundation, which exists in a Java and a C++ version. In the Java community JDOM and DOM4J are popular. These APIs have a simpler (albeit nonstandard) interface.

There are currently three DOM API levels: DOM Level 1, DOM Level 2, and DOM Level 3 (LeHors et al. 2001). Apart from other improvements, DOM Level 2 adds an event model (McCarron et al. 2001) to the DOM specification. DOM Level 3 adds an XML content model, load and save, document validation with DTD or XML Schema, and better namespace handling.

Levels

2.8.3 Binding

The Java Architecture for XML Binding (JAXB) is a recent (and still ongoing) development that can replace SAX- and DOM-based solutions in Java environments (JAXB 2001). JAXB includes a compiler that maps a DTD or XML Schema to a set of Java classes (a binding schema must manually be created to define this mapping). Document instances can then be converted to Java class instances (objects) and vice versa. Because the JAXB framework generates specific classes to represent the document type, JAXB can achieve a higher processing speed than a SAX parser (which works in interpretative mode and requires a call-back method invocation with every token processed). After importing a document, the elements and attributes can be accessed and manipulated as ordinary Java objects and fields, providing a similar if not higher degree of ease of use than DOM, but taking fewer resources. Note, however, that a DTD or schema is required to process XML documents with JAXB.

Similar technology is available with Breeze XML Studio, Software AG's Bolero (Daum and Scheller 2000), Enhydra's Zeus, and others.

2.8.4 Which API?

The decision on which of the three APIs (SAX, DOM, or JAXB) to use depends largely on the platform. If you need access via a COM interface (for example, from VBScript), you have to use MSXML, so you are limited to DOM and SAX2. In a Java environment, however, JAXB probably will be the best choice once it is released. Currently, as we stated earlier, JDOM and DOM4J are popular in the Java community, although this technology is still in beta status and provides no standard APIs.

The decision between DOM and SAX is not too difficult. If you want not only to read documents but also to update them, use DOM. If your documents contain cross-references (using ID and IDREF attributes), use DOM because you need to go back and forth to evaluate the document. If you need random access to document nodes, use DOM. If you don't know how to implement a stack, use DOM.

Otherwise use SAX. It will happily noodle even mega- and gigabyte-sized documents.

2.9 SCHEMA DEFINITION—STAGE 3

Even before the definition of the W3C's XML Schema specification, schema definition was the topic of heated debate, and it still remains so after the final recommendation. The current discussion on "when to use DTDs and when to use XML Schema" is an indication that XML Schema is not the answer to all problems. In particular, XML Schema is considered by many to be too complicated and too heavyweight. But it also misses out on some finer points of schema definition such as cross-element and cross-attribute checks, for example.

About a month after the release of the final XML Schema recommendation, OASIS published a draft for "the next-generation schema language," called RELAX NG. RELAX NG is based on the earlier RELAX and on James Clark's TREX. It is lightweight like DTDs but includes support for namespaces, for modularization (including the possibility of constructing unions, intersections, and differences of schemata), and for datatypes (incorporating XML Schema datatypes), and it also has some other improvements. Last but not least, a RELAX NG schema is—in contrast to a DTD—an XML document. Details are given in Clark and Murata (2001) and Daum (2002).

2.9.1 A Feather Duster for XML Schemata

When we earlier discussed XML Schema, we had already observed that XML Schema allows the definition of only the most basic constraints such as datatypes and uniqueness. XML Schema fails when it comes to constraints that involve several elements or attributes. If we want, for example, to enforce that attribute B must be present whenever attribute A is present, or that attributes A and B are mutually exclusive, we are out of luck. Or, if we want to enforce the presence of element C when attribute A contains an "@" character, we are similarly left on our own.

Rick Jellife's Schematron (Jellife 2001) is a tool that can do such constraint validation. Although Schematron is not a schema definition language in its own right, it can be used alongside DTDs and XML Schema.

Schematron

The concept of Schematron is as simple as it is ingenious. The technique used is a bit similar to the one used in XML Schema for the definition of `unique`, `key`, or `keyref` constraints (Jellife is a member of the XML Schema working group). Each Schematron script consists of a number of rules. Each rule first specifies a context node, via an XPath expression. On the basis of the selected context node, other XPath expressions perform tests. The success or failure of each test is reported. Since XPath is quite powerful, the range of constraints that can be checked is very wide. In particular it is possible to check for cross-element and cross-document constraints.

Technically, Schematron utilizes XSLT to validate an XML document. Using an appropriate XSL style sheet, the document is transformed into a report that gives information about invalid structures within the document. However, this requires that the XML document is already well formed; otherwise it would not be possible to process it with XSLT.

Based on XSLT

Schematron uses a two-phase concept: The first step is only applied once to a particular Schematron script and compiles it—with the help of the Schematron processor style sheet—into a validation style sheet. In the second step this validation style sheet is applied to individual document instances.

Here is an example of a Schematron script that requires that the `<lastName>` of a book author must be specified whenever a `<firstName>` was specified.

```
<schema>
  <pattern name = "author name checks">
    <rule context = "book/authors/author/name">
      <assert test = "not(firstName)
               or (firstName and lastName)">
        lastName missing in author&apos;s name
      </assert>
    </rule>
  </pattern>
</schema>
```

The context attribute in the `<rule>` element specifies the context node `book/authors/author/name`. The `<assert>` element then tests for the constraint. If the test fails, the text content of the `<assert>` element goes into the report.

Similar schema validation is possible with the Schema Adjunct Framework discussed in Section 4.4.2.

2.9.2 Elements Versus Attributes

In the XML community (and previously in the SGML community) there is a long and ongoing debate about when to use an element to model an information or data item and when to use an attribute. At times the debate has become almost a religious issue: each party is in the possession of "The Truth"—even if their respective truths are mutually exclusive (for the philosophical and logical background of this phenomenon, see Section 4.3).

We are not inclined to take the position of either side but will simply list the pros and cons of each approach. What we will find is that with the definition of XML Schema some of the arguments against elements do not hold any longer. In this respect, XML now differs from SGML.

Attribute
oriented

The following is a boiled-down version of our `<book>` example from Section 2.2 with the extensive use of attributes. The difference in size is striking, and this is also the main reason why authors use attributes to represent content.

```
<book title="The XML-Handbook™">
  <authors>
    <author aid="a1" name="Charles F. Goldfarb"/>
    <author aid="a2" name="Paul Prescod"/>
  </authors>
</book>
```

You can also see that we have cut some corners in order to make it fit. In particular we have kept only a single language for the title. To represent a multilingual title in one attribute (unlike elements, you cannot have several attributes with the same name as children of a single element), we would be required to invent a rather complex attribute format (similar to CSS-style attribute syntax):

```
title="en-us:The XML-Handbook™;de-de:Das XML-Handbuch"
```

This in turn would require us to implement a custom parser to process this complex attribute; furthermore we must postulate that no title ever contains a semicolon. Standard processors such as XSLT would not be able to break this attribute string into pieces; it would require the use of custom extension logic. Alternatively, we could create differently named attributes—one for each language.

There is no problem parsing the author's name. This attribute type could be declared as NMTOKENS, so a parser would give us a list of tokens consisting of first name, middle name, and last name. But beware: nothing stops us from specifying a name like this:

```
<author aid="a2" name="Prescod, Paul"/>
```

Now the parser would return us "Prescod," as the first name and "Paul" as the last name (assuming that we always interpret the last list element as last name). Custom logic would be required to look for a trailing "," after "Prescod" and swap the tokens accordingly (and remove the comma).

You can clearly see the drawbacks of attributes for representing complex information.

A good compromise therefore might be

```
<author aid="a2"
  <name first="Paul" last="Prescod"/>
</author>
```

or

```
<author aid="a2" first_name="Paul" last_name="Prescod"/>
```

However, in the second case we lose some structural information (that a name is comprised of a first name and a last name).

Despite the problems in our naive approach to attributes, it is, in fact, possible to represent any information structure using attributes only. This is done in a way similar to relational databases: the data is normalized and finally represented as an interrelated network of "flat" elements. The relations between the data elements are not represented through the implicit hierarchical relations between parent and child elements, but explicitly via ID, IDREF, and IDREFS attributes:

```
<book titles="title.1 title.2"
  authors="author.1 author.2"/>
<Title id="title.1" xml:lang="en-us">
  The XML-Handbook™ </Title>
<Title id="title.2" xml:lang="de-de">
  Das XML-Handbuch </Title>
<author id="author.1" aid="a1" name="name.1"/>
<author id="author.2" aid="a2" name="name.2"/>
```

Compromise

"Flat"
documents

```
<Name id="name.1"
 first="Charles" middle="F." last="Goldfarb"/>
<Name id="name.2" first="Paul" last="Prescod"/>
```

Here the structure of the document is established via matching ID and IDREFS (IDREFS) keys (@titles, @authors, @name). The advantage is that we can use the well-known relational techniques (see Section 3.1) to keep the design of such a document sound. The disadvantage is that the document is hard to read. Also it is not shorter than the original document—on the contrary, it is longer. Constructing such a document also requires some bookkeeping (to allocate unique keys to elements), and retrieving information from such a document requires much cross-referencing and joining.

Minimal XML   Juxtaposed to this design there are also concepts that throw attributes out altogether. This has culminated in the definition of MinXML (Park 2000), a minimal XML definition (without attributes, entities, CDATA, mixed elements, etc). The logic to process such XML is surprisingly simple; a parser can be formulated in 28 JavaScript statements (by Sjoerd Visscher).

```
<book>
  <title>
    <lang>en-us</lang>
    <text>The XML-Handbook™</text>
  </title>
  <title>
    <lang>de-de</lang>
    <text>Das XML-Handbuch</text>
  </title>
  <authors>
    <author>
      <aid>a1</aid>
      <name>
        <firstName>Charles</firstName>
        <middleName>F.</middleName>
        <lastName>Goldfarb</lastName>
      </name>
    </author>
    <author>
      <aid>a2</aid>
      <name>
        <firstName>Paul</firstName>
```

```
      <lastName>Prescod</lastName>
    </name>
  </author>
</authors>
</book>
```

The truth lies somewhere between these two extremes and largely depends on context and personal taste. Is it essential that the documents be as short as possible, or is it important that the processing logic be kept simple? Is the document only to be used by machines, or is it also to be read by humans? Are the documents machine generated or authored by humans, and, if the latter, with which tools?

Here are a few strong reasons to prefer attributes: Pro attributes

1. Attributes support the construction of relationships with ID/IDREF keys.
2. A DTD can define default values only for attributes.
3. A DTD allows simple type definitions (ID, IDREF, NMTOKEN, and so on) for attributes but not for elements.
4. Attributes of an element form an unordered set. This can sometimes be handy when no sequence order between information items is required.
5. Attributes are much easier to access in DOM and SAX.
6. When authoring document-centric XML in an appropriate XML editor, it is often more convenient to use attributes—as the name suggests—for attributing text. The attributes will not litter the running text, and spell checking is only applied to elements.

However, with the advent of XML Schema, these advantages of attributes vanish, especially items 1–4, because XML Schema allows the definition of unique keys, default values, types, and unordered sets for elements also.

And here are a few strong reasons to prefer elements: Pro elements

1. An element can have multiple child elements of the same kind. This is not possible with attributes.
2. Elements can be easily extended by adding child elements or attributes.
3. Attributes of an element always form an unordered set, so it is not possible to establish a sequence order across attributes.
4. Elements can contain whitespace and delimiters; whitespace handling can be specified on the element level.
5. Attributes are harder to search for in search engines.
6. Attributes do not support nil values.

7. When editing data-centric XML in an XML editor, storing content in attributes makes the editing process more difficult. Extra keystrokes are often required to view the attributes.

So, with XML Schema the scale tips toward the use of elements. But we wouldn't discard attributes completely. There are two rules of thumb on when to use what.

Rules of thumb
First, some authors recommend using elements to represent the entities of an entity relationship model (see Section 3.2) and using attributes to represent the properties of these entities. But what about complex properties? A name, for example, is clearly a property of an entity (such as a customer) but has a complex structure (first name, middle name, last name). So, we are not too sure about that case.

Second, use attributes to describe metadata (such as language identifier, element author, element version, element ID, etc.) and use elements to model content. This is more or less how we have used attributes and elements in the past. However, what is content and what is metadata can depend on the context. A good definition to distinguish content from metadata is from Elliot Kimber:

> One way to distinguish metadata from content is to ask the question "if I removed this data, would my understanding of or ability to comprehend the content change?" If the answer is no, it's metadata, if the answer is yes, it's content (or annotation, which is the third fundamental class of information).

2.9.3 XML Design Patterns

A good exercise when designing an XML Schema is to look at existing schemata. Maybe we can utilize an existing schema and extend it a bit to fit our own requirements. If this is not possible, it may still be possible to pick up a few design elements (i.e., design patterns) and utilize them for our own purposes.

Origins
Design patterns were introduced as a formal method into design by the architect Christopher Alexander (who had a background in mathematics as well). Alexander published on urban planning and building architecture in the late 1970s. In the late 1980s design patterns were picked up by software architects and found their culmination in the work of the "gang of four," Erich Gamma, Richard Helm, Ralph Johnson, and John Vlissides (Gamma et al. 1995). Since then patterns have become popular in software design.

Design patterns describe the relationship between a problem, the context of the problem, and the solution to the problem. They describe this relationship in such a generic way that it becomes possible to transfer the way of solving the problem into a different context. Design patterns are not invented: they are discovered when similar solutions are found to solve similar problems in various contexts.

Now that XML has been around for a few years, design patterns are beginning to emerge to solve problems with the design of XML documents. These patterns can be fairly generic or can be more specific, for example, to solve design problems in the area of electronic business. We therefore find various design patterns connected with the various electronic business platforms such as RosettaNet, BizTalk, or ebXML. These patterns are published either on supporting Web sites in the form of guidelines, or as reusable patterns stored in business community repositories.

A Web site dedicated to generic design patterns for XML is *www.xmlpatterns.com*. At the time of writing, this Web site contained 28 patterns: Catch-All Element, Choice Reducing Container, Collection Element, Common Attributes, Consistent Element Set, Container Element, Content Type Label, Declare Before First Use, Domain Element, Envelope, Extensible Content Model, Flyweight, Generic Element, Head-Body, Marketplace, Metadata First, Metadata in Separate Document, Multi Root Document Types, Multiple Document Types, Optional Container Element, Parallel Design, Referenced Note, Reuse Document Types, Role Attribute, Separate Metadata and Data, Short Understandable Names, Universal Root, Use XML.

Web site

Here is an example for the Extensible Content Model pattern. The pattern addresses the problem that at the time of designing a schema the designer may not be able to predict all the possible use cases for the schema and therefore wants to allow document authors to customize the schema on the instance level.

The solution is that the schema designer adds an extension mechanism to the schema definition. Since we already have discussed such a mechanism (instance subtyping) for XML Schema (see Section 2.4.2), we present here only a solution for DTDs. This solution is based on parameter entities (see Section 2.3.2), which the document author can overwrite on the instance level.

Let's discuss this for the example of our book DTD. The book element currently has only the child elements title and authors. If we want to allow document authors to add additional elements, we can do this in the following way:

Extending DTDs

```
<!ENTITY % details "">

<!ELEMENT book (title+,authors %details;)>

...
```

We have defined an empty parameter entity `details` and have appended it to the definition of element `book`.

The document author can override the definition of parameter entity `details` in the internal DTD subset and can then add additional definitions:

```
DOCTYPE book SYSTEM "http://www.book.org/book" [

<!ENTITY % details ", Price" >

<!ELEMENT Price (#PCDATA)>

]>
```

Given this definition the document body must then contain a `Price` element after the `authors` element.

2.9.4 Architectural Forms

Architectural forms were first formally defined in SGML in 1997 as part of the SGML Extended Facilities in ISO/IEC 10744:1997, Annex A.3, Architectural Form Definition Requirements (Kimber 1998). It did not take long to adapt this technology to XML; a first SAX parser enabled for architectural forms appeared with the XAF package from David Megginson (1998). A recent development is APEX, an XSLT style sheet that provides the same functionality as XAF. APEX is published as part of the National Institute for Standards and Technology (NIST) XSL Toolbox (*ats.nist.gov/xsltoolbox/*), written by Josh Lubell.

Base architectures

Now, what are architectural forms? Architectural forms (AF) could be roughly compared to a combination of interface and adaptor in object-oriented programming. Concrete XML document types can relate to one or multiple *base architectures* (which are document types, too). An AF-aware parser can then validate whether document instances satisfy the specified architectural forms. Elements that do not conform with a specified base architecture can be suppressed so that it is possible to generate different views from a single document.

This technique allows the definition of specific document schemata that implement given corporate standards. Rather than defining a single huge and unwieldy XML schema containing every possible element used within a corporation, the corporate standards are incorporated into several rather small base architectures. The document schemata created by different work groups can relate to these base architectures, and document instances created according to these schemata can be checked against these base architectures. Different vocabularies used in the base architectures are not a problem because AF allows the renaming of elements.

To use architectural forms with a document, at least one base architec-   Using AF
ture must be specified in a document in the form of an XML processing
instruction:

```
<?IS10744:arch name="Person" auto="nArcAuto"?>
```

The pseudo-attribute name specifies the name of the base architecture. The
pseudo-attribute auto controls automatic association (see below). A document may specify several base architectures simply by adding more processing instructions.

We can then use the name of a base architecture within an element
definition to map the element of a document instance to an element within the base architecture (or several base architectures). In the
following example we use three base architectures. One (<Product>) controls the layout of the <book> element; the other two (<Person> and <Per-
sonId>) control the layout of <author> elements. We have emphasized
these base architectures. We see also how the elements <author>, <first-
Name>, <middleName>, and <lastName> are mapped to <Person>, <first>,
<middle>, and <last>.

```
<?IS10744:arch name="Product" auto="nArcAuto"?>
<?IS10744:arch name="Person" auto="nArcAuto"?>
<?IS10744:arch name="PersonId" auto="nArcAuto"?>
<book Product="Product">
  <title Product="name" xml:lang="en-us">
    The XML-Handbook™
  </title>
  <title Product="name" xml:lang="de-de">
    Das XML-Handbuch
  </title>
  <authors>
    <author Person="Person" PersonID="PersonID" aid="a1">
      <name Person="name">
        <firstName Person="first">Charles</firstName>
        <middleName Person="middle">F.</middleName>
        <lastName Person="last">Goldfarb</lastName>
      </name>
    </author>
    ...
  </authors>
</book>
```

The three base architectures may look like these:

```
<Product>
  <name xml:lang="en-us">
    product-name
  </name>
</Product>

<Person>
  <name>
    <first>first</first>
    <middle>middle</middle>
    <last>last</last>
  </name>
</Person>

<PersonId aid="a1">
</PersonId>
```

Default mapping   As we have already mentioned, it is possible to use a default mapping of target document names to base architecture names. To enable this feature, the `auto` pseudo-attribute of the processing instruction is set to `auto="ArcAuto"`. The element within the target document is then mapped to an element with the same name in the base architecture. Additional syntactical elements allow us to ignore the base architecture for certain child elements, to rename or ignore attributes, and to bridge references between ID/IDREF attributes. The documentation in David Megginson's XAF package describes these features in detail (Megginson 1998).

It is, of course, not necessary to specify all these mappings in the document instance. We can easily define the attributes used to accomplish the mapping, such as `Product="name"`, as fixed-value attributes within the DTD or within an XML Schema. Similarly, we can define the processing instructions in the DTD or XML Schema, too. By using this technique, document instances do not differ from document instances that do not use architectural forms.

AF vs. XML Schema   If we compare architectural forms with the reuse mechanisms found in XML Schema, we find the following:

- XML Schema can compose a new schema from several smaller schemata and type libraries, but architectural forms cannot. Rather they allow checking given document instances against a set of "guidelines."

- Architectural forms do have a rename mechanism for element and attribute names, which the `include` and `import` facilities in XML Schema don't offer. XML Schema, in contrast, has a redefinition mechanism, allowing the type of included elements to be changed.
- With architectural forms a document element can claim conformance to multiple architectures simultaneously. This is not possible with XML Schema.

2.10 BEST PRACTICES

In this section, we list a number of best practices that are discussed in the XML community.

2.10.1 Always Use Namespaces

Small schemata are likely to be integrated into large schemata. Large schemata are often developed by separate work groups in a modular fashion. Because they prevent name conflicts, namespaces make it easier to assemble large schemata from smaller ones—even if the work group consists only of a single person. A good schema is very likely to be reused by others!

In document instances, elements should always be qualified with a namespace, either by using a default namespace or by using a namespace prefix. This is not necessary for attributes because attribute names are defined in relation to their context.

2.10.2 Do Not Reinvent the Wheel

Instead of designing every document type from scratch, use existing document types (if possible use industry standards) and extend these to your requirements. This will save you a lot of work, will usually result in higher-quality schema definitions, and will ensure that core concepts of your document are understood by others, too.

Most public repositories currently store XML schemas in the form of DTDs. Extending such a schema is done with the traditional means of cut and paste, since DTDs do not have an inheritance mechanism.

XML Schema has a powerful inheritance mechanism. Schema definitions can be composed from schema modules using `include` and `import`. Complex datatypes (i.e., nested elements) can be extended; that is, attributes and child elements can be added. The wildcard mechanism

(<xsd:any>) allows the definition of elements that follow a completely different schema (of a different namespace).

Remember that deep inheritance hierarchies can become hard to read. In object-oriented programming, where inheritance is extensively used, this phenomenon is known as the "yo-yo effect"— you have to go up and down the inheritance hierarchy repeatedly to understand the result.

2.10.3 Multipart Schemata?

Some authors (in particular, see *www.biztalk.org*) warn against using multipart schemata because they multiply the dependencies between software artifacts. These dependencies can make a system hard to maintain. Things can get very complicated—especially if you build a full inheritance hierarchy for document types and you have to maintain a corresponding taxonomy of Java (and/or C++, JavaScript, etc.) classes. (The same is true for architectural forms.) You could end up like Gulliver in Lilliput, held down by thousands of strings and unable to move.

Others, however, advocate the use of multipart schemata to construct larger schemata from smaller components and type libraries (see, for example, *www.xfront.com*).

2.10.4 Avoid External Entities

Similarly, external entities increase the dependencies between software artifacts. Additionally, not all XML processors (including some databases and messaging middleware) support external entities. For example, if you want to embellish each XML document of a site with some corporate information, it will be better to postprocess the documents using an XSLT style sheet and add the required information in this way.

2.10.5 Never Change a Published Schema

This is a good practice exercised in component-oriented systems such as COM. Instead of changing a published schema and probably burning its users, create a new schema with each change. Be prepared for users to continue to use the old schema version for a considerable time period.

2.10.6 Use Only Version-Controlled Schemata

Schemata that are not controlled by a version control system can change at any time, leaving your application "out in the rain." In particular, this is the case when you use a schema from a public repository. Make sure that the repository has a version control system in place.

If you are using multipart schemata, make sure that all parts are controlled by the *same* version control system.

2.10.7 Consider Equipping Each Document Element with a UUID Attribute

Universally unique identifiers (UUIDs) can be easily generated and can identify objects uniquely. Equipping each element in a document instance with such a UUID (as an attribute of type ID) helps to easily identify an element. One advantage is that elements can keep their identity even through transformations (for example, with XSLT), when merged with another document, or when moved to a different location.

2.10.8 Adopt a Concise Style for Schema Design

Here are a few recommendations found on the BizTalk.org Web site. (Other communities might recommend slightly different authoring styles.)

- Write element and attribute names in a style called "CamelCase." Elements reflecting an entity should be written in `UpperCamelCase`; elements and attributes reflecting a property should be written in `lowerCamelCase`. For example:

CamelCase

```
<author>
  <name>
    <firstName> ... </firstName>
    <lastName> ... </lastName>
  </name>
<author>
```

- Names should be meaningful. Names should describe the marked information item sufficiently. Avoid cryptic abbreviations. There is always a chance that humans will read the document, at least in the case of debugging. For example: do not write `odate` when you mean `orderDate`.

Meaningful names

- Elements and attributes should be named by their function, not by their position in a set. For example: do not write `<element_5>`, `<element_6>`, and so on when you can write `<firstName>`, `<middleName>`.

Avoid custom
parsing

- Do not use a complex string expression within elements that requires custom parsing. Rather, break the string into single tokens and express each token in a separate element. This will improve readability and extensibility. It also allows you to apply datatype definitions to each element when defining a schema with XML Schema.

  Note: XML Schema allows the definition of *list* datatypes. Such list datatypes allow you to write several tokens of the same datatype within a single element, separated by whitespace.

  For example: rather than writing

  ```
  <price> USD 9.95 </price>
  ```

write

  ```
  <price>
      <currency> USD </currency>
      <amount> 9.95 </amount>
  </price>
  ```

Lists like

  ```
  <luckyNumbers> 35 23 48 29 96 42 <luckyNumbers>
  ```

are okay.

Later extensions

- To model conceptual entity properties, use XML elements, not attributes. Attributes should be used for metadata such as element author, element version, element origin, modification date, and so on. (But see our discussion in Section 2.9.2.)

  The reason for this is that an element is better suited for later extension than an attribute. You can always insert child elements into an existing element, but you cannot do so with an attribute.

2.10.9 Do Not Use Exotic Language Elements

Use only language elements that are commonly supported by existing tools such as parsers, editors, viewers, and so on. For some XML-based languages the W3C has published the results of conformance tests. These reports list which language features are supported by which tools. Using only features that are supported by most tools will improve portability of your documents.

2.11 XML RESOURCES

We have selected a few important Web sites that provide either an extensive range of XML resources or other important contributions.

The World Wide Web Consortium (*www.w3.org*) is the reference point for nearly every standard mentioned earlier—and more. In particular, in case you didn't know: XML is a W3C recommendation.

www.megginson.com is the source for SAX, SAX2, and XAF.

OASIS (*www.oasis-open.org*) is a clearinghouse of XML industry standards. In particular OASIS (in collaboration with UN/CEFACT) was responsible for the ebXML standard and hosts the RELAX-NG specification.

Robin Cover's page (*www.oasis-open.org/cover/*), hosted by OASIS, contains the latest XML-related industry news and discusses new industry standards.

Also hosted by OASIS, *www.xml.org*, is a repository for XML schemata. In collaboration with ZapThink, it also contains descriptions of about 400 XML-based industry standards. This site also gives access to the XML-DEV discussion forum (*www.xml.org/xml/xmldev.shtml*).

www.xmlpatterns.com contains a collection of design patterns for XML.

www.xml.com is a site devoted to XML and related standards from O'Reilly Publishers.

www.xmlhack.com is dedicated to news related to XML core technologies.

www.xfront.com discusses programming techniques for schema authors. It also has excellent XML Schema and XSL tutorials.

www.w3schools.com offers a number of Web-related tutorials. There is also a section on XML and XML-related standards.

www.xmlresources.com is an XML-related portal with links to books, tools, tutorials, and more.

www.xmlArchitecture.org is the supporting Web site for this book.

Another good source for examples, tutorials, and tools is the XML-related pages of the various large and small software manufacturers.

Structure 3

In this chapter we discuss conceptual modeling techniques in the context of XML-based applications. After revisiting the classic entity relationship model, we introduce asset-oriented modeling—an approach to conceptual modeling that is specifically targeted at XML environments.

RDF is the W3C's official framework to model complex Web-based information structures and semantics. Currently, RDF is undergoing a revision process that will result in a new syntax and content model. If you are not particularly interested in RDF, you may want to skip Section 3.3.

Finally, we discuss how UML can be utilized with XML. UML is a de facto standard for object-oriented scenarios and is also used in some XML applications such as ebXML as the modeling method of choice.

3.1 THE EVOLUTION OF DATA MODELS

Currently, the main role of XML is certainly that of a communication format, but we also see applications for data storage and knowledge bases. The many proposals for an XML query language alone indicate that the application of XML is wider than pure message transmission. But even when used as a message format, modeling techniques become important: a BizTalk message, for example, is organized like a small database containing several business documents, business objects, and attachments.

Rationale for this chapter

Therefore in this chapter we take a close look at various modeling techniques. We think this is necessary because we know of many cases where schemata were designed that are practically unusable. You may have heard of infamous "all-in-one" documents, where a single document contains all information entities found in the problem domain, resulting in document sizes of 50 MB and more.

We have seen schemata that disregard the hierarchical possibilities of XML and store everything as a network of elements that refer to each other via ID and IDREF attributes, resulting in unreadable documents.

So, data modeling *is* an issue for XML. And because XML is very expressive, it allows us to adopt very intuitive modeling techniques. Given the current education of system and database analysts in relational modeling techniques, XML requires a rethink. Smashing complex objects into atomic pieces, as is done in the relational model, is not required for XML (in fact, it would cause poor performance and unreadable documents). That is the reason why we—after revisiting existing data models—return to the mother of all information modeling techniques, the entity relationship model. In fact, this technique has been enhanced in the meantime. With asset-oriented modeling, we will discuss a modeling technique that is more suitable for XML.

Paradigm shift

We continue here with our earlier thesis that a major paradigm shift is happening in computing. In Chapter 1 we stated that IT infrastructures moved from transactional architectures to client-server architectures in the 1980s and are now moving from client-server architectures toward navigational systems. This shift is reflected by fundamental changes in data structures:

- Transactional architectures are characterized by the hierarchical and the network (CODASYL) data models. These models started to evolve in the 1960s and are still in use today. Large amounts of operational data still reside in database systems such as IMS.

- Client-server architectures were characterized by relational data models. Relational databases became the standard database technology in the 1980s and dominated the database market in the 1990s. The relational data model structures information in a way that allows different clients to interpret data items in various combinations.
- Navigational IT architectures require a new data model, which is still evolving. It seems that data models based on regular grammars (Daum 2002) are promising. At least, XML fits into this category.

3.1.1 CODASYL

CODASYL/DBTG (Conference on Data System Languages/Data Base Task Group) dates back to 1971 (Olle 1978) and was the basis for many database implementations, including IDMS (Cullinet), DMS-1100 (Sperry Univac), IDS II (Honeywell), and UDS (Siemens).

In CODASYL schemas are defined with the Data Definition Language (DDL), while operations on the data are expressed through the Data Manipulation Language (DML). Language bindings exist to COBOL, FORTRAN, and others.

CODASYL data structures are closely related to the classical COBOL data record: A *record* consists of one or several items. Each item may have one or several occurrences (repeating group). Each record has a permanent internal identification (database key), allowing fast localization of records.

Records

Sets define the relationship between records. Each set has one owner record (or "system" for the root owner record) and one or several member records. This restricts relationships to 1:1 and 1:n relationships. As shown in Figure 3.1(a), n:m relationships must be modeled by defining two 1:n sets and one dummy record.

Relationships

Although the relationship between records within a set is strictly hierarchical, there is no global hierarchy between records. By defining several sets, a record may have several owners (Figure 3.1(b)), or records may mutually own each other (Figure 3.1(c)). It is also possible to define several differently named set types on the same record types (Figure 3.1(d)).

The record-oriented storage format makes CODASYL databases highly efficient. This is one of the reasons why a substantial amount of operational data is still stored in this format.

The problem with CODASYL databases, however, is their inflexibility. New requirements almost always require remodeling the data schema. This may affect existing applications and requires extensive integration tests.

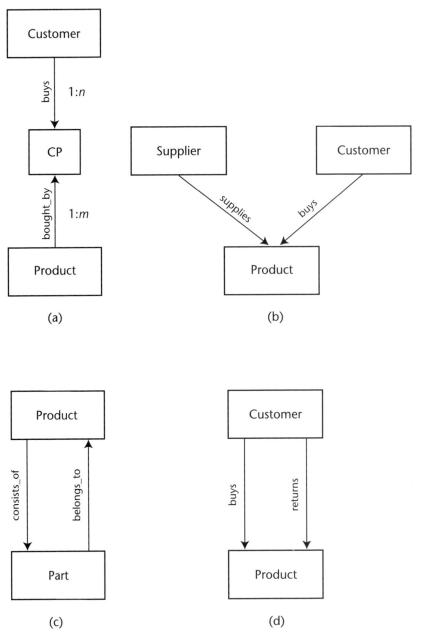

Figure 3.1 Different types of relationship sets: (a) $n{:}m$ relationship; (b) several owners; (c) mutual ownership; (d) multiple relationships.

The change of a data schema subsequently requires a reorganization of the physical database, meaning considerable downtime for the connected applications.

3.1.2 Hierarchical Databases

Hierarchical databases are similar to CODASYL databases. The main dif- Pointers
ference is that the database consists of a set of hierarchical trees. If the same record is contained in several trees or tree branches, one record is determined to be the main record. Its copies are *mirrored* through the use of pointer records. Thus, the redundancies in the database are removed.

A typical example of a hierarchical database system is IBM's IMS.

3.1.3 Relational Databases

The relational concept is based on a simple idea: the database should store data in the most atomic form, while the data structures are imposed on the data by the client (application). This concept fits well into the client-server approach, which began to evolve in the 1980s with the appearance of workstations and desktop computers that are connected to a central database server. Different clients thus can utilize the same data items in many different constellations. The introduction of new applications does not require the reorganization of the physical database. Popular representatives of this database model are IBM's DB2 and the Oracle database management system.

Relational technology is based on a sound mathematical theory—the relational algebra introduced by E. F. Codd in 1970 (Codd 1970). In rela- Tables
tional databases data is organized in *tables*. Each table represents a basic relationship between primitive data items such as customer name and customer number. Tables have *rows* (called *tuples* in relational algebra) and *columns* (attributes). The attributes are named via a schema definition; the rows, however, remain anonymous and unordered. Rows can be selected by content via a *key*.

Preparing data models for relational databases requires a sequence of normalization steps. Each step splits complex data structures into simpler constructs and reduces redundancies and dependencies between data items.

The example in Database Table 3.1, Orders-by-Supplier, shows a schema definition with the attributes SUPPLIER#, NAME, CITY, SIZE, ORDERS. As it is, this example table cannot be stored in most rational database management systems (RDBMSs) because it is not in first normal form (1NF). A table is said to be in first normal form if all attributes (columns) are atomic. The column ORDERS contains nonelementary values. It is therefore necessary to decompose this table into several tables.

The problem here is that the column ORDERS contains lists of element tuples. Lists are by definition ordered: list elements have a clearly defined sequence. Table rows, however, do not have a natural sequence. If we want to translate the list into a table structure, we have to introduce an additional attribute, POSITION, to maintain the original position of each

Database Table 3.1   Unnormalized Database Table for Orders-by-Supplier Schema.

Orders-by-Supplier

Supplier#	Name	City	Size	Orders (product#, product, amount)
44-8983	UnitedComb	Leads	small	(45A13, Comb, 50)
64-3890	Sparkle Ltd	Wellington	medium	(317-88, Toothbrush, 12)
61-7123	Softtouch	Sydney	big	(10456, Shampoo, 36), (10872, Powder, 20)

Database Table 3.2   1NF Database Table for Orders-by-Supplier Schema.

Orders-by-Supplier

Supplier#	Name	City	Size	Product#
44-8983	UnitedComb	Leads	small	45A13
64-3890	Sparkle Ltd	Wellington	medium	317-88
61-7123	Softtouch	Sydney	big	10456
61-7123	Softtouch	Sydney	big	10872

element. This would allow an application to reconstruct the original sequence by using a SORT operator (see Database Table 3.2).

Because this table combines supplier information with order data, it exhibits several anomalies:

- Supplier information cannot be stored without storing an order.
- When all orders of a supplier are deleted, the supplier information is lost.
- When the address of a supplier changes, all orders referring to that supplier must be updated.

Similar anomalies exist for the product information. For example, if all orders for a product are deleted, we lose the information about which product name belongs to which product number and who supplies which product.

At this point it becomes necessary to talk about keys. Unlike in CODA-SYL and hierarchical databases, where pointers reference a physical record (a rudimentary form of object identity), keys in relational systems relate to content. A *primary key* is a single attribute or a combination of attributes that can identify a *single* row. In our example above, the combination of SUPPLIER# and PRODUCT# is a suitable primary key.

Keys vs. pointers

A 1NF table is said to be in second normal form (2NF) if all attributes depend fully on the primary key. This is not the case in Database Table 3.2. The attribute CITY depends only on SUPPLIER#, not on the combination of SUPPLIER# and PRODUCT#. To obtain 2NF, we have to decompose the table Orders-by-Supplier into the three tables Orders, Suppliers, and Products (Database Tables 3.3–3.5).

2NF

Product	Amount	Position
Comb	50	1
Toothbrush	12	1
Shampoo	36	1
Powder	20	2

Database Table 3.3 2NF Database Table for Suppliers.

Suppliers			
Supplier#	**Name**	**City**	**Size**
44-8983	UnitedComb	Leads	small
64-3890	Sparkle Ltd	Wellington	medium
61-7123	Softtouch	Sydney	big

Database Table 3.4 2NF Database Table for Products.

Products		
Product#	**Product**	**Supplier#**
45A13	Comb	44-8983
317-88	Toothbrush	64-3890
10456	Shampoo	61-7123
10872	Powder	61-7123

Database Table 3.5 2NF Database Table for Orders.

Orders		
Product#	**Amount**	**Position**
45A13	50	1
317-88	12	1
10456	36	1
10872	20	2

Because supplier and product information now is stored separately from the order data, the anomalies mentioned earlier do not appear. However, the knowledge of how suppliers and products relate to orders is no longer contained in the database and must be provided by the application using this data.

The next step in the normalization process is the third normal form (3NF). A table is said to be in 3NF if none of the attributes depends transitively from a primary key. If, for example, the SIZE attribute in the table Suppliers (Database Table 3.3) relates to the supplier, the table is already in 3NF. But if SIZE relates to CITY, then SIZE depends transitively (via CITY) from SUPPLIER#. In this case we have to—you may have guessed it—decompose again (see Database Tables 3.6 and 3.7). Otherwise, we would lose information about cities when we delete a supplier from the table.

3NF

Database Table 3.6   3NF Database Table for Suppliers.

Suppliers		
Supplier#	**Name**	**City**
44-8983	UnitedComb	Leads
64-3890	Sparkle Ltd	Wellington
61-7123	Softtouch	Sydney

Database Table 3.7   3NF Database Table for Cities.

City	
Name	**Size**
Leads	small
Wellington	medium
Sydney	big

The normalization process continues with BCNF (Boyce-Codd Normal Form), 4NF, and 5NF. We will stop at this point—the advantages and drawbacks of the relational method are already clear.

Cleanly separating mixed information into individual tables allows client applications to apply any kind of queries without having to modify the underlying database schema. This is not possible in CODASYL databases: in these databases the access paths must be explicitly defined in the set definitions.

By using standard SQL queries it would be possible to interrogate our database for

- suppliers for a given order position
- orders for a given product
- orders for a given supplier
- products coming from "Leads"
- products supplied by suppliers in small cities

Costs

However, this flexibility comes at a price. First, database operations will be relatively slow. To read all orders from supplier Softtouch we would need five select operations, four join operations, and one sort operation. Therefore, during the design of a relational database, the sequence of normalization steps is usually followed by a series of *denormalization* and optimization steps, with the goal of obtaining a less fragmented physical data storage. The art of relational database design lies in finding the right compromise between flexibility and performance.

Second, while normalization removes the anomalies discussed earlier, it also loses structural information contained in the conceptual data model. In some cases foreign/primary key relationships can maintain some of this information. In many cases, however, structural information is hidden as join operations in applications and query expressions. For example, a foreign/primary key relationship cannot model a many-to-many relationship.

Integrity

The loss of structural information introduces integrity problems. After normalization a DBMS has no knowledge about the structural relationship between tables. Therefore the DBMS cannot control the structural integrity of the data. Deleting a CITIES tuple, for example, would leave suppliers homeless.

Relational database management systems solve this problem by reintroducing structural information into the schema definition in the form of integrity rules and triggers. These constraints and triggers allow the database system to reject violating operations or to perform additional operations that are required to keep the structure of the database intact.

For example, we could inhibit the deletion of any CITIES tuples that are referenced by SUPPLIER tuples. Or, when a SUPPLIER is deleted we could trigger the deletion of the referenced CITIES tuple if it is not referenced by other SUPPLIER tuples. It is clear that these constraints introduce additional overhead.

XML, in contrast, does not define such mechanisms. In this respect, SQL is a more mature technology. But, on the other hand, in many cases these mechanisms are not required in XML. With XML, since it is not necessary to "flatten" complex structures into third normal form, partial deletion or modification of an information structure in a database is less likely. However, to maintain the integrity of a whole information model, rules for referential integrity are required.

3.1.4 Navigational Architectures

The explosive growth of the Internet and the World Wide Web has led to a technology shift similar to that generated by the introduction of the personal computer one and a half decades ago. But progress does not stop there. At the end of the decade, practically every person in the industrial countries, and a considerable percentage of people in the rest of the world, will own one or more devices to access the Internet. When wireless technology starts to outperform standard telephone lines by orders of magnitude, this access will probably be wireless. Or, embedded into a device, it will do its work unnoticed by the user.

Because these devices must be cheap, mobile, and almost disposable, many of them will be built as thin clients (with rich multimedia and zero deployment for user friendliness, though) with a browser (perhaps a voice browser) interface—or, in the case of embedded devices, as very thin servers. The storage of strategic data and processing of information will be the duty of a vast grid of highly specialized servers, connected through powerful fiber optics backbones. At the same time, these devices will also be able to share their local resources with others. Although currently this is mostly done with MP3 records, the technology is not restricted to this format (see Section 7.4).

Thin devices

This scenario may remotely resemble the transactional scenario of the 1970s where thin clients (the famous green-black screens) were connected to powerful mainframes (powerful in the terms of the past, that is). However, there is a major difference: through the Internet the clients of today are connected not just to a single server but to a network of millions of information sources. These shareable information sources are highly heterogeneous in nature. It is unlikely that there will ever be a

Networks

common global formal model of control, administration, or registration of information sources. In addition, content, format, and availability of these information sources are under constant change.

This scenario contrasts radically with traditional enterprise scenarios consisting of multiple distributed heterogeneous database systems and data warehouses. In these systems, global data schemata are designed and decided on a priori. Databases connected to the system must comply with the global schema. "Global" in this context, of course, means "enterprisewide," not "worldwide."

New
requirements

In the world of electronic business, however, the requirements are different (Bayardo et al. 1997):

> . . . recent emerging technologies such as internetworking and the World Wide Web have significantly expanded the types, availability, and volume of data available to an information management system. Furthermore, in these new environments, there is no formal control over the registration of new information sources, and applications tend to be developed without complete knowledge of the resources that will be available when they are run. The data and the structure may bear little relationship to the semantics. Therefore, there can be no static mapping of concepts to structured data sets, and querying is reduced to search engines that dynamically locate relevant information based on keywords.

To establish, for example, a customer-supplier relationship over the Internet requires the following steps:

- Locate a supplier that provides the required services. For example: Find a supplier in the immediate vicinity of Los Angeles who can supply up to 5,000 yellow toothbrushes every two weeks. Today this is done via digital marketplaces (see Chapter 10).
- Negotiate a common trade protocol (this includes common process and data models and common semantics) with the supplier found.
- Construct collaborating workflows that orchestrate the cooperation with this supplier.
- Inform partners during the cooperation about relevant changes in business process and data model.

All of these steps add requirements to a suitable data model:

Publishing
metadata

- Metainformation must be in a format suitable for publishing to prospective partners. Metainformation describes data elements, data structures, authorship, version, origin, and so on. This is probably the most vital issue. In an open environment such as the Internet, it would be naive to believe that a single data format can fit all purposes (see also

Chapter 1). Publishing the "blueprint" of the information model (the conceptual model) together with the information set enables clients—users, software agents, and mediators—to construct their own "mind map" of the information sources and to perform searches and transformations efficiently.

- To enable public access to metadata, the relationships between information elements must be defined independently of the application. This is not the case with the relational model, where knowledge about the information structures is hardwired within applications. Metadata can either be published as an intrinsic part of a document itself, as is partly the case with XML documents, or it can be published separately, as is the case with conceptional models (see, for example, WebML in Section 7.1.2), XML schemata (see DTD and XML Schema in Chapter 2), or metadata descriptions (see RDF in Section 3.3). For electronic business, dedicated standards like WSDL (Section 6.6.3), UDDI (Section 7.3), or ebXML (Section 10.3) exist to publish metadata.

- Users should be allowed to add knowledge to published metadata, for example, to define new relationships between information elements or to add a note to a certain document type. This is necessary because no designer or system analyst can anticipate all possible use cases.

Annotation

- When querying data, it must be possible to control the choice of selection criteria and of the access paths to information elements (apart from security considerations) completely with a query expression. This is the case in the relational data model, but not in the CODASYL data model, where only predefined access paths (sets) can be used.

Flexible queries

- Document repositories should be able to maintain the integrity of documents and the referential integrity between documents. Referential integrity between the documents within an enterprise is an absolute requirement. In the open world of the World Wide Web, however, maintaining full referential integrity is not always possible—we all know the all-too-common 404 response code.

Integrity

- Documents should be easy to transform into different structures. This is important if we want to exchange business documents with partners, and if these documents follow different standards.

Transformations

- The definition of business objects must recognize the different contexts and environments the business object can interact with. This requirement is unique to the open world of electronic business, where the same business object can pass through several environments, for example, in a supply chain scenario. Such a scenario can span across several countries and continents, where different legal and administrative contexts exist that business objects have to satisfy.

Context awareness

Standard
formats

- All data formats (including metadata) should comply with international standards. Proprietary formats are counterproductive in an open environment. However, because standardization is a slow process and because standards often cover only the smallest common denominator, the use of proprietary formats is sometimes inevitable. The better choice, of course, is to extend a standard format rather than to completely roll your own.

Document
format vs.
record format

XML and XML- based technology fit well into this scenario. XML has its roots in the document standard SGML, and document-oriented formats are what is required here. For thousands of years information *exchange* between organizations was organized through document-based formats. The *storage* of information within an enterprise, in contrast, was organized through the use of index-card-based (or record-based) formats—even long before electronic data processing.

CODASYL and relational databases mimic the index-card-oriented format and are therefore well suited to cover data storage requirements within the enterprise. Records and tables closely resemble the classic index card box, where only the owner of the box knows how to interpret the data. XML breaks radically with this tradition. XML documents can be self-explanatory to human readers and are designed to be interpreted by external partners.

Let's see how XML and related standards satisfy the requirements outlined in the bulleted list above:

Publishing
metadata

- *Metainformation must be in a format suitable for publishing to prospective partners. Metainformation describes data elements, data structures, authorship, version, origin, and so on.*

    XML documents contain substantial metadata within a document. Named tags enclose every document element. Attributes can optionally be used to specify additional metainformation such as author or version for each element. Documents can have an arbitrary tree structure because document elements can be nested. Thus, a certain amount of metainformation is automatically published with each document.

    Additional metadata can be published through XML schema definitions such as DTDs or XML Schema definitions. This schema information can be used to optimize query processing, to obtain a mental model of the document type, to visualize the document structure, and to control editing tools when documents are created and modified.

    Where XML falls short is in the definition of constraints that go beyond datatypes and cross-references.

- *To enable public access to metadata, the relationships between information elements must be defined independently of the application.*

  The relationships between document elements are defined by the intrinsic document structure and are thus contained in the document. However, due to the hierarchical structure of XML documents, not every relationship can be expressed in terms of the parent-child element relationship. Also, the basic XML 1.0 standard does not define provisions to specify relations to external information items such as other XML documents and non-XML objects.

  In the following sections we discuss how to express relationships—especially relationships in the context of conceptual modeling—between documents. Relationships should be best expressed as separate "data maps" apart from the information elements.

- *Users should be allowed to add knowledge to published metadata.*   Annotation

  RDF (see Section 3.3) allows making statements about information items (in fact any resource) and publishing that knowledge. Also, topic maps (see Section 7.2) provide a mechanism to add knowledge to information items.

- *When querying data, it must be possible to control the choice of selection criteria and of the access paths to information elements (apart from security considerations) completely with a query expression.*   Flexible queries

  While XML documents adhere to a strictly hierarchical structure with nested elements, XPath query constructs allow the use of any element or element combination within an XML document as a selection criterion, and access to single elements within an XML document. However, although XPath is very powerful, it is not a full query language. There are deficiencies in the area of text retrieval, there is no join operator, and the aggregating functions known from SQL are missing. Several proposals for dedicated XML query languages have been made in the past. With XQuery, a W3C standard is now on the way (see Section 2.6).

- *Document repositories should be able to maintain the integrity of documents and the referential integrity between documents.*   Integrity

  Although XML processors can validate the structural integrity of a document against its schema definition (DTD or XML Schema), semantic integrity and referential integrity are still weak points in XML. While relational technology provides a standard way to add semantic

and referential integrity via integrity rules and triggers, XML repositories currently require application logic or the definition of proprietary
server extensions to implement semantic and referential integrity.

Transformations • *Documents should be easy to transform into different structures.*

The XSLT style sheet language allows the formulation of powerful
document transformations. In Chapter 9 we will discuss XLST in more
detail. In Section 3.2 we explain how to normalize models to allow
document transformations without information loss.

Context
awareness   • *The definition of business objects must recognize the different contexts and
environments the business object can interact with.*

The Schema Adjunct Framework (SAF) defines a two-layered approach to add behavior to XML documents. SAF allows the definition
of abstract operations that are interpreted by context-specific processors. We will discuss SAF in more detail in Section 4.4.2.

ebXML defines business objects in relation to specific contexts. It
identifies a set of context drivers for business applications. We discuss
ebXML in detail in Section 10.3.

Standard
formats   • *All data formats (including metadata) should comply with international
standards.*

XML and the related specifications are W3C standards and have
wide industry support. Topic maps are an ISO standard. There are several de facto industry standards for the exchange of business data, but
the ebXML format is a UN/CEFACT standard.

Because XML is a document standard and documents have the purpose of being exchanged, data modeling is only one aspect of an XML
architecture. Other aspects are the definition of process models, communication models, and navigation models. We will discuss these aspects in Chapters 5, 6, and 7.

3.2 CONCEPTUAL MODELING

Conceptual modeling is an early but important step in the design of information systems. While originally applied only to databases, conceptual modeling techniques are now applied to object-oriented systems,
too. In this section we will see how conceptual modeling can be utilized
for XML-based architectures.

3.2.1 The Entity Relationship Model

> Usefulness from what is not there.
> —*Lao-Tse*

Developed by Peter Chen in the 1970s, *entity relationship modeling* (ERM) can be considered to be the ancestor of all modern modeling methods (Chen 1976). The acronym ERD may be more popular—meaning *entity relationship diagram,* the graphical representation of an entity relationship model.

In the years following its original conception ERM has spun off many (~80) children and grandchildren. Among them are the following:

ERM spinoffs

- *Nijssen's Information Analysis Methodology* (NIAM) eventually became *Object Role Modeling* (ORM) (Halpin 1999).
- *Semantic Object Modeling* (SOM) was developed by David Kroenke (1995) during the same period of time.
- *Information engineering* was developed by Clive Finkelstein and became popular through collaboration with James Martin (Martin 1993).
- The *Unified Modeling Language* (UML) was published by the Object Management Group in 1997 (Booch, Jacobson, and Rumbaugh 1997). UML covers the wide area of object-oriented modeling including dynamic aspects. The data modeling part, however, closely resembles ERM. Because UML has become a de facto modeling standard in OO system design, we will discuss it in Section 3.4 in detail. UML was submitted to the International Standards Organization to become an ISO standard.
- The *Higher Order Entity Relationship Model* (HERM) by Bernhard Thalheim was developed in the 1990s (Thalheim 2000). Unlike the relatively informal ERM, HERM has a solid mathematical foundation.

Most of the later developments based on ERM had the goal of improving the conceptual design method for relational databases and, as it became popular, for object-oriented programming. Because the document metaphor established by SGML and XML does not really fit into the relational or object-oriented philosophy, we will refrain at this point from any discussion of any specialized modeling method and go back to the roots.

ERM (Thalheim 1999) models the world in terms of *entities, attributes,* and *relationships.* The scope of ERM, at the time it became popular, was to define an enterprise data model, or *enterprise scheme,* representing the overall logical structure of the enterprise database.

ERM explained

Entities

Chen described entities as ". . . a 'thing' which can be distinctly identified." Chen also said: "There are many 'things' in the real world. It is the responsibility of the database designer to select the entity types which are most suitable for his/her company."

The vagueness of this definition made ERM, in fact, a very generic concept and has probably led to the overwhelming success of the method by inviting dozens of researchers to try to improve it.

To be a bit more verbose: *An entity is an object that is distinguishable from other objects.* Entities have attributes that make them distinguishable. An entity may be a concrete object such as a person, a machine, a building, and so on, or it may be an abstract notion such as a project, a holiday, a nation, an account, and so on.

Dominant
entities

ERM differentiates between *dominant* entities and *subordinate* entities. Dominant entities exist in their own right; the existence of a subordinate entity depends on another entity. In commercial programming dominant entities are also called *business objects*.

Entity Set

An *entity set* is a set of entities of the same type, for example, a set of customers, a set of invoices, a set of trucks, and so on. Entity sets can overlap: an entity can belong to more than one entity set. For example, a student tutor belongs to both entity sets, students and teachers.

In ERM diagrams, entity sets are displayed as rectangles (see Figure 3.2).

Attributes

Entities may have attributes. In fact, there are no entities without attributes because attributes characterize entities: they define the type of an entity. An attribute consists of an attribute name and an atomic attribute value, for example, `Price: 19.95`. Formally, an attribute is a function that maps a set of entities onto a value domain.

In an ERM diagram, attributes are displayed as ellipsoids connected by straight lines to the owning entity sets, resulting in the typical ERM millipedes (see Figure 3.3).

Figure 3.2 Entity sets in an ERM diagram.

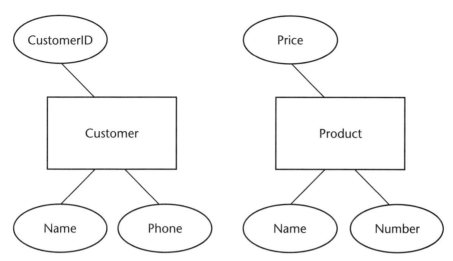

Figure 3.3 Entity sets with attributes.

In some cases it is difficult to decide what should be modeled as an attribute and what as a separate entity. Consider the entity `Driver`. The driver's license could be modeled as an attribute of `Driver`. Alternatively it could be modeled as a separate entity. The second solution would require the definition of an extra relationship `holds_license` but allows the detailed modeling of the actual license. In the first case we can only model the license as an atomic value, presumably the license number, because attribute values must be atomic.

Attribute vs. entity

We will see that the same discussion pops up again with the question of whether to use attributes or elements to specify content within an XML document. The question of whether an item should be modeled as an entity or as an attribute can only be decided on the basis of the context in which the data model will be used. Generally, an item should be modeled as an entity if it plays a role within a business process.

Keys

An attribute or a combination of attributes that uniquely identifies an entity is called a *superkey*. The smallest possible superkey (i.e., a superkey for which no subset of attributes exists that can act as a superkey) is called a *candidate key*. From the set of candidate keys, database designers can select a *primary key* to identify an entity within an entity set.

Entity sets that do not possess a primary key are called *weak* entity sets. Entity sets that do have a primary key are called *strong* entity sets. This concept is closely related to dominant and subordinate entities. Weak

Strong and weak entity sets

Figure 3.4 Subordinate entity `Transaction`.

entity sets consist of subordinate entities, while strong entity sets consist of dominant entities.

Consider, for example, the entities `Account` and `Transaction`. A transaction is usually identified with a transaction number that is unique only in the context of a given account. The set of `Transaction` entities therefore forms a weak entity set. Clearly, `Transaction` entities are subordinate to `Account` entities.

In an ERM diagram weak entity sets are displayed with a double-outlined rectangle (see Figure 3.4).

The original ERM version did not define a special notation for keys. Later versions mark unique attributes with double-outlined ellipsoids.

Relationships

Peter Chen stated: "Relationships may exist between entities" (Chen 1976). There is a little more to add: relationships associate two or more entities with each other. For example, given the entities `Customer` and `Product`, the relationship `Order` denotes a specific association between customers and products.

Role

Within a relationship each entity has a particular *role*. In our example the customer entity *issues* an order, while the product *is subject to* an order.

Arity

Relationships have an *arity*: relationships associating two roles are called *binary*, relationships associating three roles are called *ternary*, and so on.

Constraints

ERM allows the definition of certain *constraints* for relationships: roles have a *cardinality*. Roles can be restricted to incorporate a single entity, or they may incorporate multiple entities. In a binary relationship this results in four different constraints: one-to-one, one-to-many, many-to-one, and many-to-many. Our `orders` relationship is typically a one-to-many relationship because a single customer can order several product items. In addition, roles may be *optional*. That is, the role incorporates single or multiple entities only in some situations. In a binary relationship this results in 16 different constraints.

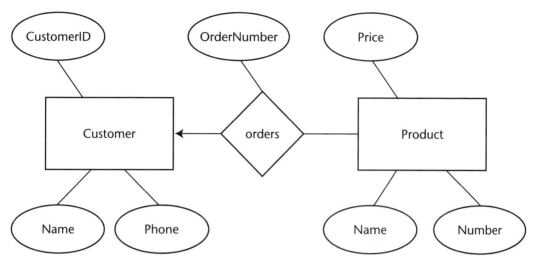

Figure 3.5 Order relation between Customer and Product.

Relationships may have attributes, too. For example, the relationship orders may possess the attribute OrderNumber.

Relationship Set

A relationship set is a set of relationships of the same type, for example, all existing orders from a given set of customers to a given set of products.

In an ERM diagram, relationship sets are displayed as diamonds and are connected by lines to the entities participating in the relationship (see Figure 3.5). The cardinality of a relationship is shown with an arrow. An arrow pointing to an entity denotes the "one" side of a relationship. Lines without arrows denote the "many" side of a relationship.

Later improvements to the ERM model replace the arrowheads with numbers below the connecting lines. This allows the specification of the minimum and maximum number of entity occurrences (cardinality) within a role; for example, (1,n) would typically replace the "one-to-many" specification. This notation also allows the specification of optional roles: (0,1) specifies a cardinality of minimum 0 and maximum 1, making the role optional.

Cardinality

Existence-Dependent Relationship

This relationship is one of three that are treated special in ERM (the other two are aggregation and generalization, to be discussed shortly). It defines the special relationship between associated dominant and subordinate

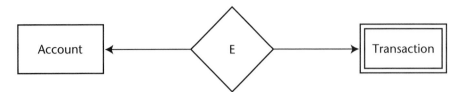

Figure 3.6 Existence-dependent relationship between `Account` and `Transaction`.

entities. Subordinate entities can only exist if the dominant entity exists. For example, `Transaction` entities for an `Account` entity only exist if the `Account` entity exists.

In ERM, existence-dependent relationships are depicted in the form of a diamond like any other relationship but with the predefined name "E" (see Figure 3.6).

Aggregation

Aggregation is a special form of relationship. What is special here is that an association of aggregated entities is treated as a higher-level entity itself. Often, subordinate entities are aggregated with a dominant entity and thus form a new complex entity. However, it is also possible to aggregate several dominant entities into a new higher-level entity. For example, the entities `Customer` and `Product` and the relationship `orders` could be aggregated into a new entity `Order`.

In an ERM diagram aggregations are depicted as ERM diagrams within a rectangle (see Figure 3.7).

Generalization

Generalization is a special form of relationship that relates entities to an abstract entity. For example, a customer may order products or services. We can model this by introducing an abstract entity `ProductOrService` and associating the concrete entities `Product` and `Service` via an `IS_A` relationship to `ProductOrService`. Although not covered as a special concept in the original version of ERM, generalization is depicted in later ERM versions in the form of triangles (see Figure 3.8).

Alternative notations

This original ERM notation is still in use today, predominantly at universities and in the scientific community. Industry has adopted notations of later ERM flavors, for example, the crow's foot notation (see Figure 3.9).

The most striking difference is that attributes are displayed within entities and that relationships are displayed as a straight decorated line. This

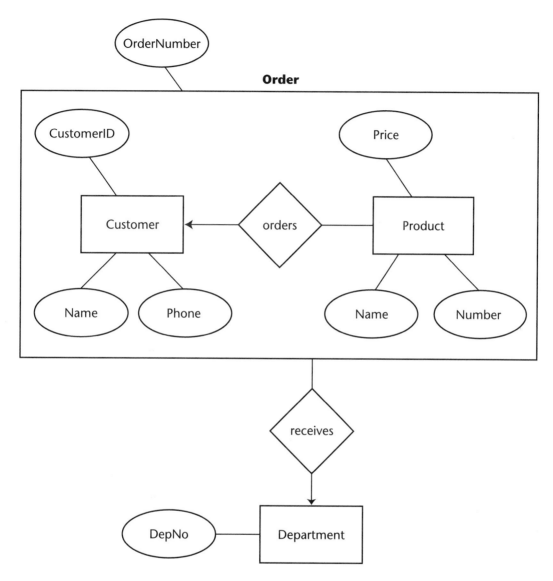

Figure 3.7 Aggregation of the "orders" relationship into a new complex entity.

makes it difficult to denote attributed relationships. Attributed relationships are therefore modeled as separate entities (see Figure 3.10).

   UML uses yet another notation. We leave this to Section 3.4, where
UML is discussed in more detail.

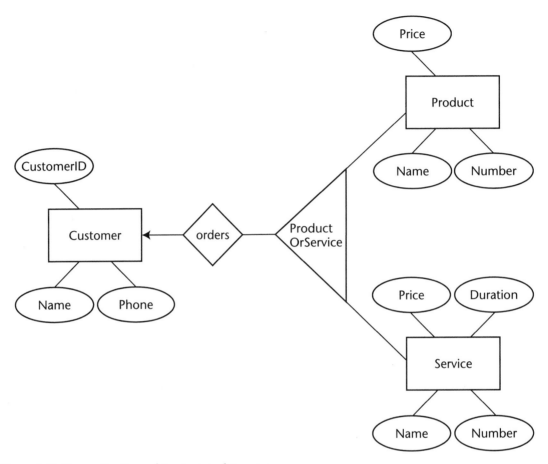

Figure 3.8 Generalization of Product and Service.

3.2.2 Asset-Oriented Modeling (AOM)

In this section we introduce a modeling method that is specifically targeted toward the construction of document-centric (i.e., XML) applications.

AOM is loosely based on the higher order entity relationship model (HERM), introduced by Bernhard Thalheim during the 1990s (Thalheim 2000). This method was developed for object-oriented modeling and includes modeling techniques for structure as well as for semantics, such as constraints and operations. It introduces a solid mathematical foundation into conceptual modeling.

Because HERM (and thus AOM) allows complex, structured attributes within entities, the structure of an AOM model can be very close to the

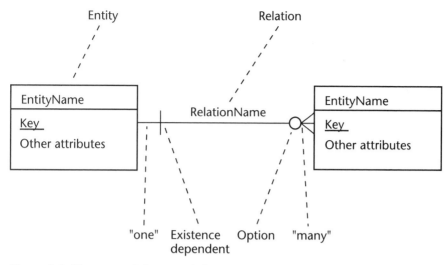

Figure 3.9 Elements of the crow's foot notation.

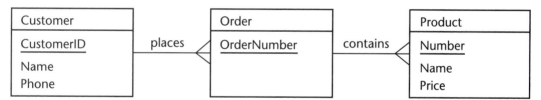

Figure 3.10 The Order example in crow's foot notation.

structure of a final XML representation. This, and the fact that HERM (and thus AOM) allows the definition of higher-order associations (i.e., associations of associations), leads to much simpler models than those obtained with ERM. AOM, in addition, does away with the artificial separation between entity type and relationship type. (It was E. F. Codd who stated that there is no reason to distinguish between entity type and relationship type (Codd 1991).) AOM also introduces a notation and an information model based on regular expressions that are closer to XML and that extend the flexibility of the method considerably.

Core Concepts
AOM is based on three core concepts: properties, assets, and arcs.

Properties can be either simple attributes or can be rather complex and deeply structured. A property can be compared to a node (element) in an XML document. We use the following notation to specify properties:

`name(…)`	Structure
`(child1,…,childn)`	Sequence (ordered)
`(child1&…&childn)`	Bag (unordered)
`(child1|…|childn)`	Alternative
`+`	Repetition $(1 \ldots n)$
`*`	Repetition $(0 \ldots n)$
`?`	Optional $(0 \ldots 1)$
`[n..m]`	Arbitrary cardinality $(n \ldots m)$ with $0 \leq n \leq m$
`lab{}`	Label definition
`lab`	Label reference

(Labels are used to define recursive property structures. For example, `lab{part(lab*)}` defines a treelike part list of arbitrary depth.)

Assets cover both entities and relationships. This means that traditional relationships known from ERM are treated as assets, too. (In terms of logic this means that relationships are immediately reified.) The advantage is that this way we can define relationships between relationships and can classify relationships, both of which the classic ERM cannot do. We use rounded rectangles to visualize an asset and unidirectional arcs to visualize how they relate to other assets (see Figure 3.11).

There are two exceptions that are not modeled as assets: the *is-a* relationship and the *has* relationship between a dominant entity and a weak entity. These relationships simply become arcs between the two assets involved in those relationships as shown in Figure 3.12. For an *is-a* relationship the subordinate asset points to the parent asset, while for a *has* relationship the dominant asset points to the weak asset. However, in many cases weak entities simply degenerate into a structured property of an asset.

The *is-a* relationship and the *has* relationship look very similar, indeed. In fact, they do almost the same thing. However, there is a subtle difference: in a *has* relationship an asset acquires the whole target asset, while in an *is-a* relationship an asset acquires only the properties of the target asset. We therefore denote an *is-a* relationship with the *role* name "is-a."

In addition, each asset has a primary *key*. Keys consist of a single property or a combination of properties. Composite keys are denoted as property sets within curly brackets, for example, {`first-name`, `last-name`}.

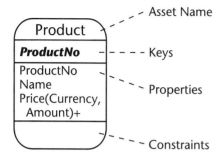

Figure 3.11 Visualization of an asset type. The constraint area is reserved for additional integrity constraints. They can be informal or formal specifications, for example, OCL expressions or Schematron (see Section 2.9.1) constraint rules.

Similar to the notation used for properties, we use DTD syntax to denote the cardinality of the relations between assets, as shown in Figure 3.13.

+	1..n
*	0..n
?	0..1
n..m	n..m

The last notation, n..m, asks for an XML Schema implementation, since DTDs cannot easily express this type of constraint. Note that this type of constraint can lead to models whose set of constraints can never be satisfied.

Arcs connect assets with each other. Each arc is unidirectional. In addition, an arc can be labeled with a *role name* at the source end.

Arcs

HERM introduces an additional construct into modeling that we also use in AOM: *clusters*. Clusters are a union of disjoint asset types. Clusters replace the generalization construct found in ERM and are denoted by a circle containing the character "|" (the XML choice operator). (See Figure 3.14.)

Clusters

Advantages

AOM has the following advantages over classical modeling methods:

- Because relationships are also represented as assets, defining higher-order relationships (relationships between relationships) is trivial.

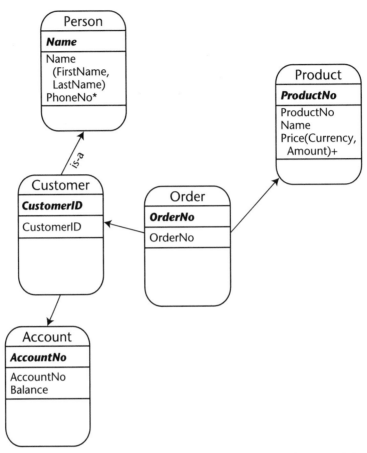

Figure 3.12 The properties Person/Name and Product/Price exhibit a deeper structure than is possible in traditional ERM diagrams. We use the notation known from XML DTDs to denote cardinality of properties, subproperties, and relations. Hence, a customer can have multiple phone numbers, and a product has one or multiple price entries (for different currencies). Classical entity types (Person, Customer, Account, Product) and relationship types (Order) are all modeled as asset types. The relationship between the dominant entity Customer and the weak entity Account degenerates to a simple arc. The same is the case for the classical *is-a* relationship between Customer and Person.

- Similarly, it is easy to define classifications over relationships (e.g., the relationship between Director and Manager would belong to the class of relationships between Employer and Employee).
- *n*-ary relationships (with *n* > 2) don't create problems.
- Implementation in XML is straightforward.
- Reverse engineering of relational databases is easy.

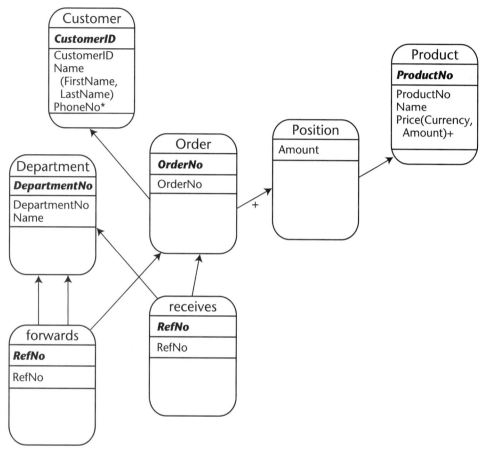

Figure 3.13 AOM diagram for a more complete Order example (Person and Account left out). We use the notation known from XML DTDs to denote cardinality of relations between assets. A department can receive multiple orders, and each order contains at least one position. Note that what would traditionally be modeled as a weak entity type—Position—is simply modeled as an asset type connected to Order.

A more detailed discussion of AOM is given by Daum (2002) and at *www.aomodeling.org.*

3.2.3 A Document-Centered Step-by-Step Approach

In this section we describe a step-by-step approach, starting with an informal description, then constructing a model using the AOM approach, and finally transforming the AOM model into an XML schema. The results are XML data structures that closely represent the model.

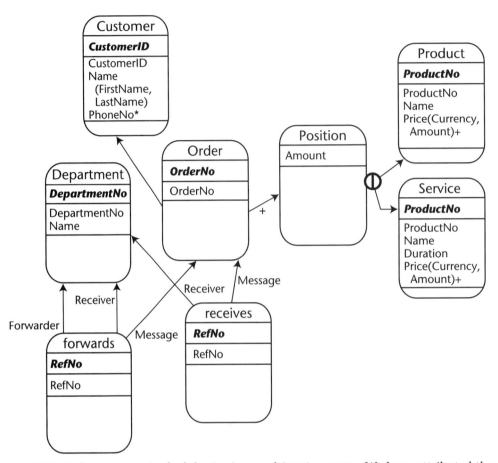

Figure 3.14 A cluster comprised of the Product and Service assets. We have attributed the arcs emanating from forwards and receives to role names.

Informal
description

Step 1

A popular method is to start with an informal verbal description of the scenario:

- Customer A orders Products or Services.
- Department B receives these Orders.
- Department B forwards an Order to Department C or D.
- An Order has Positions.
- Each Position has an amount and a Product or a Service.

A short grammatical analysis separates these sentences into nouns (Customer, Product, Service, Department, Order) and verbs (order, receive). In traditional ERM all nouns would be modeled as entities, and all verbs would be modeled as relationships. However, there is an ambiguity: the verb "orders" and the noun "Order" relate to the same concept.

Step 2

We avoid this problem by modeling both verbs and nouns as assets. We determine which properties each asset has and which property combination can act as a minimal key. We identify as asset types `Customer`, `Product`, `Service`, `Department`, `Order`, `forwards`, `receives`.

Assets and arcs

The verb "has" is not modeled as an asset. Instead, "has amount" results in a property of asset `Position`, and "has Product or Service" results in a cluster (for the "or") with arcs leading to `Product` and `Service`.

As we identify the asset types we also represent the relations between the asset types by connecting them with arcs. Because an `Order` can have more than one `Position` asset, we represent this cardinality constraint by attributing this arc to the character "+".

`Department` appears in two roles: as a forwarder and as a receiver. To differentiate between both, we label the arc emanating from "receives" with the respective role names. Optionally, we identify other roles with an appropriate role label.

Step 3

In this step, we make sure of the following:

Normalization

- Asset types are *primitive*—their properties do not contain assets that could be modeled as independent asset types. This is similar to the first normal form (1NF) in relational theory. For example, the asset type `Order` must not embed customer data.
- Asset types are *minimal*—they do not contain redundant properties, meaning none of their properties can be derived from other properties.
- Asset types should have a *key*. Keys must be minimal—they must consist of the smallest set of properties that can uniquely identify an instance.
- Asset types must be *complete*—other assets contained in the scenario can be derived from the defined asset types.
- Asset types must *not be redundant*—none of the defined asset types can be derived from other asset types.
- All asset types must have a *unique meaning*.

Step 4

An asset type is in *partitioned normal form* (PNF) if the atomic properties of an asset constitute a key of the asset and all nonatomic properties are in partitioned normal form themselves.

Partitioned normal form

The advantage of PNF assets is that their structure can be transformed without information loss. PNF is especially essential if we plan to store assets in relational databases. Relational technology requires fragmenting complex structures into flat relational tables. Keys that span complex structures are lost during such a transformation to first normal form.

In our example, all asset types are in PNF. `Customer`, for example, has the atomic property `CustomerID` as key. The nonatomic property `Name` (`FirstName, LastName`) is in PNF because the combination of the atomic subproperties `FirstName` and `LastName` constitutes a key.

In some cases, however, PNF is too strict. If we were to drop `CustomerID` from `Customer`, we would need to use `Name(FirstName,LastName)` as key. Consequently, `Customer` would not be in PNF.

Step 5

Business objects

Business objects are assets that play a role in a business process. This requires that we have a rough idea about the business process model (see Chapter 5). In our example, `Customer`, `Product`, `Service`, and `Department` are business objects (Figure 3.15). Business objects can consist of several assets. Formally we can cast any hierarchy (if we interpret the arcs as a relation between *superior* and *inferior*) of asset types into a business object. The top-level asset serves as the identifying asset of the business object.

We demarcate each business object with a rectangle and use a bold outline for the identifying asset.

Step 6

Business documents

In this step we identify business documents. Usually, business documents are exchanged between the business objects engaged in a business process. In our example, we have only one business document, consisting of `Order` and `Position`.

Formally we can cast any hierarchy of asset types into a business document. The top-level asset serves as the identifying asset of the business object. In our case this is the asset `Order`.

We demarcate each business document with a dashed rectangle and use a bold outline for the identifying asset.

Step 7

Other assets

Usually not all asset types make their way into a business document. In our example, the asset types "receives" and "forwards" are left over.

Asset types that are neither part of business objects nor part of business documents can serve various purposes. In our case "receives" and "for-

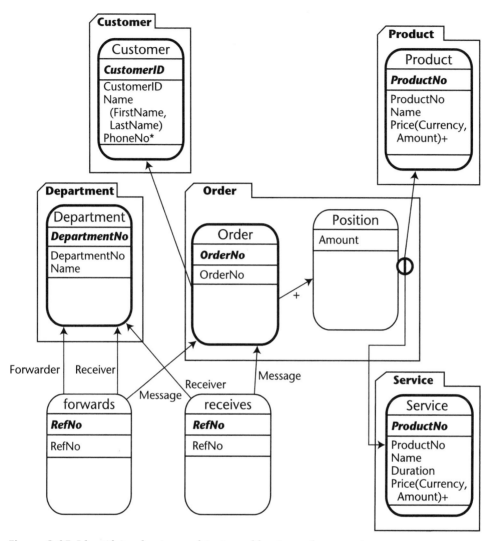

Figure 3.15 Identifying business objects and business documents.

wards" serve as audit trails for the documents received and forwarded. We would, of course, implement those assets as XML schemata, too.

Other assets that describe the relationships between business documents may result in the definition of business rules. Also in this case we would opt for an XML implementation, instead of "hard-coding" these rules into the application. The result is ease of maintenance and much higher responsiveness to change requests.

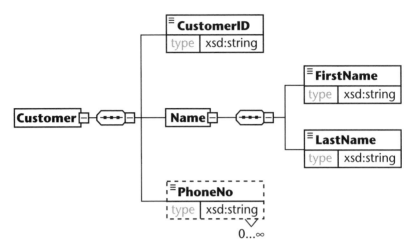

Figure 3.16 Schema diagram for Customer.

Step 8

We can now define the XML schemata. At this point we have to decide how to implement *is-a* roles. There are two options: include the properties of the target asset in the current asset, or use XML Schema's inheritance mechanisms, such as global complex types. The latter option is only applicable as long as we deal with single inheritance. Multiple inheritance is not possible with XML Schema.

Figure 3.16 shows the Customer schema (generated with XMLSpy). Here is the corresponding code:

```
<?xml version="1.0" encoding="UTF-8"?>

<xsd:schema xmlns:xsd="http://www.w3.org/2001/XMLSchema"
            elementFormDefault="qualified"
            attributeFormDefault="unqualified">

  <xsd:element name="Customer">
    <xsd:complexType>
      <xsd:sequence>
        <xsd:element name="CustomerID" type="xsd:string"/>
        <xsd:element name="Name">
          <xsd:complexType>
            <xsd:sequence>
              <xsd:element name="FirstName" type="xsd:string"/>
              <xsd:element name="LastName" type="xsd:string"/>
```

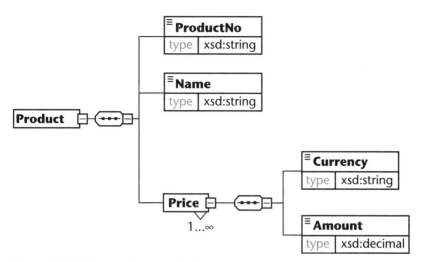

Figure 3.17 Schema diagram for Product.

```
          </xsd:sequence>
        </xsd:complexType>
      </xsd:element>
      <xsd:element name="PhoneNo" type="xsd:string"
                   minOccurs="0" maxOccurs="unbounded"/>
    </xsd:sequence>
  </xsd:complexType>
</xsd:element>

</xsd:schema>
```

Here we have implemented each property as elements, and subproperties as children of these elements.

Figure 3.17 shows the Product schema. Here is the corresponding code:

```
<?xml version="1.0" encoding="UTF-8"?>

<xsd:schema xmlns:xsd="http://www.w3.org/2001/XMLSchema"
            elementFormDefault="qualified"
            attributeFormDefault="unqualified">
  <xsd:element name="Product">
    <xsd:complexType>
      <xsd:sequence>
        <xsd:element name="ProductNo" type="xsd:string"/>
        <xsd:element name="Name" type="xsd:string"/>
        <xsd:element name="Price" maxOccurs="unbounded">
          <xsd:complexType>
```

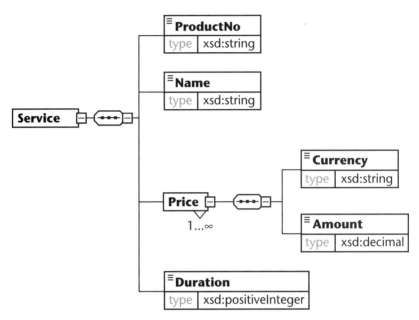

Figure 3.18 Schema diagram for Service.

```
        <xsd:sequence>
          <xsd:element name="Currency" type="xsd:string"/>
          <xsd:element name="Amount" type="xsd:decimal"/>
        </xsd:sequence>
      </xsd:complexType>
    </xsd:element>
  </xsd:sequence>
</xsd:complexType>
</xsd:element>

</xsd:schema>
```

The diagram for Service (Figure 3.18) resembles the diagram for Product. The code is also similar:

```
<?xml version="1.0" encoding="UTF-8"?>

<xsd:schema xmlns:xsd="http://www.w3.org/2001/XMLSchema"
            elementFormDefault="qualified"
            attributeFormDefault="unqualified">

  <xsd:element name="Service">
    <xsd:complexType>
      <xsd:sequence>
```

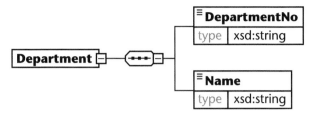

Figure 3.19 Schema diagram for Department.

```
      <xsd:element name="ProductNo" type="xsd:string"/>
      <xsd:element name="Name" type="xsd:string"/>
      <xsd:element name="Price" maxOccurs="unbounded">
        <xsd:complexType>
          <xsd:sequence>
            <xsd:element name="Currency" type="xsd:string"/>
            <xsd:element name="Amount" type="xsd:decimal"/>
          </xsd:sequence>
        </xsd:complexType>
      </xsd:element>
      <xsd:element name="Duration" type="xsd:positiveInteger"/>
    </xsd:sequence>
  </xsd:complexType>
</xsd:element>

</xsd:schema>
```

Figure 3.19 shows the schema for Department. Here is the corresponding code:

```
<?xml version="1.0" encoding="UTF-8"?>

<xsd:schema xmlns:xsd="http://www.w3.org/2001/XMLSchema"
            elementFormDefault="qualified"
            attributeFormDefault="unqualified">

  <xsd:element name="Department">
    <xsd:complexType>
      <xsd:sequence>
        <xsd:element name="DepartmentNo" type="xsd:string"/>
        <xsd:element name="Name" type="xsd:string"/>
      </xsd:sequence>
    </xsd:complexType>
  </xsd:element>

</xsd:schema>
```

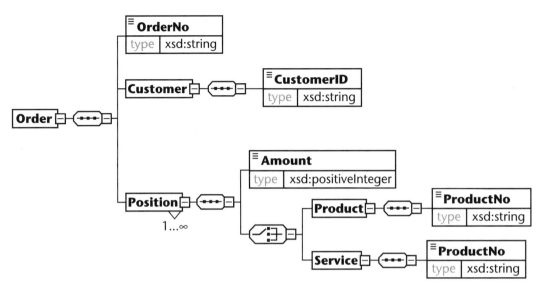

Figure 3.20 Schema diagram for Order.

The business object Order has arcs that lead to other business objects (see Figure 3.20). These are implemented as elements, too. For example, the arc leading to business object Customer is implemented as an element Customer with a child element CustomerID that contains the foreign key value.

The cluster combining the arc leading to Product and Service is implemented as a choice particle containing elements Product and Service, each with a child element ProductNo containing the foreign key value.

Here is the code for Order:

```xml
<?xml version="1.0" encoding="UTF-8"?>

<xsd:schema xmlns:xsd="http://www.w3.org/2001/XMLSchema"
            elementFormDefault="qualified"
            attributeFormDefault="unqualified">

  <xsd:element name="Order">
    <xsd:complexType>
      <xsd:sequence>
        <xsd:element name="OrderNo" type="xsd:string"/>
        <xsd:element name="Customer">
          <xsd:complexType>
            <xsd:sequence>
```

```
                <xsd:element name="CustomerID" type="xsd:string"/>
            </xsd:sequence>
          </xsd:complexType>
        </xsd:element>
        <xsd:element name="Position" maxOccurs="unbounded">
          <xsd:complexType>
            <xsd:sequence>
              <xsd:element name="Amount"
                           type="xsd:positiveInteger"/>
              <xsd:choice>
                <xsd:element name="Product">
                  <xsd:complexType>
                    <xsd:sequence>
                      <xsd:element name="ProductNo"
                                   type="xsd:string"/>
                    </xsd:sequence>
                  </xsd:complexType>
                </xsd:element>
                <xsd:element name="Service">
                  <xsd:complexType>
                    <xsd:sequence>
                      <xsd:element name="ProductNo"
                                   type="xsd:string"/>
                    </xsd:sequence>
                  </xsd:complexType>
                </xsd:element>
              </xsd:choice>
            </xsd:sequence>
          </xsd:complexType>
        </xsd:element>
      </xsd:sequence>
    </xsd:complexType>
  </xsd:element>
</xsd:schema>
```

The asset receives also has arcs that lead to other business objects (see Figure 3.21). These arcs are labeled with role names. We use these role names as names for the elements representing the arcs (Receiver and Message) and add an annotation that informs about the target asset. Here is the code:

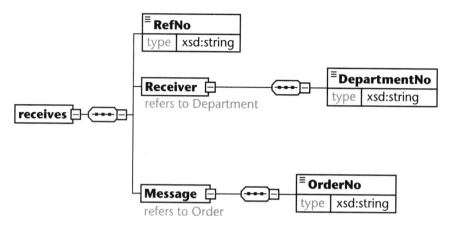

Figure 3.21 Schema diagram for receives.

```
<?xml version="1.0" encoding="UTF-8"?>

<xsd:schema xmlns:xsd="http://www.w3.org/2001/XMLSchema"
            elementFormDefault="qualified"
            attributeFormDefault="unqualified">

  <xsd:element name="receives">
    <xsd:complexType>
      <xsd:sequence>
        <xsd:element name="RefNo" type="xsd:string"/>
        <xsd:element name="Receiver">
          <xsd:annotation>
            <xsd:documentation>
              refers to Department
            </xsd:documentation>
          </xsd:annotation>
          <xsd:complexType>
            <xsd:sequence>
              <xsd:element name="DepartmentNo"
                           type="xsd:string"/>
            </xsd:sequence>
          </xsd:complexType>
        </xsd:element>
        <xsd:element name="Message">
          <xsd:annotation>
            <xsd:documentation>
```

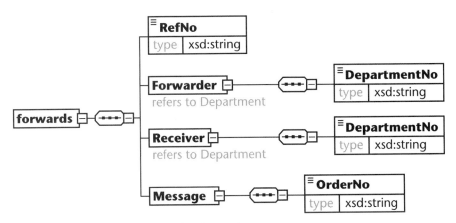

Figure 3.22 Schema diagram for forwards.

```
              refers to Order
          </xsd:documentation>
        </xsd:annotation>
        <xsd:complexType>
          <xsd:sequence>
            <xsd:element name="OrderNo" type="xsd:string"/>
          </xsd:sequence>
        </xsd:complexType>
      </xsd:element>
    </xsd:sequence>
  </xsd:complexType>
</xsd:element>

</xsd:schema>
```

The schema diagram (Figure 3.22) and code for forwards are similar.

```
<?xml version="1.0" encoding="UTF-8"?>

<xsd:schema xmlns:xsd="http://www.w3.org/2001/XMLSchema"
            elementFormDefault="qualified"
            attributeFormDefault="unqualified">

  <xsd:element name="forwards">
    <xsd:complexType>
      <xsd:sequence>
        <xsd:element name="RefNo" type="xsd:string"/>
        <xsd:element name="Forwarder">
```

```
            <xsd:annotation>
              <xsd:documentation>
                refers to Department
              </xsd:documentation>
            </xsd:annotation>
            <xsd:complexType>
              <xsd:sequence>
                <xsd:element name="DepartmentNo"
                             type="xsd:string"/>
              </xsd:sequence>
            </xsd:complexType>
          </xsd:element>
          <xsd:element name="Receiver">
            <xsd:annotation>
              <xsd:documentation>
                refers to Department
              </xsd:documentation>
            </xsd:annotation>
            <xsd:complexType>
              <xsd:sequence>
                <xsd:element name="DepartmentNo"
                             type="xsd:string"/>
              </xsd:sequence>
            </xsd:complexType>
          </xsd:element>
          <xsd:element name="Message">
            <xsd:complexType>
              <xsd:sequence>
                <xsd:element name="OrderNo"
                             type="xsd:string"/>
              </xsd:sequence>
            </xsd:complexType>
          </xsd:element>
        </xsd:sequence>
      </xsd:complexType>
    </xsd:element>
</xsd:schema>
```

This completes the definition of the schemata. Now let's look at some examples of instances of the schemata we have defined.

Here is an instance of the Customer schema:

```
<?xml version="1.0" encoding="UTF-8"?>

<Customer xmlns:xsi="http://www.w3.org/2001/XMLSchema-instance"
          xsi:noNamespaceSchemaLocation="customer.xsd">
  <CustomerID>c7790-404</CustomerID>
  <Name>
    <FirstName>John</FirstName>
    <LastName>Doe</LastName>
  </Name>
  <PhoneNo>415-555-1234</PhoneNo>
  <PhoneNo>415-555-1235</PhoneNo>
</Customer>
```

Now let's look at an instance of the Product schema:

```
<?xml version="1.0" encoding="UTF-8"?>

<Product xmlns:xsi="http://www.w3.org/2001/XMLSchema-instance"
         xsi:noNamespaceSchemaLocation="product.xsd">
  <ProductNo>p6745-3</ProductNo>
  <Name>Authoring System</Name>
  <Price>
    <Currency>USD</Currency>
    <Amount>7500.00</Amount>
  </Price>
  <Price>
    <Currency>EUR</Currency>
    <Amount>8570.00</Amount>
  </Price>
</Product>
```

Here is an instance of Service:

```
<?xml version="1.0" encoding="UTF-8"?>

<Service xmlns:xsi="http://www.w3.org/2001/XMLSchema-instance"
         xsi:noNamespaceSchemaLocation="service.xsd">
  <ProductNo>s9171-4</ProductNo>
  <Name>Training</Name>
  <Price>
    <Currency>USD</Currency>
    <Amount>1500.00</Amount>
  </Price>
  <Price>
```

```
    <Currency>EUR</Currency>
    <Amount>1730.00</Amount>
  </Price>
  <Duration>3</Duration>
</Service>
```

Here are two instances of `Department`:

```
<?xml version="1.0" encoding="UTF-8"?>

<Department xmlns:xsi="http://www.w3.org/2001/XMLSchema-instance"
            xsi:noNamespaceSchemaLocation="department.xsd">
  <DepartmentNo>d17</DepartmentNo>
  <Name>Corporate Sales</Name>
</Department>
```

```
<?xml version="1.0" encoding="UTF-8"?>

<Department xmlns:xsi="http://www.w3.org/2001/XMLSchema-instance"
            xsi:noNamespaceSchemaLocation="department.xsd">
  <DepartmentNo>d23</DepartmentNo>
  <Name>Shipping</Name>
</Department>
```

An example of an instance of the `Order` schema could look like this:

```
<?xml version="1.0" encoding="UTF-8"?>

<Order xmlns:xsi="http://www.w3.org/2001/XMLSchema-instance"
       xsi:noNamespaceSchemaLocation="order.xsd">
  <OrderNo>238</OrderNo>
  <Customer>
    <CustomerID>c7790-404</CustomerID>
  </Customer>
  <Position>
    <Amount>5</Amount>
    <Product>
      <ProductNo>p6745-3</ProductNo>
    </Product>
  </Position>
  <Position>
    <Amount>1</Amount>
    <Service>
      <ProductNo>s9171-4</ProductNo>
```

```
    </Service>
  </Position>
</Order>
```

An instance of the `receives` schema:

```xml
<?xml version="1.0" encoding="UTF-8"?>

<receives xmlns:xsi="http://www.w3.org/2001/XMLSchema-instance"
          xsi:noNamespaceSchemaLocation="receives.xsd">
  <RefNo>x832</RefNo>
  <Receiver>
    <DepartmentNo>d17</DepartmentNo>
  </Receiver>
  <Message>
    <OrderNo>238</OrderNo>
  </Message>
</receives>
```

Finally, here is an example of an instance of `forwards`:

```xml
<?xml version="1.0" encoding="UTF-8"?>

<forwards xmlns:xsi="http://www.w3.org/2001/XMLSchema-instance"
          xsi:noNamespaceSchemaLocation="forwards.xsd">
  <RefNo>f773</RefNo>
  <Forwarder>
    <DepartmentNo>d17</DepartmentNo>
  </Forwarder>
  <Receiver>
    <DepartmentNo>d23</DepartmentNo>
  </Receiver>
  <Message>
    <OrderNo>238</OrderNo>
  </Message>
</forwards>
```

Step 9

In some cases business objects and business documents can become too large. This has several drawbacks:

Segmentation

- Parsing a large document takes a long time. This affects almost any processing of XML documents (for example, transformation with an XSLT style sheet) because most processing involves parsing.

- Processing a large document with a DOM parser requires a large amount of resources. The whole document is converted into object form (each document node becomes a separate object), and this whole set of objects is kept resident in memory.
- Collaborative authoring of large documents is awkward. Some database systems (and also standards like WebDAV) support locking only on the document level. So when one author changes a document, the document is locked for others.

Therefore it is necessary to split large documents into smaller ones. This is possible on the conceptional level, for example, by splitting a large business object into a main object and aggregate parts. Each part would be modeled as a unary relationship type to which the main object relates.

Step 10

Overall layout   With XML Schema we can define the schemata for each business object and business document.

However, we still need a way to describe the overall layout of the complete model. One way to do this is to embed annotations into the schemata, similar to the ones we used in a previous example:

```
<xsd:annotation>
  <xsd:documentation>
    refers to Order via OrderNo
  </xsd:documentation>
</xsd:annotation>
```

However, this is an informal way and is hardly suitable to support automated systems. Also, by including the model structure in the schemata, the document base becomes hard to maintain. Changes in the model would require changes in many schemata.

It is much better to describe the model separately from individual schemata. One possible way is by using RDF, which we will discuss in detail in Section 3.3.

Another possibility is to describe the complete model using the AOM serialization syntax, which is XML based (see *www.aomodeling.org*). Here is a short excerpt showing the description of the assets Order, Position, Product, and Service:

```
<level2>
  <displayLabel>Order</displayLabel>
  <asset id="uuid:0016B448-EB27-47E3-AC09-9655CEF46A40"
         name="Order">
```

```
    <primaryKey
        fields="uuid:0016B448-EB27-47E3-AC09-9655CEF46A41"/>

    <property id="uuid:0016B448-EB27-47E3-AC09-9655CEF46A41"
                name="OrderNo"/>
    <arc target="uuid:0016B448-EB27-47E3-AC09-9655CEF46A20"/>
    <arc maxOccurs="unbounded"
        target="uuid:0016B448-EB27-47E3-AC09-9655CEF46A50"/>
  </asset>
  <asset id="uuid:0016B448-EB27-47E3-AC09-9655CEF46A50"
        name="Position">
    <property name="Amount"/>
    <cluster>
      <arc target="uuid:0016B448-EB27-47E3-AC09-9655CEF46A60"/>
      <arc target="uuid:0016B448-EB27-47E3-AC09-9655CEF46A70"/>
    </cluster>
  </asset>
</level2>

<level2>
  <displayLabel>Product</displayLabel>
  <asset id="uuid:0016B448-EB27-47E3-AC09-9655CEF46A60"
        name="Product">
    <primaryKey
        fields="uuid:0016B448-EB27-47E3-AC09-9655CEF46A61"/>
    <property id="uuid:0016B448-EB27-47E3-AC09-9655CEF46A61"
                name="ProductNo"/>
    <property name="Name"/>
    <property name="Price">
      <sequence maxOccurs="unbounded">
        <property name="Currency">
        <property name="Amount">
      </sequence>
    </property>
  </asset>
</level2>

<level2>
  <displayLabel>Service</displayLabel>
  <asset id="uuid:0016B448-EB27-47E3-AC09-9655CEF46A70"
        name="Service">
    <primaryKey
        fields="uuid:0016B448-EB27-47E3-AC09-9655CEF46A71"/>
```

```
<property id="uuid:0016B448-EB27-47E3-AC09-9655CEF46A71"
          name="ProductNo"/>
<property name="Name"/>

<property name="Duration"/>
<property name="Price">
  <sequence maxOccurs="unbounded">
    <property name="Currency">
    <property name="Amount">
  </sequence>
</property>
</asset>

</level2>
```

Note that the level2 elements enclose business objects. UUIDs are used to establish ID/IDREF structures between AOM items.

3.2.4 Smash the Enterprise Data Model?

The enterprise data model postulates that the data of an enterprise should be described by one coherent, complete, and consistent data model.

The idea of the enterprise data model has its roots in the classical transactional systems. When the data of an enterprise is kept in a single database, it is relatively easy to watch over constraints—for example, ensure that referenced entities are not deleted or that identifiers are kept unique. The same still holds for distributed databases that employ sophisticated transaction protocols (like the two-phase commit) to maintain the integrity of all connected databases.

However, data kept in the central repository is only a part of an enterprise's data set. A large amount of information accessible over the enterprise's intranet is kept scattered across multiple independent databases and file systems, even on the notebook computers and PDAs of the company's employees. And often the consistency and integrity of that data are in rather sad condition.

Possible drag factor

In addition, the existence of a global enterprise data model can be a drag factor for the IT infrastructure of an enterprise. Many enterprises today have a flat organization, with business units acting virtually autonomously, networking with other business units as they do with external partners. The enterprise data model, however, reflects a more hierarchical company structure. Business units that want to introduce new business policies have to apply to a central unit for a change of the data model. And vice versa—a change in the global model requires notifying every business unit about the change.

Chen, Thalheim, and Wong (1999) argue against bottom-up techniques and postulate a solid modeling concept with a top-down approach:

> It is very important to have a clean conceptual model of major components and services to guide us in this integration process. It should work like a multi-level "map," starting from a high-level map, which can be expanded into low-level maps in a hierarchical way. Each new software module constructed should follow this conceptual "guidance" model (map) and provide a self-description on details of the components and interfaces specified by the conceptual guidance map.

But, when bottom-up and quick-and-dirty methods flourish and top-down engineering techniques are avoided, there may be a reason. The reason could be that these top-down methods are not flexible enough to catch up with an ever faster changing work environment: ". . . in the flat organizations of today this kind of top-down strategies may not be suitable, as groups and local units need to control and define information resources according to their practices" (Forsberg and Dannstedt 1999).

Flat hierarchies

The mess in today's intranets is just an indication that the hierarchical enterprise data model increasingly fails to deliver. Too slow to follow the rapid changes of the business environment of today, this model made people turn to the more flexible ad hoc solutions of Web technology.

This does not mean that conceptual modeling is wrong. It simply means that conceptual modeling techniques and Web technologies have to converge. Earlier in this chapter we have shown that the way from a conceptual model to the definition of business documents and business rules is relatively straightforward. We feel that this approach is a step in the right direction. Business objects, business documents, and business rules are the constituents of business processes. Doing business on the Web implies negotiating how the business processes of the parties involved in a transaction can collaborate. We will discuss in later chapters how to model such processes.

Also required is the development of Web technologies that can make a conceptual model go live—the conceptual model can be easily transformed into a navigational structure. An example of such a transformation is given in the discussion of WebML in Section 7.1.2.

3.2.5 Best Practices

We recommend the following practices:

- Identify business objects and business documents. In the case of a purchase order, for example, the order is a business document, while order lines are subordinate assets. Model business objects and business documents as separate documents.

- Real-world entities are a good guide for detecting business objects. A customer, for example, is such an entity. The address of a customer, in contrast, is not such an entity but only a property of the customer entity. A customer address would therefore be modeled as a subordinate entity and as an element within an XML customer document.

- Using such an approach will result in an intuitive model. However, in many cases it is difficult to decide on what should be modeled as a business object. What is a dominant entity and what is not can depend on the context. When we said earlier that a customer address should be modeled as a property, we were referring to the average business case. However, in the context of a direct mailing service or the telecom industry, a street address is an asset and a business object.

- Whenever possible, use the partitioned normal form for all business objects and business documents. As we just pointed out, models can depend on the context. In electronic business, where trade relationships are hard to predict, sometimes partners will have different ideas about which entity is a business object and which is not. It is therefore essential that business objects and business documents can be structurally transformed without information loss. The partitioned normal form guarantees exactly that.

- Good starting points for identifying business objects are the electronic business standards such as Rosetta, BizTalk, and ebXML. These standards define core business objects. The definitions of these business objects are made available through public repositories. Using these definitions will increase the chance that potential business partners will "speak the same language." If you cannot find a particular business object in such a repository, you can contribute your own definitions to the repository, thus making them available to others. Remember that electronic business is not only about the collaboration of business processes but also about the collaboration of developers.

3.3 THE RESOURCE DESCRIPTION FRAMEWORK AND CONCEPTUAL MODELING

In this section we will introduce the Resource Description Framework (RDF). RDF can be seen as an enabling technology for semantic modeling, as a generic "assembler language" on top of which domain and task specific languages can be built. RDF applications include the Dublin Core and also DAML and OIL—languages for the description of ontologies that we will discuss in Section 4.2.2.

In this section we show how RDF can be used to describe the conceptual models developed in the previous chapter.

RDF has been a W3C recommendation since February 1999 (RDF 1999). The accompanying Resource Description Framework Schema Specification is, at the time of writing, a candidate recommendation (RDF 2000).

RDF provides an open standard for describing Web resources—but not just Web resources. In fact, RDF allows statements to be made about anything, even about off line resources and the weather. As long as you can identify a resource with a URI (Universal Resource Identifier), you can use RDF to say something about this resource. And because you can assign a unique URI to almost anything, including your children, your dog, and your Nintendo, RDF has a wide application range.

3.3.1 RDF Basics

We said that RDF allows you to make *statements* about resources. This is exactly the core point of RDF. RDF does not require modifying existing resources. An RDF description of a resource is a separate entity, and, as you have probably guessed, as a separate entity it can become a resource, too. So, you can make statements about statements about statements, and so on. An ideal base for gossip. And, yes, no RDF description has the exclusive rights to describe a resource. There can be many RDF statements distributed over the Web that describe the same resource.

Now, what sort of statements can you make about a resource?

RDF statements have a very simple structure. Each statement has the form of a triple, consisting of *predicate*, *subject*, and *object*. For example, in the sentence "John has phone number 415-555-6789", the subject is "John" because we are talking about him, "has phone number" is the predicate, and the object is the actual phone number, "415-555-6789".

The first RDF statement

We can see this statement from a different viewpoint. We could say that the phone number is a *property* of John. This property is called (has the name) "phone number", and the value of the property is "415-555-6789". In RDF, all statements have this form: *Subject has property*. Each property consists of a name/value pair, with property values being string literals or references to other resources.

By now you are probably asking yourself, "Isn't that similar to entity relationship diagrams where entities have attributes?" You are right, and that's why we called this section "The Resource Description Framework and Conceptual Modeling." RDF is one way to describe conceptual models.

RDF and ERM

Until now we haven't talked about relationships. In fact, RDF does not know relationships as a separate concept. In RDF relationships are nothing other than properties. The relationship "John is married to Mary" would be expressed as "John has marriage with Mary". "marriage with Mary" becomes a property of John. "marriage with" is the name of the property, and "Mary" is the value. Note that this statement does not tell us anything about Mary! It is a statement about John. To make this relationship bidirectional we would have to issue an additional statement "Mary has marriage with John".

These are more or less the basics of RDF. Simple, easy to understand, and very powerful. Before we discuss some advanced features, let us summarize the basic concepts and present a few examples. Table 3.1 lists the different ingredients of a statement.

Note that literals can be plain strings but they can also contain markup. For example, a literal could contain an XML structure. However, the RDF standard explicitly disavows a definition of equivalence between literals containing markup. This is because at the time the RDF standard was released, there existed no standard defining the equivalence between two XML documents. In the meantime, the XML canonical form has been standardized (Boyer 2001). This standard allows the comparison of two XML documents for equivalence by reducing the document layout to a canonical format. Future RDF versions may therefore contain a definition of equivalence for marked-up literals.

Nodes and arcs

RDF is an abstract, conceptual framework for defining and using metadata, independent of any concrete implementation and syntax. However, to write RDF statements we require a concrete means of expression. One possibility is directed labeled graphs (also called "node and arc diagrams"). (See Figure 3.23.)

Table 3.1   Anatomy of an RDF Statement.

Statement	Property	Domain	Example
Subject		Resource	http://www.ourfamily.org/John
Predicate	Property name		PhoneNo
Object	Property value	Resource or literal	"415-555-6789"

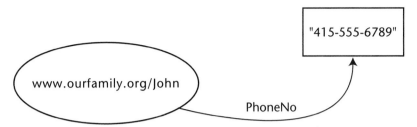

Figure 3.23 Simple node and arc diagram. The resource (ellipsoid) has one literal property value (rectangle).

In directed labeled graphs (DLGs) resources are shown as ellipsoids. Property values that are literals (strings) are shown as rectangles. An arc points from the subject to the object and is labeled with the predicate (property name). In an entity relationship diagram such a property would be represented as an attribute.

Another way to represent an RDF statement is the actual RDF syntax as defined in the RDF specification. (Currently, the RDF syntax is going through a revision cycle; see Beckett 2001.) This syntax is based on XML. Each RDF description is represented as an XML element. However, this does not mean that such a description can only describe XML resources:

Syntax

```
<rdf:RDF>
  <rdf:Description about="http://www.ourfamily.org/John">
    <p:PhoneNo>
      415-555-6789
    </p:PhoneNo>
  </rdf:Description>
</rdf:RDF>
```

As you can see, all tags defined by the RDF recommendation are prefixed with the identifier rdf:, which has been assigned somewhere to the RDF namespace URI. The about attribute identifies the subject of the statement. The property of the subject is defined as a child element of the rdf:Description element. The tag denotes the property name, while the property value is expressed as element content. The prefix p: denotes a problem domain namespace, which, for example, we could have defined using an XML namespace declaration such as

```
xmlns:p="http://www.telecom.com/schema/"
```

RDF vs. OO

If you've been well educated in object-oriented (OO) thinking, by now you probably feel a bit dizzy. If you think of resources in terms of object orientation, everything in RDF seems to be turned upside down. Where is data encapsulation? Where is information hiding? In OO, the properties of objects are private by default, unless they are published via the object's interface. In RDF, in contrast, you talk about existing resources—possibly resources at a foreign site. In most cases you would not even be able to modify a resource when you want to add a new property. RDF allows you to attach a new property from the outside.

Relationships

Now let's see how to present a relationship between two resources (see Table 3.2 and Figure 3.24). In Figure 3.24 the property value (object) is shown as an ellipsoid, too, because the value is another resource (identified by a URI). RDF allows the definition of several properties that associate two resources. This means that in terms of ERM an RDF property is equivalent to a named role within an unnamed relationship. RDF does not offer specific constructs to define named relationships. (Of course,

Table 3.2 Relationship between Two Resources.

Statement	Property	Domain	Example
Subject		Resource	http://www.ourfamily.org/John
Predicate	Property name		Marriage_with
Object	Property value	Resource or literal	http://www.ourfamily.org/Mary

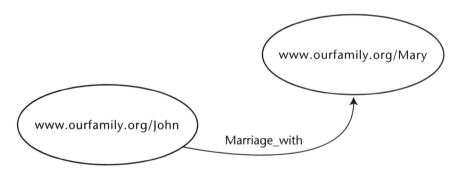

Figure 3.24 Here the property value is another resource.

you could name a relationship by making a statement about a statement, which we will discuss shortly.)

```
<rdf:RDF>
  <rdf:Description about="http://www.ourfamily.org/John">
    <f:Marriage_with>
      http://www.ourfamily.org/Mary
    </f:Marriage_with>
  </rdf:Description>
</rdf:RDF>
```

Note that we have used another problem domain namespace here. The prefix f: may be defined as

Namespaces

```
xmlns:f="http://www.ourfamily.org/schema/"
```

Authors of RDF descriptions are well advised to make extensive use of the namespace facilities available with XML. This avoids later conflicts when RDF descriptions are merged, which could be required, for example, in the case of company mergers or other marriages. Our two examples can easily be merged into one single description:

```
<rdf:RDF>

  <rdf:Description about="http://www.ourfamily.org/John">

    <p:PhoneNo>
      415-555-6789
    </p:PhoneNo>

    <f:Marriage_with
            rdf:resource="http://www.ourfamily.org/Mary"/>
  </rdf:Description>

</rdf:RDF>
```

3.3.2 From ERM to RDF

Figure 3.25 shows how a previous ERM example is transformed into RDF. This example required the description of two resources, one for a Customer instance, and another for a Product instance. The relationship between Customer and Product is modeled through a property of the Customer instance.

Note that in RDF we are talking about *instances*, while an entity relationship diagram is about *types* of entities and relationships. We will see

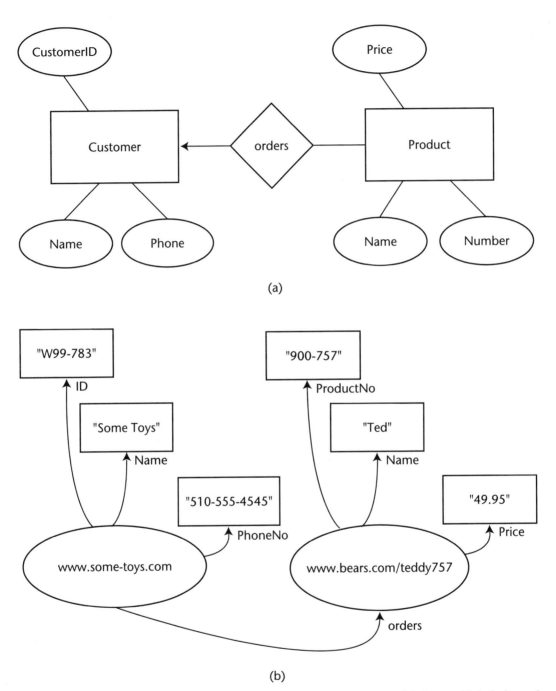

Figure 3.25 ERM converted to RDF: (a) entity relationship diagram; (b) directed labeled graph.

later how the Resource Definitions Schema Specification allows us to talk about resource types.

The following code shows the RDF serialization of the example in Figure 3.25.

```
<rdf:RDF>
  <rdf:Description about="http://www.some-toys.com">
    <sales:ID> W99-783 </sales:ID>
    <sales:Name> Some Toys </sales:Name>
    <sales:PhoneNo> 510-555-4545</sales:PhoneNo>
    <sales:orders
         rdf:resource="http://www.bears.com/teddy757"/>
  </rdf:Description>
  <rdf:Description about="http://www.bears.com/teddy757">
    <bears:ProductNo> 900-757 </bears:ID>
    <bears:Name> Ted </bears:Name>
    <bears:Price> 49.95 </bears:Price>
  </rdf:Description>
</rdf:RDF>
```

The entity relationship diagram in Figure 3.25(a) shows that the orders relationship is a 1:n relationship. We had ignored that when translating the diagram into RDF. How do we describe such a relationship in RDF?

Two RDF constructs deal with multiple occurrences: Bag and Seq (sequence). A Bag contains unordered property values; a Seq contains ordered property values. Both containers are allowed to contain duplicate values—there is no concept of uniqueness in RDF. Figure 3.26 shows our example with bags.

Bags and sequences

Technically a bag or a sequence is an anonymous intermediate resource of type rdf:Bag or rdf:Seq. (Note that the type is specified as just another property.) The RDF syntax specification, however, provides a shorthand notation in the form of tags: <rdf:Bag> and <rdf:Seq>. The elements of a bag or a sequence are identified by an <rdf:li .../> tag:

```
<rdf:Description about="http://www.some-toys.com">
  <sales:ID> W99-783 </sales:ID>
  <sales:Name> Some Toys </sales:Name>
  <sales:PhoneNo> 510-555-4545 </sales:PhoneNo>
  <sales:orders>
    <rdf:Bag>
      <rdf:li rdf:resource="http://www.bears.com/teddy757"/>
      <rdf:li rdf:resource="http://www.bears.com/teddy766"/>
```

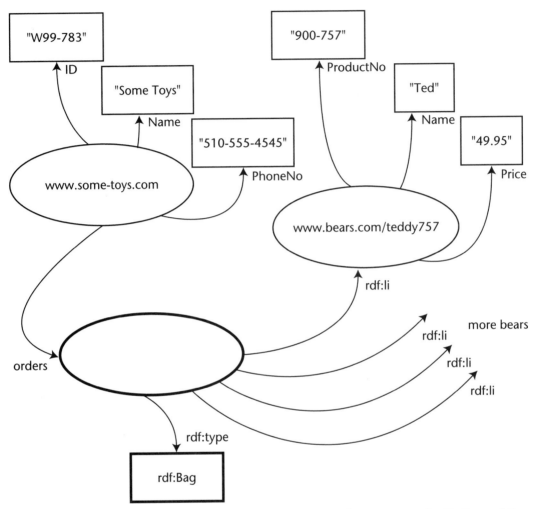

Figure 3.26 Using bags for teddies. Resource collections can be represented with Bag and Seq.

```
        <rdf:li rdf:resource="http://www.bears.com/teddy565"/>
        <rdf:li rdf:resource="http://www.bears.com/teddy123"/>
      </rdf:Bag>
    </sales:orders>
  </rdf:Description>
```

The syntax for the Seq container is similar.

An additional, third construct, called `Alt` (alternative), allows the spec-   Alternatives
ification of a list of possible property values from which one is selected.
The selection of one list element excludes the others from the relationship. In our example, using `Alt` instead of `Bag` could mean that the first
available teddy in the list is preferred and that the other bears quoted
serve as alternatives when the first bear isn't available.

Earlier we stated that RDF can describe any resource. Now, when we
define a `Bag` of resources, can we talk about this container and its contents? Of course we can.

First, we define the `Bag` as a resource in its own right:

```
<rdf:Bag ID="bag_of_bears">
  <rdf:li rdf:resource="http://www.bears.com/teddy757"/>
  <rdf:li rdf:resource="http://www.bears.com/teddy766"/>
  <rdf:li rdf:resource="http://www.bears.com/teddy565"/>
  <rdf:li rdf:resource="http://www.bears.com/teddy123"/>
</rdf:Bag>
```

This `Bag` is now its own resource, which can be identified via the URI
"#bag_of_bears". So, we can make a statement about this resource:

```
<rdf:Description about="#bag_of_bears">
  <sales:ordered_by rdf:resource="http://www.some-toys.com"/>
</rdf:Description>
```

Additionally, we can make statements about each member of the `Bag`.
To do so, RDF provides a special attribute `aboutEach`:

```
<rdf:Description aboutEach="#bag_of_bears">
  <sales:ordered_by rdf:resource="http://www.some-toys.com"/>
</rdf:Description>
```

The `aboutEachPrefix` attribute can be used to make statements about the
set of members in a container selected by a URI pattern—for example,
about all resources in a Web site:

```
<rdf:Description aboutEachPrefix="http://www.bears.com/">
  <bears:Trademark>™The Bears Company</Bears:Trademark>
</rdf:Description>
```

3.3.3 Advanced Modeling Techniques

In this section, we show how constructs known from entity relationship
modeling can be expressed in RDF.

N-ary Relationships

We have to give some consideration to *n*-ary relationships. ERM allows ternary, quaternary, and so on relationships, where one relationship associates three, four, or more entities with each other. RDF statements, however, can model only binary relationships: subject to object. Aware of this problem, the RDF specification recommends a way around it. Let's consider the following cases:

- Lecturer Miles recommends book *XML Bible* for course 3A.
- Lecturer Miles recommends book *OO Design* for course 2B.
- Lecturer Davis recommends book *SGML Praxis* for course 3A.

On the level of entity sets we could hardly split this ternary relationship into two binary relationships. We would lose information. The trick RDF uses is to introduce intermediate resources on the instance level:

```
<RDF

  xmlns="http://www.w3.org/1999/02/22-rdf-syntax-ns#"
  xmlns:rdf="http://www.w3.org/1999/02/22-rdf-syntax-ns#"
  xmlns:col="http://www.college.edu/schema#">

  <Description about="http://www.college.edu/staff/Miles">

    <col:Recommendation rdf:parseType="Resource">
     <col:recommended_reading rdf:resource=
           "http://wwww.college.edu/library/XML_Bible"/>
       <col:course rdf:resource=
                 "http://wwww.college.edu/courses/3A"/>
     </col:Recommendation>
    <col:Recommendation rdf:parseType="Resource">

    <col:recommended_reading rdf:resource=
           "http://wwww.college.edu/library/OO_Design/>
      <col:course rdf:resource=
                 "http://wwww.college.edu/courses/2B"/>
    </col:Recommendation>

  </Description>

  <Description about="http://www.college.edu/staff/Davis">
    <col:Recommendation rdf:parseType="Resource">
      <col:recommended_reading rdf:resource=
            "http://wwww.college.edu/library/SGML_Praxis"/>
      <col:course rdf:resource=
```

```
                    "http://wwww.college.edu/courses/3A"/>
      </col:Recommendation>
   </Description>
</RDF>
```

The `col:Recommendation` elements defined within the `Description` elements act as intermediate resources. Intermediate resources do not exist as real resources. They are of a purely fictive nature and are only visible within the scope of the containing element.

At this point we have to explain the `rdf:parseType` attribute. The `parseType` attribute changes the interpretation of the element content. Two values are possible: `Literal` or `Resource`.

- The value `Literal` specifies that the element content must not be interpreted by an RDF processor. For example, when an element contains some other XML or HTML markup, this value should be specified. (Note: RDF explicitly disavows definition of equivalence between literals containing markup!)
- The value `Resource` specifies that the element content must be treated as if it were the content of a `Description` element.

This technique of modeling *n*-ary relationships can also be used to model attributed relationships (see Figure 3.27). A binary relationship with one attribute, for example, is modeled in the same way as a ternary relationship without an attribute:

```
<rdf:Description about="http://www.some-toys.com">

  <sales:ID> W99-783 </sales:ID>
  <sales:Name> Some Toys </sales:Name>
  <sales:PhoneNo> 510-555-4545 </sales:PhoneNo>
  <sales:orders>
    <sales:Order rdf:parseType="Resource">
      <sales:OrderNumber> 9993-333 </sales:OrderNumber>
      <rdf:Bag>
        <rdf:li rdf:resource="http://www.bears.com/teddy757"/>
        <rdf:li rdf:resource="http://www.bears.com/teddy766"/>
        <rdf:li rdf:resource="http://www.bears.com/teddy565"/>
        <rdf:li rdf:resource="http://www.bears.com/teddy123"/>
      </rdf:Bag>
    </sales:Order>
  </sales:orders>
</rdf:Description>
```

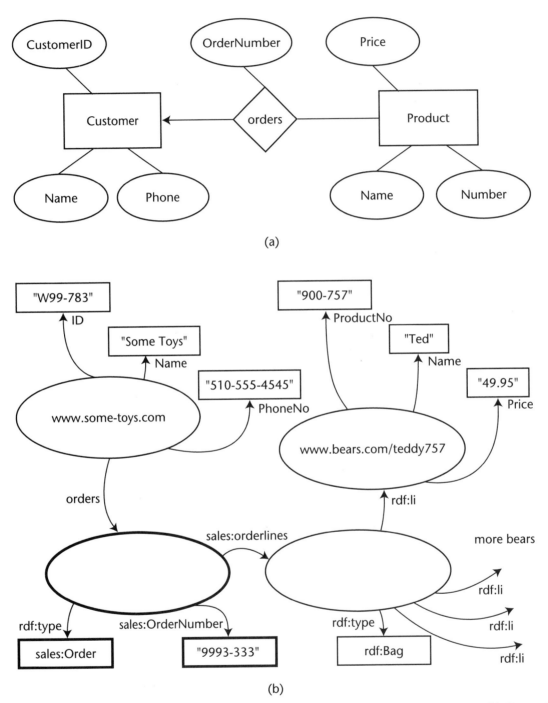

Figure 3.27 Modeling relationships with attributes: (a) entity relationship diagram; (b) directed labeled graph.

This substitution is, as we can see, very similar to what is done in ERM dialects that do not know attributed relationships when we have to model attributed relationships: the relationship is modeled as an entity; that is, it is reified. In RDF, the distinction between relationships and entities blurs because each relationship can become a resource in its own right.

Aggregations

The possibility of defining resources "on the fly" can be used to model aggregations, too (see Figure 3.28):

```
<rdf:Description about="http://www.bears.com/sales">
  <bears:DepNo> 45/3 </bears:DepNo>
  <bears:receives>
    <rdf:Seq>
      <rdf:li>
        <sales:Order rdf:ID="#order9993-333"
                     rdf:parseType="Resource">
          <sales:OrderNumber> 9993-333 </sales:OrderNumber>
          <sales:Customer
                   rdf:resource="http://www.some-toys.com"
                   rdf:parseType="Resource">
            <sales:ID> W99-783 </sales:ID>
            <sales:Name> Some Toys </sales:Name>
            <sales:PhoneNo> 510-555-4545 </sales:PhoneNo>
            <sales:orders>
              <rdf:Bag>
                <rdf:li
                  rdf:resource="http://www.bears.com/teddy757"/>
                <rdf:li
                  rdf:resource="http://www.bears.com/teddy766"/>
                <rdf:li
                  rdf:resource="http://www.bears.com/teddy565"/>
                <rdf:li
                  rdf:resource="http://www.bears.com/teddy123"/>
              </rdf:Bag>
            </sales:orders>
          </sales:Customer>
        </sales:Order>
      </rdf:li>
    </rdf:Seq>
  </bears:receives>
</rdf:Description>
```

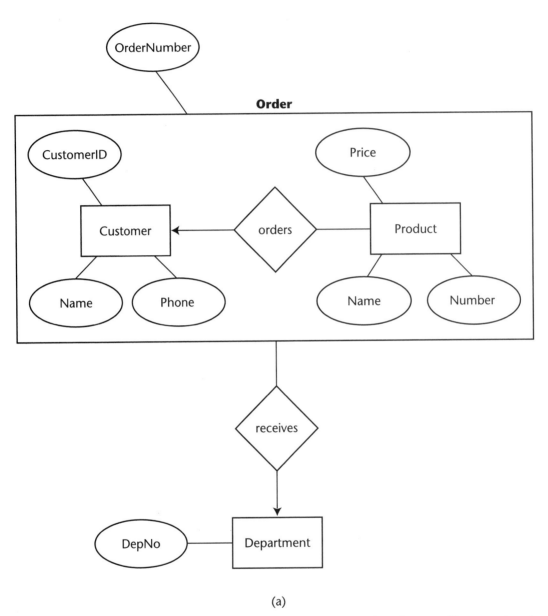

(a)

Figure 3.28 Modeling aggregation with RDF: (a) entity relationship diagram *(figure continued on facing page).*

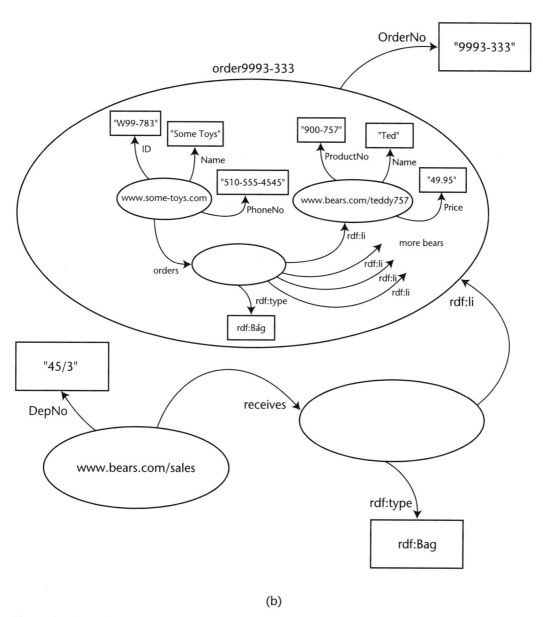

(b)

Figure 3.28 Modeling aggregation with RDF: (b) directed labeled graph.

3.3.4 Reification

Note that until now we have used RDF only to talk about resource instances. To make statements about resource classes (or resource types) on the schema level, we need to investigate the possibilities defined in the Resource Definition Schema Specification.

Statements
about
statements

But before we do this, let's explain quickly how we can make statements about statements. Because the subject of a statement has to be a resource, we have to cast the statement about which we want to make a statement into a resource—a process that is also called *reification*. "Reification" comes from Latin and means "to make into a thing." By reifying a statement into a resource, we make it into a thing that we can talk about.

Consider the following statement: "Mary has phone number 415-555-4321." We can easily model this statement in RDF:

```
<rdf:RDF>

  <rdf:Description about="http://www.ourfamily.org/Mary">

    <p:PhoneNo> 415-555-4321 </p:PhoneNo>

  </rdf:Description>

</rdf:RDF>
```

Now consider: "John says, 'Mary has phone number 415-555-4321.'" Here the statement "Mary has phone number 415-555-4321" becomes the subject X in the statement "X is attributed to John."

There are several ways to model a statement as a resource, but the easiest is to equip the `Description` element with a `bagID` attribute:

```
<rdf:Description bagID="AboutMary"
      about="http://www.ourfamily.org/Mary">

  <p:PhoneNo> 415-555-4321 </p:PhoneNo>

</rdf:Description>
```

Every statement within the `Description` element is reified and becomes a resource within a `Description` bag. We can now make statements about these resources:

```
<rdf:Description aboutEach="#AboutMary">

  <p:attributedTo> John </p:attributedTo>

</rdf:Description>
```

Warning: If we consider an RDF statement as a "thought," then reification opens the opportunity to "think" about "thoughts." So be very careful which sort of RDF statements you place on the Web—maybe it's you who caused the Web to become self-conscious!

In terms of formal logic, a set of basic RDF statements constitutes a first-order logic system. With reification (i.e., making statements about statements) we get a second-order logic system, and second-order systems have their problems. In 1931, Kurt Gödel showed that second-order systems are logically incomplete, in contrast to first-order systems, for which he had previously (in 1930) proved completeness. The basic idea of Gödel's proof of incompleteness is to construct a statement that makes a statement about itself: it claims that itself cannot be proved.

Gödel, Church, and RDF

But avoiding reification wouldn't help us much further. In 1936 A. Church proved that even for the first-order predicate logic there is no general method to decide on the correctness or incorrectness of a statement within a finite time span using a mechanical device such as a Turing machine. And since our fastest computers cannot do better than a Turing machine, we have a problem, even if we don't use reification.

However, for RDF the practical implications remain minor. Although in the design of computer languages decidability plays a crucial role (for example, Backus-Naur grammars are always decidable) because we want a parser to stop with a result after a finite time span, this is not a critical element in an open system such as the Internet. Almost always the complete set of RDF statements on the Web will be incomplete and even contradictory. A search engine that operates on such a set of RDF statements will therefore be constructed in such a way that it will successfully answer queries in most cases. In some cases, however, such a search engine would have to stop reasoning after a given time span and report its failure to find a result.

Implications for RDF

Second-order logic can be very helpful in representing the results of a query. With first-order logic, the query "Who won the U.S. election in 2000?" would simply return "George Bush or Al Gore". We wouldn't have needed a billion-dollar computer network for that sort of answer. With second-order logic, however, the answer could be something like this: "The Republican Web site claims George Bush as the winner, and the Democratic Web site claims Al Gore as the winner." Although we already knew this from TV, it gives us a much clearer picture of what is going on. To make the result of a query *traceable* we require the ability to make statements about statements.

3.3.5 RDF Schema

In the previous subsections we showed how to use RDF to describe resources on the Web and elsewhere. All this happened on the level of individual resources or collections of individual resources, that is, always on the instance level.

Taxonomy of resources

The RDF Schema Specification (RDFS) enables us to define a taxonomy of resources in terms of resource classes, superclasses, and subclasses. For each of these classes we can define which types of statements may be made about the instances of these classes, that is, which types of properties can be associated.

This does not mean that we always have to define RDF schemata when we want to describe some resource. RDF can be used without accompanying RDF schemata—the use of RDFS is optional.

This is similar to XML. Well-formed XML documents can be processed without a DTD, but when a DTD is defined, the documents that refer to the DTD as DOCTYPE can be checked for validity. In contrast with DTDs, RDF schemata do not just define the structure of an RDF statement but can also define semantic constraints. For example, it is possible to restrict the range and the value domain of given statement types.

Semantic constraints

In a previous subsection now and then we used the rdf:type property, for example, rdf:type="rdf:Bag". This property connects a resource instance to a resource type or resource class. In the case of rdf:Bag this was a predefined RDF resource class. RDFS, in addition, allows us to declare our own user-defined resource classes. In many ways, the RDFS type system is similar to the class hierarchies in object-oriented programming. However, there is a major difference: in object-oriented programming you define a class by specifying features (attributes and methods) of the class. This is usually done in the context of the class definition.

RDFS works just the other way around: properties (statements) are the subject of specification, and you describe to which resource classes they apply. This is done via the rdfs:domain and rdfs:range constraints. The rdfs:domain constraint describes to which resource classes a given property applies, while the rdfs:range constraint describes the allowed range for the property value.

In the following example we show how to model a generalization. Defined are three classes, ProductOrService, Product, and Service, with Product and Service being subclasses of ProductOrService:

```
<rdf:RDF

    xmlns:rdf="http://www.w3.org/1999/02/22-rdf-syntax-ns#"

    xmlns:rdfs="http://www.w3.org/2000/01/rdf-schema#">
```

```
<rdfs:Class rdf:ID="ProductOrService">
  <rdfs:comment>
    Abstract superclass for products and services.
  </rdfs:comment>
</rdfs:Class>

<rdfs:Class rdf:ID="Product">
  <rdfs:comment>The class of products.</rdfs:comment>
  <rdfs:subClassOf rdf:resource="#ProductOrService"/>
<rdfs:Class>

<rdfs:Class rdf:ID="Service">
  <rdfs:comment>The class of services.</rdfs:comment>
  <rdfs:subClassOf rdf:resource="#ProductOrService"/>
</rdfs:Class>

<rdf:Property ID="Number">

  <rdfs:range rdf:resource=
        "http://www.examples.com/classes#CatNumbers"/>
  <rdfs:domain rdf:resource="#ProductOrService"/>

</rdf:Property>

<rdf:Property ID="Duration">
  <rdfs:range rdf:resource="#Duration"/>
  <rdfs:domain rdf:resource="#Service"/>
</rdf:Property>

<rdfs:Class rdf:ID="Duration"/>

<Duration rdf:ID="One_day"/>

<Duration rdf:ID="Two_days"/>

<Duration rdf:ID="Three_days"/>

</rdf:RDF>
```

Note that the rdfs:Class tag starts the definition of a *resource class*. This tag is defined in the RDFS specification, hence the namespace prefix rdfs:. The ID attribute defines the class name. We define three classes: ProductOrService, Product, and Service, with Product and Service being subclasses of ProductOrService.

The elements rdf:Property define *resources* of type Property. The ID attribute defines the property name. Resource definitions are standard RDF operations, hence the namespace identifier `rdf:`. We define two properties: `Number` and `Duration`.

The element `rdfs:range` defines the value range for each property. In the case of the property `Number`, the range definition refers to a resource `http://www.examples.com/classes#CatNumbers`. We assume that the datatype `CatNumbers` is defined in this resource. For property `Duration` a new datatype is created on the spot: a class `Duration` is defined, and several resources of type `Duration` enumerate the possible values. Each property can have only a single `rdfs:range` specification.

The element `rdfs:domain` defines to which resource classes each property applies. We have specified class `ProductOrService` as the domain for property `Number`. Because the classes `Product` and `Service` are subclasses of `ProductOrService`, the property applies to `Product` and `Service`, too. In contrast, the property `Duration` applies only to class `Service`. Each property may have multiple `rdfs:domain` specifications.

`rdfs:domain` and `rdfs:range` belong to RDFS, hence the namespace identifier `rdfs:`. Because RDF and RDFS are separate specifications, they also use two different namespaces for their syntactical elements. That can be disturbing: schema authors must constantly switch between the two namespaces. Somehow, this reminds us of the tourist who drowned in Finland because all the lakes, islands, and peninsulas confused him and he ended up mistaking a lake for land.

Inheritance

As we have seen, subclasses do inherit properties from their parent classes (`Product` and `Service` inherited `Number` from `ProductOrService`). At the very top of the RDFS class hierarchy is the predefined class `rdfs:Resource`, which includes all RDF resources as instances. In RDFS, a subclass can inherit from several parent classes by using several `rdfs:subClassOf` clauses. In object-oriented programming this is called multiple inheritance. Multiple inheritance has quite a reputation in OO because inheriting from multiple parents can lead to name clashes between features with different implementations. In RDFS, however, this cannot happen because property definitions are resources in their own right and are unique within their namespace.

What is possible for classes is also possible for properties. Properties can be defined as subproperties of (several) other properties:

```
<rdf:Property ID="Number">
</rdf:Property>

<rdf:Property ID="ProductNumber">
  <rdfs:subPropertyOf rdf:resource="#Number"/>
</rdf:Property>
```

What's left? Currently, RDFS defines only a limited set of constraint properties: `rdfs:domain` and `rdfs:range`. To define additional constraints we need an extension mechanism. This is provided by means of class `rdfs:ConstraintProperty`, a subclass of class `rdf:Property`. Both `rdfs:domain` and `rdfs:range` are instances of `rdfs:ConstraintProperty`.

For example, it would be possible to define a new constraint property `myext:unique` as a new instance of class `rdfs:ConstraintProperty`:

Extension mechanism

```
<rdfs:ConstraintProperty ID="myext:unique">
  <rdfs:domain rdf:resource=
      "http://www.w3.org/1999/02/22-rdf-syntax-ns#Property"/>
  <rdfs:range rdf:resource=
      "http://www.w3.org/2000/01/rdf-schema#Class"/>
</rdfs:ConstraintProperty>

<rdf:Property ID="Number">
  <rdfs:range rdf:resource=
      "http://www.examples.com/classes#CatNumbers"/>
  <rdfs:domain rdf:resource="#ProductOrService"/>
  <myext:unique rdf:resource=
      "http://www.examples.com/classes#UniqueNumbers"/>
</rdf:Property>
```

By using this extension mechanism it becomes possible to define all sorts of constraints. However, the RDFS specification only defines the semantics of the constraints `rdfs:range` and `rdfs:domain`.

This has a reason of course: A constraint such as `unique` could hardly be handled identically in all environments. While it is easy to guarantee the value of a property to be unique within the confined space of a transactional database, the same constraint becomes impossible to guarantee in an open environment such as the Internet.

Wish List

This leaves us with some wishes (which are also wishes for other schema definition systems). Earlier in this book, in Chapter 1, we postulated that future software systems must be able to distinguish between the "required" and the "should." What we would like to see is the introduction of the concept of *soft constraints*. In contrast to hard constraints, which know only one possible policy (strict enforcement in all environments), soft constraints would know a variety of possible policies that may depend on the context.

Soft constraints

Let's look at an example. The `unique` constraint mentioned earlier could know the following policies:

- *Reject:* Reject a transaction when a property violates this constraint. This type of policy could be used in transactional systems. Here it is relatively easy to check for uniqueness, and uniqueness is absolutely necessary for certain properties (for example keys).
- *Repair:* Here an agent could travel the network and try to repair invalid properties asynchronously. This type of policy could be used within an intranet, where an agent of that kind would possess the necessary access rights for reading and modifying data.
- *Report:* Here an agent could travel the network and report any invalid properties. This type of policy could be used within an extranet, where an agent of that kind would possess the necessary access rights for reading data.
- *Ignore:* Nothing is done here. The typical environment for this policy is the Internet, where it would be completely senseless to enforce uniqueness of a certain property.

3.3.6 Reasoning with RDF

The XML syntax that we have used above for RDF statements is only one of many possible representations. The statement shown in Figure 3.23 could also be expressed in the form of a triple {predicate, subject, object}:

`(PhoneNo,www.ourfamily.org/john,"415-555-6789")`

In this form, an RDF statement can be easily stored in a relational database.

With a little bit more transformation we arrive at

`PhoneNo(www.ourfamily.org/john,"415-555-6789")`

a form that should be familiar to all readers who have some background in logic programming. In the logic programming language Prolog, for example, such a construct is called a *fact*. A Prolog program consists of a collection of facts and rules (in general rules have the form "A holds if B and/or C holds"). A query will start an inference engine that applies rules to facts in order to return a result. No procedural programming is required.

METALOG

The question that immediately springs to mind is, Why not add rules to RDF and use RDF for logic programming? This was exactly the goal of a W3C effort called METALOG.

METALOG had two objectives: First it extended RDF with the possibility of defining logic rules. Second it provided an almost natural language interface to RDF. The RDF syntax that we have presented here is not very user friendly but rather is designed to store and process RDF in an XML environment. A user-friendly syntax could greatly improve the adoption of RDF on a wider scale. As stated by Marchiori and Saarela (2000): "Metalog allows users to write metadata, inference rules and queries in English-like syntax."

The previous RDF statement could be expressed as follows:

```
"www.ourfamily.org/john" has as "PhoneNo" "415-555-6789".
```

If John has several phone numbers, we could write

```
"www.ourfamily.org/john" has as "PhoneNo" "415-555-6789" and "212-
555-0001".
```

The "and" keyword would be translated into an RDF Bag construct containing both phone numbers.

We can also use verbs as predicates:

```
"www.ourfamily.org/mary" "lives_with" "www.ourfamily.org/john".
```

This would translate into

```
lives_with(www.ourfamily.org/mary,www.ourfamily.org/john)
```

To allow the definition of rules, Metalog adds the operators "implies", "and", "or", and variables to RDF. Variables are denoted with the first character in upper case.

We can now define a rule that reasons about the two facts defined earlier:

```
if X "lives_with" Y and Y has as "PhoneNo" Z
    then X has as "PhoneNo" Z.
```

Note that the keyword "and" has a different meaning here. It is used as a logical "and", not as an indicator for an RDF Bag. Which "and" is which is decided by the context. Similarly, the keyword "or" can be used for a logical "or" or to denote an RDF Alt. The keyword "order" is used for an RDF Seq.

Finally we can query our little expert system with

```
what "PhoneNo" does "www.ourfamily.org/mary" have?
```

which would result in a new statement:

```
"www.ourfamily.org/mary" has as "PhoneNo" "415-555-6789" and
"212-555-0001".
```

3.3.7 Best Practices

We recommend the following practices:

- When writing RDF descriptions always use namespaces to identify the problem domain. This allows merging RDF descriptions at a later time without pain. The identification of problem domains, the definition of namespaces, and the definition of a namespace vocabulary are closely related to the definition of an ontology (see Section 4.2).
- When modeling relationships between two entities, make sure not only to define the relationship as an RDF property of one entity but also to define the inverse relationship as a property of the target entity.

3.4 A U FOR AN X

In this section, we discuss UML-modeling techniques in the context of XML. Due to an "impedance mismatch" between both technologies, modeling XML-based systems with UML can be tricky.

3.4.1 XML Modeling with UML

The Unified Modeling Language (UML) is a framework for modeling complex information systems that has become an industry standard within the last decade. UML emerged as the successor of three previously leading object-oriented modeling methods (Booch, OMT, and OOSE). It combines these three methods into one consistent modeling method. Additionally, it addresses problems, such as process modeling, that these methods previously did not fully address.

UML has been endorsed by the Object Management Group (OMG) as a standard modeling method. The OMG is an international organization promoting the theory and practice of object-oriented technology in software development. The OMG is also the organization behind Common Object Request Broker Architecture (CORBA), so it should not be a surprise that UML has strong links to CORBA.

Standardization   UML 1.4 has been submitted to the International Organization for Standardization (ISO) and will become an ISO standard. In addition, UML has been selected by UN/CEFACT as the standard modeling method for ebXML.

UML comprises six different models:

1. The use case model, for requirement analysis (business model)

2. The class model, for modeling the static structures of information objects

3. The state model, for modeling the dynamic behavior of objects

4. The activity implementation model, which describes work unit actions

5. The interaction model, which describes scenarios and message flows

6. The deployment model, which describes the deployment of software subsystems

UML and ERM

In the context of this section we are interested only in the class model (item 2 in the previous list). The UML class model resembles more or less the classic entity relationship model. However, the nomenclature is different (entities are called *objects*, entity sets are called *classes*, and relationship sets are called *associations*). After all, UML is an object-oriented modeling language. Figure 3.29 shows an example of a UML class diagram.

Compared to the entities in ERM the main difference is that objects are dynamic—they display a behavior. Each object has *attributes* whose values determine the *state* of the object. In addition, objects can have *operations* (methods), which can inform about the value of attributes and which can change the value of attributes (i.e., change the object's state). Objects relate to each other by sending messages (calling each other's methods) or by aggregation.

The attributes of an object determine the *type* of an object. Objects equipped with the same set of attributes have the same type. This can be compared with the entity set in ERM. Both methods and attributes of an object determine the *class* of an object. Objects with the same sets of methods and attributes are *instances* of the same class. This means that instances of a class all expose the same behavior. ERM does not have an equivalent to the class construct because ERM does not model dynamic behavior. In UML, however, it is possible to model class hierarchies. *Subclasses* can inherit features from abstract superclasses. Generalization is modeled via superclasses.

Associations can be constrained in UML at both ends by a *multiplicity* (cardinality) specification. The most common specifications are 0 .. 1, 0 .. *, 1, 1 .. * (OneOptional, ManyOptional, OneMandatory, ManyMandatory).

Associations can be bidirectional or unidirectional (*navigability*). For example, when an object sends a message to another object, the sender knows the receiver, but the receiver does not necessarily know the sender. Each end of an association may have a role name.

Margin notes: Nomenclature · Objects · Attributes · Associations

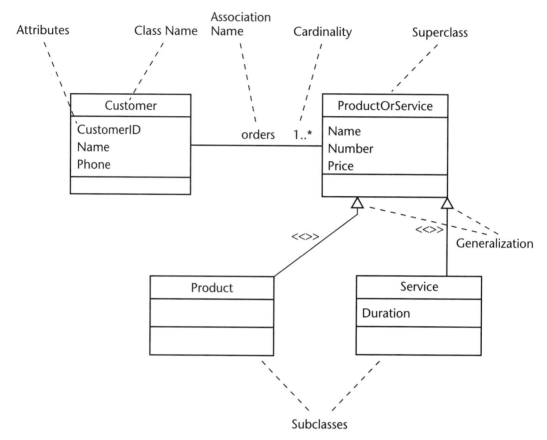

Figure 3.29 UML class diagram. Attributes are listed below the class name. Associations can be named (in addition, role names are possible). The cardinality is denoted in explicit numbers (*n:m*), with an asterisk denoting an unbounded number of occurrences. Subclasses inherit attributes from superclasses.

Stereotypes   One outstanding feature of UML is the powerful extension mechanism offered with stereotypes. A stereotype is always based on existing UML constructs but introduces new semantics.

UML and AOM

Asset-oriented models can be mapped onto UML, too. To do so we map every asset onto a UML class. The arcs between the assets become UML associations that are named with the respective role names. Compared to traditional UML modeling, this approach is very powerful. Because classical relationships are modeled as assets, too, and are thus mapped onto UML classes, we do not have problems representing relationships between relationships and *n*-ary relationships in UML.

However, UML requires the introduction of extra classes:

- Complex properties must be resolved into classes, since UML classes can possess only simple properties.
- Clusters must be represented as generalized classes in UML. The cluster members are represented as subclasses of these generalized classes.

UML and XML

XML documents can be modeled in UML as aggregations of objects, basically one UML class element per XML element plus some auxiliary elements. Conallen (2000), Booch et al. (1999), and Heintz and Kimber (1999) describe how a DTD or XML Schema can be mapped onto UML (and vice versa, how UML can be used to design a DTD):

- XML element types are modeled in UML as <<DTDElement>> stereotype elements.
- XML attributes can be mapped directly to UML attributes. XML attributes are atomic values of a certain datatype. This requires the definition of appropriate datatypes in the UML model.
- XML element content (such as character data) can be modeled as an attribute with a <<DTDElementPCDATA>> stereotype.
- XML elements of content type ANY are modeled with a <<DTDElement-ANY>> stereotype.
- XML elements of content type EMPTY are modeled with a <<DTDElement-EMPTY>> stereotype.
- The ownership between elements (parent-child) is indicated by directional associations.
- Model groups are represented by new stereotyped elements. Since model groups are anonymous, dummy names must be introduced in the UML model. Sequence groups are represented by a <<DTDSequence-Group>> stereotype; choice groups, by a <<DTDChoiceGroup>> stereotype.
- The order of sequences is captured as ordinal values in role constraints.
- Multiplicity of elements is mapped directly into the corresponding UML constraints (see Table 3.3).
- Mixed elements in XML (i.e., elements containing character data combined with child elements) can be mapped onto model groups (see earlier). A mixed element can be described as a repeated alternative of content and child elements.

Table 3.3 Cardinality Notations in XML and UML.

XML	UML
(no modifier)	1
?	$0 . . 1$
+	$1 . . *$
*	$0 . . *$

Using this technique, it becomes possible to import a DTD (e.g., an industry standard DTD) into UML, do a few modifications, and export it again. The leading UML case tools support such import and export processes.

In a similar fashion, XML Schema definitions can be mapped onto UML structures. This is described in detail by Carlson (2001).

The advantages of this technique are that DTDs and schemata can be visualized (but good schema editors can do that, too) and that the documentation is improved. It is also possible to generate program code from the UML model, such as Java code. We obtain wrapper code that is quite intuitive and allows easy access to the XML document structures.

From UML to XML

Note, however, that the UML model obtained with this method is an implementation model and not a conceptual model. This technique requires that the UML model follow the structures of the XML document. But how do we generate XML schemata from a preexisting conceptual UML model?

One possibility could be to exploit the code generation facilities of UML tools. Most UML case tools can generate program code, and some allow user-defined production rules, allowing the generation of any code including XML schemata. However, this technique relies very much on the proprietary features of the respective tool.

Using XMI   A better option is to use the fact that most UML tools can export XMI code. XMI (see Section 3.4.2) was developed to exchange modeling data between different modeling tools. Thus, XMI contains the modeling data in a standardized format. And because XMI is an XML language, we can transform XMI modeling data into any other XML format—including XML Schema—with the help of an XSLT style sheet (see Chapter 9). An example style sheet is available at the authors' Web site (*www.xmlArchitecture.org*).

So, to create XML schemata out of a UML model, we have to perform three steps:

1. Export the model in XMI format.
2. Write an appropriate XSLT style sheet (or generate it with an appropriate tool).
3. Translate the XMI data with the help of the XSLT style sheet into the target format.

UML and RDF

XML schema creation is not the only interesting aspect when looking at the relationship between UML and XML. In Table 3.4 we compare the modeling capabilities of UML with those of RDF (Chang 1998). Keep in mind that UML is an object-oriented technique, while ERM and RDF are not.

RDF and UML are fairly equivalent when it comes to modeling the static aspects of an information set. RDF has some restrictions in the constraint area: cardinality and optionality constraints are expressed via containers that only allow expressing $1:(0,n)$ relationships. This is rather weak compared to the rich set of constraint expressions that are available in UML. But keep in mind that RDF was designed for the World Wide Web, where mandatory associations are very hard to control; unresolved links are all too common on the Web.

The similarities between RDF and UML allow us to use UML as a design method for RDF resource descriptions. What is not possible, in general, is to *map* any UML model in terms of native RDF statements.

That does not mean that it is impossible to *describe* any UML model using RDF statements. For example, Melnik (2000) takes the approach of defining every identifiable UML element as an RDF resource. A set of RDF statements can thus describe any UML model. But note that these statements are statements about the UML model, and not about the real-world entities that are the subjects of the UML model—we are on a higher level of abstraction.

3.4.2 XMI: Exchange Format for Model Data

The XML Metadata Interchange (XMI) is the industry standard for encoding UML models into XML (XMI 1999). Endorsed by OMG and supported by major industry partners such as IBM and Oracle, the XMI specification can be considered as a part of the UML specification.

Table 3.4 Comparing UML with ERM and RDF.

UML	ERM	RDF
Class definition	Entity set	RDFS class definition
Single and multiple inheritance	Generalization	`rdfs:subClassOf` (single and multiple inheritance)
Attributes (named)	Attributes (named)	Named properties with literal value
Roles (named)	Roles (named)	Named properties with resource value
Associations (named)	Relationships (named)	Implicit via properties with resource value (unnamed)
Directed associations	Not supported in original ERM	Statements always have a direction (subject –> object).
n-ary associations	*n*-ary relationships	Only binary associations. Higher-order associations can be modeled via intermediate resources.
Association qualifiers	Not supported	Not supported
Aggregation	Supported via enclosing entities	Not explicitly supported. Aggregation can be modeled through properties.
Composition	Supported via existence-dependent relationships	Not explicitly supported. Composition can be modeled through properties.
Visibility control (public, protected, private)	No visibility control (everything is public)	Visibility control would not make sense. Properties are attached to resources by the public.
Operations	No means to model behavior	No means to model behavior
Interfaces	No interfaces	No interfaces
Template classes	No template classes	No template classes
Utility classes	No utility classes	No utility classes
Arbitrary cardinality constraints	Cardinality constraints: 1:1, 1:*n*, *m*:1, *m*:*n*	Multiplicity can be modeled with containers (Bag, Seq, URI pattern).
Optionality constraints are part of the cardinality constraint concept.	Optionality constraints mandatory (1,1), (1,*m*), optional (0,1), (0,*m*)	Via containers. These allow only for (0,*n*) constraints but not for (0,1) and (1,*m*) constraints.
Mutual exclusion constraint	Not supported in original ERM	Possible via the `Alt` construct
User-defined constraints	Not supported in ERM	Possible through extension mechanism
MetaModel (stereotypes)	Not supported in ERM	RDF allows making statements about anything, including RDFS definitions.

XMI is based on the OMG's Meta Object Facility (MOF). MOF is the OMG's adopted technology for defining metadata and representing it as CORBA objects. Because UML is also based on MOF, XMI presents itself as an interchange format for UML.

This origin positions XMI for possible application domains. XMI is predominantly used to exchange model data between different development tools, such as UML toolkits, development studios, and so on. The authors of the XMI specification give the following motivation for the design of XMI (XMI 1999):

> The reality is that no single tool exists for both modeling the enterprise and documenting the applications that implement the business solution. A combination of tools from different vendors is necessary but difficult to achieve because the tools often cannot easily interchange the information they use with each other. This leads to translation or manual re-entry of information, both of which are sources of loss and error.

When all of the development tools understand XMI, round-trip engineering across multivendor development platforms becomes a possibility. In addition, XMI makes it easy to exchange model data across distributed development environments. While it was difficult or impossible to exchange model parts between heterogeneous UML tools in the past, XMI opens up that possibility, provided the participating tools know how to import XMI and merge the imported parts into an existing model. Furthermore, XMI allows the development of catalogues of design patterns in a vendor-neutral format.

Finally, XMI can be used as an intermediate step when generating XML Schema definitions out of UML (see Section 3.4.1).

As an example let's look at the XMI serialization for the UML diagram in Figure 3.29. All definitions made in the model—classes, attributes, associations, cardinality—are represented as independent XML elements and identified via the `xmi.id` attribute. These elements relate to each other by utilizing XML's `ID/IDREF` mechanism.

Exchanging model data

Round-trip engineering

```
<?xml version="1.0" encoding="UTF-8"?>
<XMI xmi.version="1.0">
  <XMI.header>
    <XMI.documentation>
      <XMI.exporter>Novosoft UML Library</XMI.exporter>
      <XMI.exporterVersion>0.4.19</XMI.exporterVersion>
    </XMI.documentation>
    <XMI.metamodel xmi.name="UML" xmi.version="1.3"/>
  </XMI.header>
```

```
<XMI.content>
  <Model_Management.Model xmi.id="xmi.1"
                          xmi.uuid="127-0-0-1-ca208:e5f13cb504:-8000">
    <Foundation.Core.ModelElement.name>
      orderModel
    </Foundation.Core.ModelElement.name>
    <Foundation.Core.ModelElement.isSpecification xmi.value="false"/>
    <Foundation.Core.GeneralizableElement.isRoot xmi.value="false"/>
    <Foundation.Core.GeneralizableElement.isLeaf xmi.value="false"/>
    <Foundation.Core.GeneralizableElement.isAbstract xmi.value="false"/>
    <Foundation.Core.Namespace.ownedElement>
      <Foundation.Core.Class xmi.id="xmi.2"
                             xmi.uuid="127-0-0-1-ca208:e5f13cb504:-7fff">
        <Foundation.Core.ModelElement.name>
          Customer
        </Foundation.Core.ModelElement.name>
        <Foundation.Core.ModelElement.isSpecification xmi.value="false"/>
        <Foundation.Core.GeneralizableElement.isRoot xmi.value="false"/>
        <Foundation.Core.GeneralizableElement.isLeaf xmi.value="false"/>
        <Foundation.Core.GeneralizableElement.isAbstract xmi.value="false"/>
        <Foundation.Core.Class.isActive xmi.value="false"/>
        <Foundation.Core.ModelElement.namespace>
          <Foundation.Core.Namespace xmi.idref="xmi.1"/>
        </Foundation.Core.ModelElement.namespace>
        <Foundation.Core.Classifier.feature>
          <Foundation.Core.Attribute xmi.id="xmi.3">
            <Foundation.Core.ModelElement.name>
              CustomerID
            </Foundation.Core.ModelElement.name>
            <Foundation.Core.ModelElement.isSpecification xmi.value="false"/>
```

. . . 2 more pages . . .

```
        <Foundation.Core.GeneralizableElement.isAbstract xmi.value="false"/>
        <Foundation.Core.Class.isActive xmi.value="false"/>
        <Foundation.Core.ModelElement.namespace>
          <Foundation.Core.Namespace xmi.idref="xmi.1"/>
        </Foundation.Core.ModelElement.namespace>
        <Foundation.Core.GeneralizableElement.generalization>
          <Foundation.Core.Generalization xmi.idref="xmi.9"/>
        </Foundation.Core.GeneralizableElement.generalization>
```

```
            <Foundation.Core.Classifier.feature>
              <Foundation.Core.Attribute xmi.id="xmi.20">
                <Foundation.Core.ModelElement.name>
                  Duration
                </Foundation.Core.ModelElement.name>
                <Foundation.Core.ModelElement.isSpecification xmi.value="false"/>
                <Foundation.Core.Feature.owner>
                  <Foundation.Core.Classifier xmi.idref="xmi.19"/>
                </Foundation.Core.Feature.owner>
              </Foundation.Core.Attribute>
            </Foundation.Core.Classifier.feature>
          </Foundation.Core.Class>
          <Foundation.Core.Generalization xmi.id="xmi.9"
                              xmi.uuid="127-0-0-1-ca208:e5f13cb504:-7ff5">
            <Foundation.Core.ModelElement.isSpecification xmi.value="false"/>
            <Foundation.Core.ModelElement.namespace>
              <Foundation.Core.Namespace xmi.idref="xmi.1"/>
            </Foundation.Core.ModelElement.namespace>
            <Foundation.Core.Generalization.child>
              <Foundation.Core.GeneralizableElement xmi.idref="xmi.19"/>
            </Foundation.Core.Generalization.child>
            <Foundation.Core.Generalization.parent>
              <Foundation.Core.GeneralizableElement xmi.idref="xmi.7"/>
            </Foundation.Core.Generalization.parent>
          </Foundation.Core.Generalization>
        </Foundation.Core.Namespace.ownedElement>
      </Model_Management.Model>
    </XMI.content>
</XMI>
```

As we can see, XMI was not designed for human consumption. The intent of XMI is to exchange information between machines. But even for computers an XMI-serialized UML model can be a stress test: UML repositories of 200 MB or more are not uncommon, and the full serialization of such a model would result in XMI documents that easily break into the gigabyte class.

Meaning 4

Soon after the first XML hype ceased, software architects and engineers became aware that it is not sufficient just to know "where to put the brackets" to make systems collaborate. Even more important than syntax is agreeing about an ontology—a system of *meaning.*

In this chapter we introduce formal semantics, context, and ontologies. If you plan to implement collaborative applications, this is required reading.

One way to specify semantic aspects formally is the definition of constraints. In Section 4.1, we take a close look at constraints and how they can be defined in schemata, especially in XML Schema. Constraints are, however, only one aspect of the definition of formal semantics. Ontologies provide additional means for the declaration of formal semantics. In Section 4.2, we discuss the different levels of ontological depth

169

and introduce languages for the definition of ontologies such as DAML and OIL. In Section 4.3, we take an excursion into the Western philosophy of the past 2,000 years. We learn that context is important when interpreting the meaning of a message, especially in a globalized environment. This leads into Section 4.4, where we take a closer look at the formal treatment of context. In Section 4.4.2, we discuss a practical approach for implementing context-aware semantics with XML: the Schema Adjunct Framework.

4.1 FORMAL SEMANTICS

The Internet is about *sharing* information. This involves publishing the information, navigating to the relevant information, and interpreting that information. HTML is hardly able to fulfill these requirements, and XML was designed to fill this gap.

Semantic markup?

The markup of XML has been called by some a "semantic markup." This is in contrast to HTML, where most of the markup elements are purely representational. In XML, as common belief has it, the markup denotes the meaning of an element.

However, when we take a formal approach, we discover that the opposite is true. What conveys meaning to a human reader does not necessarily do the same to a machine. In XML, it is the tag name that allows human readers to associate a meaning with an element, provided the tag name matches an entry in the internal dictionary of the reader's brain. If the tag name is outside the scope of the reader's expertise, the tag is meaningless. Two readers with different backgrounds may even interpret the same tag as having two different meanings.

Consider the tag <motion>. A reader with a political background may interpret the tag as a motion in a deliberative assembly. In contrast, a reader with a medical background may interpret it as being related to sickness.

An XML parser does none of the above. It just reports that this is a tag and that the tag name is "motion." That's all. Parsers are about syntax, not about semantics.

With the purely representational HTML, it is just the opposite. The semantics of the tag <B> are clearly defined in the HTML specification and put into action by any Web browser. Elements enclosed between <B> and </B> are printed in bold. Tags in HTML have clearly defined semantics—of course, only in the context of document representation and navigation.

The XML specification does not define semantics for tags. Tags in XML   Semantic free
are user defined, so it is the responsibility of the user to associate a meaning with each tag. Most XML-based languages do so, but they do it in a
rather informal way. For example, SVG and SMIL, both XML-based representation languages, define the meaning of each tag. The semantics of
the tags are described in the SVG and SMIL specifications and are implemented in the SVG and SMIL browser plug-ins.

Unfortunately, there is no standard way to define semantics formally
for an XML-based language. DTDs allow only the description of the vocabulary and the structure of a document. Also XML Schema does not go
much further in this respect. This is hardly sufficient to establish communication in the global village (Doerr 1998):

> To summarise, we are on the brink of a technological revolution, which will
> render obsolete the need for homogeneous data formats for communication.
> Rather, we must engage in providing formal definitions of the underlying
> semantics in our data. Not the superficial identity of structure, but the seman-
> tic compatibility is needed. This will enable far richer services to be created
> than standardisation could ever provide.

Let's begin at the end. What is required for the correct interpretation of   Understanding
information is that both sender and receiver (or publisher and surfer) not   shared
only speak the same language, but also share the same *conceptualization* of   information
the information. This includes a shared vocabulary, a shared set of constraints, and a shared conceptual framework such as type hierarchies and
other relationships between classes of information items:

- The *shared vocabulary* guarantees that syntactical tokens (words) carry
  the same meaning for both sender and receiver. Such vocabularies
  are developed from the vocabulary used in a given community or
  industry.
- A *shared conceptual framework*—if it is complete—guarantees that the
  understanding of the information is not influenced by unspecified
  background knowledge.

Let's now see what is required to specify semantics in a formal and
machine-readable way.

4.1.1 Formal Semantics and Constraints

To understand how to formally define meaning we look at a few examples. Here is one from school:

What is our understanding of a square? A square is a rectangle where width equals height. Similarly we can define a rectangle as a four-sided polygon where all sides intersect at angles of 90 degrees.

From this simple definition we can already deduce two concepts:

- *Relation.* To define "square," we relate it to "rectangle." To define "rectangle," we relate it to "polygon."
- *Constraint.* To distinguish between "rectangle" and "polygon," we define constraints (four sides, 90-degree angles). To distinguish between "square" and "rectangle," we define additional constraints (width equals height). As a matter of fact, relations can also be seen as constraints. The fact that a square is a rectangle does certainly constrain the shape of a square.

Let's apply these simple concepts to a more complex object:

What is our understanding of a car? A car is a vehicle. It has an engine and more than two wheels. A car is driven by a driver.

Here we see different relations at work: `is_a`, `has`, `driven_by`. There is also a constraint: "more than two." Again, the relations "is a vehicle," "has an engine," and "driven by a driver" can also be seen as constraints.

Background knowledge

In addition, we can list some background knowledge that helps us to understand the meaning of the notion "car" without defining it in the strict sense:

Cars are used for transportation. Cars take part in road traffic. Cars have accidents. Cars are produced by car manufacturers and are sold by car dealers. Cars add to the greenhouse effect. And so on.

The concept of a car is thus interrelated with other concepts and gains additional meaning by that. The most important sentence here is probably the first one: concepts are best described by their practical purpose or effect. Remember that the meaning of a command in a computer language is determined by the effect the command has when the application is executed.

How humans learn

However, humans are not computers. They learn the meaning of a term in a different manner, usually in a complex process of abstraction and differentiation. When you think of "car," the first thing that probably comes to mind is the mental image of a sedan. The sedan object acts as a prototype (Gardner 1985) for the category "car" and is probably what a child first associates with "car." Only later we learn that the concept "car" also contains other car types such as race cars, railroad cars, pickups, vans, cabriolets, and so on. We learn to differentiate between these by learning the differences from the prototype.

4.1.2 Constraints in Schema Definitions

In a generic language such as XML it is possible to standardize semantics only in the most fundamental way. DTDs, for example, support only the absolute minimum. They allow datatype definitions such as NAME, ID, and IDREF only for element attributes. (A datatype definition is a constraint and thus defines semantic properties.) These datatype definitions are required for generic XML processors to function properly. Some DOM implementations can, for example, locate an element by its ID. Therefore the processor must know which element attributes must be treated as IDs. It relies on the semantics of the ID datatype.

XML Schema goes a step further and allows datatype definitions for XML elements, too. The standard already defines a rich ensemble of datatypes but also allows users to define their own datatypes. User-defined datatypes are derived from existing datatypes by adding constraining facets to them.

Datatypes

The datatypes in XML Schema allow users to specify a given document element as string, date, numeric, and so on. This allows generic XML processors to check a given document more thoroughly. It also improves XML-OO mapping: when an OO class hierarchy is generated from an XML Schema definition, the generator can automatically produce the correct datatypes for the fields representing the elements. This is not possible from a DTD.

However, this is where XML Schema stops. It only allows putting constraints in the form of datatypes onto individual elements; it does not allow the definition of constraints across multiple elements (if we forget the unique/key/keyref constraints for a moment). Let's look at an example:

Cross-field constraints

```
<size>
  <width>210</width>
  <height>297</height>
</size>
```

Here we can use datatype definitions to make sure that both width and height are numbers. We can even define minimum and maximum values for both. However, in XML Schema there is no way to define that <height> must always be <width> multiplied by 1.414, as is the case with the DIN A paper formats.

4.2 ONTOLOGIES

Semantic modeling has a tradition in knowledge engineering and in agent technology but is also applied to many other fields in information technology, such as database design, object-oriented analysis, information retrieval, and so on. In these areas, the term "ontology" is used to denote a knowledge domain or the semantic domain for an agent (Uschold and Gruninger 1996):

> Ontologies are agreements about shared conceptualizations. Shared conceptualizations include conceptual frameworks for modelling domain knowledge; content-specific protocols for communication among inter-operating agents; and agreements about the representation of particular domain theories. In the knowledge sharing context, ontologies are specified in the form of definitions of representational vocabulary. A very simple case would be a type hierarchy, specifying classes and their subsumption relationships. Relational database schemata also serve as ontologies by specifying the relations that can exist in some shared database and the integrity constraints that must hold for them. (Tom Gruber, 1994, SRKB Mailing list)

Definition   The term "ontology" has its origin in philosophy, in which it refers to the discipline that deals with the subject of existence. Ontology is the theory of "what there is" (Quine). In our context, however, the meaning of the term is slightly different: it is a formal description of the concepts and relationships that exist within a domain (and as such is not a discipline but an artifact). This means that an ontology relates to a specific vocabulary and a specific language (other than the philosophical discipline, which deals with existence but not language). Note that an ontology is an *agreement*. This agreement need not necessarily cover the whole conceptualization of a given domain but can cover just a part of it; that is, it can provide a view onto the domain. An ontology thus acts as a contract between partners, enabling them to communicate safely within the context of the information domain. For example, a software agent that commits to an ontology will be able to semantically interpret the information items covered by that ontology and to communicate with other agents committing to that ontology. Thus, an ontology establishes a community of Internet users.

4.2.1 Ontological Depth

Vocabulary   In the simplest form an ontology is just a vocabulary. In this sense, a DTD can define an ontology. If different partners agree on a DTD, they also agree on the ontology defined through the DTD because the tag names declared in the DTD define a common vocabulary. When, for example, two agents agree to share such an ontology, they can exchange messages using the vocabulary of the ontology.

However, the definition of an ontology does not stop here. As we ex- [Taxonomy] plained earlier, the meaning of terms is established by defining relationships between them. One of the most natural relationships is classification—establishing relationships between objects and classes, subclasses, and parent classes. A system of such relationships is called a *taxonomy,* and the relationships are usually called *is-a* relationships. This sort of ontology is typically established by object-oriented systems. Many existing ontologies are defined using only those hierarchical relationships.

However, ontologies can also include nonhierarchical relationships. As [Relational system] we have seen in the previous example and in previous chapters, there are many possible relationships between objects besides the hierarchical *is-a* relationships. For example, the relationship *is-driven-by* between car and driver is not a hierarchical relationship but is important enough to be described in an ontology. Such relationships are typical in entity relationship diagrams and in relational databases, and consequently each relational database schema defines its own ontology.

Besides describing relationships, ontologies can also impose con- [Axiomatic theory] straints. Constraints are defined as *axioms.* An axiom is a logical statement that cannot be proved from other statements but from which other statements can be derived. In mathematics, whole theories (like group theory or set theory) are derived from relatively small sets of axioms. In our car ontology, the statement "A car has at least three wheels" is such a constraint. In relational databases constraints are defined via *integrity rules.* Some object-oriented languages also include the ability to define constraints (e.g., *assertions* in C++ and *contracts* in Eiffel).

Thalheim (2000) classifies constraints into a hierarchy. Under *static* [Constraints revisited] constraints, he includes the following:

- *Structural:* These include conditions about the structure of the model, about relationships between entities, and so on.
- *Semantic:* These include semantic restrictions, such as multivalued (cross-field) dependencies.
- *Representational:* These are used to constrain the actual representation of the model in a system to a certain physical structure.
- *Design:* These are used to make the schema design more user friendly.

Under *dynamic* constraints, he includes the following:

- *Transition:* These restrict the application of operations depending on the current state of an object.
- *Temporal:* These constrain the possible state sequences.

Constraints may depend on the context or the application. A dynamic constraint that inhibits, for example, changing the value of the attribute `family_status` from "widowed" to "never married" makes sense in the context of a business process but must not be applied when we want to correct a wrong data entry.

While static constraints are closely related to schema definitions and databases (relational databases, for example, can protect the structural and referential integrity of data with the help of integrity rules and triggers), dynamic constraints are closely related to process models. A business process defines the possible state changes of a set of business objects, which business events cause these state changes, and which operations are triggered by these state changes.

It is not always possible to enforce constraints, especially in electronic business scenarios that involve communication across company borders. It is often only possible to postulate a desired behavior of a system.

Deontic logic

Soft constraints are used here to model the "should" instead of the "must" (Thalheim 2000). Using soft constraints requires a different logical calculus: deontic logic is used to formulate soft constraints and to reason about them. Deontic logic allows reasoning about the ideal, normative, and actual behavior of the system. Deontic logic adds three new operators to the classic predicate logic:

- Prohibitions (F) specify that certain actions or states are forbidden.
- Obligations (O) specify normative behavior—which actions and states are desirable.
- Permissions (P) specify states or actions that are permitted.

However, formulating soft constraints properly is not trivial. Deontic logic tends to produce paradoxical results, and in reality there often exist obligations that contradict each other. Such conflicts must be handled somehow, for example, by prioritizing the application of constraints.

Often, the use of soft constraints can be avoided by using context-sensitive hard constraints. (Remember that contexts can change over time.)

Our previous example is such a case. We could (sloppily) formulate that the family status "never married" should never follow "widowed." An application that would try to do so would get a warning. The better choice, however, is to make this constraint a context-sensitive "must" rule, that is, not to apply it during maintenance tasks but to enforce it in all other tasks.

Ontology levels

But back to ontologies. Guarino and Welty (1998) define several levels of ontological depth:

1. *Lexicon*: vocabulary with natural language definitions
2. *Simple Taxonomy*
3. *Thesaurus*: taxonomy plus related terms
4. *Relational model*: unconstrained use of arbitrary relations
5. *Fully axiomatized theory*

Ontologies that only implement level 1 (a vocabulary) are, however, of limited use. They may help simplify and standardize data exchange between partners but do not allow machines to reason about the meaning of an information item.

This only becomes possible at deeper levels. When we, for example, want to build a house, the machine could automatically look up a relational model to find out that we need artisans like bricklayers, carpenters, and electricians to build the house. This is possible because in this ontology these terms are related to the term "house" via a semantic web.

At this stage it is important to note that all relations within an ontology are "intentional"—they refer to conceptional items (symbols) and not to "the real thing." In our example, relations are established between the conceptional terms "house," "bricklayers," "carpenters," and "electricians," but not to real houses, real bricklayers, and so on. In Section 7.2 we will discuss how such a conceptional network of relations is finally mapped onto real resources.

The last stage in ontology definition, the fully axiomatized theory, is usually too hard to obtain in practical applications. Most applications use a limited set of constraints that are obtained from heuristic analysis but that are far from a complete and consistent set of axioms able to found a mathematical theory. Nevertheless, the use of constraints is important and adds significantly to data integrity and consistency.

Clearly, with each level more work is required to define an ontology. This is true not only for the initial definition but also for maintenance. Adding a new word to a lexicon is a fairly simple task, but on deeper levels we also have to add new relations, update existing relations, and check constraints for consistency.

When we said that a relational database schema defines an ontology, we were at the root of the problem. There are as many ontologies as there are database schemata in the world—and consequently ontologies are a hot topic. In a time of company mergers, enterprise application integration, Internet portals, and supply chain integration, ontologies clash fairly often and must be reconciled. In the past, the traditional tactic used with EDI was to negotiate bilateral agreements. However, this is hardly

A myriad of ontologies

sufficient to meet the demands of a networked and globalized business community.

Several researchers (Uschold et al. 1997; Smith and Zaibert 1997) and institutions have therefore started to define ontologies that can be used as a common platform within an industry or a sector of an industry. The introduction of XML, in particular, has led to widespread activity in the definition of shared ontologies, which has resulted in a rich collection of industry-specific XML DTDs. These definitions can only be the beginning, since simple shared vocabularies as provided by DTDs are not really satisfactory, as we stated earlier.

Building communities

The intention of these activities is not to convert existing systems, but to define a "pivot" (or top-level) ontology that can provide a common language with which incompatible systems can communicate. Such a pivot ontology can be shared by a large community of users. Instead of negotiating a communication protocol between any two partners on a bilateral basis, it is only necessary to define the translation between the proprietary system and the shared pivot ontology. By now there are a large number of such top-level ontologies. The HL-7 standard, for example, establishes a top-level ontology for the health industry. In electronic business communication the situation is a bit more fractionated, since several organizations have defined competing standards. With ebXML, UN/CEFACT has started a standardization process that should result in a top-level ontology for electronic business communication. We will discuss ebXML in Section 10.3.

Ontology types

Guarino (1998) identifies four types of ontologies:

- *Top-level ontologies:* These are shared by a large community and define only very general terms.
- *Domain-related ontologies (vertical):* These apply to a certain knowledge domain, for example, an industry sector such as the pharmaceutical industry or the computer industry.
- *Task-related ontologies (horizontal):* These apply to a certain task, for example, procurement or software requirements analysis.
- *Application-related ontologies:* These describe the concepts of an application, referring to specialization of both a domain and a task ontology. Within an application-related ontology, the items defined in a domain-related ontology appear mostly in a specific role.

When and where

Ontologies are used during different stages of the application life cycle. Software applications can be constructed as ontology-aware or ontology-driven applications—the ontology is actively used by the application at runtime. This is, for example, the case with software agents. Software agents are usually constructed as specialist applications that operate only within a narrowly defined domain. Larger-scale applications involve a variety of specialist agents that are required to communicate with each other. In order to understand the meaning of the messages exchanged, agents must be able to access and interpret the underlying ontology.

Another example is query processing. Internet portals that combine a multitude of different businesses and services under one roof, for example, must be able to relate customer queries to the underlying ontologies (mostly database schemata) of the participating partners. To interpret a query correctly, they need access to the proper ontology.

During software development the use of ontologies can save time and money. By using an ontology we can make sure that the participating software analysts, designers, and programmers talk the same language. By separating the definition of ontologies proper into top-level ontology, domain- and task-related ontologies, and application-related ontologies, we can make sure that we can reuse previous definitions. Especially for top-level ontologies, but also for domain-related ontologies, we can often reuse existing designs (such as DTDs, ebXML scenarios, or electronic business languages) that have already been defined by industry associations, standardization bodies, or manufacturers of electronic business systems. It is also a good idea to build up libraries of domain- and task-related ontologies.

There are three main areas in software systems where ontologies are used. First, most business applications are database based, and each database schema incarnates an ontology. As we mentioned earlier, navigational software systems such as Internet applications require partners to publish "maps" for their systems. This includes the publication of all or parts of the underlying conceptual models of the database schemata involved. That is, the ontology defined by the conceptual database model must be described in an appropriate way. (Publishing a database schema itself is of limited use because relational normalization and optimization can obscure the concept behind the design.)

Second, especially with relational database technology, a lot of conceptual knowledge is actually not contained in the database schemata but is contained in the application in the form of SQL commands and program logic. Applications contain knowledge not only about the data, but also about business processes. Although legacy applications contain this knowledge in hard-coded form within the program logic, the current trend is toward the explicit representation of that knowledge in the form of soft-coded business rules. Again, the explicit use of ontologies can help to document this knowledge in a consistent form, allowing this knowledge to be reused in other projects or to be utilized by software agents.

Finally, ontologies can be used with user interfaces. One possible application is the authoring of help pages. With a clearly defined and published ontology, an end user can get information about the meaning of terms and how they are related to each other.

The constraints defined in an ontology can be used to validate user input. An example of this would be XForms, which not only can validate user input according to the datatype definitions in the corresponding XML Schema but also can apply other constraints. The relations between conceptual entities defined in an ontology can be used to generate automatic document layouts. Current commercial systems (such as K-infinity from intelligent views, *www.i-views.de*) are able, for example, to produce documents where semantically interrelated topics are placed close together, if possible on the same Web page.

4.2.2 Operational Ontologies: DAML and OIL

OIL (Ontology Interchange Language) includes a whole family of languages such as Standard OIL, Instance OIL, and Heavy OIL. It has also been used as the basis for defining the ontology markup language DAML-Ont ("DAML" stands for DARPA Agent Markup Language). DAML-OIL (a version of the DAML language) is very close to Standard OIL. We will restrict ourselves to a discussion of Standard OIL (Bechhofer et al. 2000). Current implementations of OIL rely on proprietary representations or on RDF. For better readability we use here an informal notation that, if required, can easily be translated into XML or RDF.

Basic constructs   The basic constructs of OIL are classes, slots, and individuals. Individuals are instances of classes. Classes constitute a class hierarchy—a class can be a subclass of other classes:

```
class-def holding
          subclass-of enterprise

class-def enterprise
          subclass-of organization
```

Classes can have multiple parents:

```
class-def owning-director
          subclass-of director owner
```

Axioms allow the assertion of additional facts about the classes within an ontology:

- disjoint: Specifies a list of classes. No individual is allowed to be a member of more than one of the classes listed:

  disjoint enterprise government-institution

  This states that no individual can be both an enterprise and a government institution.
- covered: Specifies a class that must be covered by a list of other classes. Each individual belonging to that class must belong to at least one of the classes from the list:

  covered employee **by** director manager worker

- disjoint-covered: Same as covered, except that the classes specified in the list are also disjoint.
- equivalent: Defines a list of synonym class names.

Classes can own slots. Slots represent properties (i.e, on the instance level, slots contain values) and can be used to define relations between instances. Slots can be defined as subslots of other slots:

slot-def has-director
        subslot-of has-manager

Slots can also be defined as an inverse of an already existing slot:

slot-def manages
        inverse has-manager

So far, OIL closely resembles the entity relationship model. It exceeds the capabilities of ERM when it comes to the definition of constraints:

- Slot values can be constrained to be of a particular type:

  slot-constraint has-director
             value-type director

- Valid value types can also be declared as an enumeration of individual value types:

  slot-constraint has-partner
     value-type (**one-of** customer supplier shareholder)

- Slot values can be constrained to be of a particular cardinality:

```
slot-constraint has-director
                max-cardinality 3 director
                min-cardinality 1 director
```

- Slot values can be constrained to be of a particular value (also called *filler*). A filler value refers to one or more individuals.

```
class-def plc
          subclass-of enterprise
          slot-constraint has-company-form
                    has-filler proprietary_limited
```

- Slot value constraints can also use order relations such as min, less-than, greater-than, equal, and range to refer to individuals:

```
class-def large-company
          subclass-of enterprise
          slot-constraint employee-number
                    has-filler min 500
```

- Slot value constraints can be written as expressions using the Boolean operators and, or, and not:

```
slot-constraint external-owner
                (owner and (not owning-director))
```

Further, slots can be defined with additional properties that improve the ability to make logical deductions from slot properties. Valid properties are:

- *Transitive:* If both (x,y) and (y,z) are instances of the slot, then (x,z) must also be an instance of the slot:

```
slot-def bigger-than
         properties transitive
```

For example, if company A is bigger-than company B and company B is bigger-than company C, then company A is bigger-than company C.

- *Symmetric:* If (x,y) is an instance of the slot, then (y,x) must also be an instance of the slot:

```
slot-def business-partner
         properties symmetric
```

For example, if company A is a business-partner to company B, then company B is also a business-partner to company A.

- *Functional:* If (x,y) is an instance of the slot, then there is no z unequal to y such that (x,z) is an instance of the slot. Note that the properties *functional* and *transitive* are mutually exclusive.

```
slot-def has-sole-owner
         properties functional
```

For example, if company A is the sole owner of company B, then company B cannot be owned by another company (including the owner of company A).

In addition to the OIL definitions, OIL files contain a container element with metadata describing the file. The container element follows the Dublin Core Metadata Element Set (DCMI 2000) and contains elements such as title, creator, subject, description, publisher, type, format, identifier, source, language, and so on.

The current version of OIL suffers from a few limitations: Limitations

- *No support for constraints across slots:* Each slot constraint affects only a single slot. Multivalued constraints such as width*height*depth < 100 cannot be specified.
- *No default reasoning (only monotonic logic):* In OIL, subclasses can inherit values from superclasses but cannot overwrite inherited slot values. If we have, for example, a class bird with the slot main-method-of-movement and a filler value of "flying," we would have trouble when declaring the class emu as a subclass of bird. This could lead to major restructuring activities when an existing ontology is extended.
- *No support for second-order logic:* A reification mechanism (such as in RDF) does not exist in OIL.

4.2.3 Best Practices

We recommend the following practices:

- If a vocabulary is already used by the users in the targeted domain, use this vocabulary.
- If different vocabularies are commonly used in the targeted domain, use these vocabularies and provide a mapping between them. For example, in an ornithology ontology you would provide a vocabulary of bird names in common English and one in scientific Latin names.

Users should be able to extend these mappings (i.e., specify more synonyms).

- Provide a semantic definition for each term. This should be accessible by users who require an explanation of a term.
- Use a classification that is familiar to the user.
- Use namespaces to allow the later merging of ontologies.

4.3 PHILOSOPHICAL EXCURSUS

Aristotle

In the Western world, the Greek philosopher Aristotle (384–322 B.C.) has been the reference point for ontology questions for more than 2,000 years. For Aristotle, the formal model of logic consists of a single subject (the Me) making statements about the world of objects (the Not-Me). Within such a dualistic construction, statements are either true or false. In fact, *"tertium non datur"* (i.e., the rejection of logical values other than "True" and "False") is a fundamental axiom of Aristotelian logic.

Thomas Aquinas

The philosophical system of Aristotle was adopted for the Catholic Church by Thomas Aquinas (1225–1274) and thus has deeply influenced thinking in the Western world. During the whole medieval age the teachings of the Catholic Church served as the only possible view for interpreting the world. The majority of people lived in an ideologically consistent and coherent environment. Communities that favored a (slightly) different view of the world were prosecuted as heretics.

Copernicus and Galileo

During the 16th century, this "one and only ontology" world would be severely shattered by the developing natural sciences. Nicolaus Copernicus (1473–1543) and Galileo Galilei (1564–1642) challenged the geocentric view of the universe and replaced it with a heliocentric view of our solar system. The reaction of the Catholic Church is well recorded. Earlier, the German reformer Martin Luther (1483–1546) had challenged the ideological basis of the Catholic Church, and for the first time in medieval Europe people had a choice between two belief systems. The dominant and monolithic ideology of medieval Europe had received its first crack. There were more to follow.

Hegel

Philosophers, however, needed a bit longer to get used to the idea that there was more than one possible worldview. The possibility of multiple ontologies was first mentioned by the German philosopher Georg Wilhelm Friedrich Hegel (1770–1831).

Günther

In the 20th century it was the philosopher Gotthard Günther who combined a system of multiple ontologies (polycontexturality) with a multileveled logic calculus (Günther 1979). Günther replaced the Aristotelian one-observer view of the world with a society of multiple observers. Each of these observers may live in a different contexture (i.e., social, cultural, ethical systems) and may arrive at different models of the same world. If these observers do not communicate with each other, each of them has its own Aristotelian view of the world. The *"tertium non datur"* still holds for each of them. However, if the observers communicate and gather intelligence about each other's worldviews, they will have to drop the *"tertium non datur"* axiom. Besides their own world model, they have to recognize the world models of others. Günther formalized this model by using different levels of logical values. The immediate worldviews of an observer can be expressed in the first level of logical values, such as $True_1$ and $False_1$. A world model acquired from another observer is expressed with second-level logical values, such as $True_2$ and $False_2$. A world model acquired from another observer via a third observer is expressed with third-level values, and so on.

It is obvious that, although within the primary worldview the old Aristotelian values of "True" and "False" are still intact, they now do not have the same rigidity as before because we acknowledge the possibility that alternate worldviews might be correct as well. *Consequences*

Also obvious is that by default the communication between observers can only be of an informal nature. Consistent logical systems are only defined within a given context and, in general, cannot be used for knowledge transfer between different ontologies. The consequence for daily life is that some means of informal communication, such as natural language or heuristic mediation systems, is inevitable.

4.4 CONTEXT

The development of common, shared ontologies can formalize the previously mentioned communication process, but the development of a shared ontology (such as the negotiation of a shared XML vocabulary) must rely on informal means.

At present this task is left to humans and requires not only technical *Human skills* but also social and political skills. Although it is possible to "lift" knowledge from a limited context into a more general context and to "transcend" knowledge (McCarthy 1998) from one context into another, the rules for "lifting" and "translating" must be defined by humans. Humans can traverse multiple contexts with relative ease because they do not rely on formalized logic models. (On the other hand, they are also prone to misinterpretation and errors.) When two individuals or groups establish communication, they can rely on several things:

- Humans are usually familiar with several contexts. For example, a lawyer is not only a lawyer, but also a car driver, a husband or wife, a citizen, a cat lover, and so on. Communication with a partner becomes possible when both partners share at least one context.
- Humans share one common context: the experience of the real world. This includes the experience of one's own body. Bodily functions (e.g., eating, sleeping) are universal.
- Even foreign contexts are often very similar in structure. If you learn, for example, a foreign language or a computer language, learning a second foreign language or a second computer language will be much easier because some concepts and patterns are very similar.
- Humans can use metaphors; that is, they can transcend experience from one context to another context. In concurrent computing, for example, we say that a thread goes to sleep, thus using a term that originally describes one of our bodily functions. Or, even if I am not a mechanic, I can have a clear idea about what a T-bar is because I can associate the shape of the bar with the shape of the letter *T*.

As John McCarthy (1998) observed, the human ability to transcend between contexts is a precondition for making scientific discoveries and also for understanding somebody else's scientific discoveries.

4.4.1 Ontologies and Contexts

What now is the relationship between ontology and context? An ontology defines the vocabulary, the axioms, and the constraints of a certain problem domain. The context, in contrast, defines the set of assumptions that must hold to make the vocabulary, the axioms, and the constraints valid. The context determines which terms belong to the vocabulary and which axioms and which constraints are formulated. Depending on the context, this can even lead to contradictory statements: "Vampires do not exist" and "Vampires always hop" cannot both be true in the same ontology. Vampires that do not exist can obviously not hop. However, the first statement is valid in the context of the European Enlightenment, and the second statement is true in the context of Chinese horror movies.

Or consider a rule that might be used to control a robot: "Item A is above item B if item A is on top of item B." This sentence is obviously only true in the context of gravity. Under zero gravity the expression "on top of" makes no sense at all and should not be in our vocabulary.

Even structural relationships can depend on context. As we already mentioned in Section 3.2.5, the entity `StreetAddress` can be modeled as a property of the business object `customer` within the context of procurement but would be modeled as a business object in its own right within the context of direct mail or utilities.

Some contexts are fairly simple and include only a few assumptions. ebXML, for example, lists possible context drivers that determine the specific contextual assumptions for ebXML artifacts (see Section 10.3). But in general contexts are rich—they contain so many assumptions that they cannot be completely listed (Guha 1995):

> Contexts are objects in the domain, i.e., we can make statements about contexts. They are rich objects in that a context cannot be completely described. The contextual effects on an expression are often so rich that they cannot be captured completely in the logic. This is what leads us to incorporate contexts as objects in our ontology.

R. V. Guha and John McCarthy collaborated in the formulation of an   Lessons from Cyc
algebra of contexts. Practical application of this theory was the introduction of contexts into the Cyc knowledge base, a "common sense" knowledge base filled over 12 years with facts about this world and now containing over 1 million rules (Lenat 2001):

> The third, and perhaps most important lesson we learned along the way was that it was foolhardy to try to maintain consistency in one huge flat CYC knowledge base. We eventually carved it up into hundreds of contexts or microtheories. Each one of those is consistent with itself, but there can be contradictions among them. Thus, in the context of working in an office it's socially unacceptable to jump up screaming whenever good things happen, while in the context of a football game it's socially unacceptable not to.

Guha and McCarthy developed an algebra for operations between contexts. This algebra is based on the operator *ist(c,p)*, which stands for *p is true in context c*. Note that this statement is valid in some outer context *c'* (we cannot make statements without being in a context). Therefore the complete expression would be written as *c' : ist(c,p)*, but usually the abbreviated version *ist(c,p)* is used.

The goal of this algebra is to enable AI systems to navigate between different contexts. To solve a particular problem we can move from an outer context into a particular context (enter context *p*), solve the problem there, and move back to the outer context (exit context *p*). Statements valid in a particular context can be lifted into a more general context. For example, the statement "Item A is above item B if item A is on top of item B" is true in a context where gravity is greater than zero. This statement can be lifted into a gravity-independent context by adding a clause: "Item A is above item B if item A is on top of item B and gravity is greater than zero." The operations of entering a context, exiting a context, and lifting statements can be fully formalized. This allows the modularization of large knowledge bases (as in the case of Cyc).

Exceptions

In many cases specialized contexts can establish an exception from the more general context. Here is an example:

- A regatta is a race between boats.
- Boats travel on water.

From these two statements it should follow that a regatta takes place on water. But not so in Alice Springs, Central Australia. The annual Todd River Regatta does not take place on water for the simple reason that the river is dry. (The boats have holes in the bottom for the crew to put their feet through.) In this special context, regattas do not take place on water.

This example also explains the difference between monotonic and nonmonotonic reasoning. In monotonic reasoning, when a statement P follows from a set of statements A and additional statements are added to A, then P remains true. This is not the case with nonmonotonic reasoning. Adding new statements to A can cause P to become false. This is exactly what happens when we move from a wider context (all regattas) to a narrower context (the Todd River Regatta). Because the context now contains an additional assumption (dry riverbed), our theory about regattas comes to a different conclusion. (Prospective regatta participants should be aware that in years when the Todd River carries water the regatta is canceled.)

Nonmonotonic reasoning

The question, of course, is, Couldn't we design a correct model from the start so that we do not need nonmonotonic reasoning? The answer is that this is not always possible. When we formulate our model, we might not know all possible exceptions that could violate our knowledge base. Especially in an open environment such as the World Wide Web, it is almost certain that at some stage we will discover exceptions to the rule. Nonmonotonic reasoning allows us to add these new cases as explicit exceptions to the knowledge base, instead of completely remodeling the whole knowledge base.

But back to contexts. Although we have a formal model for the relationship between outer, more general contexts and inner, more specialized contexts, we have no model for the relationships between arbitrary contexts. We cannot formalize a general theory to *transcend* context (McCarthy 1998):

> Human intelligence involves an ability that no-one has yet undertaken to put into computer programs—namely the ability to *transcend* the context of one's beliefs.

Consequently, AI systems that must translate between different contexts have to be told how. A human knowledge engineer has to define the rules for the mediation between different contexts.

4.4.2 Binding to Contexts: Schema Adjunct

And now back to XML. Earlier we mentioned that each database schema forms an ontology. If this is so, what is the context of such an ontology? Clearly, the context of a database schema is represented by the applications (and possible future applications) that access this database schema. The definition and layout of the database schema are founded on certain assumptions about how this schema will be used. These assumptions were analyzed during the design phase of the database applications. The final applications incarnate those assumptions. The binding between applications and database schemata is usually hardwired.

A similar logic applies to XML. Although XML documents contain some of their metadata in the form of tags and attributes, they do not contain information about implicit assumptions that should be known when the document is processed. Consequently the context for XML schemata is set by the applications and services that process the XML instances.

Context in XML

A specific feature of XML is the hierarchical structure of document elements. This can be translated into a hierarchy of contexts, starting with the widest context on the root level and continuing with narrower contexts on the child level, and so on.

We can therefore describe a binding between document and context for each document element separately. For example, if we want to bind the document to an object-oriented application, the most natural way is to replicate the document structure by an isomorphic class structure. In other cases—especially if we want to bind an XML document to already existing applications or services—the binding may not be so straightforward. Traditionally, those bindings take the form of hardwired program code that in some way interprets the output of SAX or DOM parsers and takes appropriate action.

Binding to a context

SAF

A more flexible approach is possible by means of the Schema Adjunct Framework (SAF). SAF describes the binding between XML document nodes and application functions in a declarative way (Buck 2000):

> To process XML instances for a given schema, many environments need additional information which is typically not available in the schema itself. Such information includes mappings to relational databases, indexing parameters for native XML databases, business rules for additional validation, internationalization and localization parameters, or parameters used for presentation and input forms. Some of this information is used for domain-specific validation, some to provide information for domain-specific processing.

The Schema Adjunct Framework has a two-layer architecture:

- *The adjunct:* The adjunct introduces additional information not contained in the document schema. The adjunct specifies additional semantic information such as constraints and operations in an abstract way. The adjunct itself is formulated in XML syntax, too. The concept used to attach additional information to document elements is similar to the concept used in Schematron (see Section 2.9).
- *The adjunct processor:* The processor is implemented in a suitable implementation language (XSLT, Java, C++, and so on). It interprets the document instance, schema, and adjunct. Based on the abstract operations defined in the adjunct, the adjunct processor mediates between the document and a target application.

Let's look at an example (see Figure 4.1). We have defined an XML document type representing customer records. We want to map these instance documents to database tables in a relational database, and we want to generate HTML forms for updating customer entries from the XML documents. We define one adjunct that associates SQL tables and columns with the elements of our customer document. A generic adjunct processor for SQL reads the adjunct information and mediates between the XML datastreams and the SQL database. Because this processor is generic, we can use it for other document types, too.

To translate the XML documents into HTML forms, we define another adjunct that associates the document elements with abstract form elements. Here we use two different adjunct processors. One translates document instances—based on the adjunct information—into HTML. The second processor accepts the input data from the HTML form and translates it back—again based on the adjunct information—into an XML document. Although the first processor could be written as an XSLT style sheet, the second processor would probably be implemented in the form of a Java servlet. Here is the code:

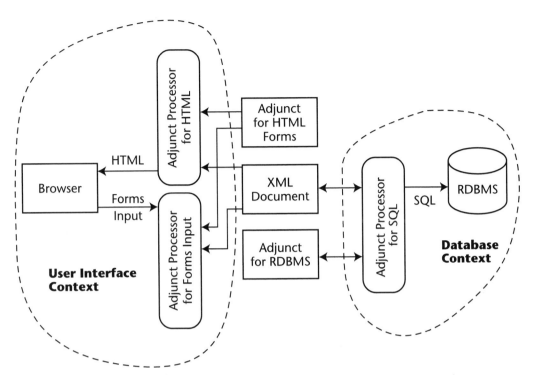

Figure 4.1 Using the Schema Adjunct Framework to build a simple XML-based application.

```
<schema-adjunct
    target = "http://www.softcorp.com/product.xsd"
    xmlns:xfg = "http://www.softcorp.com/xml-form-gen.xsd"
...>

  <element which = 'Product'>
    <xfg:form/>
  </element>

  <element which = 'Product/Name'>
    <xfg:label>Product name</xfg:label>
    <xfg:type>text</xfg:type>
    <xfg:tag>prdnm</xfg:tag>
  </element>

  <element which = 'Product/Price[Currency="USD"]/Amount'>
    <xfg:label>Price(USD)</xfg:label>
    <xfg:type>decimal</xfg:type>
```

```
    <xfg:tag>prdprc</xfg:tag>
  </element>
```

```
</schema-adjunct>
```

The adjunct refers to an XML Schema definition (`target`). Each `element` clause selects an element for processing (`which`). The child elements contained in each `element` clause define abstract operations that are to be interpreted by the adjunct processor.

By separating the semantics into an abstract layer and an implementation layer, the Schema Adjunct Framework is well suited to implementing the constraints and operations defined in a conceptual model in a flexible and portable way. The fact that adjunct definitions are XML documents themselves is an additional advantage: adjunct definitions can be created, maintained, and parsed with the usual XML tools and, if necessary, can be structurally transformed with the help of XSLT style sheets.

Modeling Processes

Why bother dealing with business processes in this book at all? Since XML could be looked at as being a technological basis for integration within the IT domain, we definitely have to take processes into account. We have seen at least two phases in IT: data integration and application integration. Giving the process paradigm appropriate weight, we can observe the phase of integrating processes of manifold kinds in different environments and with arbitrary scope in their business domains.

That is why in this chapter we will give an overview of process modeling, starting with some terminological aspects. We then present workflows as a special perception of processes. From that we will show some problems in the field of process analysis and modeling and present a somewhat uncommon perspective of business processes. These considerations are based on mechanisms that are known from research on cooperative software agents, specifically communication-based interaction, cooperation, and coordination. Finally we give some hints on applying XML technology to process modeling and implementation.

5.1 CONCEPTS OF BUSINESS PROCESS MODELING

Value creation and interaction

Business processes have proved to be an adequate paradigm in describing value-creating activities within and between enterprises—in both the old economy and the new (or Internet) economy. In turn, processes may serve to describe interactions between any participants in Internet platforms (e.g., portals, marketplaces, etc.).

Such "interactions" refer to business transactions, which encompass the collection and exchange of information, the negotiation of contracts, and the exchange of goods. This is part of what is called the "primary market transaction." The secondary transaction takes place in payment, logistics, and so forth.

Since we face interaction relationships (i.e., communication, synchronization, data manipulation, etc.) between entities, we have to consider process interfaces. XML-based formats in that context may be used to specify process contents and interfaces and thus support the interprocess understanding.

Section 11.3 will give an overview of business formats possibly able to meet this demand. For now, we present some conceptual considerations in approaching the problem of describing or specifying process-oriented contents from a model perspective.

5.1.1   Overview of Process Paradigms

Since we present XML-based modeling approaches for business processes in this section, we first have to differentiate several views of the issue. We will not discuss the pros and cons of process paradigms. Instead we will cover the modeling and exchange of process information with respect to exploiting XML and its related developments.

Most often processes are regarded as a sequence of intra- or interorganizational activities, tasks, or functions that represent some value creation. The activities may be performed by people or technical devices (e.g., computer-based systems). This perception of a process leads us to the workflow paradigm, discussed in Section 5.1.2.

Alternatively it may be helpful to consider the interaction rather than the operation. By doing so, we have to deal with communication between people and/or systems involved in the execution of a process implementation and the agreements made to perform the necessary process steps. Therefore Section 5.4 deals with contract-based, communication-based, and actor-based approaches to process modeling.

An important aspect in process analysis, modeling, and implementation is the ability to handle any changes to the process design over time. In that sense we may have to deal with process life cycles rather than with static objects. Therefore it may be important for processes to encompass the property of self-modification. This may in the first place refer to adopting changes due to external effects being relevant for the outcome of the process, and therefore the owner of the process, without any need for manual manipulation. Such an approach is closely related to the actor- or agent-based perspective. An overview is given in Section 5.4.4.

Process life cycles

5.1.2 Notion of Workflows and Modeling

The concept of a "workflow" reflects the traditional view of the implementation of processes in organizational environments. Broken down to bare techniques, the workflow view implies the modeling of business processes as sequences of complex activities that may be split into parallel sequences and/or partitioned into subsequences or elementary activities (actions). Agents, singly or in a group, are then assigned to execute these activities.

Workflow

The prevailing workflow metaphor depicts a business process as a stream or flow of documents and/or (intermediate or finished) products, processed stepwise by each agent in turn, that is, when the particular work piece comes flowing past them, and then passed on toward the next processing station. This, of course, very much resembles assembly line production. Common examples for such workflows are the assembly of a tax declaration or the processing of travel expenses.

A basic control element is given by task lists. For each agent or processing station a task list holds the tasks to be processed next at that station. An entry in the list encompasses the documents or other objects to be processed as well as the corresponding processing tools.

A workflow then is used to describe a well-structured and/or standardized process, as it can be identified in public and company administrations. It is not a useful instrument for ill-structured processes. We will defer discussion of that until later in this section.

Workflow
management
systems

Such implementations of workflows are workflow instances controlled by workflow management systems (WFMSs). In contrast the definition of workflows is part of conceptual modeling on the metalevel, that is, the workflow schema. Thus a WFMS supports the metamodeling of workflows and allows the creation of instances that it keeps track of. The Workflow Management Coalition (WFMC) has specified several components of an overall architecture, including interfaces for workflow definition and cooperation on the workflow engine level. For further information, have a look at *www.wfmc.org*.

Event-driven
process chains

Regarding common approaches to process specification, we select an example well known from the enterprise resource planning system SAP/R3: event-driven process chains (EPCs). We are not going to discuss the pros and cons of EPCs here. Instead we will present EPCs as a semiformal modeling approach within this section, a viable solution to modeling workflows. Nonetheless we will sketch some of the drawbacks to adequate modeling.

The basic idea of EPCs is to model process behavior as a sequence of events and functions. Events represent temporal or logical conditions to be fulfilled before executing a function. A function then may be thought of as a work step to be performed within the context of a business process.

Figure 5.1 shows an example of a workflow given as an EPC in ARIS (*www.ids-scheer.com*). While this is a coarse-grained top-level view, functions 1, 2A, and 2B are usually decomposed into detailed representations.

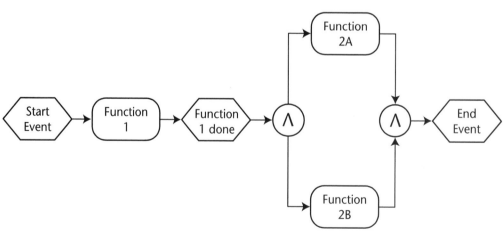

Figure 5.1 Example of an ARIS EPC.

The problems with using EPC-like modeling approaches are many. Some of them are inherent to the methodology; others arise from the inadequacy of the tools available for modeling. Here is a summary of the drawbacks that we consider important:

EPC and process modeling

- The set of constructional elements, mainly events and functions, stems from the industrial production domain, which is characterized by dealing with standardized processes. Process steps are triggered mainly by temporal conditions. The process is deterministically given by a sequence of actions. This concept is definitely valid for exactly that class of processes.
- The strict alternation of event and action in EPCs does not represent the real world adequately. Events should represent temporal and logical conditions to be fulfilled rather than functioning as syntactic separators within the sequence of functions.
- Decomposition for refinement is done on a modular basis. Once the boundaries of a component to be refined have been modeled (via so-called process interfaces), they will not change in the refined versions. So new connections with other components cannot be established without explicitly changing the complete model on higher levels of abstraction. In addition, process model graphics are more likely to be decomposed due to the limited place of output media than due to logical considerations.
- The decomposition problem gives proof that reverse engineering is not supported—or, if so, just to a very limited extent—by the corresponding tools.

Section 5.2 includes a further discussion of this topic and the demands of today's business environment.

5.1.3 Metamodeling Aspects

Metamodels describe the elements and their relationships within a specific model type. This means that syntax as well as semantics is defined. Concrete models therefore are built on the concepts that the metamodels describe. Figure 5.2 shows a simplified metamodel of EPCs, given as an entity relationship model. The connectors, also represented in the metamodel, allow the process analyst and modeler to express parallel and alternative paths within an EPC, using logical AND, OR, and XOR operators. Additionally a function may be associated with an organizational

Metamodel for EPCs

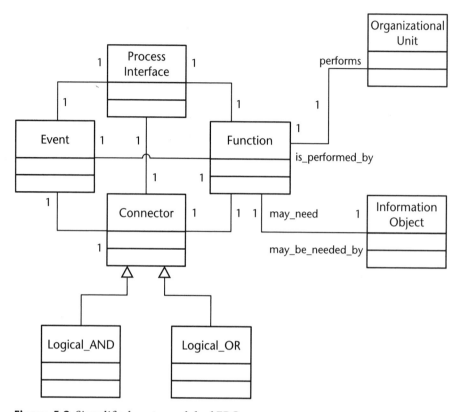

Figure 5.2 Simplified metamodel of EPCs.

unit that performs the function and an information object needed to perform the function. From the IT or implementational view, an information object then may be mapped to a data element stored in a database.

The metamodel developed here clearly does not meet the modeling semantics of EPCs. The construction procedure would require ordering rules such as "events and functions are strictly alternating when hiding the connectors" or "let an EPC start with either an event or a process interface," where a process interface may represent either an event or a function.

Metamodels are important components in business process management, and we will make use of them in the following section. From the conceptual perspective they semiformally explain the modeling elements in the particular context. From the perspective of frameworks that support modeling they build the basis for checking mechanisms as well as for model generation (e.g., via appropriate rule-based engines).

Metamodels, roughly speaking, function as information models, as do   Information
ontologies (see Section 4.2). In the process management context they   models
hold process-related knowledge or metainformation to be worked with or
to be communicated between software entities.

XML may be employed to specify workflows from the perspective of
metamodeling as well as from the perspective of the concrete instance of
a workflow. DTDs may be used for the exchange of such specifications as
well as for the storage of the specification in appropriate repositories. The
exchange of workflow information between two interacting software
components could be realized using advanced schema definition mechanisms, such as the Resource Description Framework (RDF), discussed in
Section 3.3.

A concrete application area for the exchange of process information   Workflow
would be the migration of workflows in distributed workflow manage-   migration
ment environments (e.g., for the purpose of load balancing). Since a
workflow system can control only the workflows that it has some understanding of, passing control of a workflow instance from engine to engine
would imply sending the metadata (i.e., the workflow schema) as well.

An example more complex than what we have presented here can
be found at *www.ebxml.org/project_teams/business_process/wip/metamodel/
version2.0.pdf*. Section 10.3 presents ebXML as a process-related XML
technology.

5.2   BUSINESS PROCESS MODELING AND SYSTEMS DEVELOPMENT

In this section we first sketch the current situation in business process
(re-)engineering (BPE) and point out shortcomings in practice, especially
for a certain class of business processes that can be structurally characterized as being highly dynamic. These are likely to be found in service businesses. We present an approach to business processes that in general
promises more adequate engineering of such conventionally rather
intractable processes.

5.2.1   Background

These days there is a growing dissatisfaction with the established way of
analyzing and describing business requirements and deriving IT solutions
for the processes thus defined. This is true even though the concrete
understanding of the modeling of, and IT support for, business processes
differs from case to case.

Business process engineering

We consider business process engineering as a paradigm for investigating business information for use in appropriate IT development. We will focus on currently observable practice, in which processes are mostly considered as plain workflows, as has been sketched earlier. As a result, and to simplify matters, we generally call these conventional approaches the "workflow view" of business activities.

Workflow classification

The main technique for describing this kind of workflow view is a chart, a graphical network, the nodes of which are either events or actions (often called "functions"). In this chart, a starting event precedes an action and a result event follows the action—or more than one result event if there are alternative outcomes of an action. The result event of one action usually serves as the starting event for the next one, or result events of several actions are somehow connected to start an action. Alternative paths (i.e., mutually exclusive paths) and parallel paths through this kind of event-action-chaining net are distinguishable only by the kind of "connectors" (with propositional logic semantics) at path branches or junctions. Well-known examples are event-driven process chains in ARIS (Scheer and Nüttgens 2000), as seen earlier, and the activity diagrams in UML (Fowler and Scott 1997).

Workflow classification

Workflows can be executed using a workflow management system (WFMS). In a WFMS configuration, people or systems (applications, machines) are assigned to perform the actions by processing documents or work pieces that are usually supplied by WFMS service components. Often workflows are classified into (ill-structured) ad hoc, semistructured, and (well-structured) standard workflows. Standard workflows are completely supportable by WFMS; semistructured, partly; and ad hoc workflows, not at all (Back and Seufert 2000).

Divergent design and implementation

Unfortunately, the structure class of a workflow is often recognized only after implementing it and then observing its mismatch with reality. The result of the analysis and conception phase may be a nice workflow graphic that is commonly agreed upon to exactly describe what happens in the departments under investigation. But the WFMS solution set up accordingly may turn out not to be workable because the workflow had almost completely "evaporated" in the course of its implementation and trial. This may be due to the fact that the initially analyzed process is ad hoc and highly dynamic rather than well structured.

For greater flexibility, newer WFMSs have been equipped with exception-handling mechanisms or some means for explicitly allowing deviation in practice. Watering down the workflow principles this way demands, naturally, a kind of metacontrol. This may be based on a means of process monitoring to detect diverging behavior of the actors.

The fact that such divergence happens (and that workflow designers have provided for "emergency exits") is evidence of the inadequacy not just of a particular workflow but rather of the whole traditional workflow concept when applied to business processes that are not really well structured.

The established workflow view (the activity- and work-piece-centered view of business processes) is probably inadequate for a whole class of business processes for the following reasons (among others): Workflow appropriateness

- It requires a rigid, fixed process structure.
- It presupposes that all choices are decidable.
- It views agents as being event-triggered. That is, they are called, by the workflow, to work on a certain object in a precisely defined way and then sit idle until the next work piece comes flowing by.

The class of processes for which the workflow view is inappropriate can be identified as being complementary to the class of processes for which the workflow view initially was conceived (namely, the industrial production processes). For these, the conditions listed in the preceding paragraph hold. But for administrative or service processes, or for highly dynamic business processes generally (those that deal interactively with people), another view is needed. This especially applies to businesses acting in changing market conditions and therefore being subject to permanent organizational changes. Dynamic business processes

The degree to which a business process is dynamic affects its potential for automation, which in turn corresponds to the degree of the possible shift or delegation of responsibility from units involved in the performance of a business process to units designing (the automation of) a business process. Instead of narrowing the responsibility of actors to single work steps within a workflow, designers need a much wider scope. In other words, as far as any actor (human or machine) is intended to be a logical part of some transaction (in the IT sense), decentralized responsibility is not possible. And, since responsibility and flexibility are the flip sides of the same coin, hopes for introducing flexible reaction into a workflow will always be dashed.

5.2.2 What Is a Business Process?

Capturing the dynamics of business processes certainly necessitates additional concepts in modeling: communication, parallelism, nondeterminism, and mobility. These concepts have a sound basis in formal process calculi, especially Milner's π-calculus (Milner 1999).

Definition
of a "business
process"

Let's first look at the definition of a "business process." We regard a business process as

- a network of interacting abstract agents, each of them playing certain business-related roles,
- working concurrently, organizing their cooperation using preestablished or ad hoc–created communication channels,
- implicitly or explicitly using or negotiating contracts with clients or other agents, realizing a cascade of contracts specifying the value creation, where a distinct contract is to achieve given and explicitly stated goals or subgoals, and
- where real world agents are assigned to work for the roles they play (i.e., because of their competence), with such assignments spanning organizational structures.

The benefits we expect from this view are many. The degree to which these benefits really become visible, however, depends on the kind of business and, to a lesser degree, on the kind of enterprise organization: the more service oriented the business and, therefore, the higher the process dynamics, the greater the benefits of this approach! Let's look at the benefits from three different perspectives.

Benefits in Process Design

Process
construction

The design of a new business process can profit substantially from the following method: We start by (1) stating and decomposing the goals that the business process is to meet, then we proceed to (2) derive initial contracts to serve the business goals and to identify "contractors" and the roles they play in a cooperation net. This forward business process engineering may be continued by (3) defining the internal nature of the roles and their external communication behavior, eventually arriving at a model in which (4) resources are allocated to roles and tasks and where we, finally, can (5) use this model configuration to derive requirements for IT systems to support tasks, roles, and even whole interaction structures.

Benefits in Process Reengineering

Process
reconstruction

Optimization of an existing business process is also greatly facilitated by the changed view of the circumstances. Reengineering a business process first requires an "as is" model of the process. This means in particular the modeling of what it has actually grown into, not what it once was conceived to be and therefore is believed by some managers to still be (but perhaps never was). In such a model, we must determine the degree of support for newly defined or persisting business goals by the existing business process. Degrees of support can never really be measured if, from the findings, all aspects that do not fit into an idealized notion of the business must be cut away, as is often the case with the Procrustean bed of the workflow view. When an adequate business process model has been reached, we can reconstruct the roles and, further on, the (implicit!) contracts according to which the roles are observed to act. By examining the reconstructed contracts, the gap between the actual and the desired goal support will become visible, and we can see how contracts and/or roles will have to be changed, or what changes have to be made to the inventory of contracts, roles, and tasks, in order to close the gap.

Figure 5.3 summarizes the elements of the reverse and forward engineering approaches to process design and their relationship as it is commonly found in real world projects. "Reverse engineering" denotes the reconstruction of real contracts from given physical situations. "Forward engineering" is constructing ideal contracts from the goals of an enterprise. A gap analysis on the contract level may also contribute to the evaluation of process implementations.

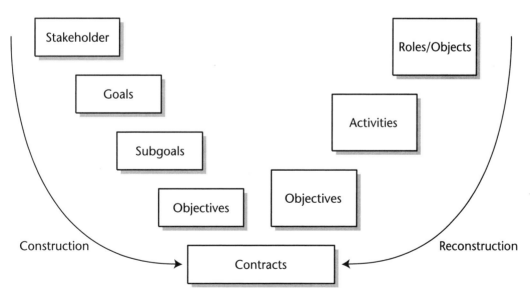

Figure 5.3 Integrating construction and reconstruction in business process analysis.

Benefits in Process Optimization

Not surprisingly, one way to optimize an existing business process is to optimize its IT support. This is the usual motivation for business process modeling and BPE. The real problem in improving IT support is determining its purpose and its scope; that is, the problem is identifying the "real" requirements for better IT systems. Directly asking the actual human agent will yield a much too narrow view. But asking a manager will yield a view that is usually more and more idealized and removed from reality the higher up the management hierarchy you go. So, instead of directly asking for requirements, we have to inductively build a model of the whole business environment of an IT system. This procedure might start by asking agents to whom they are talking; what information they are exchanging this way; how they would categorize what they are doing today and what they did yesterday and the day before that; which resources they use; how they see their work supported by IT systems; to whom they turn for advice; and so on. That is, we gather information pieces that allow us to build a model of what is really going on (e.g., what interdepartmental shortcuts exist, often with undocumented data flow; what undocumented resources are used and in what undocumented ways; what undocumented procedures have come into existence; how people have tried to optimize their tasks, often only locally and thus sometimes degrading global performance; and much more).

From what has been said so far, it appears that a WFMS is normally not the proper software choice to support business processes in business areas where BPE really shows its benefits. In these cases, a collaborative support system (CSS) may be more appropriate. But, usually, software is needed that is specially geared to the service tasks of the business in question. And there it is important to know the requirements as exactly as possible. So "off-the-shelf" products might not be the answer.

Although such knowledge of real requirements might also be gained in other ways, business process reverse engineering is a viable solution in order to get the basis for optimal IT support of whole business processes or the appropriate parts. Even if only partial support is needed, it is important to reverse engineer the whole business process—or at least as much as can be done within the limits of a project—in order to get a complete enough picture.

To sum up, we see the benefits of our approach

- for forward engineering of business processes, in which design of much more flexible processes is facilitated, but also

- for business process reverse and reengineering, in which much more adequate modeling allows for more complete and more correct representation of established processes.

There is another area where the new view promises substantial benefits, although we have not yet explored it sufficiently and we do not know exactly, at the present time, how to handle it technically. It is the area of continuous change management, a hot topic in the age of e-business. We expect the mobility concept to be very useful for integrating changes to business processes directly, on the same level, into the business process model. Traditionally, workflow changes must be managed in a metalevel model, whose objects are the different versions of a workflow model. That means changes are done *to* the workflow model, not *within* it. Workflows share this fate with program sources, of course: that is how the ordinary source management system works. And as with changes to programs, adapting a workflow means a whole run through an editing–recompiling–retesting–reinstalling cycle.

Continuous change management

In a collection dealing with business process management (van der Anlst, Desel, and Oberweis 2000), where all contributors work strictly within the workflow view, an essay (Ellis and Keddarn 2000) asserts that "a workflow change is a workflow," thus underscoring the metalevel problem. Although the modalities of change as listed in the article, as well as the techniques for change description presented there, are also important for a π-calculus-based change management, the mobility feature of π-calculus seems to allow changes to be an integral part of the business process model. Alas, even if we knew how to handle such dynamism within business process engineering, there still remains the nontrivial task of reflecting such changes within the IT systems supporting dynamically changing business processes. Component-based software, however, seems to facilitate the needed flexibility. Actually, adding and exchanging components in a running IT system is a research field presently addressed on the basis of π-calculus (Henderson 1997). So, the hope is to demonstrate in the not-too-distant future that business process change is not a business process but an integral feature of a differently, more adequately, engineered business process. We will pick up this aspect again in Section 5.4.4.

Workflow change

5.2.3 Employing Formal Modeling

Imposing an inappropriate "grid" for process description results in the distortion or complete loss of important information. The degree to which this inadequacy becomes obvious depends very much on the business sector. Workflow-oriented business process modeling may indeed be appropriate for industrial manufacturing, where we usually find well-structured processes, but it is definitely inadequate for service branches, especially in the financial sector, such as insurance companies and banks (although the term "production process" is used in such organizations as well). The latter business sectors do not have the rigid structure of industrial production. Instead, there is much more dynamism and change, quite often imposed by the rapidly changing social and legal environment of these businesses. That is, we find mainly ad hoc or semistructured processes. This is certainly true in the current wave of mergers and acquisitions in the financial sector, with all its organizational implications, which leads us back to the problem of change management.

π-calculus

Although we have been dealing with rather descriptive aspects so far, this chapter will present a formal modeling approach, based on the concepts of Milner's π-calculus (Milner 1999). Although this is not the place to fully introduce π-calculus, we will briefly sketch its main features, as far as they are relevant to BPE.

A *calculus* is a collection of elements and rules that specify how to combine these elements. A *process calculus* then is a collection of formal elements that represent physical, social, or formal processes and rules to construct and combine process elements.

Such calculi have been developed to describe and understand the behavior of complex systems by abstracting from specific attributes. In particular, this may refer to state transitions and concurrency in such systems. Examples are petri nets, Hoare's Communicating Sequential Processes (CSP), and the Calculus of Communicating Systems (CCS). Complex "real world" systems to be investigated may be found as technical, social, or natural processes in machines, electronic devices, communication systems, organizations, enterprises, societies, and other dynamic systems.

CCS

CCS, also developed by Milner around 1980, is meant to describe the observable behavior of parallel processes in process systems. The behavior is given by the interaction, that is, the communication between single processes. Furthermore behavioral equivalence between process systems can be determined, which allows the analysis of systems with regard to building process classes. Process calculi may also allow the description of nondeterminism. So the π-calculus basically adds the concept of mobility.

Communication channels

Let's first have a closer look at communication in the π-calculus. Communication in that context is a formal act of synchronization or handshaking between two interacting processes rather than a mechanism to exchange structured messages. Technically communication is performed via channels, referred to by channel names. Channel names can be used only for bilateral communication—but by more than two processes, leading us to one type of nondeterminism.

Process systems are processes existing in parallel, each of which is formulated by a so-called process term. These terms basically are sequences of possible communications. Since communications are directed, terms normally encompass sending (outgoing) as well as receiving (incoming) communications.

In Figure 5.4 a process system is given by two parallel processes Travel-Agency and Traveler. The two processes communicate via a channel named by the pair $\overline{\text{confirm}}$ (for an outgoing communication) and confirm (for an incoming communication). They may be thought of as ports of a virtual connection. Note that communications are always directed.

Consider this short example:

```
TravelBusiness := TravelAgency | Traveler

TravelAgency := request . offer . book . confirm . 0

Traveler := request . offer . book . confirm . 0
```

The process system named TravelBusiness includes the two parallel processes TravelAgency and Traveler from Figure 5.4. Each of these processes is described by a process term. The dot indicates the sequence (i.e., the flow of communicational steps of single processes). The sequence of performing communications leads to what is understood as process evolvement. Roughly speaking, when a process comes to a receiving communication in its process term, it blocks until the communication is performed; that is, it is triggered by receiving the handshake communication via the channel in question. It then evolves to the next state. So, having performed a handshake communication, both process terms evolve to the next step. This is close to state transitions in automata, but

Figure 5.4 Communication channel between processes.

Process terms — margin note

Process evolvement — margin note

not necessarily finite or deterministic. By the way, the ".0" indicates the evolvement toward the termination of the process. It may be left off for abbreviation.

Nondeterminism   Since more than two processes can use the same channel, with precisely the same name, nondeterminism can be expressed. Consider again the following simplified example for our travel business (see also Figure 5.5):

TravelBusiness := TravelAgency1 | TravelAgency2 |
                    Traveler

TravelAgency1 := request . $\overline{\text{offer}}$. book . $\overline{\text{confirm}}$

TravelAgency2 := request . $\overline{\text{offer}}$. book . $\overline{\text{confirm}}$

Traveler := $\overline{\text{request}}$. $\overline{\text{request}}$. offer . $\overline{\text{book}}$. confirm

Here we do not know how the process system evolves (i.e., which of the travel agencies wins the race with its offer). In this simple example both travel agencies are identical, and both receive the traveler's request (probably sent to both by $\overline{\text{request}}.\overline{\text{request}}$) and make an offer. The traveler will book at only one agency. The "losing" agency will block at the

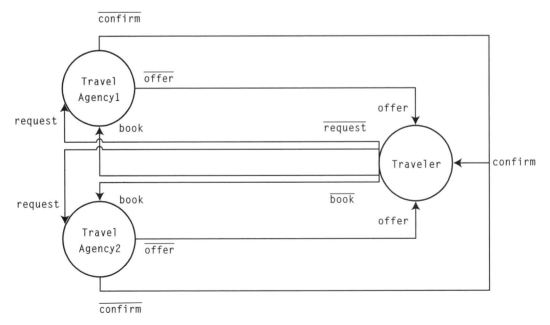

Figure 5.5 Nondeterminism in process systems.

book step. By the way, we also do not know which agency receives the request first. Although this example is rather simple, it shows that the π-calculus provides us with mechanisms to model real world situations that cannot be clearly expressed at modeling time. Our example leaves totally open which travel agency the traveler will get a ticket from after all.

Mobility is one mode of evolvement given by means of communi-   Mobility
cation links (or channels) that die or are dynamically created during the lifetime of the process system. So we can describe the fact that a communication channel is moved from one component of a process system (or "agent" in our terminology) to another. The set of communication links of an agent describes its neighborhood and, as a consequence, its location. Then we can also move the agent itself by moving its communication links and thereby creating a new location.

In our previous example we can think of the situation where the travel agency cannot handle a request in time and therefore delegates the task of preparing an offer to its subagency (see Figure 5.6). For that purpose a new channel reply is established that is moved via names offer1 and offer2 from TravelAgency1 to TravelAgency2 (indicated by the block arrow). The reply channel functions as a process handle that is passed along to TravelAgency2. By that mechanism, TravelAgency2 is able to send its offer to Traveler although it does not even directly know the

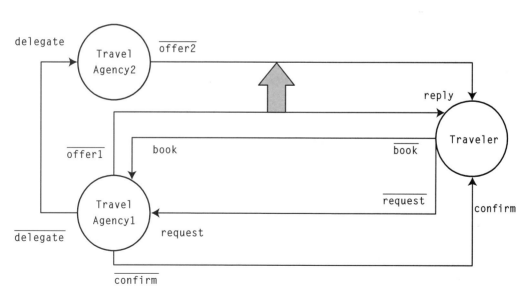

Figure 5.6 Mobility in process systems.

reply channel. TravelAgency2 just works out the offer; booking and confirmation in our example are dealt with by TravelAgency1 and Traveler.

The π-calculus notation of this example is as follows:

TravelBusiness := TravelAgency1 | TravelAgency2 |
                        Traveler

TravelAgency1 := request(offer1) . $\overline{\text{delegate}}$<offer1> .
                     book . $\overline{\text{confirm}}$

TravelAgency2 := delegate(offer2) . $\overline{\text{offer2}}$

Traveler := (new reply)$\overline{\text{request}}$<reply> . reply .

            $\overline{\text{book}}$. confirm

π-calculus-based business processes

We will now incorporate the features sketched so far into a modeling approach. Modeling based on π-calculus means viewing a business process as a system of what we will call "π-processes," processing concurrently, in parallel. A b-process is performed (1) by the interaction of such π-processes (this interaction is externally observable) and (2) by activities internal to these π-processes.

Business process representation

So, a business process is actually represented on two layers: (1) the interaction layer and (2) the elementary task layer. At first sight, this does not seem to differ so much from the workflow model, but in fact it does so significantly: In the π-processes system, there is no globally imposed scheduler, and no predefined network of interaction flow. The interaction structure of a "π-system" emerges as its π-processes evolve, that is, as single π-processes proceed (advance their state) by communicating with other π-processes. This means a decentralized control structure, organized by cooperation. As long as mobility is neglected, a structure of possible communication channels can be determined a priori for a π-system by examining the individual structures of the π-processes, that is, by looking up which "front ends" or "back ends" of channels appear within a term (expression) defining a π-process. An instance of π-calculus communication, as stated earlier, is directed and a singular event, meaning, loosely speaking, a channel is one-way and used at most once. But since concurrent π-processes can compete simultaneously for the same channel, it is often impossible to predetermine who will win and which communication will take place. Similarly, within a π-process, the evolution path can branch, and it is often not possible to decide locally in advance which path will be taken. We will come back later to these kinds of nondeterminism.

Mobility now adds the creation of new channels "on the fly," establishing new front or back ends, or both. This way "process handles" can be passed along, which is logically equivalent to moving processes. This feature, which we explained earlier, is quite useful and is applicable to diverse cases of real world modeling. Milner gives the technical example of a mobile phone in a car that must disconnect from, and reconnect to, transmitters as it is moved over cell boundaries. Here "mobility" is the movement of the cellular phone's link to another transmitter rather than the movement of the phone as the car is moving. Typical business process examples could include the following:

- Servicing moving clients, such as travelers or customers in big shopping centers, with special information (e.g., pertaining to places, possible activities, possible contacts, etc.)
- Maintaining or offering service relations when customers (people as well as companies) move their site of operation (e.g., by shifting services for relocated customers to another branch of a bank)
- Introducing people or entire units into organizations and business networks and helping them within such environments (e.g., initiating new employees in the processes of their departments and of the whole company, or guiding and supporting students at universities, or providing citizens with communal and other public services)
- Accompanying a product life cycle, for material products as well as for service products (e.g., as offered by banks), especially when different phases of a product life cycle necessitate different services

Rather than just treating the symptoms, inadequacies in the workflow view are remedied to a large extent only if a business process model is built around the concepts of communication, parallelism, nondeterminism, and mobility, derived from π-calculus. With these concepts, the reality of an enterprise or organization can be modeled much more adequately. Such a model prominently features agents:

1. Agents cooperate actively to reach the goals set for a business process.
2. Agents work concurrently and interactively.
3. Agents know who is the expert for a particular job step, or who routinely performs particular tasks.
4. Agents communicate with each other about orders or completion reports of orders, information, and availability of material or (intermediate) products.

Agent-oriented aspects

5. In certain situations, agents decide for themselves what to do next or whom to ask for help with a task.

6. In special problem situations, agents try to find somebody who can help or who knows whom to consult for help.

7. In the case of new goals, agents may accept new duties and establish new communication links in order to react flexibly to a changing world.

The concept of communication accounts substantially for items 1, 2, 3, and 4; parallelism, for items 1 and 2; nondeterminism, for item 5; and mobility for items 6 and 7, in this very incomplete list of cooperation aspects.

Nondeterminism

Nondeterminism is certainly not a desirable feature for an IT system specification, but it is a requisite for modeling business processes—certainly in service-oriented business sectors and probably also generally. Nondeterminism can be understood as modeling the fact that the modeler either does not have (or does not want to spend the effort to supply) enough information to always exactly determine a process evolvement (i.e., to exactly differentiate between the conditions for each individual path of a branch) has no way to determine beforehand which one of equally possible communications within a system of parallel processes may succeed. Such situations are more likely to occur the more concurrency exists in the system realizing a business process. Thus, to model (some) business processes really precisely and in detail requires the deliberate introduction of nondeterminism into the model.

Contracts

Moreover, nondeterminism in a business process model reflects a high degree of decentralized control in the performance of this business process. To describe the organization of this kind of decentralized control (i.e., cooperation), an additional concept is needed—contracts. A contract specifies how a provider services a client, where both service consumer and service supplier are peers. This distinguishes contracts from orders or commands in a traditionally viewed organization and identifies them as a means of modeling cooperation and delegation, rather than hierarchical function decomposition. Obviously, this distinction also corresponds to the view of a business process as "stretching horizontally" through an enterprise as opposed to "climbing up and down" a Tayloristically structured organization hierarchy.

Contracting agents

So the previous enumeration of features to be modeled for agents according to the new view has to be complemented with the feature of contracting. The contracting ability of an agent means that the agent is authorized to negotiate the way he or she produces and delivers a result, or to decide to responsibly employ the help of other agents for a partial process. In such a way, a cascade of contracts may be found in an adequate business process model.

An additional notion has proved helpful: we denote what agents contribute to a certain business process as the role they play in that business process. This abstraction allows us to make clear that the same agent may, probably at different times, be part of different business processes, playing different roles. The notion of roles also allows us to describe a business process without naming concrete people or IT systems.

The main reason for obtaining more adequate business processing models is to make a shift in the perception of business—the shift from a view of structured activities to a view of communicating agents, actively cooperating to achieve common goals, and with a contracting ability of their own. This is roughly expressed by the slogan that calls for a transition from "process-driven people" toward "people-driven processes," or more generally toward "agent-driven processes."

Shift toward agent-driven processes

This "shifted view" is actually a view dual with the traditional way of viewing business processes: instead of focusing on activities and their sequence, the dualistic view entails focusing on roles that agents play, and on their interaction, structuring, and organizing of the b-process "from the inside" (i.e., by cooperation) instead of being fixed into a rigid structure controlled from the outside.

Dualistic view of processes

Some interesting points can be made with regard to this dualism: The basic elements of the workflow concept, events and (complex) activities—corresponding respectively to states and transitions (e.g., as known from Petri Nets)—are purely abstract entities. The new basic elements, agents (as players of roles) and communications, however, can be directly observed.

In a workflow, agents do not initially appear, although they may appear in a workflow configuration as actors assigned to activities. So, comparing workflow configurations with our b-processes, we might assert the following correspondence:

- Agent (in a role, π-process) $\leftrightarrow$ actor (assigned to activity)
- Communication $\leftrightarrow$ event
- Internal task $\leftrightarrow$ elementary activity

Mapping dualistic concepts

The sore point of this correspondence is the comparison of "communication" and "event." There is an additional convention needed, something like "An event as a result of an activity performed by actor X shall be understood as a sending communication by an agent in role X; an event starting an activity performed by actor Y shall correspond to a receiving communication by role Y." Whether this actually works generally is not yet clear.

This "dualistic transformation" is trivialized if we first apply a dimension-reducing projection from the new onto the old view's "space": if nondeterminism and mobility are completely removed, and parallelism partly, from the new view, what is left over can easily be transformed into a workflow (configuration).

The last point, the conditionally possible "projection" from the "space" of the new view onto that of the old one, is another way of saying that the new view encompasses the old. In other words, the conventional workflow view is just a special case of the new view of business process engineering.

5.2.4 A Business-Centered Modeling Approach

Enterprise modeling may have several goals. So far we have focused on business process modeling. Its basic goal from the IT perspective is to analyze the behavior of an organization and get a summary of the information demands. Data modeling is much more technology centered and

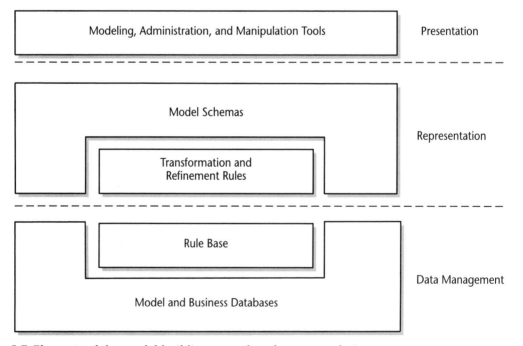

Figure 5.7 Elements of the model-building procedure for process design.

deals with the identification of structural elements and relationships to be mapped into the IT world.

Basic elements of a business-centered view of process modeling can be divided into three tiers, as shown in Figure 5.7.

Business-centered method

The main layer is the representation of model information on the metalevel. Here the model schemas are given for several methodological views:

- The business domain model, representing the business structure
- The contract model, defining the parameters of collaborative value creation
- The process model, defining the behavioral aspects in process systems
- The valuation model, representing all task-oriented information
- The allocation model, linking physical to virtual entities in the overall model.

Figure 5.8 shows an ERM of a sample metamodel representing the business domain information.

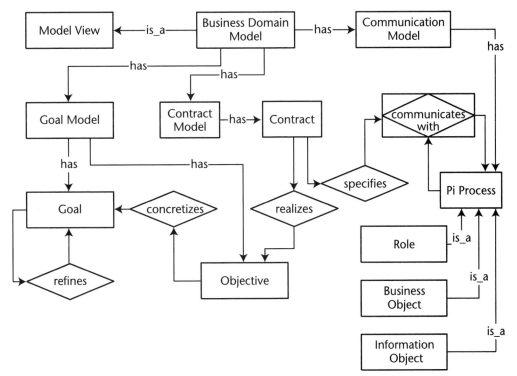

Figure 5.8 Sample metamodel view of the business domain model.

Additionally the modeling procedure and seamless integration of model views are supported by a mechanism for transformation in the horizontal direction and refinement in the vertical direction, both forward and backward in the ideal case. This approach heads in a rule-based direction.

5.2.5 Process Design and Object Orientation

Reinterpretation of UML diagrams

After all, why not use OO modeling for adequate BPE? You could employ UML diagrams to visualize facts contained in a model according to the new view. For example, UML collaboration diagrams (Fowler and Scott 1997) are handy for presenting the interaction structure of roles, displaying the roles as object symbols and the channels (i.e., the possible communications) as message arrows. That is, we are using UML constructs in a very special way. When showing such a diagram to someone familiar with UML, we have to point out this reinterpretation in order to avoid misunderstanding.

Inadequacy of OO

The trouble is that the OO approach is a solution only on the technical level, on the software level, not on the BPE level. This is a significant difference: a business process is not just another view of an IT systems landscape; a business process encompasses IT support but comprises much more than the IT side. Especially in the service businesses, we may see business processes only very sparingly supported by IT. An OO model is, in the first place, a model of some software system or, in other words, a technical specification of some software. A business process model describes the business domain ideally without any IT aspects in mind, which is certainly not the case in workflow modeling.

Relation between OO and process modeling

Nonetheless, business process modeling and OO modeling are related:

- In forward business process engineering, one of the results of building a business process model and of its evaluation can be a specification of an OO model—a specification of a specification of some software.
- In business process reengineering and reverse engineering, an OO model is an important input for (re-)constructing the business process model.

5.3 COMMUNICATION AND COOPERATION: TOWARD AGENT-BASED SYSTEMS

Management of communication

In the previous section we argued for a paradigm shift in regarding and dealing with business processes in today's organizations, by replacing the management of structures with a management of communication. Complex business transactions take place in highly dynamic cooperative networks rather than rigid sequences of production steps vertically or horizontally placed along the so-called value chain (Porter 1998).

Agent-oriented technologies have become of increasing interest for the design and development of software systems. There are high expectations: "the next significant breakthrough in software development" and "the new revolution in software" (Jennings and Woolridge 1998). In turn, huge market opportunities with billions of dollars of revenues are foreseen (Guilfoyle 1998). Since agent technologies are discussed in various contexts, we first give a short overview.

5.3.1 The Notion of Agent-Based Systems

Agents, or software agents, were originally part of artificial intelligence (AI) research work. Thus many concepts in the field of multiagents systems are closely related to AI concepts. Instead of contributing to the discussion about what an agent really is (for a discussion of that topic, see Müller and Jennings 1997), we will summarize several aspects as being basic attributes of agents.

Software agents

Figure 5.9 gives an overview of agent attributes. *Reactivity* is the ability of an agent to perceive information from its environment and perform an action accordingly. It may have either sensors for that purpose or an internal model of its environmental system (deliberative agent). Depending on its goals, an agent may also be self-induced and perform actions that may influence its environment (goal orientation and proactivity). The ability to learn implies the ability to deduce from its observations and adapt accordingly. Here we find AI concepts such as knowledge or rule bases.

Agent attributes

Autonomy is one of the most important aspects that makes agent technology interesting for software development. Agents perform their tasks autonomously in the sense that interaction with a controlling entity such as a human user is not needed—or, if so, only to a small degree. To achieve its goals an agent may move among nodes within a communication network (*mobility*) to reduce the communication overhead. Such migration approaches are known from distributed computing.

Another essential attribute is *communication*—interaction both with human users and with other agents. The latter case requires the existence of agent languages with appropriate protocols (a subject of later discussion). Communication also serves to coordinate agents performing complex tasks cooperatively. Thus cooperation is only possible if agents can communicate with each other.

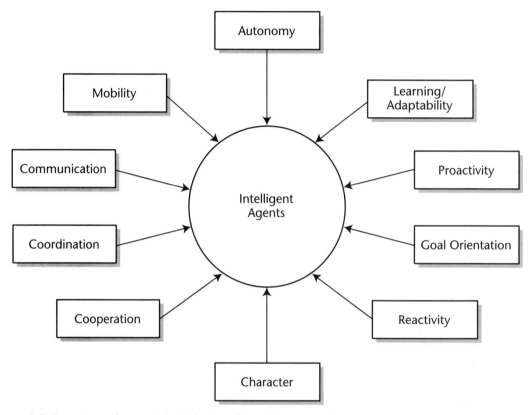

Figure 5.9 Overview of essential attributes of intelligent agents.

Attributes such as autonomy, communication, reactivity, and proactivity are commonly considered essential for agents. From the perspective of AI, mental attributes may be added, such as knowledge; belief, desire, and intention; emotion; and creativity. Mobility is usually considered to be optional.

5.3.2 Typology and Applications of Agents

The attributes discussed in the previous subsection may serve as classification factors for agents, leading to the typology shown in Figure 5.10. This is just a sampling of the approaches observable in the field of agent-based research and applications. This classification allows for combination; for example, we may find applications of smart, collaborative, mobile agents (Franklin and Graesser 1997).

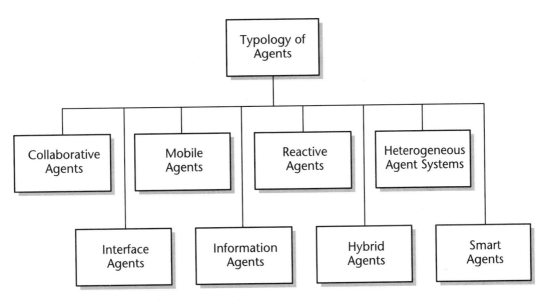

Figure 5.10 A typology of agent concepts.

The concept of agents has been given a great push by the Internet. The Internet agents
shift toward information processing in changing networked environments has led to the problem of efficiency in dealing with increasing
amounts of information. So the class of interface and information agents
has become of particular interest—for example, robots that preselect
information from mailboxes, lists, and similar resources, or personal
assistants that help to find resources on the Web.

Much of the research in the field of interface agents has been done
at the Massachusetts Institute of Technology (MIT). We will mention just
some of the applications developed there. Prominent examples are Cal-
endar Agent, for the management of appointments (Kozierok and Maes
1993); NewT, to train agents for news selection (Maes 1994); and Kasbah,
an agent-based marketplace for music titles (Chavez and Maes 1996).
Currently we face a new wave in personal assistance in Web-based
applications. Constructed with 3D modeling techniques, these agents
have a human appearance and interact with users through natural speech
interfaces.

Another class is given by the more general concept of collaborative Collaborative
agents—autonomous software units that perform tasks on behalf of a sin- agents
gle user or a group of users. Autonomy, as stated earlier, means that an
agent decides on the basis of its own (e.g., rule-based) knowledge. Agents

may be mobile—they may move within a computer network to get their jobs done and return with the result.

Since tasks may be diversified, agents may also be grouped into agent systems to perform complex tasks. If agents of several types are grouped, we may consider the result a heterogeneous (multi-)agent system.

There are further categories and applications of agents that we will not discuss here but that are documented in a variety of publications: document retrieval, air traffic control, management of telecommunication networks, computer integrated manufacturing, medical care systems, and many more.

The large number of agent-based approaches demonstrates that agent-oriented computing is a viable technical solution for mapping certain classes of complex systems to the IT world. In particular, to come back to our original problem, this is true for the support of business processes, from conceptual modeling to implementation, via computer-based techniques and systems.

5.3.3 Agent-Oriented Concepts

An essential concept of agents is communication, which builds the basis for the "social" capabilities of agents. This implies that agents interact on the basis of an agent communication language. ACL is an example of such a language. ACL has three components: a vocabulary, the outer language KIF (Knowledge Interchange Format), and the inner language KQML (Knowledge Query and Manipulation Language).

Agent communication is performed by message passing. ACL messages are expressions that are defined using the KQML. These expressions consist of terms and sentences in accordance with the vocabulary, which is context specific and defined in an extensible dictionary.

A KQML message is abstract; that is, it is independent from its content, which is just one component of the KQML message itself. The vocabulary is often referred to as the "information model" or the "ontology." A receiver has to understand the ontology to be able to process the message on the semantic level. Ontologies were discussed in Section 4.2 (see also Uschold and Gruninger 1996). On the message-passing level, speech acts are defined. Since speech acts will be discussed later in Section 6.4, we will just outline the idea here.

Messages are of a certain speech act type. A concrete instance of a speech act type is called a *performative*. Several types are defined, such as tell to transmit a message, ask-one to check for a fact, or broker-one to delegate the execution of a speech act (Finin et al. 1993). Here is an example that asks for a stock rate (Mayfield, Labrou, and Finin 1996):

```
(<ask-one>
    :content   (PRICE IBM ?price)
    :receiver  stock-server
    :language  LPPROLOG
    :ontology  NYSE-TICKS
)
```

The speech act or statement defined in the content field is based on what has been defined within the language field. The general structure of a performative thus is fixed by the given fields. Finally, to give an impression of the relevant aspects and complexity, Figure 5.11 shows the overall structure of language concepts in the field of agent technology.

Many types of agents in a variety of applications rely on cooperation to perform their tasks. So far we have said nothing about how the necessary exchange of services is coordinated. At least two types of communication can be identified: deliberative and negotiation.

An example of negotiation-based agent coordination is the contract net approach (Dauts and Smith 1983). Services are exchanged according to service level agreements (SLAs) that have been negotiated among the participants. These SLAs may be considered as contracts in the sense of our notion of business processes discussed earlier. **Negotiation**

A contract net specifies a network of nodes given by agents that act according to market mechanisms. In multiagent systems, special managers are usually implemented and provided with the necessary knowledge to tender services. Processors then supervise the contract building.

Alternatively, auction-based mechanisms have been proposed for the coordination of service exchange. We will not discuss the economic implications of negotiation and auctions in detail, but we will just state that auctions give much more transparency to the market and therefore promise more efficiency in resource allocation.

Additionally the conditions are commonly known in advance. This reduces the complexity for modeling the realization of appropriate mechanisms in agent systems. The appropriate strategies differ from type to type since we may deal with the English, the Dutch, or Vickrey auction, to mention just a few. Some parameters are still up to the single participant to define.

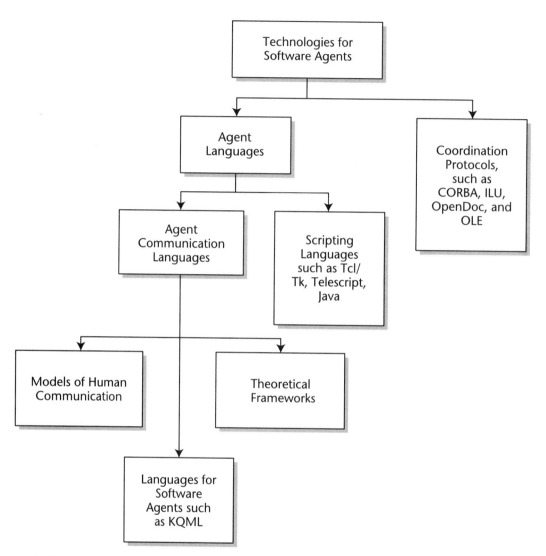

Figure 5.11 Agent communication languages in the context of agent technologies.

Agent
architectures

The question of how to communicate and coordinate in agent systems is answered by architectures. Architectures support the organization of the cooperation within multiagent systems (Genesereth and Ketchpel 1994). From the perspective of communication, there are two cases: (1) directly (i.e., bi- or multilaterally by broadcast mechanisms or specific channels) and (2) supported (i.e., via special components that pass the messages from a sender forward to the receiver).

In the first case, either service requests or service profiles (specification sharing) are sent. On that basis receivers can act according to their goals and answer (react) appropriately. In the second case, services are normally registered in central directories or knowledge containers of the coordinating entities, and the sender does not need to know the receiver.

Such entities are called *facilitators* in federated systems that specifically support agent coordination. Agents delegate some of their autonomy to the facilitator, which acts on their behalf by sending messages on the basis of general information and requirements about its clients.

Agent architectures aim at abstracting from proprietary approaches and providing a conceptual framework for the design and development of agent systems. Examples of architectures are InteRRaP, GRATE, and ADEPT. ADEPT is the topic of the following subsection.

5.3.4 ADEPT

An architecture of particular interest is the Advanced Decision Environment for Process Tasks (ADEPT). It aims to support business processes with agent-based IT solutions. ADEPT has been a research project under the participation of British Telecom. Its basic results and concepts will be outlined here (for more details, see Norman et al. 1996 and Jennings et al. 1996).

Business process support

ADEPT allows the mapping of simple or complex organizational units to an *agency*. Agencies deliberately provide services to and/or request services from other agencies. An agency can be thought of as executing part of a business process that may have been modeled conceptually as a result of a business process reengineering project.

Agencies

An agency may encompass other agencies or agents. The responsible agent controls its agency, coordinates its services, and represents them to the rest of the system world. From an organizational perspective, it could be considered the head of a department, with the agency being the department. According to our earlier arguments, we will not consider the allocation of real world objects to conceptual elements in detail.

Figure 5.12 shows the logical structure defined by ADEPT. Agency Y consists of agencies E, F, and G and the responsible agent. TD1, TD2, TE1, and TE2 are atomic tasks to be performed by agents, that is, by the responsible agent and in turn by so-called subsidiary agents within the agency.

Atomic tasks

In agency E we have zoomed into the responsible agent, which encompasses five logical and functional components. Services provided

ADEPT models

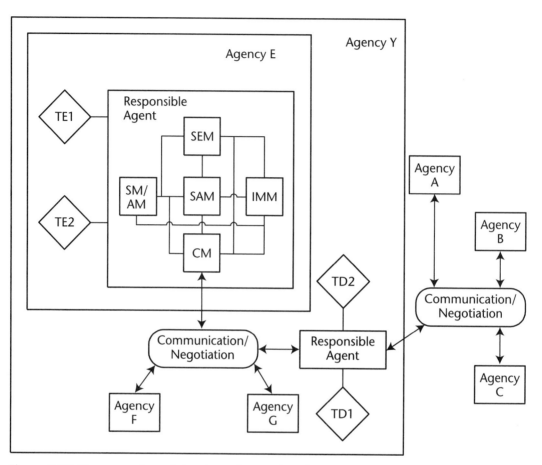

Figure 5.12 Components and structure of agent-based process management in ADEPT.

by the agency are mapped to the self model (SM), which additionally holds the execution schedules of agents. The acquaintance model (AM) encapsulates knowledge about other agents, including their capabilities and a history of service requests. The execution schedule is maintained by the situation assessment module (SAM). For that purpose it needs several types of information, such as requests by other agents, services that it has already agreed upon, and service- as well as negotiation-oriented information.

The service execution module (SEM) initializes and manages the services that the agent has committed to provide. It also requests services required from other agents. The interaction management module

(IMM) represents the interests of an agent in the negotiation procedures. It is triggered by the SAM.

The exchange of information and services is based on communication performed among the communication modules. They pack messages and pass them toward the receiving agent. On the implementation level, CORBA services (i.e., the object request broker) may be employed for that purpose.

CORBA-based communication

The communication protocol in ADEPT is based on speech acts that express the intent of an agent. The content may be coded in KIF syntax; the semantics are given by the ontology, as we outlined in the previous subsection. So the structure of a message follows the KQML approach. Some examples of negotiation-oriented actions are propose, counter-propose, accept, reject, confirm, and deny. The basic structure is the following:

ADEPT speech acts

```
(message

    (action:       <communicative-act>)

    (sender:       <agent-id>)

    (recipient:    <agent-id>)

    (conversation: <conversation-id>)

    (service:      <service-name>)

    (info-model:   <model-id>)

    (content:      <expression>)

)
```

The CM not only manages the logical distribution of messages, but it also encodes and decodes the content according to the language. This allows agents that "speak" different languages to communicate with each other, as long as the CM has access to the necessary information in the AM.

We will not discuss the outcome of the project in detail, but we should mention that ADEPT has been applied to some business processes at British Telecom (BT), for example, the Provide Customer Quote Service (see *www.mmrg.ecs.soton.ac.uk/nrj/projects/paam96/paam2.html*). Research on collaborative agents at BT laboratories has resulted in the development of the agent-building tool kit ZEUS (*www.labs.bt.com/projects/agents.htm*).

5.4 PROCESS CONCEPTS AND XML

So far we have put a lot of effort into describing our notion of business processes, the necessary paradigm shift for adequate process modeling, and agent-oriented techniques to support business process modeling and execution. Now we will finally give some hints as to what the contribution of XML to these topics might be. Since this is a field of ongoing research and practical work, the purpose of some of the statements made in this section is more to give an idea than to present the solution.

5.4.1 Actor-Driven Processes

The heading of this subsection generalizes to a certain extent what we stated earlier: a paradigm shift from process-driven people to people-driven processes. We have to overcome conceptual and implementational patterns that have been well elaborated in assembly line industrial production.

Instead we have to consider active and collaborative entities, whether we call them "agents," "actors," or whatever. These entities contribute to value creation, which is the goal of a business process, assuming they have a common understanding of the process or business domain or at least compatible targets.

Since collaboration requires interaction, communication is a main attribute of such considerations. We first discuss a special aspect of communication in the next subsection. This is followed by a discussion of contracts, another important feature, that aims at specifying the conditions of value creation steps between collaborating entities.

5.4.2 Open Communication Processes

The design and implementation of IT systems will lead to much better results if designers and system architects understand the business domain that is supposed to be supported by IT solutions. Business process analysis and modeling may be a helpful approach to gaining the necessary information.

Interaction   In larger business contexts, processes do not perform without interacting with their environment. In particular, they exchange information and work pieces with other processes. So, instead of dealing with single isolated processes, we deal with systems of interacting processes, interaction performed by communication.

Communication in the real world as well as in computer systems is the common means of exchanging information and/or services among several entities. In informatics the concept is used in a variety of approaches, for example, client-server architectures in general, or CORBA to mention just one in particular. Agent-based systems seem especially promising at this point.

But there are still some unanswered questions. In the context of com- **Dynamic** munication, the feature of dynamics encompasses the possibility of **adaptation** changing communication channels between interacting entities or— what is even worse—entities may migrate, disappear, or appear arbitrarily. In a real world business, think of a service unit or a whole department that moves to another location, has been closed, or is newly established. These events lead to changes in the communication structure of the process system.

Although migration or closing down could be handled by communicating the new contact information to the known partners in advance, the problem of communicating with unknown entities still has to be solved. There are two possible situations: (1) a process seeks another process (e.g., for the reason of collaborating or exchanging services), or (2) a new process has been established and it needs to integrate with a process system "at runtime."

These two situations share a common problem: how can a process find **Anonymous** other processes to get its job done? First, the processes must be a proper **communication** fit for one another in terms of offering the required services. Second, they must have compatible interfaces. And third, a mechanism must exist to publish this information.

The first two requirements are answered by mechanisms that may be implemented using XML-based technologies and incorporating concepts from other fields such as agent communication languages. The third requirement, however, is a lot more difficult without central mechanisms such as directories or broker services. The third requirement is, at the same time, the most interesting since in real world systems we often find many chaotic aspects that do not rely on fixed structures or predefined knowledge of "how to do something." On the other hand, we often find lots of business cases where centralized mechanisms make sense.

Bi- or multilateral communication between agents usually is session **Message passing** oriented. Sessions can only be established if agents are able to identify each other. Centralized (i.e., broker-based) communication is commonly realized via message passing. Message passing is the mechanism of choice in many communication-oriented services and protocols, such as CORBA in object-oriented systems and KQML/KIF in the context of agent technologies.

Broadcasting

For "anonymous" publishing mechanisms (i.e., the sender does not know the receiver(s)), our first thought would be a broadcast service that provides an infrastructure that messages can be pushed at. A potential receiver would have to actively and deliberatively poll over such a public message queue.

5.4.3 Contract-Based Interaction with tpaML

tpaML (Trading Partners Agreement Modeling Language) is a markup language specification proposed by IBM. It has been integrated with IBM's B2B e-commerce products, particularly the WebSphere B2B Integrator, which has been built on top of the WebSphere Commerce Suite.

TPA contract

The basic idea is to set up an electronic contract (TPA) on the basis of XML. A TPA defines how trading partners interact on several layers. In particular, it defines contract terms and conditions, participant roles, identification, communication properties, security properties, actions, sequencing rules, and error handling or recovery procedures (Sachs et al. 2000; Ennser et al. 2000).

The language to stipulate all this information is tpaML. The resulting contracts are enforced by the integration software that controls the business transactions of two partners over the Internet.

TPA layers

There are three concrete layers for TPAs. First, the business protocol layer is the interface between the business application functions and the TPA-defined actions. It provides rules for sequencing the messages between servicing parties. Second, the document exchange layer provides abstracting services for document handling between the business protocol and transport layers, including time-stamping, logging, auditing, and nonrepudiation. Finally, the transport layer delivers messages according to the selected communication protocol, including security aspects.

A TPA is an XML document described by a DTD or schema. From this description the document code is generated on the computer systems of the trading partners that agreed on the TPA. The following is the basic structure of a TPA as a snippet of XML, enriched by some additional tags in the transport section:

```
<TPA>

    <TPAInfo> <!-- Preamble: TPAname, role, definitions,
            participants, etc. -->

    </TPAInfo>

    <Transport> <!-- communication and transport security -->
```

```
<HTTP>

    <Version>version</Version>

    <HTTPNode> <!-- one for each party -->

       <OrgName Partyname=name/>

       <HTTPAddress> <URL> … </URL> </HTTPAddress>

    </HTTPNode> …

  <HTTP>

  <!-- communication and transport security
      information -->

</Transport>

<DocExchange> <!--exchange and security --> </DocExchange>

<BusinessProtocol>

   <ServiceInterface>

      <!--Action definition etc. for each provider -->

   </ServiceInterface>

</BusinessProtocol>

</TPA>
```

Such a TPA has to be set up and then agreed upon by the partners. Then code is generated on either side, including the local registration information and the code necessary to enforce the corresponding rules of interaction.

5.4.4 Self-Modifying Processes

The attribute of self-modification comes into play for adaptations of business entities due to environmental changes. *Change management* is a structured procedure for performing all necessary organizational transformations that keep an enterprise competitive. Usually short-term changes are considered that are supposed to meet current client demands, technological innovations, political or economic circumstances, and so on.

Short-term changes

Additionally we may also consider long-term changes that influence "long transactions," using an IT-related term. As an example, we can think of a process that manages all activities related to the financial demands of a customer. The process then covers the "life cycle" of the

Long-term changes

customer. At some point a bank account is needed, then some life insurance, followed by some investments, a mortgage, asset management, and so on.

Changing processes on the conceptual level leads to changing process implementations on the fly or at runtime. This is done by replacing some implementations by other implementations. Therefore mechanisms are needed that allow the generation of process instances. This is what we consider a metalevel problem.

Minor changes in processes may be dealt with by parameterization. For example, an audit mechanism could control processes by tuning them with appropriate parameter values. The behavior of processes may be dealt with on the implementation level as well, for instance, through artificial intelligence such as rule-based mechanisms. Structural changes in processes, however, must be considered on the metalevel.

Metamodels   A metamodel describes a process or a class of processes (i.e., its structure, the relationship of its components, and its behavior). From that description an instance of a process may be derived, including appropriate real world allocations for process objects. The π-calculus (see Section 5.2.2) provides the modeler with an advanced means to anticipate certain types of changes, mainly through the mobility feature.

A solution on the conceptual level implies having formal transformation mechanisms for forward and reverse engineering that allow the incorporation of changes at the implementation site backward into the corresponding model views and, in turn, the generation of appropriate process instances from changed metamodels.

Since the support for such a task through formal means is still an open research field, automated adaptation and self-modification are a future result. Nonetheless the BPMI, presented next, claims to enable process implementations to change across systems, over time, and dynamically in response to changing conditions.

5.4.5 The Business Process Management Initiative (BPMI)

The Business Process Management Initiative (*www.bpmi.org*) aims at promoting and developing standards for the design, deployment, execution, maintenance, and optimization of business processes, particularly collab-

BPML and BPQL   orative processes in electronic business. Two open specifications have been defined, the Business Process Modeling Language (BPML) and the Business Process Query Language (BPQL).

A business process describes some transaction, based on a finite-state machine, between two business partners. Interaction takes place through a common (i.e., public) interface, supporting the exchange of information among the private process implementations. The private implementations are considered to be participants in the process. The public interface may be supported by common protocols such as ebXML, to be discussed in Section 10.3.

Although the private implementations could be specified using the BPML, the execution of business processes is supported using the BPQL. Figure 5.13 presents an architectural overview of the scope of BPMI.

Similarly to XML, which describes data on the metalevel, the BPML allows the modeling of business processes on the metalevel and independently of any existing back-office system or protocol. The schema for BPML can be thought of as building the basis for the specification of processes in a specific business process modeling language. BPML representations encompass control, data, and event flows as well as support for defining business rules, security roles, and transaction contexts.

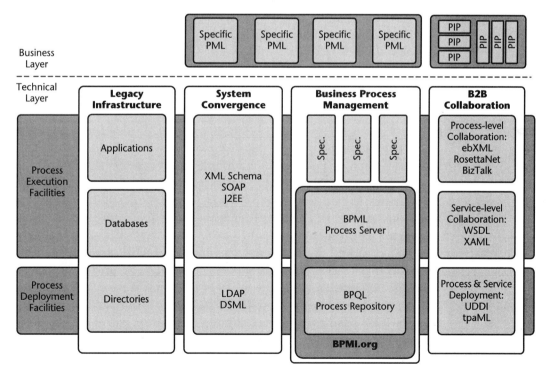

Figure 5.13 Scope of the BPMI specifications.

A draft of the BPML specification is available from *www.bpmi.org*. Here is a short excerpt from the BPML XML Schema, defining the process element:

```
<xsd:element name="process">
  <xsd:annotation>
    <xsd:documentation xml:lang="en">
      Process definition
    </xsd:documentation>
  </xsd:annotation>
  <xsd:complexType>
    <xsd:complexContent>
      <xsd:extension base="processDefinition">
        <xsd:sequence>
          <xsd:group ref="extension"/>
        </xsd:sequence>
      </xsd:extension>
    </xsd:complexContent>
  </xsd:complexType>
</xsd:element>
```

The complex type `process definition` encompasses metadata for advertising, searching and categorizing, rule sets to express conditions and dependencies, complex activities representing flows of control, and simple activities to perform data processing, communication, and system operations or actions. These entities again are defined in further detail by the schema definition.

Process integration

As stated earlier, the BPMI specifications deal with processes in electronic businesses. They aim at process integration in intra- and inter-enterprise computing. Therefore distributed transactions (synchronous as well as asynchronous) are supported that allow the embedding of applications within business processes. Process integration with BPML refers to the following targets:

- Integrating applications as process components
- Interleaving processes and transactions

- Process model exchange between business process management systems

The BPQL is an interface to the execution-oriented components of process management infrastructures. Such infrastructures typically encompass a component that controls the execution of processes (i.e., a process server), which may be compared to a workflow engine. Additionally a component is available to hold data such as process descriptions and related information (i.e., a process repository).

The execution of process instances can be controlled through an interface based on SOAP (see Section 6.5.2). The repository can be queried through an interface based on WebDAV, a set of HTTP extensions to collaboratively edit and manage files on remote Web servers (*www.webdav .org*). Process models managed by the process repository through the BPQL interface can be exposed as UDDI (Section 7.3) services for process registration, advertising, and discovery purposes.

5.4.6 Business Rules

Business rules contain business knowledge that describes the parameters (i.e., policies and procedures) of transactions and work processes in a "what to do if something happens under certain conditions" manner. A common example of such a business rule would be the specification of when and how a buyer can make changes to his or her order (see the following subsection). For example, this would encompass temporal conditions followed by corresponding reactions.

Business-rule-related topics encompass their formulation or specification, how to mine them from existing data, possibly the building of rule-driven business systems, and their management in evolving business environments. In this subsection we focus on the formulation and specification of business rules. Traditionally business rules, like other business logic, have been hard-coded in business application code or buried in other IT components, such as stored procedures in DBMSs, and could not be easily accessed or even managed by nontechnical staff. XML-based specification is a solution to this problem.

Formulation and specification

That type of formulation might rely on more general principles, such as ontologies and knowledge representation, with background from artificial intelligence, such as inference and deduction. We will not discuss this in detail. Instead we present some general approaches to XML-based business rule definition. A more extended overview of the topic is given by Thorpe (2001).

Business Rules in Contracts—The BRML

Agent communication was the starting point for business rule research at IBM (*www.research.ibm.com/rules/home.html*). In the Business Rules for E-Commerce (BREC) project, rule-based business processes for e-commerce were investigated.

ACL messages (see Section 5.3.3) can be regarded as containers that hold the business rules described in an appropriate language. ACL's outer language, KIF, was not designed to be the proper choice for this. Instead Courteous Logic Programs (CLP) are used, which are an extension of as well as a complement to KIF.

BRML

Aiming for the integration of such a language with the Web would require coding CLP in XML. Such an XML DTD is given as the Business Rules Markup Language (BRML). The BREC research aimed at supporting the translation of rules to and from heterogeneous rule systems or languages, as well as to and from KIF (*logic.stanford.edu/kif*), along with providing an XML-based interchange language, such as BRML, to perform such translation.

Consider the following rule: "A customer may modify an order 14 days or more prior to delivery if he or she is a preferred customer." Given as a logic program expression, this rule would result in

```
<leadTimeRule>orderModificationNotice(?Order, days 14)

            preferredCustomerOf(?Buyer,?Seller)

        ∧ purchaseOrder(?Order,?Buyer,?Seller)
```

The "?" indicates a logical variable. Let's translate this into BRML notation:

```
<?xml version="1.0">

<!DOCTYPE brml SYSTEM "brml.dtd">

<clp>

   <erule rulelabel="leadTimeRule">

     <head>

        <cliteral predicate="orderModificationNotice">

           <variable name="Order"/>

           <function name="days 14"/>

        </cliteral>
```

```
    </head>

    <body>

      <and>

        <fcliteral predicate="preferredCustomerOf">

          <variable name="Buyer"/>

          <variable name="Seller"/>

        </fcliteral>

        <fcliteral predicate="purchaseOrder">

          <variable name="Order"/>

          <variable name="Buyer"/>

          <variable name="Seller"/>

        </fcliteral>

      </and>

    </body>

  </erule>

</clp>
```

As stated before, IBM aimed at having a language that supports a common understanding of business rules in contracts among agents and the modification, communication, and execution of rules by agents. An implementation of BRML is IBM's Common Rules Java Library (*www.research.ibm.com/rules/commonrules-overview.html*), which is a follow-up to the ABE agent framework.

BRML implementation

The Rule Markup Initiative

The Rule Markup Language (RuleML) is based on an initiative that several parties (including the BRML group) participate in. The design of RuleML (*www.dfki.uni-kl.de/ruleml/*) is grounded on a hierarchy of rules (see Figure 5.14). The hierarchy represents specialization relations, starting from the top-level reaction rules.

RuleML

Reaction rules are known in active database research as event-condition-action constructs. Such rules are triggered if the defined event occurs, which requires some observation mechanism. Then the condition,

Reaction rules

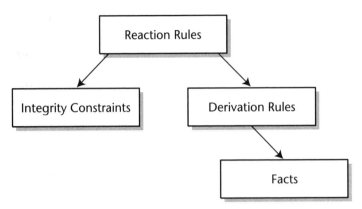

Figure 5.14 Rule hierarchy in RuleML.

simple or complex, is checked. Finally, if the condition evaluates to true, the action is fired; that is, the procedure it contains is executed. This is a straightforward application of rules of that type.

Integrity
constraints

Integrity constraints are also forward oriented. They check for inconsistency and signal if the conditions are fulfilled. Events are given by manipulation operations on databases.

Here is the structure of a reaction rule, including an action to signal an inconsistency, which would be based on the definition of a corresponding integrity constraint that it implements.

```
<rule>

    <_body>

        <and> premises </and>

    </_body>

    <_head>

        <signal> inconsistency </signal>

    </_head>

</rule>
```

Derivation rules

A *derivation rule* is a specialization of reaction rules where the action is to draw a conclusion if the condition is fulfilled. These rules can be applied in either direction: forward assertion of conclusions from conditions as well as backward assertion of conditions from conclusions. *Facts* are a further specialization having an empty list of premises so that the conclusion is always drawn.

So far the main effort of the initiative has been toward derivation rules and facts. RuleML has been hierarchically modularized into a directed acyclic graph of DTDs for these rules, which is open for further sublanguages.

Exchange via Rule Engines—The SRML

The Simple Rules Markup Language (SRML) is a proposal for a general-purpose interlingua that allows the definition of rules on the basis of XML for their exchange between rule engines (*xml.coverpages.org/srml.html*). A major goal is to abstract the process rules from concrete rule engines, and thereby be vendor independent.

SRML

This idea is based on providing a DTD to the rules community that specifies a subset of common rule engine language constructs. Rules defined according to that schema can be translated and executed appropriately on the target system.

An example in traditional syntax is

```
rule Discount {

  when { ?s:ShoppingCart (purchaseAmount > 100) ; }

  then { update ?s { discount = 0.1 }; } }
```

which rule marked up becomes

```
<rule name="Discount">

  <conditionPart>

    <simpleCondition className="ShoppingCart"
                     objectVariable="s">

      <binaryExp operator="gt">

        <field name="purchaseAmount"/>

        <constant type="float" value="100"/>

      </binaryExp>

    </simpleCondition>

  </conditionPart>

    <modify>
```

```
                <variable name="s">

                <assignment>

                  <field name="discount">

                  <constant type="float" value="0.1"/>

                </assignment>

              </modify>

            <actionPart>

            </actionPart>

          </rule>
```

So, not very surprisingly, SRML rules have a condition part and an action part. Actions provided by the schema are `modify`, `assert`, and `retract`. The condition is built from one or more test expressions.

5.5 CONCLUDING REMARKS

Since we have been working on several different concepts in this chapter, let's summarize the main results and relations. So, what was this chapter all about? Recall our initial and still overall argument that process engineering is needed in today's business-oriented information management. The process paradigm is powerful and is adequate for the analysis and description of business knowledge. The resulting models may be used in either (re-)organization projects or IT development. In both cases, we expect to gain a sound basis for higher-quality solutions.

We also introduced a process-oriented approach based on the concepts of the π-calculus. It included the features of mobility and nondeterminism for the following two reasons:

• First, since business organizations and environments are subject to increasing dynamism, change management should be supported. Therefore formal mechanisms are needed to provide a basis for realizing integrated process engineering methodologies. Such an approach includes information analysis, modeling, seamless forward and reverse engineering, and finally simulation of process designs. The π-calculus provides concepts and an algebraic notation that may contribute to an appropriate solution at this point.

- Second, we argued for business concepts given in terms of a management of communication rather than of structures, as well as people-driven processes rather than process-driven people. This results from the observation that business activities are interactions, and interaction is either communication or the exchange of goods. The prevailing workflow-oriented view of business processes may be appropriate for industrial processes, but it is not appropriate for service processes. So we need a modeling approach that is communication based. The π-calculus promises to help at this point, too, by describing systems of communicating processes.

On the technical level the approach that we outlined in the first two sections of this chapter is very similar to what is known from agent-oriented technologies, where we find many concepts and research results that may be applied to the process context. These range from the understanding of communication protocols to the formulation of business knowledge in terms of rules, for instance. We then gave an overview of software agents and systems, leading us to the ADEPT system to support service processes in telecommunication.

Finally, the role of XML in the field of business-process-oriented approaches had to be made clear. To do this, we summarized the initiatives taken and results gained so far in this area. We focused on the formulation of process features in XML that have been identified before, all for the purposes of representation and exchange. This chapter outlined the BPMI architecture, and other efforts such as ebXML will be dealt with in Chapters 10 and 11.

Communication

For early transactional systems, data storage was one of the most challenging aspects of computing. Today, with ubiquitous networks, the focus of software engineering has moved to communication. In this chapter we first introduce the conceptual aspects of communication. After describing a layered communication model, we look at the transportation environment for messages: channels and ports. Then we discuss the theory of speech acts that helps us to structure the exchange of messages and leads to protocol patterns.

In Section 6.5, we look closer into the anatomy of message implementation, and we discuss SOAP and XML Protocol as practical examples. In Section 6.6, we discuss both the classical ACID transactions and the newer, process-oriented, long-living transactions and how those transactions concepts can be applied to Web services. Security issues are covered in Section 6.8. This includes a discussion of two security-related standards: XML Signature and XML Encryption.

241

6.1 HISTORY

McCarthy's CBCL   As early as 1975 John McCarthy proposed a Common Business Communication Language (CBCL) (McCarthy 1999). As McCarthy observed, "Developing an expressive Common Business Communication Language has proved unexpectedly difficult." The problem is not so much the syntax but that the problem is open-ended. You cannot stop at some stage and claim that all aspects are covered. For each business rule that is covered by the model, it is easy to find a more complicated business rule that is not yet covered. Just take the following rules describing shipment orders as an example:

1. Ship by express mail.
2. Ship by standard mail, but insure the parcel up to a value of $1,000.
3. Ship by truck, provided the truck is air-conditioned.
4. Ship by integrated rail/truck door-to-door service, provided the refrigeration chain is not interrupted for longer than 90 minutes. Request printed temperature protocol from pickup to delivery.
5. And so on.

We can see the problem. What would be required to cover all possible cases is a language with the expressive power of natural language. Natural language, however, is awkward to process with computers.

McCarthy solved the problem by devising an extensible business language based on a language popular for building artificial intelligence applications: LISP. In CBCL the shipment orders could look like this:

```
(shipment (carrier mail) (method express))
```

```
(shipment (carrier mail) (method standard) (insurance
(insured sum 1000)))
```

and so on.

LISP vs. XML   We can easily translate these rules into XML. Each list head makes a tag, and nested lists make child elements:

```
<shipment>
    <carrier> mail </carrier>
    <method> express </method>
</shipment>

<shipment>
    <carrier> mail </carrier>
    <method> standard </method>
```

```
<insurance>
<insured_sum> 1000 </insured_sum>
</insurance>
</shipment>
```

and so on.

People trained in LISP will like the CBCL format better because it is more compact. However, we find that XML makes it easier to determine the end of each structure: there is no need to count parentheses. A document standard such as XML was needed to bring John McCarthy's idea of an extensible business communication language to widespread adoption. No wonder: exchanging documents is at the core of all business communication.

6.2 LAYERS OF COMMUNICATION

The classical process model as it is used in enterprise application integration (EAI) and workflow applications is not really applicable in an open electronic business scenario. These process models are described in terms of *state transition diagrams, Petri nets,* and *message sequence charts* (such as *activity diagrams* in UML). These techniques are well suited to the closed world of enterprise business processes and workflows and for "closed world" long-term business relationships as we find them in typical EDI partnerships.

The situation in electronic business, however, is different. Electronic business processes typically cross the boundaries of companies and long-term partnerships. Especially with smaller businesses (and for larger corporations that use the concept of autonomous work groups), there is a high degree of autonomy between the business partners. Collaborations frequently change and often are mediated through a market mechanism. For example, a manufacturer who wants to ship certain items to a customer will not use a single shipper but will dynamically select a shipper according to price, availability, quality, and so on. In some cases it may be necessary to use alternative services, for example, when the pilots are on strike or the rivers are flooded. In these cases, the manufacturer must be able to quickly align his or her own business processes with those of a temporarily selected shipper.

Temporary partnerships

Traditional modeling techniques such as state transition tables or Petri nets have problems with this kind of required flexibility. Early experiences with the application of these techniques to electronic business scenarios have led to the conclusion that the models become too complex when we want to cover each possible exception and contingency.

New methods required

Researchers have therefore looked into ways to make the traditional process model more flexible or to use alternative methods to describe open processes. In the previous chapter, we looked at Milner's π-calculus as one possibility. In this chapter we will take a close look at the *speech act theory* (SAT) and communication patterns, so-called protocols, which are a basis for modeling transactions and access to Web services in electronic business. In later chapters we will see that some recent technologies such as ebXML and RosettaNet are based on similar principles.

Layered metamodel

These concepts follow a layered metamodel, as in Figure 6.1 (Weigand, van den Heuvel, and Dignum 1998):

- *Messages* are the most elementary part of such an architecture. A message can be a simple signal, such as an acknowledgment, or it can be quite complex, containing one or several business documents. A message may relate to its operational context (i.e., the transaction that it is a part of).
- *Transactions* are composed of messages (or other transactions). That means that transactions can be nested, allowing the construction of complex transactions from simple transactions. A transaction is considered as a logical unit of work that transforms the states of the participating systems from one valid state to another valid state. In the simplest case a transaction consists of two messages, a request and a re-

Figure 6.1 Layered communication architecture in electronic business.

sponse. Transactions can be classical ACID transactions or long-running transactions (see Section 6.6.2). Transactions occur in the context of a business process or a business service.

- *Business services* implement generic business processes such as services for funds transfer, credit card validation, invoicing, or remittance.
- *Business processes* orchestrate transactions into an organic process. In their simplest form, business processes involve just two partners, but business processes involving more than two partners can be constructed by composing several simple business processes. Business processes occur in the context of a business contract.
- A *business contract* is negotiated between the partners involved in a prospective business process. The contract determines the concrete form of the business process and defines the rights and responsibilities of each partner within the business process. The partners also agree on shared vocabularies (or ontologies), or on how to mediate between different ontologies.

  Business contracts are usually legally binding. A business contract is negotiated in the context of a business scenario.
- *Business scenarios* describe the context in which contracts are negotiated and business processes take place. These descriptions include partner profiles, describing the capabilities of each partner (technical capabilities, supported message protocols, and so on). They also describe common context information, such as the national and cultural environment. Additionally business scenarios describe the interrelationship among several business contracts that are in effect simultaneously.

6.3 CHANNELS AND PORTS

Channels organize the communication between end points, so-called ports. Messages are interchanged between these end points through the channels. A partner within a business process must own at least one port; otherwise it will not be able to communicate and take part in the process. Channels that organize the communication between exactly two end points are 1:1; channels that organize the communication from a single end point to multiple end points (multicast) are 1:m. Often 1:m channels are implemented using a fire-and-forget strategy; that is, the sender does not expect an acknowledgment from the receiver (typical broadcast situation).

Channel
parameters

The type of channel is defined by the *protocol*—the valid sequences of messages between the partners. There are additional parameters that can characterize a channel:

- *Binding:* The transport method used. Popular choices to transport messages are HTTP, SMTP, and FTP.
- *Reliability:* A channel can be implemented as a persistent channel; that is, it guarantees the delivery of a message once the message has been accepted. This requires more overhead since the channel must implement a persistent message store, where messages can survive a system crash.

   An alternative solution is to use a nonpersistent channel. In this case it is preferable that the sender receives an acknowledgment when the message has been delivered. This may happen immediately or lazily (i.e., the acknowledgment is returned in a bundle with some other traffic that travels in the opposite direction). In this case it might happen that a message is sent twice (when the system is restarted after a crash). Either the channel or the receiver should therefore display idempotent behavior (i.e., discard duplicate messages).
- *Synchronicity:* A channel may act synchronously or asynchronously. To receive a message synchronously, the client has to request a message. It then has to wait for the message (or to poll for it). A client who wants to receive messages asynchronously has to register with the channel and is notified when a message arrives.
- *Security:* A channel may encrypt messages to transport them safely and enforce digital signature technology to ensure that no unsolicited messages are sent.
- *Scalability:* Channels may open alternative routes in case of heavy traffic. Some channels may have a higher priority than other channels or may give certain messages a higher priority than other messages.

6.4 SPEECH ACTS

Speech act theory (SAT) goes back to John L. Austin's *How to Do Things with Words* (Austin 1975). Austin postulated that language statements not only transport a meaning but also accomplish something; that is, an issued statement has a practical purpose. It is that purpose that defines the *illocutionary force*[1] of a message. Messages can thus be categorized

---

[1]The illocutionary force of an utterance is the speaker's intention in producing that utterance.

according to their illocutionary force (Moore 1996). The following categories are defined: advise, ascribe, assent, assert, concede, confirm, deny, describe, dispute, dissent, inform, offer, permit, predict, prohibit, promise, question, report, request, require, retract.

Scott A. Moore and Steven O. Kimbrough have defined a set of formal languages for business communication (FLBCs) on the basis of these message categories. Examples of the application of these FLBCs in message management systems are found in Kimbrough and Moore (1994). (The paper also contains a lovely example of supply chain management in a bicycle shop.) Only recently an XML DTD has been published for the formal definition of these FLBCs through XML. Here is a short example of a question expressed in FLBC:

FLBCs

```
<flbcMsg>
  <simpleAct id="ask-if" speaker="me" hearer="you">
    <illocAct force="question">
      <!- content of question goes here ->
    </illocAct>
  </simpleAct>
  <context>
    <resources>
      <actors>
        <person id="me"/>
        <person id="you"/>
      </actors>
    </resources>
  </context>
</flbcMsg>
```

For our requirements the following five basic categories (Dignum 2000) seem to be sufficient:

Basic categories

- *ASSERT:* Messages of this type inform the receiver about a given fact. They do not require immediate action from the receiver. The receiver is free to believe the message or to ignore it. For example: "The authors of The XML-Handbook are Charles F. Goldfarb and Paul Prescod." ASSERT messages also include simple acknowledgments like "Your message has arrived."
- *OFFER:* Offers (or proposals) invite the receiver to request something or to commit to something (see DIRECT and COMMIT). For example: "Buy this book before next Saturday and get 15% off."
- *DIRECT:* This message type is used to transmit orders or requests to the receiver. This usually results in an obligation for the receiver that the

receiver may choose to follow or not. For example: "Show me all books about XML."

- *COMMIT:* The COMMIT message type is used to create obligations for the sender itself; that is, the sender commits itself to do something. COMMIT messages often follow the reception of a DIRECT request. For example: "We will deliver within three days."
- *DECLARE:* This message type is used to create new facts. For example, it may be used to equip the receiver with certain access rights. This message type is mostly used during the negotiation phase and is hardly used in later stages of the communication. For example: "You have full access to all of my accounts."

Message
patterns

By categorizing messages into such classes, we are able to construct metapatterns of possible transactions. An example of such a metapattern could be:

1. Party A sends a request to Party B.
2. Party B sends an acknowledgment to Party A, to acknowledge the reception of the message.
3. Party B sends a commitment to Party A, to indicate that it is willing to process the request.
4. Party A sends an acknowledgment to Party B to indicate that it has received the commitment.

Such a transaction could be described as a DIRECT-ASSERT-COMMIT-ASSERT pattern. The pattern also defines an abstract protocol for both partners. Software instances could be created that are able to handle these abstract protocols. These software instances can then be reused whenever such a communication pattern occurs—the abstract message categories are simply instantiated with concrete message types.

6.5 MESSAGES

In this section, we further investigate the anatomy of messages and how this anatomy is covered by messaging specifications such as SOAP.

6.5.1 Simple and Complex Messages

A message typically wraps a business document or a set of business documents plus attachments into an envelope. The envelope is responsible for security; it can provide encryption and digital signatures (see Section 6.8).

A special class of messages is *signals*—messages that do not carry a pay-   Signals
load of documents but are simply used to trigger an event in the receiving
process. Such signals are typically used to acknowledge the reception of a
message or to inform about an exception.

A message can contain additional metainformation in the *message*   Message header
header describing the documents, their current state, and processing instructions for the documents.

The message header may contain the following information:

* The encoding used for the message
* Supported XML namespaces
* Source and destination of the message
* An identity pointer to identify the message uniquely, for example, a
  UUID or a URI
* Date and time when the message was sent
* Date and time when the message expires
* A pointer to the context where the message is valid, such as a business
  process instance, a contract, or a scenario
* Pointers to vocabularies used in documents and attachments
* A description element, describing the topic of the message
* A manifest, listing the documents and attachments contained in the
  message
* A flag indicating if it is required to acknowledge the reception of the
  message
* A flag indicating if it is required to acknowledge the positive commit-
  ment to process the message

Concrete specifications of messaging architectures are described in Sections 6.5.2 (SOAP), 10.3 (ebXML), and 11.3.3 (BizTalk).

6.5.2 SOAP

SOAP (Simple Object Access Protocol) started as a Microsoft initiative (in
collaboration with UserLand Software and DevelopMentor) to use XML
for remote method calls as a serialized transport format between distributed objects.

SOAP has its roots in XML-RPC (XML-RPC 1999). RPC stands for   XML-RPC
"remote procedure call." XML-RPC addressed a problem existing in heterogeneous environments. Distributed component systems use remote
procedure calls to invoke a method in a remote object. The calling object
has to transmit parameters to the called method. And, vice versa, results
must be returned to the caller. Since both parameters and results can be

arbitrarily complex objects, it is necessary to convert them into a byte-stream in order to transmit them over the wire. This process is called *serialization* in Java and *marshalling* in DCOM and CORBA. As you can guess from the different names, the different component systems use different serialization formats, too. To call a CORBA method from DCOM, for example, extra "bridge" software is necessary. This software translates between the two serialization formats. XML-RPC solves this problem by providing a single serialization format: XML. Thus XML-RPC makes it possible for CORBA objects to directly interoperate with DCOM or Java, and so on.

SOAP vs. XML-RPC

SOAP evolved directly from XML-RPC. UserLand, which signed for XML-RPC, was also involved in the development of SOAP. One key difference from XML-RPC is how method parameters are identified. XML-RPC represents parameters without parameter names—parameters are identified by position. SOAP represents parameters with their names, so sequence does not matter. This is the better choice because it is easier to identify parameters. It is also more XML-like.

Message composition

In addition to the serialization issue, SOAP also addresses the issue of message composition. A typical SOAP message consists of an envelope, optional headers, and the message body.

The envelope defines the namespaces and encoding used in the message. Here is an example from the SOAP 1.1 specification. It starts with the usual HTTP header, indicating a POST operation and declaring the content as "text/xml":

```
POST /StockQuote HTTP/1.1
Host: www.stockquoteserver.com
Content-Type: text/xml; charset="utf-8"
Content-Length: nnnn
SOAPAction: "Some-URI"
<SOAP-ENV:Envelope xmlns:SOAP-ENV=
          "http://schemas.xmlsoap.org/soap/envelope/"
        SOAP-ENV:encodingStyle=
          "http://schemas.xmlsoap.org/soap/encoding/">
...
</SOAP-ENV:Envelope>
```

Multiple headers are allowed in SOAP messages. Each header describes a certain aspect of the message such as quality of service, security, or transactional behavior. Here is a hypothetical header to define transactional behavior (currently not supported in SOAP):

```
<SOAP-ENV:Header>
  <t:Transaction xmlns:t="some-namespace-for-transactions"
                 SOAP-ENV:mustUnderstand="1">
    5
  </t:Transaction>
</SOAP-ENV:Header>
```

The body carries the payload of the message—the serialized parameters of the action (or method) invoked (a complete example will come later).

SOAP is not a high-speed communication method: the use of both **SOAP adoption** HTTP and XML takes its toll in terms of performance. Instead, SOAP addresses the need for a loosely coupled transport protocol that can work across company boundaries and between different component models. In the beginning, SOAP was somewhat COM centric; however, with version 1.1, SOAP is now neutral to component models and transfer protocols. Many other manufacturers (Ariba, CommerceOne, Compaq, HP, Iona, IBM, Lotus, SAP, Sun Microsystems) have joined the SOAP opera, and in the meantime SOAP has become a de facto standard. The Apache organization, for example, has adopted the IBM SOAP4J implementation as the basis of an open source reference implementation. Using SOAP, component-oriented platforms such as DCOM, CORBA, and Enterprise Java Beans can interoperate with each other through HTTP, SMTP, POP3, or FTP. Because of the use of HTTP, SOAP gets around firewall problems. (However, administrators can configure firewalls not to accept SOAP messages.) The purpose of SOAP is described in Box et al. (2000) as the following:

> SOAP is a lightweight protocol for exchange of information in a decentralized, distributed environment. It is an XML based protocol that consists of three parts: an envelope that defines a framework for describing what is in a message and how to process it, a set of encoding rules for expressing instances of application-defined datatypes, and a convention for representing remote procedure calls and responses.

SOAP is used as a transport protocol in XML-based standards for electronic business such as BizTalk and ebXML.

The following example shows a typical SOAP request/response datastream using HTTP as the transfer protocol (SOAP can use other protocols, too):

```
POST /Validation HTTP/1.1 Host: www.cardservice.com
  Content-Type: text/xml; charset="utf-8"
  Content-Length: nnnn
```

```
SOAPAction: "CardValidation-URI"
<SOAP-ENV:Envelope
  xmlns:SOAP-ENV="http://schemas.xmlsoap.org/soap/envelope/"
  SOAP-ENV:encodingStyle=
            "http://schemas.xmlsoap.org/soap/encoding/">
  <SOAP-ENV:Body>

    <m:ValidateCard xmlns:m="CardValidation-URI">
      <RetailerID>393837</RetailerID>
      <TransactionNo>907</TransactionNo>
      <CreditcardNo>4578987898990</CreditcardNo>
      <ValidUntil>06/04</ValidUntil>
      <Currency>USD</Currency>
      <Amount>99.95</Amount>
    </m:ValidateCard>

  </SOAP-ENV:Body>
</SOAP-ENV:Envelope>
```

The SOAP body indicates that method `ValidateCard` in namespace `CardValidation-URI` within www.cardservice.com/validation should be invoked. The application at www.cardservice.com/validation can be any type of Web service, such as a CGI script or a servlet. After execution of the invoked method, the results are returned via a SOAP response message:

```
HTTP/1.1 200 OK
 Content-Type: text/xml; charset="utf-8"
 Content-Length: nnnn
 <SOAP-ENV:Envelope
  xmlns:SOAP-ENV="http://schemas.xmlsoap.org/soap/envelope/"
  SOAP-ENV:encodingStyle=
               "http://schemas.xmlsoap.org/soap/encoding/"/>
 <SOAP-ENV:Body>
   <m:ValidateCardResponse xmlns:m="CardValidation-URI">
     <TransactionNo>907</TransactionNo>
   </m:ValidateCardResponse>
  </SOAP-ENV:Body>
</SOAP-ENV:Envelope>
```

Features   SOAP supports all the built-in datatypes defined in XML Schema plus a number of complex datatypes such as variants and unions, structures ("struct"), records, and arrays including multiple and nested arrays. All data is passed by value, not by reference. Apart from defining standards for message envelopes, message encoding, and remote procedure calls, SOAP does not cover other transport aspects, such as schema-based message validation, object creation and destruction, bidirectional synchronous communication, distributed transactions, persistent messaging, or recovery from exceptions. These tasks are left to higher-level standards such as BizTalk or ebXML.

6.5.3 XML Protocol (SOAP 1.2)

SOAP is a de facto industry standard. It is not a W3C recommendation yet, but it has been submitted to the W3C for consideration. This has resulted in a new W3C activity called XML Protocol (XMLP) (Williams and Jones 2001). The XMLP activity was inspired by SOAP but includes more advanced features and will eventually be the successor of SOAP. It now has been named SOAP 1.2.

Most important, XMLP is not an end-to-end protocol. Inspired by the definition of SOAP-RP (Nielsen and Thatte 2001), it allows one or several intermediaries to forward a message. Intermediaries can remove blocks from a message and add new blocks to it (i.e., a modified block is a new block). This allows a kind of pipelined communication structure where a message can pass through several processing stages—an interesting approach to establishing collaboration between various Web services.

Pipelined messages

6.6 TRANSACTIONS AND PROTOCOLS

The classical notion of a transaction is connected to the OLTP world. First restricted to single database management systems, the classical ACID transaction concept has subsequently been extended to distributed databases and to other transactional services such as transactional *message-oriented middleware* (MoM). Applications access these resources by means of interfaces as defined by the XA (Transaction Authority) standard (e.g., the Java Transaction API, JTA). XA is a popular standard protocol to orchestrate ACID transactions over distributed databases.

6.6.1 ACID Transactions

ACID is an acronym for the four primary attributes ensured to any OLTP database transaction:

Definition of ACID

- *Atomicity:* A transaction cannot be divided into smaller parts. Either all or none of the data elements involved in a transaction are committed to a transaction.

- *Consistency:* A transaction leads to a new and valid state. In case of a failure, the transaction is reset to the previous valid state.
- *Isolation:* A pending transaction must remain isolated from any other transaction.
- *Durability:* Once data has been committed it must stay—regardless of system failures or restart—in its committed state.

A COMMIT is the last step in a successful database transaction. ROLLBACK is used to abandon the current transaction and return the resources involved in the transaction to their original state.

Two-phase commit

In distributed OLTP database systems, the ACID characteristics are achieved by means of the two-phase commit. In the first phase all partners involved in a transaction receive a signal "Prepare to commit." Each partner responds with a "Ready to commit." Only when all partners have signaled a "Ready to commit" is the final "Commit" issued.

XA

XA supports the two-phase commit by introducing the concept of resource managers and transaction managers. The transaction manager is responsible for controlling the distributed transaction and coordinating the resource managers involved in the transaction. Resource managers are usually databases but can also be other transactional services, for example, a MoM server. Resource managers can be heterogeneous—systems from several manufacturers can engage in one distributed transaction.

6.6.2 Transactional Web Services

New requirements

However, for orchestrating Web services, the classical two-phase commit is too strict. The classical two-phase commit requires resource managers to lock the resources involved in a transaction during its whole duration, from the beginning of the transaction until the final commit. With Web services this could take a long time. Remember that a Web service may encapsulate other business processes and even human activity. Locking resources for such a long time would lead to Web services that perform badly when traffic increases.

On the other hand, when resources are not locked, they cannot be rolled back if the transaction fails. Another—competing—transaction may have changed a resource in the meantime. When the resource is reset to its original status, the changes made by the second transaction are lost.

Take for example a credit card validation service. In transaction A, the credit card service is asked to charge $400 against the customer's credit card account. Now, while transaction A is still pending, another transaction B charges $300 against the same account and commits. Then transaction A fails. Because it fails, everything must be set back to the original state (rollback). The consequence is that the charge of $300 from transaction B is lost. This is clearly unacceptable, and this is why OLTP databases lock their resources during a transaction.

The solution for non-OLTP environments such as electronic business or Web services lies in the introduction of compensating actions. When transaction A fails, it will not physically roll back all resources involved in a transaction but will trigger compensating actions. In our case it will credit $400 to the account, thus compensating the previous $400 debit.

Long-running transactions

Because these compensating actions work on a semantic level, they require additional development effort. The programmer cannot just rely on the rollback mechanisms of the resource managers but has to implement compensating actions.

Typically, long-running transactions are integrated into orchestration services (see, for example, the BizTalk orchestration services discussed in Section 11.3.3). To support long-running transactions, providers of transactional Web services are therefore required to offer for each transactional Web request type a corresponding request type for a compensation action.

6.6.3 The Web Services Description Language (WSDL)

The interface to a service (transactional or not) is described by a certain sequence of messages (for example, following a pattern as discussed in Section 6.3) and the format of these messages (i.e., a protocol). Usually such a protocol is defined for a given port, and each Web service can possess several ports; that is, it is able to support several protocols. Such protocols can be defined with the Web Services Description Language (WSDL).

The Web Services Description Language, a proposal to the W3C (Christensen et al. 2001), is a joint initiative of Ariba, IBM, and Microsoft. The same collaborators also started an initiative for the definition of UDDI (see Section 7.3), which complements WSDL in that it specifies the registration and discovery of Web services. Other companies joined the initiative, including Hewlett-Packard, which—after some political quarrels—opted to integrate its own development, e-speak, with WSDL and UDDI.

Politics

WSDL describes "Web services" in an abstract way. A *Web service* is defined as a collection of end points (or *ports*) capable of performing operations and exchanging messages. WSDL covers only synchronous operations.

The abstract definition of each end point can then be bound to a concrete communication protocol. The necessary binding mechanism is defined in WSDL, too. Special predefined bindings currently exist in SOAP, HTTP GET/POST, and MIME.

A port thus establishes a binding between a sequence of operations and a concrete message protocol and format. Because a Web service can incorporate several ports, it can accept several message sequences (and perform operations on them) and can communicate using several message protocols.

Elements
of a WSDL
description
A WSDL description consists of five major elements:

1. `<wsdl:types>`
2. `<wsdl:message name=...>`
3. `<wsdl:portType name=...>`
4. `<wsdl:binding name=... type=...>`
5. `<wsdl:service name=...>`

`<wsdl:types>` contains the datatype definitions that are used to describe the messages exchanged between the ports. WSDL does not introduce its own type system but uses the XML Schema type system (see also Chapter 2). XML Schema expressions are directly embedded between `<schema>` ... `</schema>` tags in the form of `<element name=...>` elements. Each element occurrence defines one type.

`<wsdl:message name=...>` represents an abstract definition of the data being transmitted. Each message consists of one or multiple parts, and each part definition refers to a type definition (see above). This allows us to compose a message from several type definitions (i.e., one message can transport several business documents). There may be several `<wsdl:message>` definitions.

Each `portType` contains one or several `<wsdl:operation name=...>` elements. These define abstract operations. Each operation element may contain `<wsdl:input name=... message=...>` and `<wsdl:output name=... message=...>` elements that refer to input and output messages.

Additionally, an operation element also may contain a `<wsdl:fault name=... message=.../>` element for error messages.

Operation types
There are four different operation types:

- *One-way:* The end point receives a message. `portType` contains only an `input` element.
- *Request-response:* The end point receives a message and sends a correlated message. `portType` contains a sequence of `input`, `output`, and `fault` message elements.

- *Solicit-response:* The end point sends a message and receives a correlated message. `portType` contains a sequence of `output`, `input`, and `fault` message elements.
- *Notification:* The end point sends a message. `portType` contains only an `output` element.

`<wsdl:binding name=... type=...>` describes to which concrete protocol and data formats the operations and messages of a particular `portType` are bound. (The attribute `type` refers to a specific `portType`.) Child elements map each abstract operation and its input and output messages to concrete operations and data formats.

The mapping of abstract input and output messages to concrete messages involves the transformation of messages if both message formats differ. Thus, clients are not required to use the concrete message format of the Web service.

`<wsdl:service name=...>` describes a complete service. Each `service` element can contain one or several `<wsdl:port name=... binding=...>` elements. Each of these `port` elements represents a communication end point and refers to a specific binding element. Additionally, it specifies the network address of the end point.

Here is an example of a WSDL Web service description, based on Christensen et al. (2001):

```
<?xml version="1.0"?>
<definitions name="StockQuote"

targetNamespace="http://example.com/stockquote.wsdl"
        xmlns:sqw="http://example.com/stockquote.wsdl"
        xmlns:sqt="http://example.com/stockquote.xsd"
        xmlns:soap="http://schemas.xmlsoap.org/wsdl/soap/"
        xmlns="http://schemas.xmlsoap.org/wsdl/">

    <types>
      <schema
        targetNamespace="http://example.com/stockquote.xsd"
        xmlns="http://www.w3.org/2000/10/XMLSchema">
        <element name="TradePriceRequest">
          <complexType>
            <sequence>
              <element name="tickerSymbol" type="string"/>
            </sequence>
          </complexType>
```

```
          </element>
       <element name="TradePrice">
        <complexType>
         <sequence>
            <element name="price" type="float"/>
         </sequence>
        </complexType>
       </element>
     </schema>
  </types>

  <message name="GetLastTradePriceInput">
    <part name="body" element="sqt:TradePriceRequest"/>
   </message>

  <message name="GetLastTradePriceOutput">
    <part name="body" element="sqt:TradePrice"/>
  </message>

  <portType name="StockQuotePortType">
    <operation name="GetLastTradePrice">
      <input message="sqw:GetLastTradePriceInput"/>
      <output message="sqw:GetLastTradePriceOutput"/>
    </operation>
  </portType>

  <binding name="StockQuoteSoapBinding"
           type="sqw:StockQuotePortType">
    <soap:binding style="document"
        transport="http://schemas.xmlsoap.org/soap/http"/>
    <operation name="GetLastTradePrice">
    <soap:operation
        soapAction="http://example.com/GetLastTradePrice"/>
      <input>
        <soap:body use="literal"/>
      </input>
      <output>
        <soap:body use="literal"/>
      </output>
    </operation>
  </binding>
```

```
<service name="StockQuoteService">
  <documentation>My fiirst service</documentation>
  <port name="StockQuotePort"
        binding="sqw:StockQuoteBinding">
    <soap:address location="http://example.com/stockquote"/>
  </port>
</service>

</definitions>
```

This WSDL example first defines two complex XML datatypes, Trade-PriceRequest and TradePrice, using XML Schema as the specification language. It then defines two message types, GetLastTradePriceInput and GetLastTradePriceOutput, that use these datatypes for the definition of their respective message bodies. Next it defines a port type named Stock-QuotePortType. This port supports one operation, GetLastTradePrice, which takes GetLastTradePriceInput as the input message and GetLast-TradePriceOutput as the output message. The next section then describes SOAP as the transport service for the operation GetLastTradePrice. The last section describes the whole service, StockQuoteService, by listing its operations with their bindings.

At present, WSDL can describe Web services only in a static way. There   Limitations
is no way to describe how the operations can be orchestrated into a business process or workflow. This is left to future versions of WSDL.

6.7 SEMANTICS OF COMMUNICATION

The semantics of a message not only matters to the source and the target of a message, that is, the sender and the receiver. In many cases it will also be necessary that the content of a message be interpreted by the channel, too, in order to provide services such as ontology mapping and content-based routing.

6.7.1 Content-Based Routing

In many cases it is necessary to change the route and even the destination of a message based on content. For example, a customer might send an order to a company but not know which department handles the specific order. An intelligent router can look at the message, apply business rules to determine the receiving department, and change the destination address accordingly.

6.7.2 Ontology Mapping

When the two partners do not share an ontology, they have to use a *mediation process* to translate the message from one ontology into another. In the simplest case this is a translation of vocabularies or taxonomies, but it can amount to more complex transformations in document structure. This is a typical job for an XSLT style sheet (see Chapter 9). Carlson (2001) has an example of an XSLT style sheet that translates from a RosettaNet ITTD taxonomy to the CatML taxonomy.

However, the naive approach of direct translation from one ontology into another usually causes havoc—the number of transformations simply explodes with an increasing number of ontologies. A more sophisticated approach lies in the definition of a generic pivot ontology that can cover a wide range of existing ontologies. Messages that must be translated from ontology A into ontology B are translated in two steps: first from ontology A into the pivot ontology, then from the pivot ontology into ontology B.

6.8 SECURITY

Security is an important aspect of communication. On the Internet a whole arsenal of security techniques has been developed over the years.

Physical level

On the physical level, Secure Socket Layers (SLL) allows safe communication between communication end points. However, it solves only part of the problem: what happens before or after the end points is not protected by SSL.

Application level

Seamless security can only be achieved by applying security techniques on the application level. Popular methods for achieving security on the application level are Pretty Good Privacy (PGP) and Secure MIME (S/MIME). However, both methods require that applications support these methods. Also, both methods can only encrypt either a whole document or nothing. This is not always required and not always wanted: a document may contain parts that must be readable to the public, and other parts that must be kept confidential.

In early 1999 the W3C began with the definition for a security architecture for XML. We will see that this architecture can provide flexible security not only to XML documents but also to all objects that can be addressed through a URI.

6.8.1 Basics

A security architecture is based on the following security services:

- *Confidentiality:* A confidential document should not be read by un-authorized persons. This can be ensured by encrypting the data.
- *Integrity:* Integrity means that the unauthorized modification of data can be detected. Integrity can be ensured by computing message digests (see below).
- *Authentication:* Authentication ensures the origin of data or the identity of communication partners. Data origin authentication is achieved by computing digital signatures and message authentication codes (MACs). These are message digests that can only be computed and checked with a secret key.
- *Nonrepudiation:* Nonrepudiation combines data integrity with data origin authentication, so that the sender of the data cannot repudiate modifications that he or she applied to the data, for example, digitally signing the data. This makes legally binding digital contracts possible.

The technologies to implement these services are well known:

- *Symmetric encryption keys:* This encryption method uses the same key for encryption and decryption. This encryption method is fast, but, because sender and receiver must possess the same key, the transmission of the key poses a security risk. Keys with a length of at least 128 bits are considered safe. Examples are AES (128–256 bits), Blowfish (64–448 bits), and Twofish (128–256 bits).
- *Asymmetric keys:* These keys always come in pairs: a public key is used by the sender to encrypt the message, and a private key (which must be kept secret) is used by the receiver to decrypt the message. Examples of such keys are RSA (Rivest-Shamir-Adleman) and ECC. The advantage of asymmetric keys is that they do not involve an insecure step (exchange of keys) and don't require much management. However, the algorithms used are very slow.
- *Hybrid keys:* This technique involves a pair of asymmetric keys and a symmetric key. As a first step, sender and receiver exchange the symmetric key but encrypt this exchange with the asymmetric key. The following communication can then be safely encrypted with the symmetric key.
- *Message digests:* Message digest algorithms are used to compute a hash value from data that must be protected against tampering. The

algorithms used are fast and guarantee that any change in the message content will cause a significant change in the hash value. To be safe the minimum length of hash values is 160 bits. Popular algorithms to compute hash values are MD5 (but already classified as unsafe), SHA-1 (Secure Hash Algorithm, Revision 1), and RIPEMD160 (RACE Integrity Primitives Evaluation Message Digest).

- *Digital signatures:* Digital signatures use an asymmetric technique to generate a signature from the content of the signed document. The signer uses a private key to generate the signature value, while the reader uses a public key to check the validity of the signature. Again, because asymmetric algorithms are slow, hybrid techniques are used. First, a message digest is computed from the document content; then the digest value is protected by the asymmetric key. Popular methods for digital signatures are DSA (Digital Signature Algorithm) and RSA.

- *Certificates:* The problem with public keys is that a third party may intercept the publication of a public key and replace it with its own public key. Thereafter it could read any messages encrypted with that public key. This problem is solved by certifying public keys. A certification authority (CA) certifies public keys by embedding them into a certificate. A sender that wants to use the public key of the message receiver can ask for a certificate containing this public key. To check the authenticity of the certificate, the sender can validate it against the public key of the CA. Public keys of CAs are hard-coded into client software such as Web browsers or signature programs.

6.8.2 XML Security

The XML security architecture is based on cryptography methods such as DSA and RSA. In the next two subsections we will discuss the two standards, XML Signature and XML Encryption, that deal with cryptography. Based on these two standards are security architecture components such as the following:

- The Security Assertion Markup Language (SAML) is used for the safe exchange of user privileges.
- The XML Access Control Language (XACML) allows the definition of access rights to XML data.
- XML Key Management Services (XKMS) provides an XML interface to public key infrastructures.

6.8.3 XML Signature

XML Signature describes the syntax and processing model of XML-based signatures and has the status of a W3C proposed recommendation (Eastlake, Reagle, and Solo 2001). XML Signature allows the digital signature of any kind of Web objects including XML objects. In contrast to existing systems like S/MIME, XML Signature can sign not only a single object but also multiple objects. Also new is the possibility of embedding a signature into objects. XML Signature uses a distributed concept by allowing the reference of signed objects, signature algorithms, and transformation algorithms through URIs.

When signing XML documents or elements, signature algorithms use the character representation of the document or element to compute the signature. This creates a problem: since the same XML information set may have different character representations, this would result in different signatures for the same content. XML Signature therefore allows the transformation of an XML document or element into a canonical form before computing the signature.

There are three signature flavors in XML Signature:

- *Enveloping signature:* An enveloping signature wraps the signed content. The signature element contains the signed content element as a child element.
- *Detached signature:* The signature refers to a remote content element (within the same document or in another document).
- *Enveloped signature:* The content element contains the signature element as a child element.

Signature flavors

The following example shows a simple detached signature:

```
<Signature Id="MyFirstSignature"
        xmlns="http://www.w3.org/2000/09/xmldsig#">
  <SignedInfo>
    <CanonicalizationMethod Algorithm=
       "http://www.w3.org/TR/2001/REC-xml-c14n-20010315"/>
    <SignatureMethod Algorithm=
       "http://www.w3.org/2000/09/xmldsig#dsa-sha1"/>
    <Reference
       URI="http://www.w3.org/TR/2000/REC-xhtml1-20000126/">
      <Transforms>
        <Transform Algorithm=
```

```
            "http://www.w3.org/TR/2001/REC-xml-c14n-20010315"/>
        </Transforms>
        <DigestMethod Algorithm=
            "http://www.w3.org/2000/09/xmldsig#sha1"/>
        <DigestValue>j6lwx3rvEPOOvKtMup4NbeVu8nk=</DigestValue>
      </Reference>
    </SignedInfo>
    <SignatureValue>MCOCFFrVLtRlk=...</SignatureValue>
     <KeyInfo>
       <KeyValue>
        <DSAKeyValue>
          <P>...</P><Q>...</Q><G>...</G><Y>...</Y>
        </DSAKeyValue>
       </KeyValue>
     </KeyInfo>
   </Signature>
```

The signature elements explained the following:

- The element Signature acts as a container element for the whole signature.
- The element SignedInfo acts as a container for the references to all signed objects.
- The element CanonicalizationMethod points to the algorithm used to transform the SignedInfo element into canonical form before it is digested as part of the signature operation.
- The element SignatureMethod points to the algorithm that is used to convert the canonicalized SignedInfo into the signature value. This algorithm consists of a combination of the digest algorithm, a key-dependent algorithm, and other algorithms.
- The Reference elements point to the single signed objects. For each object, it is possible to define a transformation algorithm that is applied before the digest value is computed, the digest algorithm, and the digest value that signs the object.
- SignatureValue contains the computed signature for the SignedInfo element and thus secures the SignedInfo element against manipulation.
- The optional element KeyInfo contains information about certificates, public keys, or key identifiers.

6.8.4 XML Encryption

XML Encryption, currently a W3C working draft, defines how arbitrary data can be represented in encrypted form in XML (Eastlake and Reagle 2001). The standard addresses the following encryption targets:

- Arbitrary binary data
- Complete XML documents
- XML elements including start and end tags
- Element content

Here is an example of the encryption of XML element content:

```
<?xml version='1.0'?>
<PaymentInfo xmlns='http://example.org/paymentv2'>
  <Name>John Smith</Name>
  <CreditCard Limit='5,000' Currency='USD'>
    <EncryptedData xmlns='http://www.w3.org/2001/04/xmlenc#'
    Type='http://www.w3.org/2001/04/xmlenc#Content'>
    <CipherData>
      <CipherValue>A23B45C56</CipherValue>
    </CipherData>
    </EncryptedData>
  </CreditCard>
</PaymentInfo>
```

The element `EncryptedData` is the result of an encryption process. The attribute `Type` shows that `EncryptedData` contains element content, not a whole element. Similarly, the element `EncryptedKey` (not shown here) is used to transport encryption keys to a communication partner as required with hybrid encryption methods.

The `CipherValue` element contains the encrypted content. If this value is not supplied directly, a `CipherReference` element may instead point (through a URI) to a resource containing the encrypted content.

Optionally, the `EncryptedData` element may contain an `EncryptionMethod` element to specify the encryption algorithm.

In addition to the definition of its own syntactical elements, XML Encryption utilizes the concepts and syntax of XML Signature to specify things such as transformations or key information.

Navigation and Discovery

The most characteristic navigation method for the World Wide Web is the hyperlink as supported by HTML. The XML specification, in contrast, does not define a navigation method. In Section 7.1 we first discuss XLink, a W3C recommendation that introduces powerful hyperlink techniques into the world of XML. A discussion of WebML completes this section. WebML is a modeling method that integrates a structural model, a navigational model, and a presentational model.

Concepts such as RDF and topic maps extend the hypertext metaphor to semantic navigation. RDF (see Section 3.3) was developed in order to describe Web resources, while topic maps had their first application in the area of knowledge bases and interactive encyclopedias. We will discuss topic maps in detail in Section 7.2.

Hypertext techniques are based on the signpost metaphor—the end user is led through the Web, link by link. This is not always sufficient, as the existence of search engines proves. Services that lie beyond the horizon cannot be seen by the surfer. In Section 7.3 we discuss UDDI, an XML-based language that supports the registration and discovery of Web services through public repositories.

Peer-to-peer technology relies on a different concept. Systems such as Gnutella or Freenet do not rely on signposts or central repositories but work by "word-of-mouth propaganda." To find certain information items, you simply ask your neighbors. They in turn ask their neighbors, and so on. We will discuss peer-to-peer technology in Section 7.4.

7.1 HYPERMEDIA

Originally, the World Wide Web was designed as a huge library. The protocol for the Web, `http:`, was designed for the collaborative authoring of documents. We have to remember that the Internet has its roots in the scientific sphere. The Internet was used directly by the end users (i.e., humans) for the authoring, exchange, and retrieval of documents and files. The main metaphor for the Web, the hyperlink, has its roots in scientific texts and encyclopedias; highly hyperlinked texts look very scientific indeed but can drive nonacademic users nuts. Hypertexts existed long before the Web, and even then the expression "lost in hyperspace" was popular.

Therefore, it is not wrong to look at the experience of the multimedia and hypermedia camp. XML applications—despite the origins of XML as a puritan document standard—can possess rich multimedia layers. There are already a couple of XML-based standards that make this possible: SVG and SMIL. Also, in terms of navigation, a lot can be learned from the sophisticated models developed in the hypermedia camp.

7.1.1 A Short History of Hypermedia

The history of hypertext dates back to 1945. In that year Vannevar Bush published an article, "As We May Think" (Bush 1945), that pushed the idea of associative indexing:

> It affords an immediate step, however, to associative indexing, the basic idea of which is a provision whereby any item may be caused at will to select immediately and automatically another.

The actual terms "hypertext" and "hypermedia" were coined by Ted Nelson in 1965, in an article published in *Literary Machines* (Nelson 1982):

By "hypertext" [we] mean nonsequential writing—text that branches and allows choice to the reader, best read at an interactive screen.

The first hypertext system was originally developed by van Dam for IBM in 1967. It was later used for project documentation in the Apollo space program. Other hypertext milestones include the following (Nielson 1997):

- 1968: NLS by Doug Engelbart (who also invented the mouse) at Stanford Research Institute
- 1978: The Aspen Movie Map by Andrew Lippman of MIT Architecture Machine Group
- 1981: The never-implemented Xanadu by Ted Nelson
- 1985: Xerox's NoteCards
- 1987: HyperCard by Bill Atkinson of Apple Computer

7.1.2 Hypermedia Navigation

Often, the logical relations that exist between information items in a conceptual model or a presentation-neutral XML implementation are misunderstood as navigation structures. Although these logic relations form the basis for navigation structures, they are not identical with them. The design of navigation structures must not only take logic into account, but also has to focus on themes such as user friendliness, perception, psychology, different usage patterns, and so on.

The following guidelines apply to almost any hypermedia system:　Guidelines

- *Pages must be self-sufficient.* They must explain a topic without requiring the user to jump between different pages. This can require a certain amount of repetition and redundancy between pages, a "no-no" in the conceptual model.
- *Pages must allow the discovery of related pages and navigation to them.* This often requires adding additional information to a page. Take for example the relationship between a purchase order and a customer document (see also Figure 3.15 in Section 3.2.3). Because the conceptual model requires only an arrow leading from the purchase order to the customer document, the reader of the customer page would not notice the existence of orders made by this customer. So, the customer page should inform the reader about purchase order pages pointing to this customer page. It should include hyperlinks that allow the reader to jump to these pages.

This requires a transformation from a presentation-neutral, structural content model to a navigational model and finally into a presentation format. Later in this section, we will discuss as an example WebML, an integrated system that does exactly that. But before we do this, let's take a close look at XLink, a W3C recommendation that allows the specification of hyperlinks in XML presentation formats.

Linking between Documents (XLink)

XLink specifies the syntax and semantics of links between and within XML documents. Links in XML can be compared to links in HTML that are specified using the HREF attribute. However, the functionality of XLink goes far beyond that of HTML (DeRose, Maler, and Orchard 2001).

A typical HTML link could look like the following:

```
<A HREF="http:www.bookshop.com/books/isbn0-8833-9898-4">
  The comic book
</A>
```

Simple links

XLink had to find another syntax for representing links. There is no <A> tag in XML—there aren't any predefined tags. Instead we want to be able to equip any XML element with link information. This is only possible if all link information is added in the form of attributes. A simple link in XLink—which has more or less the functionality of a link in HTML—looks like this:

```
<bs:catalogItem
  xmlns:bs="http:www.bookshop.com/books"
  xmlns:xlink="http://www.w3.org/1999/xlink"
  xlink:type="simple"
  xlink:href=
    "http:www.bookshop.com/books/isbn0-8833-9898-4"
>
  The comic book
</bs:catalogItem>
```

After specifying a user domain namespace prefix bs and an XLink namespace prefix xlink, the actual link information is given: the link type (always required) is set to "simple", and with href the location of the remote resource is specified.

Link ingredients

That doesn't look too different from HTML, and it does the same thing. Let's now take a closer look at the ingredients of a link:

- Each link establishes a working relationship between several *resources*. In the previous example, we have exactly two resources: the element that contains the link forms the *local* resource, and the target URI locates a *remote* resource. Remote resources can be any Web object, including non-XML objects such as images, sound files, video clips, and so on.

If we generalize this concept to *n:m* relationships, we get links that lead from *n* resources to *m* resources.

- The relation between any two resources can be represented by an arc. Within a relation each participating resource can take a specific role. An arc can also be associated with an `arcrole`, which is useful when there are several arcs pointing from or to a resource.

- When a link is *actuated*—usually when the user requests it—the current focus traverses from a "from" resource to a "to" resource. In a browser, for example, the new resource usually replaces the current resource in the browser window. However, it is also possible that the new resource is *shown* in a separate window or in another frame.

Let's look at another HTML example:

```
<IMG SRC="cover0-8833-9898-4.JPG" ALT="The comic book">
```

Although not a hyperlink, this element represents a link between two resources: the `<IMG>` element as a local resource and the JPEG file as a remote resource (see Figure 7.1). But there are a few things different from the previous example. First, the link is actuated not by a user request but when the containing Web page is loaded. The remote resource (the image) neither replaces the current window content nor is shown in a separate window. Instead, it is embedded into the current window content. Finally, this link is equipped with a title (the `ALT` attribute), which is shown as long as the remote resource is not loaded, or when the mouse hovers over an image.

Using XLink we could express such a behavior as

```
<bs:coverImage
  xmlns:bs="http:www.bookshop.com/books"
  xmlns:xlink="http://www.w3.org/1999/xlink"
  xlink:type="simple"
  xlink:href="cover0-8833-9898-4.JPG"
  xlink:actuate="onLoad"
  xlink:show="embed"
  xlink:title="The comic book"
/>
```

As we can see, XLink can cover the full linking functionality in HTML with simple links. Extended links go far beyond this functionality. In particular, they allow many-to-many links.

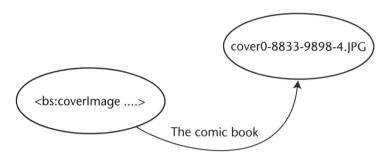

Figure 7.1 A simple link is a unidirectional connection between two resources.

Link properties

Let's first give an overview of possible link properties:

type	simple, extended, locator, arc, resource, title, none
href	Specifies the location of a remote resource via a URL
role	The specific role of a resource
arcrole	The specific role of an arc
title	The link title
show	new, replace, embed, other, none
actuate	onLoad, onRequest, other, none
label	Identifies a resource for link purposes
from	Specifies "from" resource via a label
to	Specifies "to" resource via a label

Extended links

The link types locator, arc, resource, title, and none are used for the further specification of extended links. But how can we apply them? xlink:type is an attribute, and in XML we aren't able to define properties for attributes. The problem is solved with a trick: An element with the xlink:type="extended" attribute is said to be an extended link element. This element is equipped with child elements, which in turn have attributes like xlink:type="locator" and so on.

```
<bs:bookAuthorLink
  xmlns:bs="http:www.bookshop.com/books"
  xmlns:xlink="http://www.w3.org/1999/xlink"
  xlink:type="extended">
  <bs:bookres
    xlink:type="resource"
    xlink:label="book"
    xlink:role=
```

```
        "http://www.bookdomain.com/linkprops/books">
      The comic book
  </bs:bookres>
  <bs:authorloc
    xlink:type="locator"
    xlink:href="http:www.freelist.com/ggoose"
    xlink:label="aut"
    xlink:role=
        "http://www.bookdomain.com/linkprops/authors"
    xlink:title="Gustave Goose" />

  <bs:authorloc
    xlink:type="locator"
    xlink:href="http:www.cartoonworld.com/mpiggy"
    xlink:label="aut"
    xlink:role="http://www.bookdomain.com/authors"
    xlink:title="Miriam Piggy" />

  <visitAuthors
    xlink:type="arc"
    xlink:from="book"
    xlink:to="aut"
    xlink:title="Visit the authors' homepages"
    xlink:actuate="onRequest"
    xlink:show="new" />
</bs:bookAuthorLink>
```

An extended link is constructed from resource elements, locator elements, and arc elements. Each arc element constructs a link from a group of resource elements to a group of locator elements. Groups are identified by the label attribute of each element: Elements with the same label value belong to the same group.

Here we have specified one resource type element <bookres>. This element acts as a local resource. It belongs to a one-element group named "book". Then we have two locator type elements specifying the respective home page URLs for each author. Both elements belong to the same group named "auth". Finally we have one arc type element (see Figure 7.2). This element establishes a link from all elements with label "book" to all elements with label "aut". In our case this would result in a 1:2 link because we have one element with label "book" (the local resource) and two elements with label "aut". We could, of course, have modeled these relationships with two simple links. However, the behavior would be different. In an XLink-aware browser, two simple links would show up as

Local resources

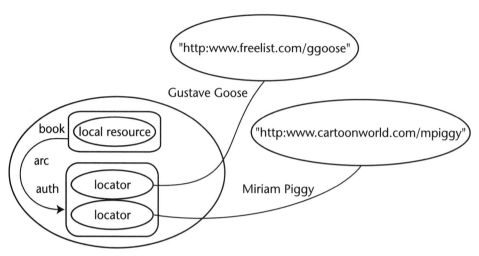

Figure 7.2 The arc element connects the local resource contained in group book with the two external resources specified in group auth.

two separate items. This extended link would show up as a single item instead. If it is actuated, the browser can immediately open two new windows displaying the home pages of each author. Or it could show a context menu containing the menu items "Gustave Goose" and "Miriam Piggy" and allow the user to select one.

Multiple arcs   Extended links can contain more than one arc. For example, we could have added additional locator elements pointing to book reviews and an additional arc element titled "Read book reviews":

```
<bs:reviewloc
  xlink:type="locator"
  xlink:href="http:www.toons.com/reviews/july2000_5"
  xlink:label="rev"
  xlink:role=
      "http://www.bookdomain.com/linkprops/reviews"
  xlink:title="cartoons.com" />

<bs:reviewloc
  xlink:type="locator"
  xlink:href="http:www.review.org/2000/the_comic_book"
  xlink:label="rev"
  xlink:role=
      "http://www.bookdomain.com/linkprops/reviews"
  xlink:title="review.org" />
```

```
<readReviews
  xlink:type="arc"
  xlink:from="Book"
  xlink:to="rev"
  xlink:title="Read reviews"
  xlink:actuate="onRequest"
  xlink:show="embed" />
```

This is another 1:2 arc, leading from the <bookres> resource to both reviews. In this case, we embed the review into the current page but only when the user requests it.

As a special service to the authors, we could make the reviews available to the authors' home pages, too:

```
<reviewsForAuthors
  xlink:type="arc"
  xlink:from="aut"
  xlink:to="rev"
  xlink:title="Reviews for 'The Comic Book'"
  xlink:actuate="onRequest"
  xlink:show="new" />
```

This 2:2 arc, however, creates a problem because now we have defined an outgoing arc from remote resources (the authors' home pages). How should the authors' home pages know that this link exists? The solution is to modify the authors' home pages and to include a pointer to the document that contains these link definitions. Such a document is called **Linkbases** a link database, or *linkbase*. A pointer to a linkbase can be expressed with XLink just as well and is identified by a special xlink:arcrole specification:

```
<comicBookLinks>
  <res1
    xlink:type="locator"
    xlink:label="r1"
    xlink:href="index.xml"/>

  <linkbase
    xlink:type="locator"
    xlink:label="linkbase"
    xlink:href=
        "http:www.bookshop.com/books/the_comic_book"
  />
```

```
<loadLinks
  xlink:type="arc"
  xlink:arcrole=
    "http://www.w3.org/1999/xlink/properties/linkbase"
  xlink:from="r1"
  xlink:to="linkbase"
  actuate="onLoad" />

</comicBookLinks>
```

Loading linkbases

Such a definition can be enclosed in each author's home page (which we have assumed to be named "index.xml"). When the page is loaded, the link is actuated. In this case the actuation of the link causes the link definitions defined in the linkbase to be loaded. They can then be evaluated by the browser and presented to the user (see Figure 7.3).

Using linkbases can drastically reduce maintenance efforts for a Web site, especially when the same link definitions are used in many documents. To subsequently modify the link structure of a site, it is only nec-

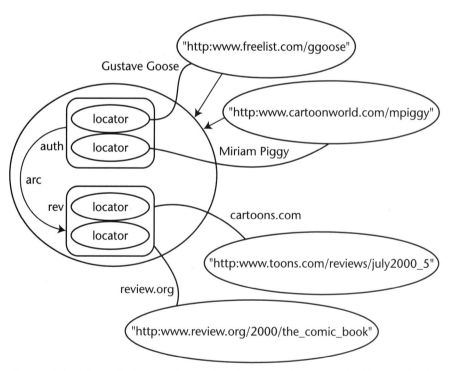

Figure 7.3 Using a linkbase. The authors' pages point to the linkbase, which contains all the necessary link information. This makes this information available to the authors' pages.

essary to modify the linkbases. The content pages can remain untouched. The linkbase can be made known to the client by embedding a link pointing to the linkbase into each document or, even better, by registering the browser with the linkbase.

WebML

Although it is possible to embed hyperlinks into XML documents using XLink, there are currently very few browsers that can handle this type of link (Mozilla and Amaya can handle simple links). Instead, the typical solution is to transform XML documents on the Web server into HTML (XHTML) or WML, which can contain links that the browser can understand. As an example let's consider an integrated XML-based architecture that supports the construction of hypermedia-based Web sites from conceptual design to representation layer.

WebML (Web Modeling Language) was the result of a research effort under the W3I3 project, funded by the European Community. The project was driven by the requirements of two major European Web developers, the German Otto-Versand, specializing in e-commerce, and the Dutch PPT (KPN), specializing in Web hosting services.

> History of WebML

WebML addresses the high-level, platform-independent specification of data-intensive Web applications and targets Web sites that require such advanced features as the one-to-one personalization of content and the delivery of information on multiple devices, like PCs, PDAs, digital televisions, and WAP phones (Ceri, Fraternali, and Bongio 2000).

The project has also produced a supporting CASE environment called WebRatio (*www.webratio.com*), which covers the entire life cycle of Web applications and follows a model-driven approach to Web design, centered on the use of WebML. WebML is clearly positioned for the development of hypermedia-based Web sites; it is not an appropriate tool to model collaborative Web applications such as supply chains and other peer-to-peer applications. It has its roots in classic hypermedia modeling methods such as HDM (Garzotto, Paolini, and Schwabe 1993) and OOHDM (Rossi, Schwabe, and Lyardot 1999). What interests us here is the consistent use of XML from the conceptual model to the finished Web site, and how the navigational model can be derived from the conceptual model (Ceri, Fraternali, and Bongio 2000):

> Integrated environment

> WebML enables the high-level description of a Web site under distinct orthogonal dimensions: its data content (structural model), the pages that compose it (composition model), the topology of links between pages (navigation model), the layout and graphic requirements for page rendering (presentation model), and the customization features for one-to-one content delivery (personalization model).

Structural Model   The structural model describes the information items of the site in terms of entities and relationships. WebML does not introduce new modeling methods, but it can collaborate with existing modeling methods such as the classical ERM or UML class diagrams.

The structural model consists of several ENTITY elements.

```
<ENTITY id="Product">
...
</ENTITY>

<ENTITY id="ServiceProvider">
...
</ENTITY>
```

ENTITY elements, in turn, contain ATTRIBUTE elements, COMPONENT elements, and RELATIONSHIP elements as child elements.

Simple properties

ATTRIBUTE elements describe the name and type of entity attributes. Types are restricted to String, Text, Number, Integer, Float, Date, Boolean, Image, URL, and WebMLURL. (When WebML was created, XML Schema was still far away. WebML therefore uses its own type system.) User-defined enumeration types are also possible by declaring them in separate DOMAIN elements.

```
<ATTRIBUTE id="weight" type="Float"/>
```

Complex properties

COMPONENT elements are used to describe complex multivalued types. They can contain several ATTRIBUTE elements and can specify minimum and maximum cardinality:

```
<COMPONENT id="Price" minCard="1" maxCard="N">
    <ATTRIBUTE id="currency" type="String"/>
    <ATTRIBUTE id="amount" type="Float"/>
</COMPONENT>
```

RELATIONSHIP elements are used to describe the relationships to other entities. They can specify the target and role of the relationship, minimum and maximum cardinality, and an inverse relationship:

```
<RELATIONSHIP id="ProductToServiceProvider"
              to="ServiceProvider"
              inverse="ServiceProviderToProduct"
              minCard="1" maxCard="1"/>
```

Query language

In addition, WebML introduces an OQL-like query language that allows the specification of derived attributes. Here is an example that computes a derived attribute "shippingCost" from attribute "weight":

```
<ATTRIBUTE id="shippingCost" type="Float"
        value="Self.weight * 3.50"/>
```

A special case of deriving an attribute is to import an attribute from another entity:

```
<ATTRIBUTE id="ServicePhoneNo" type="String"
      value="Self.ServiceProviderToProduct.PhoneNo"/>
```

"Self" identifies the entity to which the `<ATTRIBUTE>` element belongs. Here we imported the attribute `PhoneNo` from a related `ServiceProvider`.

With a similar syntax is it also possible to derive new relationships from existing relationships. Derived relationships can be important in the navigation model for the definition of shortcuts.

Hypertext Model The hypertext model defines one or more hypertexts that can be published in the site. Each different hypertext defines a *site view*, which in turn consists of two submodels. The root element of the hypertext model is the `SITEVIEW` element.

Composition Model The composition model specifies which Web pages belong to a hypertext and which *content units* belong to a Web page. The content units are defined on top of the structural model—the designer specifies how content units relate to the entities defined in the structural model.

A composition model is represented by the `PAGE` element, which is a child of the `SITEVIEW` element and which identifies a certain region within a hypertext. For example, a `PAGE` can be implemented by an HTML frame or a WML card. `PAGE` elements can in turn contain other page definitions or `UNIT` elements that refer to one of the following unit definitions.

```
<SITEVIEW ...>
  ...
  <PAGE id="outerFrame">
    <PAGE id="leftFrame">
      <UNIT id="ProductIndex"/>
    </PAGE>
    <PAGE id="rightFrame">
      <UNIT id="shipping"/>
    </PAGE>
  </PAGE>
  ...
</SITEVIEW>
```

Margin notes: Derived attributes and relationships

Content units

There are six types of content units: data units, multidata units, index units, filter units, scroller units, and direct units.

Data units publish the information of a single information item (e.g., an instance of an entity or of a component). They can select specific attributes of the displayed information item:

```
<DATAUNIT id="shipping" entity="Product">
  <INCLUDE attribute="weight"/>
  <INCLUDE attribute="shippingCost"/>
</DATAUNIT>
```

Multidata units publish information about a *set* of information items (e.g., all the instances of an entity). They can contain several data units:

```
<MULTIDATAUNIT id="allProducts" entity="Product">
  <DATAUNIT id="productData" entity="Product">
    <INCLUDEALL/>
  </DATAUNIT>
</MULTIDATAUNIT>
```

Index units show a list of information items. The INDEXUNIT element contains a DESCRIPTION element that specifies the attribute from which the index list is composed:

```
<INDEXUNIT id="ProductIndex" entity="Product">
  <DESCRIPTION Key="name"/>
</INDEXUNIT>
```

Filter units allow a search value to be entered in order to display only the matching items. Inside a FILTERUNIT element one or several SEARCH-ATTRIBUTE elements can be specified. Each defines the name of an attribute and a predicate such as eq, neq, gt, gteq, lt, lteq, like:

```
<FILTERUNIT id="ProductFilter" entity="Product"/>
  </SEARCHATTRIBUTE name="name" predicate="like">
</FILTERUNIT>
```

Scroller units present commands that allow navigation in a set of information items:

```
<SCROLLERUNIT id="ProductScroll" entity="Product"
  first="yes" last="yes"
  previous="yes" next="yes"/>
```

Direct units do not display information but are used to denote a one-to-one relationship between semantically related information items:

```
<DIRECTUNIT id="ToServiceProvider"
            relation="ProductToServiceProvider"/>
```

Navigation Model The navigation model describes the *navigational structure* of a hypertext, that is, how pages and units are linked together. This is defined by *links*. Links lead from a source unit to a target unit. This can happen across pages. All of the previous unit elements may contain one or both of the following link elements: INFOLINK and HYPERLINK.

When used in a DATAUNIT, the link type INFOLINK carries instance information from the source to the target. The information in the target unit therefore depends on the instance in the source unit. For example:

```
<DATAUNIT id="ServiceProviderData"
          entity="ServiceProvider">
  <INCLUDEALL/>
  <INFOLINK id="indexLink" to="ProductIndex"/>
</DATAUNIT>

<INDEXUNIT id="ProductIndex" entity="Product">
  <DESCRIPTION Key="name"/>
</INDEXUNIT>
```

This definition would create a link within the ServiceProviderData unit that leads to the unit ProductIndex. This unit would display only those products that are related to the ServiceProvider instance shown in the first unit.

We see that the INFOLINK element exploits the knowledge contained in the RELATIONSHIP elements in the structural model. But what if we use INFOLINK in other units?

- For *multidata units* the context information associated with the data units nested within the multidata unit determines the content in the target unit.
- For *index units* the key value selected from the index list determines the content in the target unit.
- For *filter units* the attribute values entered by the user determine the content in the target unit.
- For *scroller units* the identifier of the object selected by using the scrolling commands determines the content in the target unit.
- *Direct units* are treated similarly to data units.

HYPERLINK does not carry instance information from the source to the target. The information in the target unit is therefore independent of the instance in the source unit.

If we modify the previous example to

```
<DATAUNIT id="ServiceProviderData"
          entity="ServiceProvider">
  <INCLUDEALL/>
  <HYPERLINK id="indexLink" to="ProductIndex"/>
</DATAUNIT>

<INDEXUNIT id="ProductIndex" entity="Product">
  <DESCRIPTION Key="name"/>
</INDEXUNIT>
```

the difference is that the unit ProductIndex shows *all* product instances.

Look and feel

Presentation Model   The presentation model describes the layout and graphic appearance (look and feel) of pages by means of an abstract XML syntax. This description is device independent. WebML pages are rendered according to a style sheet.

Users and user groups

Personalization Model   The personalization model describes *users* and *user groups*. These are modeled explicitly as predefined entities in the structural schema. The properties of these entities can be used to store user or user group preferences and other personalization data. This data can be used to construct derived attributes of other entities, in the composition of content units, and in the definition of the presentation model.

For example, a user entity contains an attribute discountRate. The entity product contains an attribute listPrice. With the help of an OQL-like expression we could compute a derived attribute effectivePrice for the entity product from listPrice and discountRate.

Business rules

In addition to these declarative definitions, the personalization model allows procedural specifications, too, in the form of business rules that describe the reaction of the system to user interaction (clicks or text entry) and other events.

A business rule is specified as a triple event-condition-action. When a specified event occurs, the specified condition is tested, and if the condition is found true, the action is performed. Typical actions triggered by a business rule are the assignment of users to specific user groups (good customers, bad customers), the notification of users (for example, in case of price changes), the logging of user actions (for data warehousing), and so on.

7.2 TOPIC MAPS

Using hyperlinks that are embedded into documents is not really a good idea. Everybody who has surfed the Web for more than half an hour has probably come across the infamous 404 response code: a URL pointed to a resource that no longer exists in the specified location—probably because the Web master had the brilliant idea of reorganizing the directory structure of his Web site. Moving resources to another location requires that all URLs in all of the Web pages that point to this particular location must be updated—and by all, we mean worldwide! This usually doesn't happen.

One solution to this problem is offered by XLink with linkbases, as discussed in Section 7.1.2. Linkbases can contain all the links of a set of Web pages and thus reduce the maintenance efforts to the linkbase. When the location of a Web page changes, it is only necessary to make modifications to the linkbase instead of modifying each page individually. With linkbases it becomes much more likely that hyperlinks are kept in good shape.

Hyperlinks (and also hyperlinks contained in a linkbase) are links between physical Web resources. Navigation through such a structure is almost always like walking through a town without a roadmap. You can follow signposts, but only the signposts that are in your viewing range. It is easy to get lost.

Hypermedia and encyclopedia editors have known this for a long time. Therefore they supply their users with a variety of navigational access structures: table of contents, index, guided tour, history, and so on. One of these access structures is the semantic map. Semantic maps allow users to navigate on an *abstract* level and then to drill down to the actual resources.

A prominent form of this is the *topic map,* probably one of the most important developments in the area of knowledge representation and navigation in a long time.

7.2.1 A GPS for the Web

Topic maps are an ISO standard (Biezunski, Bryan, and Newcomb 1999). Charles Goldfarb, the father of SGML, has described topic maps as "GPS for the Web." In fact, navigation was one of the prime design issues for topic maps. Topic maps originated in the SGML community and have their roots in HyTime. The standard, however, does not rely on a specific

Dangling pointers

Separate link layer

The virtues of a map

implementation language. One implementation of the topic map standard is XTM 1.0 (XML Topic Maps) (Biezunski and Newcomb 2000, 2001).

Nodes and arcs

Like entity relationship diagrams (see Chapter 3), topic maps consist of nodes and arcs. The difference, however, is that the nodes are "topics," not "entities," and the arcs are called "associations," not "relationships." There are some similarities. Compare Peter Chen's statement:

> An entity is a "thing"' which can be distinctly identified.

to Steve Pepper's statement (Pepper 1999):

> A topic, in its most generic sense, can be any "thing" whatsoever—a person, an entity, a concept, really anything—regardless of whether it exists or has any other specific characteristics, about which anything whatsoever may be asserted by any means whatsoever.

You cannot get much better than that. However, the similarity of these descriptions could be misleading. A topic is not equivalent to an entity. Despite the claim that topics are "things," they actually are not. They are rather themes around which "things" are grouped. ISO specification 13250 defines the structure of a topic map as

Topic map defined

- groupings of addressable information resources around topics (occurrences), and
- relationships between topics (associations).

In this sense, a topic can be better compared to an *entity set* in Chen's model, but in a less typed way. Topics are abstract notions such as "20th century history," "Marilyn Monroe movies," "Otto Preminger movies," and so on.

Associations can relate topics to each other; for example, "20th century history" includes "Marilyn Monroe movies." Unlike the relationships in ERM, associations are always bidirectional; that is, our "includes" association can be read backward as "is included by."

What is important here is that associations are established not between the information resources but between the abstract topics. The semantic network consists only of topics and associations and can be formulated independently from the underlying base of information resources. In fact, it is possible to project a topic map onto different sets of information resources.

One map, two resource pools

Let us look at an example (see Figures 7.4 and 7.5). The same topic map is applied onto two different sets of information resources. In Figure 7.4, the map imposes a structure onto a pool of AVI files, while in Figure 7.5, the information resources consist of HTML files. A topic map can be

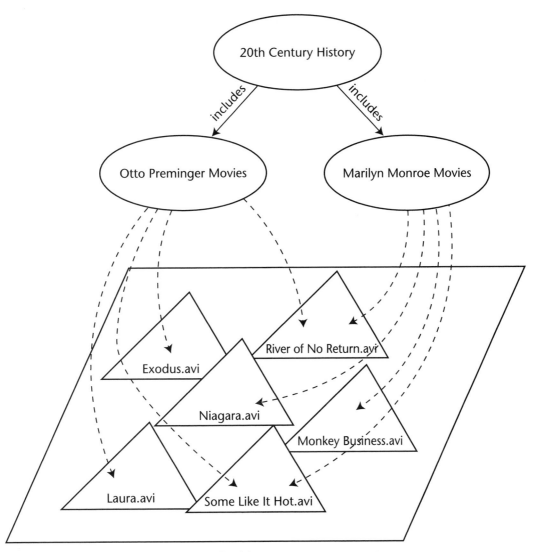

Figure 7.4 Topic map for an online video library.

imposed on such an information pool without even touching the information resources. The links between topics and information resources are all defined in the topic map.

This also allows us to impose different topic maps onto the same information pool (see Figure 7.6).

These links can, as we see in Figures 7.4 and 7.5, establish a connection between two topics. Although there is no direct association between

Two maps, one
resource pool

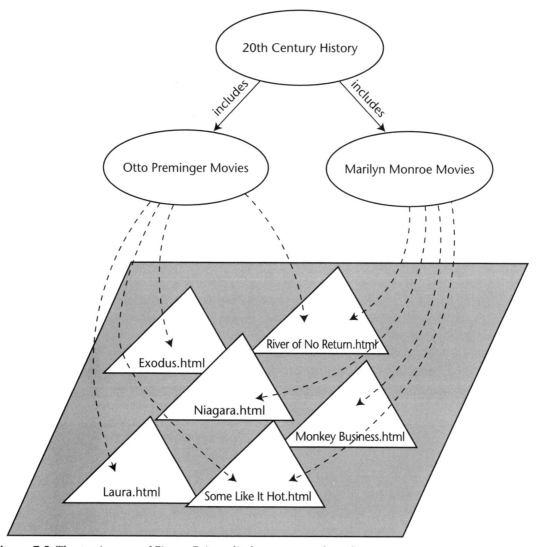

Figure 7.5 The topic map of Figure 7.4 applied to an encyclopedia.

"Marilyn Monroe movies" and "Otto Preminger movies," a connection exists because both topics share the same information resource (*River of No Return.avi* in Figure 7.4, and *River of No Return.html* in Figure 7.5).
Specification 13250 states:

> Two topics may be connected through an association, and they can also be connected by virtue of sharing an occurrence.

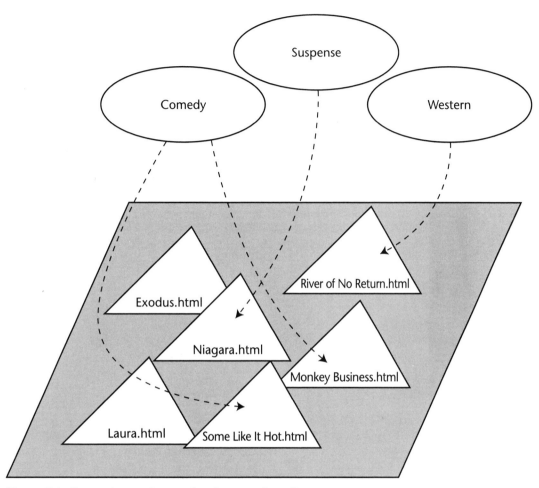

Figure 7.6 Alternative topic map for the encyclopedia.

However, a topic map should not rely on occurrence sharing. Concepts should be "spelled out" by means of associations, not by occurrence sharing. Otherwise, important aspects of a concept could get lost when a topic map is applied to a different information pool.

Occurrence sharing

In our example, the connection between Otto Preminger and Marilyn Monroe obviously relies on the presence of an information resource about *River of No Return*. This anomaly is due to a poor design of the semantic Web. A better approach would be to model each movie as a separate topic, independent of information resources. This would result in a proper topic map describing the movie world (see Figure 7.7). This topic map is completely independent of the underlying information resources.

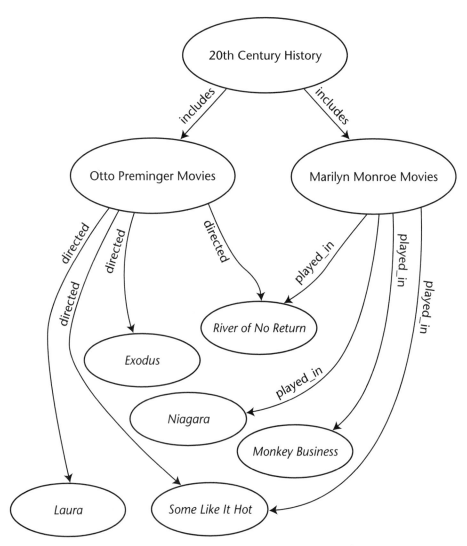

Figure 7.7 The complete semantic network.

It describes the concepts completely, but it can be easily mapped onto different information pools.

Topics in Detail

Subject defined   The concept of topics is closely related to the concept of a subject. XTM 1.0 defines the term *subject* as

> . . . the organizing principle of a topic.

It also makes the following distinction between a subject and a topic:

> A topic aggregates information which shares the characteristic of being about a given subject. In other words, the subject is the ineffable thing which is at the heart of a topic.

Steve Pepper (2000) puts it a bit more philosophically:

> We might think of a "subject" as corresponding to what Plato called an *idea*. A topic, on the other hand, is like the shadow that the idea casts on the wall of Plato's cave: It is an object within a topic map that represents a subject.

Any topic represents a subject, and a subject is represented by exactly one topic. Nevertheless, there is a possibility that more than one topic definition represents the same subject, for example, when the same subject is represented in different topic maps or in different sections of the same topic map. Let us return to Plato's cave: an idea can have multiple shadows if there are multiple light sources.

Therefore there must be a way to establish the identity of topic definitions that represent the same subject. There are two ways to do this:

Topic identity

- Topics are identical if they have the same `baseName` (see below) and the same *scope*.
- Topics are identical if they refer to the same *published subject indicator* (PSI). This allows us to establish the identity of subjects across topic maps, and even across Web sites. A published subject indicator represents each published subject with a unique URI. (A similar technique to obtain globally unique identifiers is used for XML namespaces.)

Let's now look at XTM topics in detail. Within the XTM 1.0 DTD, a topic is defined by

```
<!ELEMENT topic
  (instanceOf*,subjectIdentity?,(baseName|occurrence)*)>
```

Topic element

The first element `instanceOf` classifies the topic. A topic can belong to one or multiple topic classes. Topic classes define a type for each topic. A topic class itself can be defined as another topic (so it is possible to link information resources to it and to include it in associations). Also published subject indicators can act as topic classes. This is especially true when no `instanceOf` definition is supplied. In this case the topic type defaults to a predefined top-level published subject indicator "topic":

```
(http://www.topicmaps.org/xtm/1.0/#psi-topic)
```

In our example, all movie topics such as "River of No Return", "Some Like It Hot", and so on could be instances of a parent topic "movie".

The second (optional) element `subjectIdentity` defines a unique *subject identity point* for the topic and thus establishes the topic's subject identity. `subjectIdentity` is either (1) a reference to an information resource, (2) a reference to a published subject indicator (see above), or (3) a reference to another topic. In the first case, the specified resource *is* the subject of the topic. In the second case, the specified PSI *identifies* the subject. In the third case, the identity *is inherited* from the topic pointed at, and both topics will merge.

This last technique allows the introduction of short names for the lengthy PSIs:

```
<topic id="ronr">
   <subjectIdentity>
      <subjectIndicatorRef xlink:href=
         "http://www.cine.org/
         preminger/river_of_no_return"/>
   </subjectIdentity>
</topic>
```

With this definition in place it is now sufficient to refer to topic "ronr" whenever we want to refer to the subject with identity `"http://www.cine .org/preminger/river_of_no_return"`.

The element `baseName` defines a name for the topic in natural language. A topic may have none, one, or several `baseName`s. Base names can be constrained by a `scope` element that declares the base name valid only within a specified context such as a specific language, geographical area, or historical period. (Topics with the same base name and the same scope will merge.)

For each `baseName` it is possible to define an arbitrary number of `variant` elements (e.g., for display or for sort purposes). The definition of variants is recursive, so you can have variants of variants, and so on.

Finally the `occurrence` elements define all the occurrences to information resources. Occurrences can also have a `scope` defining the context in which they are valid. Occurrences can have a type (only one) that is defined through their `instanceOf` child element. This type definition defines the role of the occurrence. (If no `instanceOf` type definition is supplied, the type of the occurrence defaults to a predefined top-level PSI "occurrence".)

Occurrences can also possess (only one) `baseName`. Processors can use this base name to display a label for a link to a resource. The linked information resource is usually given in the form of an `xlink:` reference, but it can also be supplied in the form of literal data.

Let's now look at an example of a topic definition:

```
<topic id="River_of_no_Return">
    <instanceOf><topicRef link:href="#movie"/></instanceOf>
    <subjectIdentity>
      <topicRef xlink:href="ronr"/>
    </subjectIdentity>
    <baseName>
      <baseNameString>
        River of No Return
      </baseNameString>
    </baseName>
    <occurrence>
      <instanceOf>
          <topicRef xlink:href="#video-avi-format"/>
      </instanceOf>
      <resourceRef xlink:href=
"ftp://www.movielib.com/western/preminger/no_return.avi"/>
    </occurrence>
    <occurrence>
      <instanceOf>
          <topicRef xlink:href="#html-online-description"/>
      </instanceOf>
      <resourceRef xlink:href=
          "ftp://www.clops.com/preminger-no_return.html"/>
    </occurrence>
</topic>
```

In this example we have defined two occurrences for the topic "River of No Return" with different roles "video-avi-format" and "html-online-description", mapping the topic into both information pools. Both roles "video-avi-format" and "html-online-description" would be defined as topics, too. This would allow us to link information resources to each role, for example, describing how to use these particular data formats.

Associations

Associations are defined as

```
<!ELEMENT association ( instanceOf?, scope?, member+ )>
```

Association elements

The first element `instanceOf` again specifies a class (or type) to which the associations belong. This means that associations can also be typed. Association classes are either topics themselves or published subject indicators.

Associations can be constrained by a scope element that declares the association valid only within a specified context such as a specific domain, version language, geographical area, or historical period. Scopes are defined as references to another topic, to an information resource, or to a published subject indicator.

Finally, member elements define the items that participate in the association. That can be topics, information resources, or published subject indicators. Each member definition can comprise a role specification, that is, a reference to another topic or published subject indicator representing the role. Also possible are *n*-ary associations, with $n > 2$.

Merging Maps

The concept of topic identity allows the merging of topic maps. This is an important aspect because it allows separate work groups to develop separate topic maps and then to merge them. Also, in the case of company mergers or when establishing a virtual company, it will be necessary to merge semantic networks, for example, to merge thesauri for product descriptions and so on.

Modular maps

Also possible is the modular development of topic maps and the reuse of such modules. In Figure 7.8 we have modularized our example topic map by slicing it into two layers. The top layer defines the semantic network, while the lower layers do only the mapping of the topics to their respective information resources.

The merging of topic maps is accomplished through the mergeMap element:

```
<!ELEMENT mergeMap
        (topicRef|resourceRef|subjectIndicatorRef )* >

<!ATTLIST mergeMap
    id              ID        #IMPLIED
    xlink:type      NMTOKEN   #FIXED 'simple'
    xlink:href      CDATA     #REQUIRED   >
```

The xlink:href attribute of mergeMap points to the topic map to be merged into the current map. The mergeMap element can be used recursively; that is, a map that is merged in via a mergeMap element can contain mergeMap elements itself.

The mergeMap element can contain a child element defining one or more scopes for the map merged in. These scopes are defined as references either to another topic, to an information resource, or to a published subject indicator.

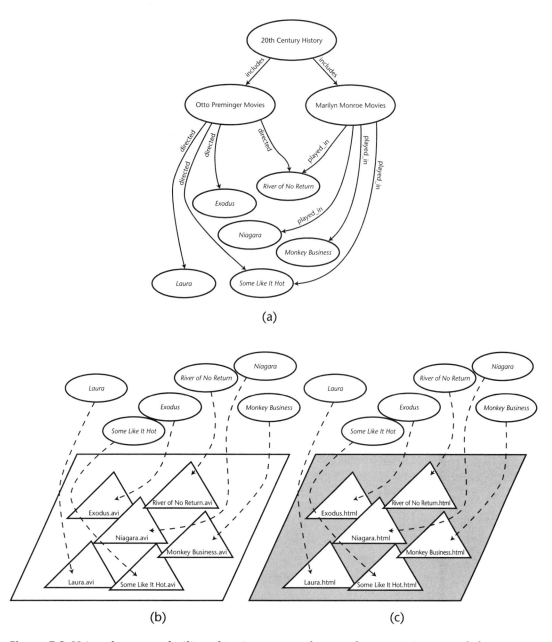

Figure 7.8 Using the merge facility of topic maps to abstract the semantic network from concrete resources. (a) This topic map defines only a semantic network. It can be applied to an information pool by merging it with one of the other topic maps. (b) This topic map maps only the topics from the semantic network to our video library. (c) This one does the same for the encyclopedia.

Attaching Properties to Resources

Annotating
resources

ISO specification 13250 defines for topic maps the concept of *facets*. A facet is a property that can be attached to an information resource from the outside, without modifying the information resource itself. This is similar to RDF's capability to make statements about resources without modifying the resource. However, facets have been dropped from the XTM specification. In XTM an information resource is also a topic by default. It is relatively easy to attach a property to a resource, so there is no need for an extra mechanism.

In the next example we do exactly this. We define a topic that has as subject the resource

`"ftp://www.movielib.com/western/preminger/no_return.avi"`.

Using an occurrence element, we attach a name/value (baseName/ resourceData) pair saying that the movie will be screened soon:

```
<topic
 id="ftp://www.movielib.com/western/preminger/no_return.avi">
  <subjectIdentity>
   <resourceRef xlink:href=
    "ftp://www.movielib.com/western/preminger/no_return.avi"/>
  </subjectIdentity>
  <occurrence>
     <baseName>
        <baseNameString>Availability</baseNameString>
     </baseName>
     <resourceData>
        To be screened soon
     </resourceData>
  </occurrence>
</topic>
```

Applications

Topic maps are ideally suited for structuring complex knowledge bases and thesauri. They enable semantically driven navigation between information items, semantically driven automatic layout of Web and help pages, and so on.

7.2.2 Another Philosophical Excursus

As we have seen, topic maps make a clear distinction between information resources and topics. While the information resources represent the entities in an information system, the topics refer to subjects that exist independently of a particular information system. The concept of subjects has its foundation in the theory of *substance,* formulated over 2,000 years ago by Aristotle.

Substances exist on their own, they keep their identity throughout their life span and their life span is continuous through time, they are "one" (i.e., they do not consist of other substances and cannot belong to another substance), they have a complete and determinate boundary, and they take up space and are spatially connected (Smith 1998).

Substances can be classified. Classification introduces higher-level substances—*second-order substances*—such as apple, computer, desk, and so on. These are abstract notions referring to real instances: a particular apple, computer, desk, and so on (Partridge 2000).

Substances have attributes, but attributes are never substances. A cat may have a smile, but (if we forget Lewis Carroll for a moment) there isn't a smile without a cat. For a first-order substance, attributes are concrete. For example, my computer screen has a screen size of 17 inches, no more, no less. For a second-order substance such as "computer screen," the value "screen size" may be undefined; it may, however, be constrained to a certain value domain, say 15 to 22 inches. For other second-order substances, such as "17-inch computer screen," the value may be well defined.

Attributes such as "screen size" can apply to various substances, for example, to computer screens, television screens, projector screens, and so on. This encourages us to classify attributes independently from the substances hierarchy. Thus we arrive at *second-order attributes,* such as "color," "size," "weight," "complexity," "price," and so on. These second-order attributes are not concrete (although their values may be constrained to a certain domain), nor do they belong to a particular first- or second-order substance.

Substances can be related. In the substance-attribute model, relationships can be assigned to substances as attributes. However, this poses a problem. Most relationships are bidirectional; for instance, the relationship "Lewis Carroll wrote *Alice in Wonderland*" implies the reverse relationship "*Alice in Wonderland* was written by Lewis Carroll." Aristotle was well aware of this problem:

> All relatives have their correlatives. "Slave" means the slave of a master, and "master" in turn implies slave. "Double" means double of its half, just as "half" means half of its double. By "greater," again, we mean greater than this or that thing which is less, by "less" less than that which is greater. So it is with all relative terms.

Margin notes:
Aristotle again

Classification

Attributes

Relationships

This concept of correlatives, however, introduces redundancies because a relation between two substances is here described twice—once for each substance. For many-to-many relationships, things get completely out of hand.

As we saw earlier, topic maps take a different approach. Relations (or "associations" as relations are called in the context of topic maps) are defined as separate items, not as properties. Associations are always bidirectional, so topic maps do not introduce the previously mentioned redundancy. This is quite in contrast to RDF.

7.2.3 Topic Maps versus RDF

Similarities

Both topic maps and RDF are designed to model semantic networks. Both use the same paradigm to do this: graphs consisting of nodes and arcs. In the definition of ontologies, both fall short by not offering language elements for the definition of constraints.

Differences

What now are the differences between topic maps and RDF? As the name says, the main organizing principle for topic maps is topics. It is possible to define complete topic maps without even talking about resources. If resources are present, topic maps construct links from known semantics to resources. In contrast, for RDF the main organizing principle is resources. RDF constructs pointers from existing resources to known semantics. Semantic networks are constructed on the basis of existing resources. We could say that topic maps work top down, while RDF works bottom up.

Also, a topic map intentionally defines a whole semantic network. In practice, a semantic network, however, could be defined by several topic maps and the resulting semantic network obtained by merging them. In contrast, an RDF description intentionally makes statements about a single resource. The semantic network is formed by the RDF statements defined in a given domain. Ultimately the whole Internet becomes one semantic web.

Topic maps therefore lend themselves better to a client-server environment. Typically topic maps are found in knowledge servers and content management systems, and they are used to structure a clearly bounded information base. RDF is designed to support open environments. It can support navigational systems (e.g., search engines, agents, etc.) and is posed to convert the Web into a huge knowledge base.

The "closed system" approach of topic maps has advantages and disadvantages. It can be expected that the definition of a topic map is more consistent than a collection of RDF statements that are possibly made by different people, at different times, in different places. On the other hand, a topic map can quickly become outdated and needs constant maintenance by its author. This is beautifully shown by an example topic map published on the Internet: the map lists all free XML tools on the Web. By the time this topic map was published, it was probably already out-of-date. With RDF the definition of a semantic network would be incremental. Every time a new XML tool is published, corresponding RDF statements can be published as well.

RDF is a low-level language. Modeling a knowledge base in RDF can result in a huge and unwieldy collection of RDF statements. In contrast, topic maps provide a much more structured approach to the task of knowledge modeling: topic maps are more problem oriented.

RDF allows second-order constructs by reifying RDF statements into RDF resources. Topic maps do not provide such a possibility; associations cannot be treated as topics (i.e., it is not possible to define associations about associations). This restricts the expressiveness of topic maps somewhat.

7.3 DIRECTORY SERVICES (UDDI)

Directory services are to computers what the Yellow or White Pages are to humans. They contain the addresses of people, organizations, and other resources. Service providers that have a service to offer can publish their service in a directory. Clients that require a certain service can search a directory for that service.

The Universal Description, Discovery, and Integration (UDDI) specifications define a way to publish and discover information about Web services (UDDI 2000). UDDI is a joint initiative of Ariba, IBM, and Microsoft. The companies involved in the definition of the standard are committed to providing free directory services based on UDDI to the public.

The information stored in a UDDI registry consists of three components:

- *White Pages* contain the addresses, contact information, and identifiers of businesses and services.
- *Yellow Pages* categorize services along industrial categorizations based on standard taxonomies.
- *Green Pages* contain technical information about the advertised services, including references to further documentation and discovery mechanisms.

UDDI is designed for the discovery of technical features of a service or of a business. It is not designed for discovery queries such as "Give me the supplier of toothbrushes with the lowest price," or "Find the brass factory closest to New Orleans." Such queries can be answered by services such as marketplaces or business portals; these services rely on UDDI to locate only the Web services that are technically fit to satisfy the request.

Here is a simple UDDI request searching for a business name:

```
<?xml version="1.0" encoding="UTF-8"?>
<Envelope xmlns="http://schemas.xmlsoap.org/soap/envelope/">
  <Body>
    <find_business generic="1.0" xmlns="urn:uddi-org:api">
      <name>Microsoft</name>
    </find_business>
  </Body>
</Envelope>
```

UDDI requests (in bold) must be wrapped into a SOAP envelope; the prescribed encoding is UTF-8.

A UDDI query like this one would be answered with a list of businesses and services that match the specified business name (Lovett 2000):

```
<businessList generic="1.0" operator="Microsoft Corporation"
              truncated="false" xmlns="urn:uddi-org:api">
  <businessInfos>
    <businessInfo
         businessKey="0076B468-EB27-42E5-AC09-9955CFF462A3">
      <name>Microsoft Corporation</name>
      <description xml:lang="en">
        ...
      </description>
      <serviceInfos>
        <serviceInfo
            businessKey="0076B468-EB27-42E5-AC09-9955CFF462A3"
            serviceKey="1FFE1F71-2AF3-45FB-B788-09AF7FF151A4">
          <name>Web services for smart searching</name>
        </serviceInfo>
        ...
      </serviceInfos>
    </businessInfo>
    ...
  </businessInfos>
</businessList>
```

As you can see businesses and services are identified via `businessKey` and `serviceKey` attributes whose values are given as UUIDs (universally unique identifiers). Further queries may use these identifiers to drill down in the information structure and get details about the services, for example. This type of identification used in UDDI should be well known to COM and DCE programmers. The initiators of UDDI probably chose this form of identification because this way it is easier to leverage existing naming service and registry implementations for UDDI. UUIDs are globally unique and have some advantages over domain-name-based identifiers. They can be easily computed without the help of a central registry instance, and they don't depend on a physical location. However, to the human eye, they appear inscrutable.

Information in a UDDI registry is stored in XML format. It contains much more information than `businessInfos` and `ServiceInfos` (Boubez et al. 2000).

There are four main groups:

- *Business information:* The top-level element to store information about a business is the `BusinessEntity` element. It contains details such as the business name, business identifier, address, contact information, and optional elements for categorization.
- *Service information:* The business information for services is contained in the `BusinessService` elements, which are child elements of the `BusinessEntity` element. These elements contain the service name, identifier, and optional elements for categorization.
- *Binding information:* Technical data such as the address of the service (e.g., a URL) or routing options is contained in the `bindingTemplate` element, a child element of the `BusinessService` element. This element also contains pointers to technical specifications.
- *Interface information:* A client process that wants to use a service not only needs the address of the service, but also has to know how to interface with the service. This interface is described in a `tModel` element. A `bindingTemplate` (see above) can reference a `tModel`. A `tModel` describes a specification. It contains the name, the publishing organization, identifiers and optional elements for categorization, and a URL pointer to the actual specification. Such a specification would describe the wire protocol, the interchange format, and interchange sequencing rules. Examples for such specifications are found in standards such as RosettaNet, ebXML, or the various EDI standards.

A `tModel` thus acts as a kind of fingerprint for an interface specification. Companies that agree on a `tModel` can be sure that their

UUIDs

UDDI registry

exchange formats are compatible without having to look deeper into the interface specification.

Business identifiers

Both `BusinessEntity` and `tModel` elements can contain additional identifiers. Typical identifiers for businesses include Dun & Bradstreet D-U-N-S numbers, tax identifiers, or any other kind of organizational identifiers. The purpose of these identifiers is to allow others to find published information through these more formal identifiers.

Business categories

As we have seen, `BusinessEntity` elements, `BusinessService` elements, and `tModel` elements may contain information for categorization. Categorization associates these elements with industry codes, product or service categories, or regional classification. Categories can be chosen from defined taxonomies. This category information can be used for searches in the Yellow or Green Pages.

Taxonomies

Three taxonomies are predefined in UDDI operator registry sites: the North American Industry Classification System (NAICS), the Universal Standard Products and Services Classification (UNSPSC), and a geographic taxonomy.

Both category taxonomies and identification systems can be represented by `tModels`, too. `tModel` references can therefore be used for categorization and identification purposes. Operator registry sites provide a number of useful `tModels`, including U.S. tax codes, NAICS, UNSPSC, and a geographic taxonomy.

7.4 PEER-TO-PEER ARCHITECTURES

Napster

Peer-to-peer (P2P) architectures have recently received a lot of publicity, especially in the Napster controversy. Napster offered its users a directory service for MP3 song titles. Users interested in a song would source it with the help of this directory. The directory would point them to another user who owns a copy (but not the copyright) of the song. He or she could then download the song directly from the computer of this user, provided this user was online. Although the exchange of the MP3 files worked on a P2P basis—from user to user—finding the location of a file relied on the central Napster directory. This was where Napster was vulnerable, and the music industry won a court case against Napster forcing them to remove millions of titles from the directory.

Gnutella

While this technology is not really new in electronic business—finding a service in a directory and then using it is a well-known technique in component-based architectures such as CORBA—things become more interesting when we look at Napster's competitors. Gnutella and others are not as vulnerable as Napster was: they don't use a central directory. Here's how they do it.

After installing the software, you must find a Gnutella site that is already operating. That may be a friend or some advertised site. In the future you will only communicate with this partner site (or, if you selected several sites, with these sites). If you are searching for a file, your Gnutella client will issue a request to your direct partners. Either they will be able to satisfy your request, or they will forward the request to all the sites they are connected with. And so on. Once a file is found, its address is passed back from site to site—like the famous bucket—until you get it. You can then download it from its original location. To avoid a request circling around, each request has a unique identifier, and each node on the way keeps a log of the requests it has already forwarded. This enables these nodes to prune out circling requests.

This all works well in a small community. But if the population of the network goes into the millions, your request is replicated a million times. It will even be replicated in some areas of the network after you have already received the file you wanted! And this is the effect of a single query. If a million users issue queries at the same time, the consequences are obvious: the network goes down. Gnutella solves this by introducing an aging process for queries. A query dies after it has been replicated a specified number of times. This restricts network traffic to tolerable amounts but limits the horizon of a query, so a file might not be found even if it exists somewhere in the network.

Some of these performance issues are addressed by a new development, Freenet. The objectives of Freenet are, however, different. Its goals are to guarantee freedom of speech, not freedom of copyright infringement. It does so by anonymizing and replicating files, making it impossible to destroy a file or to track its origin.

Freenet

Freenet answers the request for a file not with the address of the requested file but with the file itself. This means that the file travels all the way down from the place where it was found until it reaches the requester. A copy of the file is kept resident on each node it passes. (Nodes may, however, decide not to store a copy.) After some time it will expire if it was not requested again. Each node acts as a cache. The effect is that popular files are kept almost anywhere, so requests don't have to travel far to find such a file. A side effect is that sites that produce popular material don't have to buy into expensive server equipment. The delivery process is "outsourced."

In addition, Freenet uses another search strategy. When a client receives a request it cannot satisfy, it will not forward the request to all connected clients but will forward it to a single peer only. If the response of that peer is negative, it will continue with the next peer. (It will start with the peer that had the most hits in the past.) This depth-first strategy avoids the unnecessary query replication of Gnutella. Freenet, therefore, scales much better, but it has some problems of its own. Currently, Freenet does not support free text searches. Even if it would, users couldn't be sure that the version they have found is the most recent version. It may be an outdated copy residing somewhere between requester and submitter. Document authors are therefore well advised to include a pointer to the most recent version of the document in the document itself (a standard practice, for example, in W3C documents). But then—wouldn't one goal of Freenet get lost: anonymity?

Apart from those teething problems, these early P2P implementations may perhaps indicate the future direction of the Web. More recent implementations are file-sharing programs such as Morpheus. Microsoft is actively researching a serverless symbiotic distributed file system under the code name FarSite based on peer-to-peer technology.

So, central directories could become almost extinct, as did the operator-controlled telephone exchange. White and Yellow Pages? Well, some of the largest cities in the world have done without them for decades. P2P fits well into the nonplanned settlement of the Internet.

Presentation Formats

U p to this point, we have discussed XML as a representation format for managing and interchanging structured data. We have said nothing so far about how we are able to view XML-based data on typical front-end devices.

In this chapter we will give an overview of several formats for presenting XML data, with a focus on Web and multimedia applications. First, we will discuss the attributes of data formats that serve representational and presentational purposes. We will base our discussion on results from multimedia research.

Dealing with several formats is of interest to multipurpose Web publishing—providing Web publishers with a means to present content on a range of client systems, such as browsers, mobile devices like PDAs, and even phones. The current standardization effort will help to provide this ability. Challenges to be solved include device independence, reusability of content, and encodings that meet the limitations presented by network transfer capabilities. The W3C has made important recommendations—and more are expected—about several formats, including HTML, XML, and CSS. All of them will be considered in this chapter.

8.1 PRESENTATION AND REPRESENTATION

Information system tasks

When dealing with arbitrary data in today's information systems, there are five tasks that must be supported by computer systems:

- The creation or definition of data
- The processing or manipulation of data
- The storage of that data
- The exchange of data
- The presentation of data to end users

Although each of these tasks may need a particular data format, we may reduce our discussion to exactly two classes of data formats: presentation and representation formats.

Data formats

Data formats encompass both content and descriptive data. Content is the information that a user wants to have processed by a computer system; descriptive data defines the context that is necessary for the computer system to deal with that data appropriately. Since we have identified five tasks to be supported by computer systems, we may find that descriptive data or metadata differs from task to task. Therefore several formats are necessary to hold that particular metadata.

8.1.1 Results from Multimedia Research

XML and multimedia

That this book deals with multimedia is not very surprising. First, there is a requirement to enrich Web applications with more sophisticated media than just text. Later in this chapter, we will present XML-related solutions to multimedia (re)presentation techniques. Second, some fundamental considerations for multimedia also apply in the XML field. Although our discussion may appear somewhat academic, the properties to be identified may be helpful in evaluating XML developments. So we decided to give a little room to this topic.

What Is Multimedia?

In the early 1990s, multimedia was the buzzword for application systems and user interface design. *Multimedia* is the computer-based combination of different media elements (e.g., text, graphics, video, and music). Text and graphics are visual. Music is auditory. Video is a combination of both visual and auditory elements.

Another way to categorize different media is their appearance over time. Text and graphics don't change; video and music do. The former are *static* or *time independent;* the latter are *dynamic* or *time dependent.* A multimedia show can encompass both static and dynamic media elements.

Another aspect of multimedia is that some means are required to describe the presentation and to specify the representation of media and applications. Presentation deals with the problem of how to present a show to the viewer (eventually independent of the client platform). Representation deals with management and storage problems (on the server side, if we are speaking about distributed multimedia services realized through a client-server architecture). A lot of research has attempted to answer these different questions.

From Multimedia to the Web

Two areas may be identified in multimedia research: stand-alone applications (e.g., on terminal systems or on CD-ROMs) and applications in distributed environments (usually on two- or three-tier client-server architectures).

A multimedia show must be defined in an appropriate format (i.e., a scripting language format or an output format produced by an authoring tool). This format will describe the spatial and temporal relationships between the media objects incorporated into the multimedia show. For the purpose of reuse, we can store the media objects separately from the description of the show, and eventually on different nodes in the distributed environment (for example, each node could be dedicated to store one type of media object). Video servers and image databases are examples of such nodes as part of a computer network.

As stated earlier, multimedia, in a narrow sense, is the combination of several media types in a computer-based application, which usually is organized into documents. Hypertext is characterized by the ability to navigate inside and between documents, as long as the application just deals with text. Gopher, a predecessor of the Web, is a hypertext-based system. Integrating both hypertext and multimedia gives us *hypermedia.*

Hypermedia systems or applications encompass media elements of several different types and provide the end user with navigational function-

Definition of multimedia

Media types

Multimedia shows

Hypertext

Hypermedia

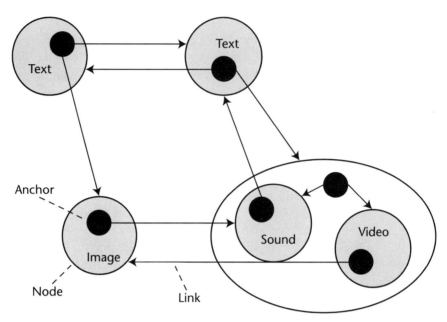

Figure 8.1 Media integration and navigation in hypermedia presentations.

ality. Navigation is typically realized by adding links to be followed from one informational chunk to the next, often located in different documents (see Figure 8.1). In what follows, we will not differentiate between multimedia and hypermedia.

Web-based applications

Web-based applications are characterized by the features that we just outlined (i.e., media integration and navigation as one form of user interaction). Although early applications were based on HTML, and therefore limited to text and graphics, authors today have access to more advanced technologies and features. These may have been developed to fulfill the requirements of specific applications, such as mobile business, or they may rely on general-purpose specifications.

Problem layers

In Web-based applications, we face three problem layers:

- Appropriate representation of arbitrary elementary and aggregated content
- Its presentation to end users on a variety of devices (user agents)
- A model of how to flexibly access Web resources, implemented through a navigational layer

As we stated earlier, we will focus on presentational and representational aspects in this chapter.

8.1.2 Dimensions of Multimedia Composition

Multimedia applications are composed of media elements that consume either space or time or both when presented to the user. Therefore a multimedia programmer has to deal with both spatial and temporal composition. For example, media elements must be positioned on the screen, in a window, or on a stage, when using the Macromedia Director authoring tool. The programmer must also deal with interaction elements and the actions associated with them.

Spatial Composition

The spatial composition of visual media objects is essential to the appearance of the multimedia show. Positioning occurs in three spatial dimensions. Although a computer screen is two-dimensional, the third dimension becomes obvious when one media object overlays another. That way the screen is given virtual depth.

Virtual depth

Take Figure 8.2 as a simple example. Two visual objects may each be positioned relative to the origin, which is the upper-left corner of the screen. This is called *absolute positioning*. Alternatively we may set objects into a spatial relation, just as the rectangle has been positioned relative to the center point of the circle in Figure 8.2(b). This procedure is called *relative positioning*.

The positions of the objects in absolute positioning are given by the coordinates (x, y). In relative positioning, we use the difference of the coordinates, for example, $(x - 3, y + 1)$.

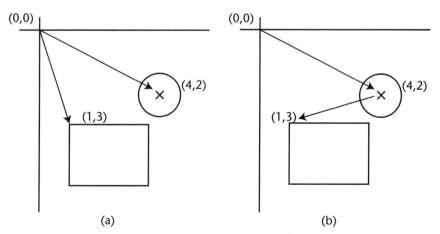

Figure 8.2 Positioning of spatial data objects in multimedia shows: (a) absolute positioning; (b) relative positioning.

Interaction

The presentational flow may be influenced by user interaction. For that purpose visual interaction elements are defined and integrated into the multimedia presentation. Using an interaction object will result in the performance of an action associated with that interaction object. In multimedia research, interaction falls into one of the following categories:

- *Scaling actions* change the appearance of a presentation (e.g., the size of the windows that the presentation is performed in).
- *Film actions* change the direction or speed of the presentation (e.g., start, stop, forward, backward, and so on). These features are familiar from VCRs or similar electronic devices.
- *Choices* influence the flow of the presentation: the user may choose a certain information branch and thus take an individual path through the informational landscape defined within the authored frame.

Since interaction objects are visual, they consume space and are subject to the mechanisms outlined in the context of spatial composition.

Temporal Composition

What we have said about spatial composition also holds for the temporal positioning of dynamic or time-dependent media objects, as shown in Figure 8.3. Temporal composition can be either absolute (usually measured against the starting point of a presentation) or relative.

A number of common relationships in temporal composition have been formulated. For example, in Allen's time calculus (Allen 1983), there are seven temporal relationships: before, meets, overlaps, finishes, during, starts, and equals. Each, except for equals, has an inverse relationship.

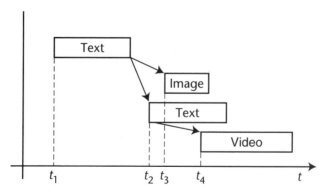

Figure 8.3 Absolute and relative temporal composition.

The representation used in Figure 8.3 is called a *timeline model.* It has the same expressiveness as Allen's time calculus: both can be transformed into the other without any loss.

This equivalence between the interval-based and point-based represen- Interval-based
tations of time can easily be seen when mapping the starting and end and point-based
points of intervals to time axes and giving time stamps to the points. representation
Then the temporal aspects can be expressed using Allen's calculus. Wahl
and Rothermehl (1994) and Little (1994) give overviews of the representation of time.

Synchronization

When incorporating time-dependent media (e.g., sound and video sequences) into a multimedia presentation, the temporal requirements
have to be met at presentation time.

Synchronization mechanisms can affect single media objects (*intra-* Intramedia and
media synchronization) or the relationship between two or more media ob- intermedia
jects (*intermedia synchronization*). representation

Another dimension in synchronization is coarse- versus fine-grained.
Coarse-grained synchronization handles the starting and ending points
of one or more presentation intervals. Fine-grained synchronization handles the temporal relationship within presentation intervals.

Consider a video sequence and its corresponding soundtrack. First, the
start of both objects has to be controlled. Second, the difference between
the two timelines must stay within certain acceptable bounds.

Of course, in distributed environments the control of temporal definitions at presentation time is closely related to Quality of Service (QoS)
parameters, which may also be incorporated into representations of
multimedia applications. But we will not consider this aspect in further
detail here.

8.1.3 The Advantage of Audiovisual Information

Web-based applications have been driven from the business perspective
by sales and marketing goals (commerce) and also by learning/training
goals, so we will say a few words regarding the psychological aspects of
the processing of information. In this section we will focus on the efficiency of conveying information through presentations based on a technical environment such as the Internet.

One area of multimedia research is determining to what extent multimedia techniques influence the ability of the user to recall information.
This includes the combination of media types as well as the power of

Increased
information
reception

interaction. The underlying mechanisms are the same for both Web-based applications and stand-alone multimedia applications.

Jeffcoate and Templeton (1992) measured the efficiency of the reception of information. They found that a person receives 10% of visual information, 20% of audio information, and 50% of audiovisual information. Other studies have slightly different results, but they support the hypothesis that the combination of both visual information (such as text and graphics) and audio information (such as spoken text and sound) will increase the efficiency of information transmission. An even better effect can be obtained by involving the user, as is the case with interactive elements.

These results may be an additional motivation for integrating multimedia information into Web-based environments, at least for a set of applications. One approach in that direction is outlined in the following section.

8.1.4 Multimedia Data Models

Data models and
formats

All functions of multimedia/hypermedia systems, as they have been characterized before, rely on the availability of appropriate data models implemented with corresponding formats. Data formats may be differentiated into several hierarchical interchange categories: general containers such as ASN.1 or Bento; monomedia for graphics, video, and others (e.g., JPEG or MPEG); metalanguages; and special-purpose object containers for data interchange on an object-oriented basis. We will shortly introduce HyTime and MHEG as representatives of metalanguages and object containers, respectively.

Data interchange is normally performed through APIs in multimedia systems for application interchange, for storing and archiving in file systems or database systems, and for presentation in networked environments. The last aspect, of course, is of special interest in our context.

MHEG

While monomedia formats just specify single media elements for the purpose of interchange, the definition of structural information is the objective of the Multimedia Hypermedia Information Encoding Group (MHEG). Structural information describes the interrelationships between the different pieces of multimedia presentations.

OO multimedia
composition

The MHEG format defines an object-oriented model for composing multimedia presentations. MH-Object is considered the root of the MHEG class hierarchy (see Figure 8.4). MHEG is intended for the inter-

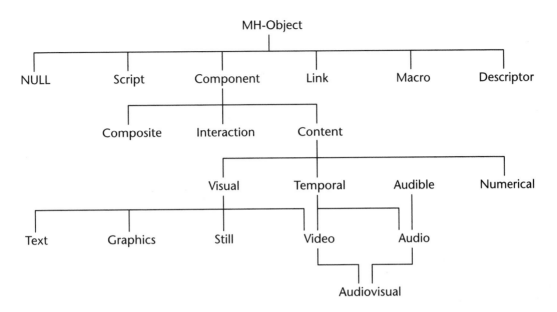

Figure 8.4 Example of an MHEG class hierarchy (Koegel 1992).

change of final-form presentations; that is, it supports delivery rather than authoring.

The MHEG classes provide abstractions and inheritance rules. The standard does not specify methods that would define actions on the objects. The first part of the MHEG standard gives a formal specification of the data structures using the ISO notation ASN.1. MHEG objects are then instances of the classes created to compose a multimedia presentation.

Abstraction and inheritance

To perform a presentation on a target platform, MHEG objects and media elements have to be transmitted from their origin. Therefore an additional transfer syntax is needed. The presentation is shown to a user via an MHEG engine that interprets the MHEG object and reconstructs the structure of the multimedia composition.

Transfer syntax

Further elements of the MHEG model are the content data (i.e., the pieces of information given by text, graphics, and so on), the behavior (i.e., the actions that reflect the appearance of the presentation regarding the temporal and spatial relationships), and user interaction (i.e., choosing from alternatives or modifying data through entry fields).

HyTime

Another format is the Hypermedia/Time-Based Structuring Language (HyTime), an SGML-based approach to multimedia interchange. SGML/

HyTime supports the coexistence of disparate multimedia information objects by a uniform object identification representation. It further provides a uniform representation of metainformation about notation data objects and a uniform multimedia information structure.

HyTime modules HyTime consists of the following six modules:

- The *base module* is similar to SGML and encompasses several utility architectural forms.
- The *location address module* creates pointers to information of any form and at any location.
- The *hyperlinks module* deals with the navigational relationships between information pieces. It therefore relies on the location address module that identifies these pieces.
- The *measurement module* handles the numerical dimensions such as time, space, and digital datastreams.
- The *scheduling module* represents the compositional relationships by describing coordinate spaces whose axes correspond to domains of measurement and events. Information objects are "located" in that space accordingly.
- The *rendition module* provides constructs for projecting events within the coordinate spaces and modifying the objects of events.

The scheduling and rendition modules together define the scheduling facilities of HyTime. Figure 8.5 shows the structuring facilities that enhance SGML.

The hyperlinked structure allows arbitrary relationships between nodes (i.e., information pieces), providing high flexibility by allowing links to have any number of link ends. A basic feature of HyTime is the Finite Coordinate Spaces (FCS). This is given by the scheduled structure, which is application-neutral. Different associative lists may be created from an FCS that all refer to information objects maintained once. This means that an FCS provides ordered views of the same content elements. The interpretation of the ordering within the lists (i.e., the semantics) is left to the application, although an FCS can provide instructions for spatiotemporal rendering or formatting of data. Newcomb, Kipp, and Newcomb (1991) and Kretz and Colaitis (1992) provide early overviews of HyTime.

8.2 VIEWING XML DATA ON THE WEB

In the previous section, we dealt with some groundwork and formal aspects of presentation and representation of (multimedia) information.

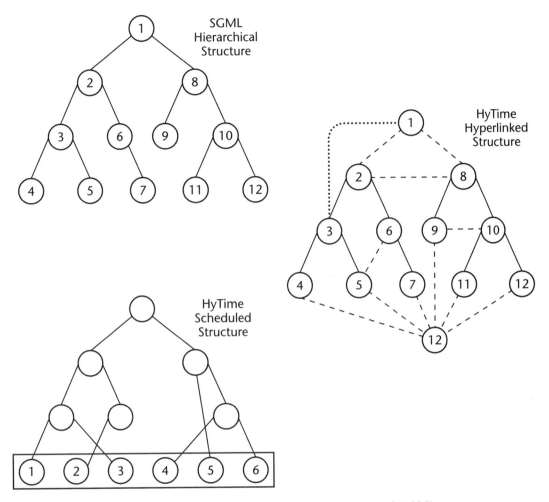

Figure 8.5 From SGML structuring to HyTime scheduling (Newcomb 1995).

Now we come to more concrete aspects of the presentation of XML-based information. The main application in that context, of course, is the Web.

8.2.1 Overview of Viewing XML Data

The basic idea of markup languages is the separation of the content of a document from its form (i.e., how it is presented to a user). Therefore extra processing is needed before viewing marked-up information on a Web front end. For us, two mechanisms are of particular interest: formatting

Markup languages

and transformation. From the latter perspective, XML may have to be transformed into another format, an HTML document, for instance. Transformation aspects will be covered later.

Formatting and style sheets

The formatting of XML documents may be achieved by using style sheets. They may be regarded as collections of rules to transform abstract XML information into formatted information to be passed on toward an output device. The transformation is done by a style sheet processor that will read the XML input along with the style sheet given. From that the processor generates the output accordingly, as long as the style sheet follows a notation the processor understands. This process may be performed on the server as well as on the client side of an Internet-based information system. The basic idea is illustrated in Figure 8.6 from the general perspective of SGML.

Client- vs. server-side generation

The decision on whether to process an XML document on the server or to pass it to the client depends on the application. As long as we only wish to view XML-based information, we may perform the processing on

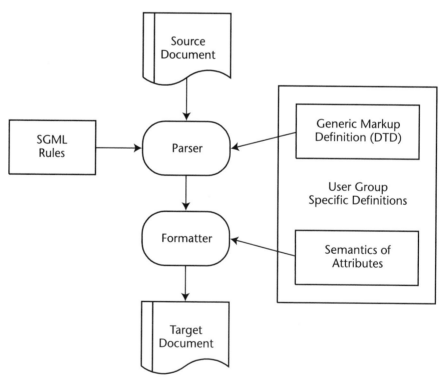

Figure 8.6 Overview of creating final form documents in SGML (Steinmetz and Nahrstedt 1995).

the server. If an application requires XML data for decentralized processing on the client side, we have to send the XML document along with the
style sheet. This may be the case in e-commerce applications, for example, when exchanging product information or ordering data.

8.2.2 HTML

The Hypertext Markup Language (HTML) is the well-known tagged language for setting up Web sites for Internet applications (i.e., Web publishing). It may be regarded as an application of SGML; that is, the HTML tag
set is defined using SGML notation.

The HTML specification is currently available from the W3C as version
4.01, which is a revised version of HTML 4 (HTML 1999). Here "revision"
means changes to the HTML DTD. We will not be discussing HTML in
principle here; we will assume you are familiar with the concepts of
HTML. Nor will we elaborate the elements of the revision here. Rather
we will give an overview of the basic features of HTML and its future
direction.

While earlier versions of HTML, namely, 2.0 of 1995 and 3.2 of 1997,
focused on supporting textual and multimedia content as well as hyperlink features, HTML 4 goes much further. The major goal in the development of the HTML versions was to achieve a broad consensus on the lan-
guage-supporting interoperability between manifold platforms and
presentations on client devices. The additional features incorporated into
HTML 4 include the following:

- More multimedia options (e.g., support for embedding external   HTML 4 features
  objects).
- Scripting languages to support dynamic Web applications (e.g., forms
  that react to user input).
- Style sheets to give authors more control of the rendering of HTML
  content. Style information may be specified internally in the document as well as in external documents associated with the HTML document. We will come back to style sheets in the next subsection.
- Better printing facilities for larger source documents that are divided
  into several HTML documents. These parts may be interconnected by
  the "link" element or by RDF, described in Section 3.3.
- Better accessibility for users with disabilities, through the support of
  more clearly distinct documents with regard to structure and presentation. Style sheets contain new features for nonvisual rendering, access
  keys, semantic grouping of controls, and so forth.

- Internationalization of documents, including the representation of international characters, text direction, punctuation, and other world language issues, to support the publishing of documents written in any language as well as the indexing for search engines.

Adding Style to HTML Documents

When considering formatting information in the context of Web design in HTML, the Web designer has two options: (1) formatting single elements in single documents using specific attributes or (2) employing internal or external styles.

Formatting

Formatting is supported by the inclusion in the HTML specification of tags and attributes, for example, the bold element <b> or the "font size" attribute. This way of creating a Web page layout may be viable for very small Web sites but is certainly not for large Web sites with dozens, hundreds, or even thousands of Web pages.

CSS

A solution to this problem is style sheets. Style sheets allow the central definition of formatting information for elements of tagged documents. Cascading style sheets (CSS) are a well-known method of formatting HTML documents. Take a corporate Web site as an example. Since a style sheet document may be assigned to an arbitrary number of HTML documents, a consistent look and feel for the site can be guaranteed just by developing a CSS document that follows the corporate design requirements. An additional benefit of using CSS is that maintenance of Web sites is much easier for layout.

The use of a CSS with HTML is de facto optional: standard browsers such as Netscape Communicator and Microsoft Internet Explorer have internalized the HTML document type definition. The browsers know the elements of HTML and have a predefined formatting for them.

Using Style Sheets with XML

CSS and XML

The presentation of HTML through standard browsers for end user presentation does not require an extra style sheet. XML has in any case to be associated with style sheets. The use of CSS is not very common with XML, although the Mozilla browser (*www.mozilla.org*), for instance, provides the feature of directly viewing XML content on the basis of the internalized conversion to HTML.

Principal elements of CSS are assignments of the kind

```
Selector(s) { declaration }
```

with the declaration given as

```
property : value.
```

An example taken from HTML would accordingly be

```
H2, H3 { font-family: roman; font-size: 14pt }.
```

Additionally, properties may be assigned in a context-sensitive way. Let's have a look at the following example:

```
H1 EM { color: red }
```

The effect is that the content of element EM to be emphasized in H1 will be displayed in red. This feature is helpful for a variety of definitions, such as numbering lists, to mention just one.

Style sheets will be associated with XML documents following the corresponding W3C recommendation, available from *www.w3.org/TR/xml-stylesheet/*. The recommendation provides the xml-stylesheet instruction to process the style sheet document specified within the XML document in question. Here is an example, first as an instruction in an HTML document, then the corresponding XML version.

```
<LINK href="mystyle.css" rel="stylesheet" type="text/css">
```

```
<?xml-stylesheet href="mystyle.css" type="text/css"?>
```

8.2.3 XHTML

The Extensible Hypertext Markup Language (XHTML) is a collection of document types and modules specified by the W3C "that reproduce, subset, and extend HTML 4" (XHTML 2000a). The document types are XML based; that is, XHTML is an HTML version that uses XML syntax. The element types are the same as for HTML. Documents written in XHTML always have to be well formed and valid. XHTML has been designed to work with XML-based user agents. A user agent denotes a system that | User agents provides functionality and services to retrieve and process documents containing, for example, XML or XHTML content.

The basic idea behind XHTML is to provide Web developers with a | Richer Web standard that allows for richer Web pages on a wider variety of client de- | pages vices and yet still be in accordance with the rigorousness of XML. The increasing range of browser platforms and applications is being met by the modular design of XHTML, to be discussed later in this subsection.

The main benefit to be gained from using XHTML is the flexibility for | Flexibility Web application developers. This refers to the future interoperability within and among various XHTML environments as well as to the potential of enhancing the language with new elements that will be needed for future applications.

XHTML 1.0 (XHTML 2000a) was recommended in January 2000. It is the first document type in the XHTML family and is based on HTML 4.01. It is thus a reformulation of the three HTML 4 document types (flavors) using XML 1.0, resulting in the following:

- XHTML 1.0 Strict is for documents that do not contain any tags associated with layout. Layout effects are then defined together with W3C's CSS language.
- XHTML 1.0 Transitional supports users whose browser versions do not understand style sheets. It allows the adjustment of markups with layout-oriented attributes.
- XHTML 1.0 Frameset supports the partitioning of the browser window into HTML frames.

XHTML 1.0 may be used to specify content that is XML conforming. It also works with client applications that conform to HTML 4. Therefore XHTML documents may be viewed, edited, and validated with standard XML tools. HTML may be checked using a tool provided by the W3C, the "HTML Tidy" (*www.w3.org/People/Raggett/tidy*). It also allows HTML content to be rolled over into XML to be delivered in XHTML.

The following is a small example of an XHTML document. The DOCTYPE declaration prior to the root element <html> has to reference one of the three DTDs mentioned earlier. Along with the root element, the XHTML namespace is specified accordingly. Additionally the namespace is used along with another namespace defining MathML, which is used to semantically specify mathematical formulas to be presented on Web clients.

```
<?xml version="1.0" encoding="UTF-8"?>

<!DOCTYPE html

    PUBLIC "~//W3C//DTD XHTML 1.0 Strict //EN"

    "DTD/xhtml1-strict.dtd">

<html xmlns=http://www.w3.org/1999/xhtml

        xml:lang="en" lang="en">

    <head>

        <title>A Math Example</title>

    </head>

    <body>
```

```
<p>The following is MathML markup:</p>
<math xmlns=http://www.w3.org/1998/Math/MathML">
    <apply> </log>
        <logbase>
            <cn> 3 </cn>
        </logbase>
        <ci> x </ci>
    </apply>
</math>
<p>MathML reference available from
    <a href="http://www.w3.org/Math">W3C Website</a>
</p>
</body>
</html>
```

In order to be compatible with HTML, some guidelines have to be followed. There are also some differences with HTML that have to be taken into consideration. (See section 4 and appendix C of XHTML 2000a for a corresponding overview.)

In the next step of the W3C's XHTML roadmap, the elements and attributes have been modularized into convenient collections for use in documents that combine HTML with other tag sets (XHTML 2001a). "Modularization" in this context means to break up XHTML into smaller sets of elements since not all client platforms will need the complete definition.

XHTML modularization

An example of such a set of modules is XHTML Basic (XHTML 2000b), which is targeted at mobile applications. XHTML content can be exchanged among PDAs, mobile phones, desktop computers, and TV sets. Numerous companies in the fields of communication and content have announced that they will support XHTML for mobile business applications. XHTML Basic subsets HTML such that a document can be shared among a maximum number of user agents. Of course, it may be extended to meet particular requirements of a community and still support the presentation of XHTML Basic content.

Mobile applications

A reduced set of HTML features has been the starting point for the design of XHTML Basic, including basic text (headings, paragraphs, and lists), hyperlinks and links to related documents, basic forms, basic tables, images, and metainformation. All of these are part of the corresponding XHTML modules, which are listed later in this subsection, given as current version XHTML 1.1.

These features may also be found in document types representing subsets and variants of HTML for the type of user agents outlined earlier. Examples include Compact HTML (Kamada 1998), the Wireless Markup Language (WML), and the "HTML 4.0 Guidelines for Mobile Access" (Kamada et al. 1999). WML will be considered in Section 8.4.

XHTML 1.1 (XHTML 2001b) defines a new XHTML document type based upon the modularization work of W3C. Unlike XHTML 1.0, it provides a consistent basis for future document types being cleanly separated from the deprecated, legacy functionality of HTML 4. In turn it is a reformulation of XHTML 1.0 Strict.

Well-formed markup   Thus the goal of XHTML to move Web content from malformed, nonstandard into well-formed markup, given by XML, has been approached a lot more closely by XHTML 1.1. The motivation of XHTML 1.0 was to migrate HTML-based content to XHTML and XML. With the modularization of XHTML, support for deprecated elements and attributes has been removed from the XHTML family.

The basic idea is to support the provision of markup content from a semantic perspective rather than with presentation-oriented functionality, as is given with XHTML Transitional and Frameset document types. Many of the presentation features of XHTML 1.0 are avoided.

The XHTML 1.1 document type is based upon a set of XHTML modules defined in XHTML (2001a). Here are the features associated with each XHTML module.

- Structure module: `body`, `head`, `html`, `title`
- Text module: `abbr`, `acronym`, `address`, `blockquote`, `br`, `cite`, `code`, `dfn`, `div`, `em`, `h1`, `h2`, `h3`, `h4`, `h5`, `h6`, `kbd`, `p`, `pre`, `q`, `samp`, `span`, `strong`, `var`
- Hypertext module: `a`
- List module: `dl`, `dt`, `dd`, `ol`, `ul`, `li`
- Object module: `object`, `param`
- Presentation module: `b`, `big`, `hr`, `i`, `small`, `sub`, `sup`, `tt`
- Edit module: `del`, `ins`
- Bidirectional text module: `bdo`
- Forms module: `button`, `fieldset`, `form`, `input`, `label`, `legend`, `select`, `optgroup`, `option`, `textarea`
- Table module: `caption`, `col`, `colgroup`, `table`, `tbody`, `td`, `tfoot`, `th`, `thead`, `tr`

- Image module: `img`
- Client-side image map module: `area, map`
- Server-side image map module: attribute `ismap` on `img`
- Intrinsic events module: event attributes
- Metainformation module: `meta`
- Scripting module: `noscript, script`
- Style sheet module: `style` element
- Style attribute module: `style` attribute (deprecated)
- Link module: `link`
- Base module: `base`
- Ruby annotation module: `ruby, rbc, rtc, rb, rt, rp`

XHTML 1.0 and XHTML 1.1 are recommendations of the W3C, the latter as of May 31, 2001. XHTML 1.0 Second Edition is currently a working draft as of October 4, 2001. The first draft of XHTML 2.0 is scheduled for early 2002. XHTML Modularization is a proposed recommendation as of February 22, 2001. Further steps on the W3C roadmap are to be determined.

XHTML may be viewed and processed using standard XML tools. Additionally, Web browsers can read XHTML. The first editor for XHTML has recently been presented by Mozquito. "Mozquito Factory" supports the authoring of Web content in XHTML as well as the import of HTML documents and their translation into XHTML. The Mozquito approach will be discussed in Section 8.3.2.

8.2.4 Formatting Objects with XSL

In this section, we will discuss an approach to formatting documents that goes beyond the options of CSS. The focus of our discussion will be on formatting objects that represent structural units in documents.

XSL and XSLT

The Extensible Style Language (XSL) is a language to define style sheets, as was discussed in Section 2.7. It is similar to CSS in that it separates formatting information from content. It also supports printing options and the transmission of XML documents across various platforms. The XSL specification contains three parts: the XSLT language for transformation (see Chapter 9), the XPath language to access parts of or whole XML documents (see Section 2.5.1), and finally XSL formatting objects, which will be discussed later in this section.

The Extensible Style Language Transformation (XSLT) is the language that is used within XSL documents to transform XML documents into other documents, either XML again or HTML. This allows content to be represented in several XML documents for particular applications.

DSSSL

The relationship between XSL and XSLT can be shown with Document Style Semantics and Specification Language (DSSSL), which although perhaps outdated still serves to visualize the key procedure here. It was developed to process SGML documents, and many of its concepts have been incorporated into XSL and XSLT. The transformation and formatting process is shown in Figure 8.7, where the gray elements are specified by DSSSL.

Formatting objects

As previously stated, XSLT provides transformation and XSL provides formatting. XSL then may be considered as a specific document type. Its elements are *formatting objects* (FOs). These FOs define formatting semantics and are generated by a preceding transformation step, performed, not so surprisingly, by XSLT. The XSL-FO then may be converted into arbitrary final formats such as HTML for online presentation, RTF for text processing, or PostScript or PDF for printing. An example of printing XML via PDF is given at *www.dpawson.co.uk/xsl/print.html*. We may also use XSLT to generate other documents such as XHTML or WML (see Section 8.4.2).

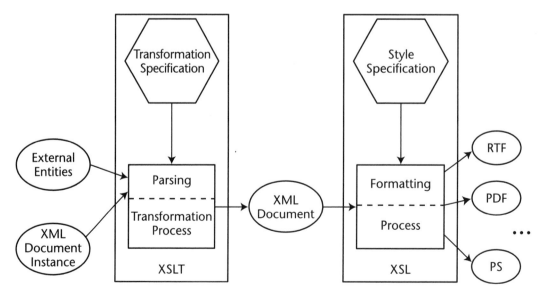

Figure 8.7 Overview of the DSSSL processing of SGML documents (Behme and Mintert 2000).

XSL Formatting Objects

XSL Formatting Objects (XSL-FO) makes up almost two-thirds of the XSL
specification (*www.w3.org/TR/xsl/slice6.html#fo-section*). It describes how
to present page-oriented output. Although XSL-FO code can be produced
manually, the more usual way would be to transform an XML document
into another XML document using XSL-FO vocabulary. This transformation from a semantic to a presentational representation is done with
XSLT. Since browsers cannot display XSL-FO documents directly, apart
from X-Smiles (see Section 8.3.2), a further transformation to final output
has to be done, most likely to PDF (see later in this subsection).

The content of XSL-FO documents is organized into *areas,* which can
be thought of as rectangular boxes containing the formatting objects that
represent the content. The areas form a kind of hierarchy. The spatial positioning of the areas is done by an XSL formatter. When being processed,
the formatting objects document is broken up into pages, normally one
for Web presentation and individual pages for printed output. Each page
then contains a number of areas.

While CSS is mainly used for Web presentation, XSL-FO goes further
and provides a more sophisticated layout model that also supports multipurpose publishing. We will not reproduce the definition of all the formatting objects here. Instead we will summarize them in a condensed
list, giving some hints where the FO names are not self-explanatory. The
recommendation documents encompass the following FOs:

- *Pagination and layout formatting objects:* definition of master pages and
  page sequences, particularly of interest for printed output
- *Block formatting objects:* formatting of text-based information such as
  paragraphs, titles, and captions given as block objects
- *Inline formatting objects:* portions of text inside block formatting
  objects; for example, adding the word "Page" to a running foot for
  pagination
- *List formatting objects*
- *Table formatting objects*
- *Out-of-line formatting objects:* floating objects and footnotes to be placed
  at the next possible position in the output document
- *Other formatting objects:* for example, wrappers for property heritage
  and markers for running heads and feet

The order of the FOs listed here, roughly speaking, corresponds to the
order in which content is placed. Further formatting details, however,
are specified by attributes assigned to the individual FO. Many of these

XSL-FO

Areas

formatting properties have CSS equivalents (e.g., `font-family`); others do not.

The set of standard XSL-FO properties includes the following:

- *Common absolute position properties:* absolute positioning including size
- *Common aural properties:* rendition of FO content for output via voice processors
- *Common border, padding, and background properties*
- *Common font properties*
- *Common hyphenation properties:* line breaking including language-dependent hyphenation
- *Common keeps and breaks properties:* column and page breaks
- *Common margin properties:* spacing and indents
- *Other properties:* specific to certain FOs, such as character- and color-related properties, conversions, pagination and layout, dynamic effects, and many more

Final-form PDF   The two preceding lists give a first glimpse of what XSL-FO is about, particularly for publishing purposes. A tutorial on using XSL-FO with XEP to produce final-form PDF documents, just to mention one application, can be found at *www.renderx.com/Tests/doc/html/tutorial.html*. We will come back to this topic in Section 8.6.1.

Here is a short example of the use of formatting objects, taken from Harold (2001), available online at *www.ibiblio.org/xml/books/bible2/*.

```
<?xml version="1.0"?>

<fo:root xmlns:fo="http://www.w3.org/1999/XSL/Format">

  <fo:layout-master-set>

    <fo:simple-page-master master-name="only">

      <fo:region-body/>

    </fo:simple-page-master>

  </fo:layout-master-set>

  <fo:page-sequence master-name="only">

    <fo:flow flow-name="xsl-region-body">

      <fo:block font-size="20pt"

          font-family="serif" line-height="30pt">

        Hydrogen

      </fo:block>
```

```
<fo:block font-size="20pt"

    font-family="serif" line-height="30pt" >

    Helium

  </fo:block>

</fo:flow>

</fo:page-sequence>

</fo:root>
```

Here we can see the hierarchy mentioned earlier, starting with the root element including the other nested FOs. The content itself is specified in the two elements given by fo:block, including the corresponding text formatting properties.

Generating Final-Form Documents for Presentation

Obviously we have a lot of choices of which technique to use for presentation. Figure 8.8 summarizes some of the available alternatives.

Which do we choose? CSS, for example, has proven to be very useful **CSS vs. XSL** for presenting HTML content. But XSL is XML technology. There is no one right answer along the lines of "CSS if you can, XSL if you must." Table 8.1 compares the major aspects of CSS and XSL.

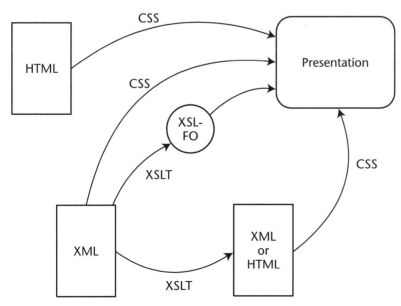

Figure 8.8 Presentation techniques using CSS and XSL (W3C 2000a).

Table 8.1 Comparison of CSS and XSL.

	CSS	XSL
Can be used with HTML	yes	no
Can be used with XML	yes	yes
Transformation language	no	yes
Syntax	CSS	XML

Finally a word about practical application. So far we have been dealing with only conceptual considerations, and reality may bring us back to earth. The specifications are in different states of completion, and therefore accepted standardization and wide market penetration may be some years away, for example, for XSL-FO.

So, unless the different components of Web-based environments—ranging from authoring to data management and business middleware, to the variety of standard and exotic output devices—fully implement and support these specifications, we will have to make pragmatic compromises.

We expect the support for XSL by client devices, such as browsers, handhelds, and so on, to be on the server side rather than the client side. The server will handle the presentation of XML content by transforming it into HTML, probably enhanced with CSS. In mixed environments, different style sheets could be set up for the output devices that are XSL enabled and for those that are not.

8.3 USER INTERACTION WITH XFORMS

User input

Forms to capture user input have become commonplace in Web-based applications, particularly with the more advanced requirements of e-commerce. So we will give a short overview of XForms as the XML-based proposal for adequately handling user interaction through forms, followed by sample implementations.

8.3.1 Concepts of XForms

Traditional Web forms as known from HTML and XHTML have become an important feature in interactive Web applications that collect data from users. As stated earlier, the current W3C efforts aim at separating the structural information defining elements in Web documents from their appearance in the Web browser or other user agents.

In accordance with that goal, XForms (*www.w3.org/Markup/forms*) in- troduces abstract concepts to decouple data, logic, and presentation of Web forms, making XForms a successor to XHTML forms. The main components of XForms are the following:

Main components

- The *XForms model* describes the forms independently from device-specific rendering. The presentation options are attached separately.
- The *XForms user interface* provides the necessary visual form controls (i.e., widgets for user interaction) that can be used inside different XML documents (e.g., XHTML and SVG).
- The *XForms submit protocol* defines the method by which a form sends and receives data.
- The *XForms processor* is an implementation of the XForms model. Its components, behavior, and mechanisms are described by a corresponding reference model.

Figure 8.9 summarizes the major components of XForms.

The different components—particularly XForms model, instance data, and form controls—are connected with bindings. The binding expressions of XForms are based on XPath (see Section 2.5.1); that is, they use XPath datatypes.

If we consider forms to consist of a purpose, a presentation, and data, we could argue that earlier implementations of Web technologies did not

Appearance vs. purpose

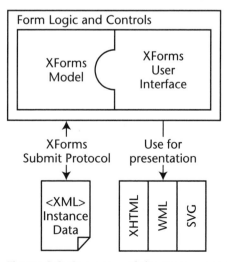

Figure 8.9 Overview of the major components of XForms.

separate the presentation of a form (i.e., its appearance) from its purpose. This separation would definitely be helpful in adding conditional or input-dependent dynamics. That is, forms should be able to differentiate several user input cases and adapt accordingly. Let's look at an example. First the XHTML code:

```
<form action="http://example.com/submit" method="post">
    <span>Select Payment Method:  </span >
    <input type="radio" name="paytype"
            value="cash">Cash</input>
    <input type="radio" name="paytype"
            value="credit">Credit</input><br/>
    <label>Credit Card Number: <input type="text"
            name="cc"/></label> <br/>
    <label>Expiration Date: <input type="text"
            name="exp"/></label> <br/>
    <input type="submit"/>
</form>
```

This sample code produces two radio buttons to select the payment method, input fields for credit card number and expiration date, and a submit button.

Now have a look at the corresponding XForms code:

```
<selectOne xmlns=http://www.w3.org/2001/06/xforms
            ref="paytype">
    <caption>Select Payment Method</caption>
    <choices>
        <item value="cash">Cash</item>
        <item value="credit">Credit</item>
    </choices>
</selectOne>
<textbox xmlns="http://www.w3.org/2001/06/xforms" ref="cc">
    <caption>Credit Card Number</caption>
</textbox>
```

```
<textbox xmlns="http://www.w3.org/2001/06/xforms" ref="exp">

  <caption>Expiration Date</caption>

</textbox>

<submit xmlns="http://www.w3.org/2001/06/xforms"/>
```

Here we have basically the same interaction elements. But in contrast to XHTML, the radio buttons are not hard-coded, the input elements such as `textbox` are predefined, and the input is submitted as XML data.

Most important from a presentational perspective, the rendering of specific elements can be done by different devices. This refers to the `selectOne` element that replaced the radio buttons in the XHTML sample code.

This decoupling allows Web authors to create richer Web applications with advanced forms logic, multiple forms per page, or multiple pages per form. In turn, as in other XML initiatives, the international aspects are improved and a variety of devices are supported.

8.3.2 Implementations

In the previous sections, we discussed the concepts of XHTML. XHTML technology has already been implemented in the Mozquito and X-Smiles tools that we present next.

Mozquito

Mozquito is an example of XHTML technology that has been enhanced   XHTML-FML
with additional features. Since the support for forms has been a focus, the XHTML-FML (Form Markup Language) has been defined for advanced form functionality. Further efforts will lead in the direction of fully integrating FML with XForms.

The basic idea of Mozquito is to transform its documents into HTML documents with JavaScript code that can be processed by any Web browser. This is done on the server side, thus taking some of the load off the Web client. JavaScript was chosen so as to be independent from installing new browser versions or plug-ins.

Since most Web site code is produced by authoring tools on the client side, Mozquito provides a corresponding authoring environment that includes an XML parser to check on well-formedness and validity. An overview of the Mozquito Factory can be found at *www.mozquito.org/html/ lang-english/beginning.html*. There you will also find FML references and specifications.

X-Smiles

X-Smiles (*www.x-smiles.org*) is a nonprofit Java-based XML browser that supports several XML technologies. Although XForms and SMIL are features of X-Smiles, SVG, XSLT Transforms, and XSL-FO are supported through third-party components. A detailed overview of what is currently supported can be found at *www.x-smiles.org/xsmiles_features.html*.

The main objective of X-Smiles is the support for desktop solutions and for embedded solutions. Both of these may be mixed in a single document. An additional goal is the processing and streaming of multimedia content.

X-Smiles is still in the prototype stage (version 0.45 was released on October 26, 2001). The next steps, among others, are compliance with SMIL 2.0, full support of XForms models, and reimplementation of the formatting objects renderer.

8.4 EXCHANGING INFORMATION THROUGH WAP DEVICES

Mobile information access seems to be the current wave in information management and processing. An increasing importance has been attached to m-commerce, to mention just one buzzword, in business-to-business as well as business-to-consumer relationships. This raises the need for appropriate techniques and formats as well as for applications and technical devices. For our discussion, since we are only interested in XML-related presentation formats for mobile devices, we will give a short introduction to the WAP technology followed by a description of the corresponding markup language, WML.

8.4.1 What Is WAP?

The Wireless Application Protocol (WAP) is an open specification that allows mobile access to, and exchange of, information and services. It embraces handheld devices such as mobile phones and palmtops/PDAs, as well as pagers and, to a lesser extent, car radios.

Interoperability   Since WAP is not based on a particular transmission standard (e.g., UMTS or GSM), interoperability is guaranteed for such applications. Most of the manufacturers of mobile devices have committed to supporting the specification, which therefore can be regarded as a de facto standard.

While WAP specifies only the transmission of data to and from compliant devices, a language is needed to define the contents for WAP applications. This language is WML, which is covered in the following subsection.

Devices need an appropriate WAP-enabled microbrowser to display information. Most mobile phones now come with such a browser. For other applications and devices, browsers are available for a variety of operating system platforms: Microsoft Windows, PalmOS, and JavaOS, to mention just a few.

The WAP standard is based on an OSI architecture, the WAP stack, which consists of five major layers. They specify the front-end interface to the devices, the session handling, transmission, security, and transport at the back-end interface to the network.

Typical applications for WAP are communication (e.g., mailing and chatting) and unidirectional information (e.g., the weather forecast or the movie schedule of your local theater). Bidirectional information exchange (i.e., user action and response) is required for financial applications (e.g., online banking or brokerage services), shopping, electronic organizing, navigation and tour guiding, and home automation (i.e., the remote control of devices in your house). The last is expected to be an important feature in the near future.

Part of the WAP effort is the Wireless Application Environment (WAE), specified in WAE (2000). It aims at building a general-purpose and interoperable application environment using Web technologies to provide applications and services for wireless platforms. Several techniques contribute to the WAE specification, including the specifications of Wireless Markup Language (WML), WMLScript, WAP Binary XML Format (WBXML), and Wireless Telephony Application (WTA).

The WAE architecture is based on a client-server model, as are traditional Web services. Content and services are hosted on standard Web servers using standard URLs. In addition to the basic client-server model, a gateway provides encoding and decoding mechanisms as well as WMLScript compilation for content exchange between server and mobile client and the handling of user action. Thus, on the server side, standard Web content is produced at a client's request. The encoding enables a user agent to navigate through Web content on the basis of the WML and WMLScript. The WTA in this context specifies extensions for call and feature control mechanisms in telephony applications. Figure 8.10 gives a very basic architectural overview.

For more information about the standard, technical equipment, and development aspects, you may start your investigation at the WAP Forum (*www.wapforum.org*), the Web site of the industry association that developed the standard. You may also find helpful information at *www.wap*

Microbrowser presentation

WAP stack

WAE

WAE architecture

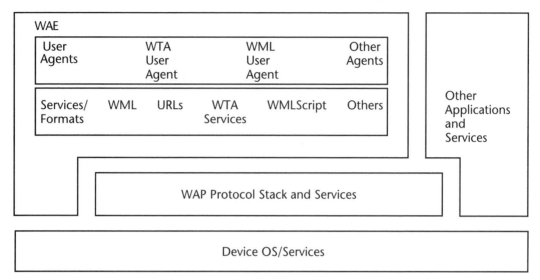

Figure 8.10 Architectural model of WAP efforts (WAE 2000).

.net. An overall overview of WAP is given in the WAP Forum white paper (WAP 2000). A basic goal of the WAP Forum is to work together with the Web Coalition (W3C) and the Internet Engineering Task Force (IETF) to integrate WML with next-generation HTML and HTTP.

8.4.2 WML

Wireless Markup Language (WML) is used to provide static information for WAP applications in an appropriate way. It has to meet the limitations of current wireless communication. Therefore reduced information has to be provided according to the presentational capabilities of the devices and the low transmission bandwidth.

Cards

Decks

Both WML and HTML are markup languages, based on tags. But, by looking closer at WML's structure, you will find that it is formed of well-defined units of user actions, called *cards*. The basic concept of accessing information in WAP applications is navigating between cards that may be dispersed in several WML documents. Cards may be grouped into sets, called *decks*, each describing an interaction with the user. This design meets the limitations of even the small-size displays of handheld devices. The concept of organizing information in cardlike units is similar to HyperCard, an early authoring approach for the development of multimedia applications, which is still available and in use (*hypercard.apple.com*). Here is a small WML example (WML 2000a):

```
<wml>

  <card>

    <p>

      <do type="accept">

        <go href="#card2"/>

      </do>

      Hello world. This is the first card …

    </p>

  </card>

  <card id="card2">

    <p>This is the second card. Goodbye.</p>

  </card>

</wml>
```

The main features of WML are the following:

WML features

- Support for text and images, providing the author with elements for specifying such content and laying it out to a certain extent.
- Support for user input such as controls for text entry, selection from several options, and task invocation. These controls may be presented by the user agents as being bound to physical keys, voice commands, or sections of the screen presentation.
- Navigation and history stack. The former keeps track of user actions on the basis of WML's several URL-based navigation mechanisms.
- Abstract specification of layout and presentation for independence from particular interfaces and devices.
- Optimization for narrow-band devices, mainly through the minimization of server requests and the amount of data to be exchanged.
- State and context management (i.e., the provision of variable states). These may be used to modify the content of parameterized cards and can be shared among decks without server communication.

8.4.3 WMLScript

WMLScript enhances JavaScript in order to program user agents (i.e., mobile devices). It allows the design of more advanced user interfaces for mobile applications by enriching browsing and presentation on the basis of WML by behavioral capabilities. It allows the performance of client-based processing to be fully integrated with the WML browser.

Client-based processing

Examples of client-based action include any interaction with the user in general, checking user input before passing a request to the server, or accessing device facilities and peripherals. The invocation of WMLScript may be triggered by events caused by user interaction or by the environment.

WMLScript supports several operations (e.g., assignment, arithmetical, logical), script functions (defined internally or externally), and library functions (e.g., for floating point and string handling) defined in the WML Standard Libraries Specification (WML 2000b).

8.4.4 WBXML

The WAP Binary XML Content Format (WBXML) has been designed as a means to reduce the transmission size of XML documents on channels with low bandwidth (WBXML 2000). The element structure of XML is preserved without losing any functionality or semantic information.

Reduction of document size is based on tokenization of the XML syntax. This means that any entity, tag, attribute, and so forth is mapped to a token. The following example specifies a tokenized WML deck and demonstrates variable and attribute encoding and the use of the string table (WML 2000a). Let's look at the source deck first:

```
<wml>

   <card id="abc" ordered="true">

     <p>

        <do type="accept">

           <go href="http://xyz.org/s"/>

        </do>

        X: $(X) <br/>

        Y: $(&#x59;) <br/>

        Enter name : <input type="text" name="N"/>

     </p>

   </card>

</wml>
```

We will not give a complete overview of the tokenized form here. To give an impression we have listed a subset of annotated token streams in Table 8.2, representing the first two lines of the source deck code.

Table 8.2 Example of Tokenized Source Deck Code.

Token Stream	Description
7F	wml, with content
E7	card, with content and attributes
55	id=
03	Inline string follows
'a', 'b', 'c', 00	String
33	ordered="true"
01	END (of card attribute list)

Table 8.3 Overview of WAP-Related Tools.

Tool	Platform	Link
WAPUniverse 0.3.0 Build 5	PalmOS	*http://download.sourceforge.net/wapuniverse/ WAPUniverse_0_3_0_Build5.zip*
AU Systems Browser	PalmOS	*http://www.ericsson.com/developerszone/ uploadedfiles/wapbrowser161.zip*
EzWAP	Windows CE	*http://www.ezos.com/Main.asp*
Ericsson R380s WAP Emulator 3.0	Windows 95/98/NT	*http://www.ericsson.com/developerszone/*
WinWAP 2.3 Light	Windows 95/98/NT	*http://www.slobtrot.com/winwap/*
ccWAP Browser	Windows 95/98/NT	*http://www.checkcom.de/download.htm*
iobox Surfer WAP simulator	Browser window	*http://www.iobox.de/static?&PAGE=core/ mainpage&ITEM_ID=11000#*
waptiger-Emulator WAP Simulator	Browser window	*http://www.waptiger.de/waptiger/*

8.4.5 Links to WAP Tools

WAP-related tools include browsers, emulators, and simulators that can be used to experiment with WAP applications, since WAP is not supported by standard browsers. Table 8.3 provides a list of Web sites that such tools may be obtained from.

8.5 GRAPHICAL AND MULTIMEDIA PRESENTATION WITH XML

With the increasing penetration of the Internet into business and private life, efforts are being made to integrate multimedia with Web applications. Specifically, script languages seem to be the target of many researchers and developers since the normal markup structure of HTML is not very promising for further enhancements. An example of such an initiative is the Virtual Reality Markup Language (VRML). Although there are some interesting applications for simulation (Luttermann and Grauer 1999) and scientific visualization, VRML has not become a market success.

VRML

In this section we will focus on current efforts to combine several media or multimedia features with the Web, starting with SMIL and proceeding toward speech integration.

8.5.1 SMIL

The Synchronized Multimedia Integration Language (SMIL) is an XML document type for the description of multimedia presentations. It allows the positioning of media objects as well as spatial and temporal synchronization (i.e., along the third and fourth dimension, respectively).

Let's consider to what extent SMIL meets the requirements composing multimedia presentation, as they have been rolled out in Section 8.1.2.

Media integration

First, SMIL allows the integration of several media elements since there are text, graphics, audio, and video formats. When working with SMIL, however, we have to take into consideration the capabilities of the different SMIL players that are available. Table 8.4 gives an overview of media types, the corresponding tags used in SMIL, and whether or not the media are supported by the players (Helio 1999).

SMIL skeleton

We will start with a short introduction to the features of SMIL. The following code is a skeleton for SMIL documents. The head section is primarily for layout definitions, and the body section is primarily for specification of media and synchronization parameters:

```
<smil>
  <head>
    <meta name="Author" content="B. Daum and U. Merten" />
    <layout>
      <!-- layout tags -->
    </layout>
```

Table 8.4 Overview of SMIL Attributes and Player Support.

Media	Tag	G2	GRiNS	Soja
GIF	img	OK	OK	OK
JPEG	img	OK	OK	OK
Microsoft Wav	audio	OK	OK	—
Sun Audio	audio	OK	OK	OK
Sun Audio Zipped	audio	—	—	OK
MP3	audio	OK	—	—
Plain text	text	OK	OK	OK
Real text	textstream	OK	—	—
Real movie	video	OK	—	—
AVI	video	OK	OK	—
MPEG	video	OK	OK	—
MOV	video	OK	—	—

```
    <head>
    <body>
        <!-- media and synchronization tags -->
    </body>
</smil>
```

Positioning of Media

SMIL provides absolute as well as relative positioning. Everything about the layout of the SMIL application goes into the layout section of the SMIL document. For instance, have a look at the following code fragment:

Spatial composition

```
<layout>
    <root-layout width="300" height="200"
                 background-color="white"/>
    <region id="picture-region" left="25" top="25"
            width="150" height="100" z-index="2" fit="fill"/>
    <region id="text-region" left="125" top="100"
            width="100" height="50" z-index="1"/>
</layout>
```

The attributes of the root-layout tag define the layout of the overall presentation window. Two regions for an image and a text object are specified by their absolute coordinates. The z-index gives priority along the *z*-axis and thereby governs overlapping. In our example the text will overlay the image. The fit attribute can have different values: fill makes the picture fit into the region, slice and meet make the picture grow without distortion, and scroll is used if the region is too small and the picture is to be scrolled over. Relative positioning is achieved by assigning percentages to the top and left attributes.

Now we have to specify the objects that must be placed in the regions defined so far. This is done in the body section of the document:

```
<body>
    <text src="some.txt" region="text-region"/>
    <img src="some.gif" alt="Here is a picture"
         region="picture-region"/>
</body>
```

Synchronization

SMIL allows the definition of the duration of the presentation of a media element (e.g., the time period that a picture will be shown to a user). This is intramedia synchronization; intermedia synchronization refers to at least two elements (e.g., sequential playing of two video objects). Furthermore we may define that an element becomes apparent only after some period of time (i.e., it is delayed).

This may be done absolutely by setting the presentation time relative to the starting point of the SMIL application. The word "relative" is not really appropriate since relative synchronization refers to the temporal positioning of a media element with regard to another element within the SMIL show. Here is an example of sequential presentation with delayed start and duration attributes:

```
<body>
  <seq>
     <img src="some.gif" alt="Here is a picture"
          region="some_picture" dur="10s"/>
     <img src="another.jpg" alt="And another one"
          region="another_picture" dur="5s" begin="1s"/>
  </seq>
</body>
```

Finally, we may also want to define the presentation of some media elements in parallel, which SMIL provides for with a corresponding tag <par>. More advanced features include the event-based relative synchronization of media objects.

Switching

SMIL also supports user preferences including some types of service parameters. This is done by defining options using the switch tag. An example is switching between several language versions of text elements according to the user settings. Another would be the evaluation of the transfer rate of a user's Internet connection and changing the image resolution accordingly. We could have a high-resolution image for high bandwidth and a low-resolution image for low bandwidth. This aspect in turn also affects the appearance of the presentation, as does a possible adaptation to the screen resolution given by a front-end system. The following listing gives an impression of how to use these features within SMIL:

Service parameters

```
<body>

   <switch>

      <par system-language="en"> <!-- English only -->

         <text src="you_are_english.txt" region="main_message"/>

         <switch> <!-- testing the screen size -->

            <text src="800_600.en.txt" region="size"
                  system-screen-size="800X600"/>

            <text src="1024_768.en.txt" region="size"
                  system-screen-size="1024X768"/>

         </switch>

      </par>

      <par system-language="fr"> <!-- French only -->

         <text src="vous_etes_francais.txt"
               region="main_message"/>

         <switch> <!-- testing the screen size -->

            <text src="800_600.fr.txt" region="size"
                  system-screen-size="800X600"/>
```

```
        <text src="1024_768.fr.txt" region="size"
              system-screen-size="1024X768"/>
    </switch>
  </par>
  <text src="unknown_language.txt" region="main_message"/>
</switch>
</body>
```

Here we have a nested `switch`: the outer one for the language choice and the inner ones for the screen resolution in either language followed by a "default" case (i.e., an unknown language).

Finally Integrating Multimedia with the Web?

The dynamics currently observable in XML-related developments not only affect the traditional (re)presentation and transformation of text content. Quite a lot of effort goes into providing developers with standards that allow for richer applications, for example, by adding more advanced interaction and multimedia elements.

SMIL has been presented as an XML document type that provides authors with the fundamental mechanisms identified in Section 8.1.1, in particular, the spatiotemporal composition of content being coded in different media types. The current version, SMIL 2.0 (*www.w3.org/TR/smil20*), is at the status of a W3C recommendation as of August 7, 2001, while SMIL 1.0 is the version supported, for example, by X-Smiles.

Multimedia awareness

What we expect from the SMIL initiative is that the Web will become more multimedia aware. But, even to a larger extent than with other XML-related standards, market penetration will take a while and there will need to be a more general shift from HTML-oriented toward XML-oriented applications. So we may have to wait for next-generation client-side tools that are not only SMIL enabled, but that also allow integration with other XML technologies that go beyond today's Flash-like presentations.

8.5.2 SVG

Scalable Vector Graphics (SVG) is an XML application that provides a language to describe two-dimensional graphics (SVG 2001). These graphics are built from three types of objects: vector graphics, images, and text.

Images, or raster graphics, denote graphical objects that are pixel based, that is, built from dots. The visual information is coded by describing each single pixel of the image, usually by a set of values for color, intensity, and so forth. The data size for such images may be determined directly by calculating the number of pixels times the number of bits or bytes needed for coding each pixel. Examples of corresponding image formats are TIFF, GIF, JPEG, and bitmap.

In contrast, vector graphics are much more efficient in the description of content and operations including transmission, presentation on output devices, and necessary recalculations due to scaling, zooming, and so forth. Vector graphics are more flexible in their appearance and usually consume less space than images do because the visual information is represented directly by polygons. An object therefore is not a subset of pixels but is described as a path of lines and curves as geometric elements. An example is Corel Draw.

SVG has several benefits. Because it is a vector format, it leads to smaller file sizes than regular bitmapped graphics, and it is resolution independent, so that images can scale down or up to fit proportionally into any size display. Because it is based on XML technology, it provides text labels and descriptions for searchability, and it has the ability to link to parts of an image.

Furthermore it provides the feature of complex animation either by embedding corresponding SVG elements or by scripting. SVG objects can be assigned event handlers, which give the Web designer using SVG animations similar opportunities as, for example, with Macromedia Flash (*www.macromedia.com/software/flash/*) presentations.

Following the principles of XML, SVG works by assigning attributes to elements. For instance, the `<svg>` element may have positioning attributes such as `x`, `y`, `height`, and `width`. It is the outermost element that defines the image. The `allowZoomAndPan` attribute gives the author control over zooming in and panning over the image. Other elements define shapes and lines, others define opacity, and others define ways to embed JPEGs and PNGs (W3C's successor to GIF) into the SVG image. Still, these are only a few SVG elements; there are many more.

The following example describes a rectangle (see the `<desc>` element in the listing for further detail) with a shadow. One specialty here is the ordering of the visual elements. The rectangle specified second will be shown as the frontmost. This builds a virtual third dimension, as has already been outlined in Section 8.1.2 and with the `z-index` of our SMIL sample. (To proceed further with this example, leading to a product presentation for a fictitious shop, see Eisenberg 1991.)

Raster graphics

Vector graphics

SVG benefits

```
<svg id="body" width="21cm" height="13.5cm"
    viewBox="0 0 210 135">
    <title>Part of a shop example</title>
    <desc>
        Rectangle with red border and light blue interior,
        with gray shadow rectangle.
    </desc>
    <rect x="10" y="20" width="150" height="70"
        transform="translate(3, 3)"
        fill="#999999" stroke="#999999" stroke-width="1"/>
    <rect x="10" y="20" width="150" height="70"
        fill="#eeeeff" stroke="red" stroke-width="1"/>
</svg>
```

Currently, SVG images are not supported by standard Web browsers; therefore, either a user must download an SVG viewer, or a plug-in is needed to view SVG within the browser window.

Compatibility with SMIL

Among other efforts the W3C seeks compatibility with SMIL by incorporating features from SMIL (e.g., the `<switch>` element) and extending the general-purpose animation capabilities given by SMIL. In turn, future versions of SMIL will use SVG content as media components.

PDF generation

To anticipate the section on type setting, we will mention an approach to generating PDF files from SVG here (*www.digapp.com/ newpages/svg2pdf .html*). This approach aims at giving an example of how to convert Web content into printable form on the basis of XML technology rather than using PostScript as an intermediate format, as is usually done for PDF.

8.5.3 VoiceXML

Speech and the Web

The Voice eXtended Markup Language (VoiceXML) is a proposal that has been made to the W3C and is part of its "Voice Browser" activity (W3C 2001b). The goal is to integrate speech-based services with Web applications. In particular, the use of the telephone to access Web resources is investigated. The Web author thus does not have to deal with low-level services and resource management on the level of voice services.

VoiceXML is an XML schema specified by the dialog markup language of W3C. Originally it was an initiative of the VoiceXML Forum (*www .voicexml.org*), a program of IEEE-ISTO. The VoiceXML 1.0 specification is available as a W3C note (VoiceXML 2001). The W3C has worked out a set of requirements and working draft language specifications that the dialog markup language is part of. The working draft of VoiceXML 2.0 is out as of October 23, 2001.

VoiceXML describes the human-machine interaction provided by voice response systems, which includes output of synthesized speech (text to speech), output of audio files, recognition of spoken input, recognition of DTMF (touchtone) input, recording of spoken input, and telephony features such as call transfer and disconnect.

Conceptually, a *voice service* is a sequence of interaction dialogs between a user and an implementation platform. The dialogs are units of interaction provided by document servers that also maintain the overall service logic and system operations. The dialogs are conducted by a VoiceXML interpreter. User input within a dialog results in further requests submitted to a document server. The reply then may be another VoiceXML document containing dialogs to continue the session.

This section will give an overview of these conceptual aspects as well as of the architectural model. Refer to *www.w3.org/Voice* for a list of vendors that have implemented VoiceXML 1.0 in conformance with the markup languages in the W3C Speech Interface Framework. Additional resources that may be of interest include the VoiceXML DTD (*www .voicexml.org/voicexml1-0.dtd*) and a series of tutorials for developers (*www .voicexml.org/tutorials/index.html*).

Architecture

The design of VoiceXML may be explained along a high-level architecture (see Figure 8.11). It encompasses several components that interact by following client-server principles.

A *document server* is a Web resource (node) that produces VoiceXML documents on request from a client application. This application is the VoiceXML interpreter, which operates within the VoiceXML interpreter context. The documents returned by the server are processed by the VoiceXML interpreter. The VoiceXML interpreter context acts as an "event listener," monitoring user inputs in parallel with the VoiceXML interpreter. Examples are special user interactions (escape phrases) that need particular attendance and reactions such as taking the user to a high-level personal assistant or changing user preferences.

A third tier in this client-server model is given by the *implementation platform*. It is controlled by the VoiceXML interpreter context and by the VoiceXML interpreter. This is necessary since we have events produced by the implementation platform due to user interactions or the system itself.

[margin notes: Voice response system; Interaction dialog; Client-server architecture]

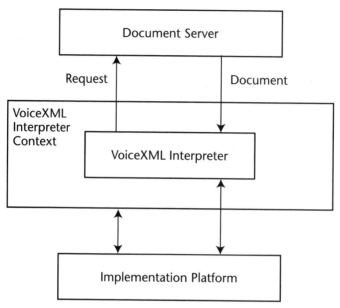

Figure 8.11 Client-server architectural model of VoiceXML (VoiceXML 2001).

Some have to be processed by the interpreter (e.g., user response) as far as it is part of the specific dialog. Others have to be acted upon by the interpreter context (e.g., incoming phone call and initialization of the dialog).

Concepts

A VoiceXML application is a set of *documents*. Each document forms a conversational finite-state machine. The states of the machine are the dialogs. A user is always in only one state at a time. Each dialog determines the next dialog (and possibly document) to transition to, specified by URIs. If a dialog does not specify a successor, the conversation ends.

Forms and menus

As stated earlier, dialogs are either *forms* or *menus*. A field-gathering input may specify a grammar of valid values. A menu offers the user a choice of options leading to the corresponding dialog. Subdialogs may be defined that can be considered like function calls.

Sessions

The sequence of interactions is called a *session*. A session may be terminated by either the user, a document, or the interpreter context.

Documents of an application share the same *application root document*, which is always loaded with the application. That way "global" variables

and grammars can be defined and set to be valid for the duration of the
application. *Grammars* for speech and/or DTMF are associated with dialogs and active when the user is in the dialog. In *mixed initiative* applications, the execution flow may transition from one active grammar to another as if a statement had been made in that other grammar.

Grammars

Besides the gathering of normal user input by forms, VoiceXML supports the handling of events thrown by the platform due to special user reactions or semantic errors detected by the interpreter. In accordance with well-known event-handling mechanisms, behavior event catching elements can be specified at any level and apply to all lower levels.

Simple Conversation Example

The following example formulates a dialog between a user and a machine concerning the selection of a drink. The root element is <vxml>, which is a container for dialogs given as either forms or menus. Forms present information and require input; menus offer choices of what to do next.

```
<?xml version="1.0"?>

<vxml version="1.0">

    <form>

    <field name="drink">

        <prompt>Would you like coffee,

            tea, milk, or nothing?</prompt>

        <grammar src="drink.gram"

            type="application/x-jsgf"/>

    </field>

    <block>

        <submit next=

            "http://www.drink.example/drink2.asp"/>

    </block>

    </form>

</vxml>
```

Our example has a single form, which contains a field and a block.
A *field* is an input field that a user has to provide a value for before

Fields

proceeding to the next element in the form. This may be regarded as the machine asking for a choice ("Would you like . . .") and the user answering. The block contains a *submit* element that passes the user's valid choice forward to another document given by URI specified. Since the form does not specify a successor dialog, the conversation ends.

8.6 DOCUMENT-BASED TYPE SETTING

So far we have focused on how to present XML-based data on the screens of personal computers, PDAs, and other mobile devices. The root of Web-based publication goes back to SGML, and SGML was driven by the publishing industry. So we will also devote some space to notes on how to transform XML content into printable forms.

8.6.1 PDF

PDF generation

The Portable Document Format (PDF) is an open de facto standard from Adobe for electronic publishing. PDF is platform independent and preserves formatting information from any source document. The common procedure relies on PostScript: First, a PostScript document is created from the source document. Then it is read by the Adobe Acrobat Distiller tool and transformed into a target PDF document. Alternatively, applications may generate PDF directly through API calls to specific printer drivers.

PDF documents

A PDF document is a collection of objects that together make up one or more pages. Associated with the objects is structural information. The appearance of a page is represented by a content stream that contains all layout and formatting information specified by the application that created the document. PDF is regarded as a page description language. Therefore the page representation in PDF may be considered as holding graphical objects to be painted on the page.

The cross-platform functionality of PDF is based on a two-stage process. First, a device-independent description of the output is generated. Second, this description is interpreted and rendered on a specific output device.

PDF syntax

Regarding the syntax of PDF, four components can be identified: objects, file structure, document structure, and content stream. Objects are composed within a data structure building the PDF document. PDF supports basic types such as Boolean, integer and real values, strings, and arrays. The file structure specifies structural object handling within the PDF file. The document structure specifies the use of objects to represent components like pages, fonts, and so forth. The content stream, as stated earlier, describes the appearance of entities by sequences of instructions. All PDF information is given as a stream of 8-bit bytes within a character set or as binary data (e.g., for included images). (For further information on PDF, see PDF 2000.)

Transforming XML content into PDF documents may be performed using XSL Formatting Objects (XSL-FO), as we saw in Section 8.2.4. Here we would also like to mention an Apache project called FOP (*xml.apache.org/fop*). FOP is a Java application based on XSL-FO that allows the conversion of formatting objects into a PDF document for printing. FOP also serves as a transcoder in the Batik toolkit (*www.apache.org/batik*) to produce PDF output from SVG.

Since transformation using XSL will be elaborated on in Chapter 9, we will not discuss the single steps here in detail. Instead we refer you to a tutorial available on IBM developers' site (*www-106.ibm.com/developerworks/education/transforming-xml/index.html*).

8.6.2 (La)TeX

LaTeX and TeX—which we will refer to together as (La)TeX—are commonly used in the community of natural sciences as a markup environment for text editing. It therefore has most of the advantages that we have already discussed in earlier chapters.

Since (La)TeX is widely used for editing and publishing purposes, the question arises, How do we generate XML content from (La)TeX documents, or vice versa? The latter direction is of primary interest in the context of this chapter.

A number of proposals, papers, projects, and similar research have been aimed at solving this particular problem. An overview as well as a list of resources is given at the XML Coverpages Web site (*xml.coverpages.org/ sgml-tex.html*), where there is a focus on SGML. Here we will pick up one example to convert XML to (La)TeX content, TeXML (*www.alphaworks.ibm.com/tech/texml*). **XML to (La)TeX**

TeXML encompasses a DTD (TeXML.dtd) and a corresponding Java program (TeXMLatte.java) that parses the input conforming to the DTD and outputs TeX. XSLT is employed to transform an arbitrary XML document into one that conforms to the DTD.

The following listing shows the original XML documents for a small MathML example, which includes the term (a+b)2:

```
<?xml version="1.0" ?>

  <msup>

    <mfenced>

      <mrow>

        <mi>a</mi>

        <mo>+</mo>

        <mi>b</mi>

      </mrow>

    </mfenced>

    <mn>2</mn>

  </msup>
```

The XML document first has to be transformed into TeXML. The generated TeXML document is given below. It already contains some content specific to (La)TeX. For instance, documentclass will be needed to link the appropriate document template. The corresponding value would be article in this case.

```
<?xml version="1.0" encoding="UTF-8"?>

<TeXML>

  <cmd name="documentclass">

    <parm>article</parm>

  </cmd>

  <cmd name="title">

    <parm>Some Math</parm>

  </cmd>

  <env name="document">

    <cmd name="maketitle"/>
```

```
<cmd name="["/>
    <group>(<group>a+b</group>)</group>
    <spec cat="sup"/>
    <group>2</group>
  <cmd name="]"/>
</env>
</TeXML>
```

The outcome of TeXMLatte should be something like the following TeX listing, but with a few more linefeeds. Without explaining the TeX syntax, we find that the mathematical term has been finally set to \[{({a+b})}^{2} \], which is the TeX representation of our sample:

```
\def\TeXMLmath#1{\ifmmode#1{}\else$#1{}$\fi}\def\TeXMLnomath#1{\i
fmmode\hbox{#1{}}\else#1{}\fi}
```

```
\documentclass {article}
```

```
\title {Some Math}
```

```
\begin{document}
```

```
\maketitle
```

```
\[ {(({a+b}))}^{2} \]
```

```
\end{document}
```

Transformation

Document transformation is an important issue for XML. Because XML allows the storage of information in a presentation-neutral format, it becomes necessary to transform this content into a presentation format such as HTML, WML, or PDF when clients ask for that information.

In this chapter we will give a short overview of XSLT, an XML-based transformation language. We introduce two opposing programming styles and discuss the virtues and deficiencies of XSLT. Because XSLT draws heavily on XPath, please refer to the discussion of XPath in Section 2.5.1.

XSLT has a reputation of not scaling very well. Although this doesn't matter for the purposes of prototyping and ad hoc solutions, it is an issue when it comes to enterprise computing. We will discuss performance problems and look for alternatives.

Historically XSLT was a part of the XSL (Extensible Stylesheet Language) specification, but then XSL was split into three parts: XPath, XSLT, and Formatting Objects (XFO). XSLT is now a recommendation in its own right (Clark 1999a). The purpose of XSLT is to enable style-sheet-controlled transformations from one XML document format into another document format (XML or non-XML, but mostly HTML).

When you think about it, XSLT can unleash substantial power:

- XSLT can be used to transform presentation-neutral XML data into presentational formats such as XHTML, XForms, WML, SMIL, SVG, and so on.
- It can be used to convert document instances when a new version of a schema is introduced. It can be used to harvest RDF statements from the XLink elements in a document, or to generate XML Schema definitions from XMI.
- As we saw in Section 2.9, it can even be used to check the validity of data against a set of constraints (Schematron and APEX).

Although XSLT is quite powerful, we have to say that not everybody likes it. One commentator even described it as an "ugly, difficult language" (Leventhal 1999). One reason for such dislike is that XSLT is a rule-based, declarative language. Programmers who are used to imperative languages such as Java or C sometimes find it hard to think in these terms. But also the inconsistent use of (source) document node sets and (result) tree fragments can be disturbing.

Another reason for this dislike is the syntax. The XSLT syntax itself is XML. This makes sense when you want to indulge in metaprogramming (i.e., apply XSLT transformations onto XSLT style sheets), but it can be difficult for the human eye to read. For this problem, at least there is help: Paul Tchistopolskii's (*www.pault.com*) XSL Script has a much more legible syntax yet can be translated into 100% XSLT.

Usually, the XSLT control elements are prefixed with an identifier for the XSLT namespace. Here, we use the prefix xsl:.

9.1 PROCEDURAL TRANSFORMATION

There are two programming styles that can be used with XSLT. In the *procedural* programming style, also known as the "pull" model, the programmer describes to the XSLT processor exactly what to do and in which sequence. This programming style is easier to understand for programmers educated in imperative languages such as C or Pascal. The XSLT style sheet will look very much like the target document, with interspersed XSLT instructions to fill in the blanks. This technique has similarities to the programming approach used in Java Server Pages (JSP).

The *rule-based* programming style, also known as the "push" model, is a more declarative approach. Rules describe how the elements of the input document should be transformed. Rules are applied recursively based on a pattern-matching mechanism. Nonprogrammers and programmers educated in declarative languages such as PROLOG, expert systems, and so on should find it easier to work in this way.

Of course, it is also possible to mix both programming styles.

Procedural XSLT instructions include operations such as the following:

Procedural operations

- *Control structures:* XSLT instructions such as `xsl:for-each`, `xsl:if`, and `xsl:choose` provide procedural control structures like conditional execution or loops. It is possible to sort the result of an `xsl:for-each` instruction with an `xsl:sort` instruction. Additionally, the results can be numbered with the `xsl:number` instruction.
- *Accessing content:* The `xsl:value-of` instruction writes the content of the current node (or of an explicitly specified node) to the target document.
- *Call by name:* Named templates can be invoked via the `xsl:call-template` instruction, similarly to how a subroutine is invoked in a mainstream programming language. It is possible to pass parameters to these templates, but it is not possible to return result values.

Here is an XSLT example that converts the book order example from Chapter 2 into some HTML using the procedural programming style. Figure 9.1 shows what we want to obtain.

Figure 9.2 shows how the resulting HTML document is compiled from the original XML file with the help of an XSLT style sheet.

Figure 9.1 Screen representation of a book order.

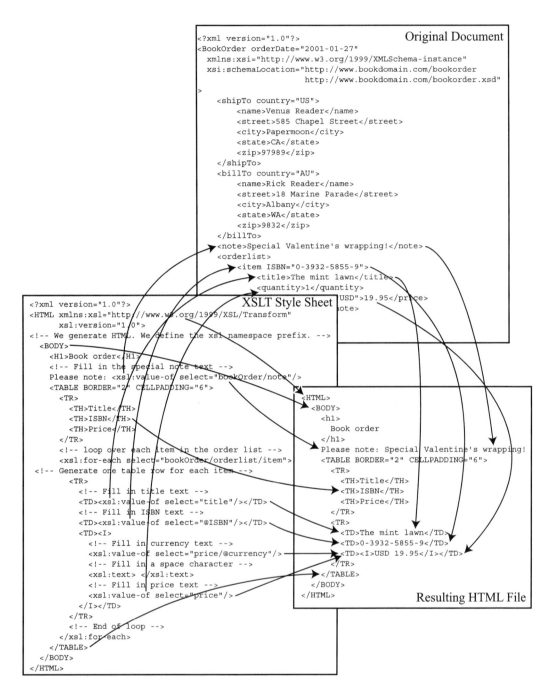

Figure 9.2 Generating output the procedural way. The XSLT style sheet determines the layout of the output document. Data is pulled out of the source document and placed into the appropriate slots in the output document.

9.2 RULE-BASED TRANSFORMATION

With rule-based transformation, the main XSLT control elements are templates (`<xsl:template>`). Each template consists of a head and a body. The head of a template decides on the context in which the template shall become active. This is done by using the attribute `match=` and specifying an XPath expression to select the context nodes. The template body describes what to do. This is specified with the help of XSLT instructions.

The instruction `xsl:apply-templates` applies all templates defined in the style sheet recursively but only to the nodes within the context selected by the `select=` attribute—template processing is applied recursively.

`xsl:apply-templates` can additionally be equipped with an optional `mode` attribute. This allows the application of different sets of templates depending on context, since templates can also be equipped with a `mode=` attribute that must be matched.

It is possible to sort the result of an `xsl:apply-templates` instruction with an `xsl:sort` instruction. Additionally, the results can be numbered with the `xsl:number` instruction.

Procedural XSLT instructions (see earlier) can be used for conditional processing or to write content to the target document.

In cases when the heads of several templates match a certain context, the template with the best match is selected for execution:

Rule-based operations

- Templates in the current style sheet win over templates from imported style sheets.
- The more specific a matching expression in the template head is, the better is the match.

Figure 9.3 shows a rule-based example style sheet that produces the same output as the previous procedural style sheet.

A rule-based style sheet usually contains a template rule that matches the root node ("/"). In the root node rule we set up the global layout of the target document, including global styles. The rule then applies all rules recursively to the children of the root node.

The next rule applies to the `<bookOrder>` element. It outputs a header for the order and applies all the rules again to its children. The value of the `<note>` element is extracted with the `xsl:value-of` instruction.

The next rule applies to the `<orderlist>` element. It sets up a table, outputs a table header, and applies all the rules again to its children. It then closes the table element.

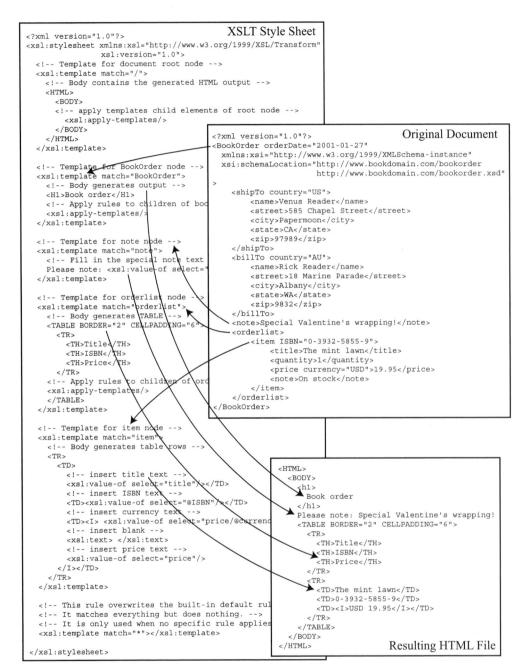

```
                                                    XSLT Style Sheet
<?xml version="1.0"?>
<xsl:stylesheet xmlns:xsl="http://www.w3.org/1999/XSL/Transform"
                xsl:version="1.0">
 <!-- Template for document root node -->
 <xsl:template match="/">
    <!-- Body contains the generated HTML output -->
    <HTML>
      <BODY>
        <!-- apply templates child elements of root node -->
          <xsl:apply-templates/>
      </BODY>
    </HTML>
 </xsl:template>

 <!-- Template for BookOrder node -->
 <xsl:template match="BookOrder">
    <!-- Body generates output -->
    <H1>Book order</H1>
    <!-- Apply rules to children of boo
    <xsl:apply-templates/>
 </xsl:template>

 <!-- Template for note node -->
 <xsl:template match="note">
    <!-- Fill in the special note text
    Please note: <xsl:value-of select="
 </xsl:template>

 <!-- Template for orderlist node -->
 <xsl:template match="orderlist">
    <!-- Body generates TABLE -->
    <TABLE BORDER="2" CELLPADDING="6"
      <TR>
        <TH>Title</TH>
        <TH>ISBN</TH>
        <TH>Price</TH>
      </TR>
      <!-- Apply rules to children of ord
      <xsl:apply-templates/>
    </TABLE>
 </xsl:template>

 <!-- Template for item node -->
 <xsl:template match="item">
    <!-- Body generates table rows -->
    <TR>
      <TD>
        <!-- insert title text -->
        <xsl:value-of select="title"/></TD>
        <!-- insert ISBN text -->
      <TD><xsl:value-of select="@ISBN"/></TD>
        <!-- insert currency text -->
      <TD><I> <xsl:value-of select="price/@currenc
        <!-- insert blank -->
      <xsl:text> </xsl:text>
        <!-- insert price text -->
      <xsl:value-of select="price"/>
      </I></TD>
    </TR>
 </xsl:template>

 <!-- This rule overwrites the built-in default rul
 <!-- It matches everything but does nothing. -->
 <!-- It is only used when no specific rule applies
 <xsl:template match="*"></xsl:template>

</xsl:stylesheet>
```

```
                                                 Original Document
<?xml version="1.0"?>
<BookOrder orderDate="2001-01-27"
  xmlns:xsi="http://www.w3.org/1999/XMLSchema-instance"
  xsi:schemaLocation="http://www.bookdomain.com/bookorder
                       http://www.bookdomain.com/bookorder.xsd"
>
    <shipTo country="US">
        <name>Venus Reader</name>
        <street>585 Chapel Street</street>
        <city>Papermoon</city>
        <state>CA</state>
        <zip>97989</zip>
    </shipTo>
    <billTo country="AU">
        <name>Rick Reader</name>
        <street>18 Marine Parade</street>
        <city>Albany</city>
        <state>WA</state>
        <zip>9832</zip>
    </billTo>
    <note>Special Valentine's wrapping!</note>
    <orderlist>
        <item ISBN="0-3932-5855-9">
            <title>The mint lawn</title>
            <quantity>1</quantity>
            <price currency="USD">19.95</price>
            <note>On stock</note>
        </item>
    </orderlist>
</BookOrder>
```

```
<HTML>
  <BODY>
    <h1>
      Book order
    </h1>
    Please note: Special Valentine's wrapping!
    <TABLE BORDER="2" CELLPADDING="6">
      <TR>
        <TH>Title</TH>
        <TH>ISBN</TH>
        <TH>Price</TH>
      </TR>
      <TR>
        <TD>The mint lawn</TD>
        <TD>0-3932-5855-9</TD>
        <TD><I>USD 19.95</I></TD>
      </TR>
    </TABLE>
  </BODY>
</HTML>
                                            Resulting HTML File
```

Figure 9.3 In a rule-based style sheet the execution of templates is triggered by the elements of the source document as this document is processed. The sequence of elements in the output document thus depends on the sequence of elements in the original document. Note that the rule for element "item" still uses procedural techniques in order to change the order of elements.

The next rule applies to `<item>` elements. For each item element it outputs a table row.

The last rule is used to disable XSLT's built-in default rules. The effect of those rules is that the XSLT processor outputs text and attributes of all attributes that are not caught by a specific rule. In our case this is unfortunate because we do not want to output the content of the `<shipTo>` and `<billTo>` elements. Therefore, we add a "catch-all" rule that does nothing:

```
<xsl:template match="*"></xsl:template>
```

This template applies when no other template applies to an element (because its matching expression is the least specific one), so the default rules are never called.

Although both style sheets produce the same output, they actually define different transformations. We can see a difference when we rearrange the elements in the input document. If we placed the `<note>` element behind the `<orderlist>` element, there would be no effect on the output document in the case of the procedural style sheet. In the case of the rule-based style sheet, however, the output `Please note: ...` would appear after the table. This is because in the rule-based style sheet the transformation is defined in a declarative manner. So, the input document drives the sequence of processing, and consequently the layout of the input document determines the layout of the output document. In the procedural style sheet, in contrast, the layout of the output document is determined by the layout of the style sheet.

Procedural vs. rule based

9.3 WHAT XSLT CAN DO

In this section, we discuss some of the outstanding features of XSLT. Later, in Section 9.4, we look into its weaknesses.

9.3.1 Variables

XSLT has variables; however, these variables are read-only variables. The value is assigned at the time the variable is defined and cannot be modified afterward. Templates can specify variables as formal parameters, too, so that it is possible to pass parameters to templates.

9.3.2 Keys

Cross-
references

Some XML documents make extensive use of cross-referencing. XSLT provides an extra construct to make the navigation across such structures easier:

```
<xsl:key
  name="mykey"
  match="//author"
  use="@aid"/>
```

This construct imposes a new key structure onto the document. We can then use this key in other XPath expressions: `key("mykey","1")/name` would result in the name of the author with `@aid="1"`.

9.3.3 Multiple Input Files

IO

The `document()` function allows access to additional documents by specifying their URI as a parameter.

9.3.4 Various Output Methods

XSLT can transform an XML document tree structure into another XML document tree structure. This means that the input document must be a well-formed XML document, and, by default, the output document is a well-formed XML document, too.

However, a special XSLT instruction allows the modification of that behavior:

- `<xsl:output method="xml"/>` is the default output method. The output document is a well-formed output document. Tags contained in the style sheet must obey the XML rules for well-formedness. An HTML tag `<br>` without a closing tag `</br>` would not be allowed. In contrast, the corresponding XHTML tag `<br/>` would be allowed.
- `<xsl:output method="html"/>` allows the specification of HTML 4.0 tags in the style sheet, even if they violate the well-formedness of the style sheet. So it is possible to specify tags of empty elements such as `<br>` or `<p>` without a closing tag. This output method also keeps the strings in scripts intact, supports minimized attributes (attributes without a value), recognizes HTML tags regardless of case, and more. The input document, however, must always be well-formed XML.
- `<xsl:output method="text"/>` strips all tags from the output, so that only the text contained in the elements of the output tree appears in

the output document. This allows the creation of almost any output format, as long as it is text output. The `media-type` attribute can be used to set the MIME type of the output file.

9.3.5 Metatransformations

XSLT is an XML-based language itself. This makes any XSLT style sheet a possible subject to a transformation by another XSLT style sheet. This technique can be used to extend the XSLT language. Here are two examples:

- We have already described Schematron earlier in this book (Section   Schematron
  2.9). Schematron scripts are used to check XML instances for compliance to certain constraints. These constraints are described in a Schematron script. After authoring the script it is compiled into a validation style sheet. This is done with the Schematron compiler, which is nothing more than a predefined XSLT style sheet. The resulting validation style sheet, also an XSLT style sheet, is then applied to the XML document instances. The result of this transformation is a document containing a list of errors and warnings.
- The loop compiler. Implemented by Oliver Becker (*www.informatik.hu-berlin.de/~obecker/XSLT/#loop-compiler*), this XSLT preprocessor converts non-XSLT statements such as

```
<loop:for
    from="expression" to="expression" step="expression">
...
</loop:for>
```

into standard XSLT expressions. Needless to say, the preprocessor is implemented as an XSLT style sheet.

More examples of the unorthodox use of XSLT are found at the "Gallery of Stupid XSL and XSLT Tricks" at *www.incrementaldevelopment .com /xsltrick/*.

9.3.6 Modules

XSLT style sheets can be developed in modules. Two instructions—include and import—allow the combination of several style sheets into one. While include adds the included style sheet to the current style sheet, import allows the imported style sheet to override existing definitions in the current style sheet.

Since all names in XSLT (such as template names, mode names, or key names) are qualified names (i.e., they can be specified with a namespace prefix), it is possible to avoid name clashes when style sheets are imported or included.

9.4 WHAT XSLT CAN'T DO

While in many cases XSLT allows sophisticated document transformations, there are other cases where the required transformations are met by restrictions:

No "real" variables

- There is no destructive assignment for variables in XSLT. This can make certain tasks (like counting) difficult, especially for programmers with a background in procedural programming. (The destructive assignment can be simulated via recursive calls to templates, passing the updated value as a parameter with each call.)
- XSLT does not have a complete set of mathematical operators. For example, there are no built-in trigonometric functions and no random number generator. This can make some tasks tedious and error prone.
- Because an XSLT style sheet is always a single document tree, we cannot split output into several files—a feature that is desperately needed when we want to convert a complex XML file into a set of interrelated XHTML, SVG, and SMIL files.

XSLT 1.1

   However, this issue is addressed in XSLT 1.1 (Clark 2001), which is currently in draft status. An xsl:document instruction will allow the redirection of the output stream.

- XSLT converts an input document into an output document, but it does not produce a binding between both. This is fine for mere representation purposes, but it does not really support user interactivity. For example, we can easily write a style sheet that converts a representation-neutral XML file into an XForms file, but we have no way to map the user input back to the original XML file. (Section 4.4.2 discussed how this is still possible.)

9.5 EXTENSIONS

These limitations are asking for an extension technique, which XSLT fortunately provides. Several XSLT processors exist that allow extensions, most notably Michael Kay's Saxon (Kay 2001) and Xalan from the Apache Group.

However, although the extension technique is standardized, the extension implementation is not standardized, so you have to decide on a specific processor and stay with that processor. The good news is that there are community efforts to create a standard set of extensions: have a look at *www.exslt.org*.

XSLT extensions come in three flavors: Extension flavors

- *Extension attributes*. Extension attributes can be used to influence the behavior of the XSLT processor. For example, an extension attribute may be used to switch on the processor's trace function.
- *Extension elements*. Extension elements perform actions by calling an extension routine. For example, an extension element can redirect the output stream, so that it becomes possible to create several output files from one style sheet. Extension elements may contain attributes, text nodes, and child elements. This content is passed to the associated extension routine. Values that are returned to the extension element are inserted into the result tree.
- *Extension functions*. Extension functions are called in the same way as XSLT core library functions are called. Function arguments are passed to the associated extension routine, and the value returned by the routine is passed back as the function result.

Several XSLT processors support extensions, most notably Saxon and Saxon
Xalan. The Saxon XSLT processor is well renowned for its robustness, speed, and extensibility. It is also one of the few processors that supports the XSLT key construct. It is freely available at *users.iclway.co.uk/mhkay/saxon/*. Saxon allows the implementation of extension elements, extension attributes, and extension functions in the form of Java classes. The Saxon package comes with a rich collection of built-in extensions.

Xalan uses the Bean Scripting Framework (BDF) to incorporate ex- Xalan
tension routines. This allows independence from particular scripting languages. Thus, Xalan supports a wide range of scripting languages such as Mozilla Rhino, NetRexx, BML, JPython, Jacl, JScript, VBScript, or PerlScript. In addition, it is possible to call methods of Java objects, too.

Here is a simple example of a Xalan extension function:

```
<?xml version="1.0"?>
<xsl:stylesheet
      xmlns:xsl="http://www.w3.org/1999/XSL/Transform"
      version="1.0"
      xmlns:lxslt="http://xml.apache.org/xslt"
      xmlns:my-ext="ext1"
      extension-element-prefixes="my-ext">
```

```
<!-lxslt:component defines the JavaScript
    extension function ->

<lxslt:component prefix="my-ext"
                 functions="logscale">
  <lxslt:script lang="javascript">
    function logscale(x)
    { return Math.ln(parseInt(x))*Math.LOG10E*20; }
  </lxslt:script>
</lxslt:component>
```

...

```
<xsl:template match="sales-figure">
  <rect style="stroke:green;fill:lightgreen"
        x="100" y="400" width="50">
    <xsl:attribute name="height">
      <xsl:value-of select="my-ext:logscale(.)"/>
    </xsl:attribute>
  </rect>
</xsl:template>
```

...

```
</xsl:stylesheet>
```

The lxslt:component element defines all extension components, in this case only one function (log). This must be declared in the functions attribute. This function accepts one argument and adjusts it to a logarithmic scale. The function is then used in the template that matches sales-figure. Here we generate an SVG element to draw a rectangle. We see how we can use the XSLT instruction xsl:attribute to dynamically create an attribute for element <rect>.

Here is a simple example of file redirection:

```
<xsl:template match="shipTo">
  <redirect:write select="envelope.xml">
    <envelope>
      <xsl:apply-templates/>
    </envelope>
  </redirect:write>
</xsl:template>
```

This template matches the <shipTo> element in our bookOrder example. For the whole processing of this element it redirects the output stream to a file called `envelope.xml`. After the element has been processed, the output stream is switched back to its previous destination. (The `redirect` extension is a predefined extension shipped with the Xalan package.)

9.6 AUTHORING AND TESTING OF XSL STYLE SHEETS

There are quite a few XSLT authoring tools. The W3C XSLT Web site lists a comprehensive set of them. We can classify these tools into three categories:

- *Generic XSLT editors:* These editors allow the writing of XSLT style sheets. The XSLT code is checked for correctness, and the style sheet can be tested against existing XML documents. These editors require a good knowledge of XSLT.

  One prominent example is IBM's XSL editor, which is available under the usual 90-day license from the alphaworks Web site. Implemented in Java, this tool allows the display of the source document, the style sheet, and the resulting output side by side. All three documents can be viewed in text mode and tree mode. A debugger allows the tracing of the execution of the style sheet and the setting of breakpoints.

- *Visual XSLT editors:* These editors are targeted toward the creation of style sheets that transform XML into HTML. The target HTML document is composed by visual means (similarly to how it is done in a visual HTML editor). The author associates these display elements with the elements of the source XML document. The tool generates XML templates appropriately. In most cases authors will not have to write XSLT. Typical examples of such tools are eXcelon's Stylus, Whitehill's <xsl>Composer, and XML Spy (all commercial products).

- *Generic XSLT generators:* These tools allow the association of the elements of source documents and target documents with the help of a mapping function. Users can select from a variety of available mapping functions. The tool will then create appropriate XSLT style sheets. An example of such a tool is XSLerator, again from alphaworks.

9.7 PERFORMANCE ASPECTS

The first XSLT processors, such as James Clark's XT, were implemented in Java using the DOM API (see Section 2.8.2). These processors are quite resource hungry because any node in the input document and in the

XT

style sheet is represented by a first-class object. However, XT is still one of the fastest XSLT processors around, especially when large documents are to be transformed.

Saxon

But Saxon also seems to have kept pace. By using caching techniques for transformed pages, performance levels better than obtained with Java Server Pages (JSP) technology have been reported.

Xalan

The Xalan processor (also implemented in Java) reduces the object-oriented overhead by representing XML nodes with integer array elements instead of full objects, thus requiring far fewer resources.

Sablotron

C++ implementations such as Sablotron and Informiix generally achieve a better performance than Java implementations when small documents are processed, with Sablotron slightly outperforming XT for large documents, too.

Sun's XSLT compiler

Sun Microsystems, in the meantime, has developed an XSLT compiler. The compiler takes an XSLT style sheet as input and generates a hierarchy of Java classes, packed into a "translet." This translet will then accept XML documents as input, apply the specified transformations, and deliver output documents. The compiler covers virtually all of the XSLT 1.0 specification, but it has only limited support for extension and cannot split the output into several files.

Performance improvements by a factor of 2–3 can be expected. In one case reported, the time to transform a large document was reduced from 8 minutes (obtained with an interpreting XSLT processor) to 25 seconds (i.e., a factor of 19).

Sun has donated the XSLT compiler to the Apache organization, where it has become part of the Xalan distribution. The compiler, however, cannot handle extensions in the way Xalan does.

Compiling to C++

Another development is the XSLT compiler by Olivier Gerardin. This compiler translates XSLT style sheets into C++ classes with similar performance gains. This compiler is available under the GNU license from *www3.cybercities.com/x/xsltc/*.

Caching

Although performance gains can be achieved by the selection of the right XSLT processor, the best performance gains in heavy traffic situations are achieved via caching. XML documents are transformed into the target format such as HTML when requested, but the result of the transformation is stored in a cache. Subsequent requests that access the same document are served directly from the cache. However, update operations to the original XML document must be carried forward to the cached transformations.

9.8 OTHER LANGUAGES

XSLT is not the only way to transform an XML document. Transformation is also possible with general-purpose languages such as Java, C, C++, Pascal, SmallTalk, Eiffel, Visual Basic, JavaScript, and so on—even with assembler, if you really want. Some of these languages have access to SAX or DOM APIs that reduce the effort to parse the XML document. In particular, Java has the most complete XML support, as virtually all new implementations of XML processors are done in Java first.

General-purpose languages

Then there are the languages that feature strong pattern-matching facilities. In particular, languages with good support for regular expressions are well suited to process XML. Here are a few examples.

Languages with pattern matching

9.8.1 Omnimark

Omnimark is a commercial product by stilo that is designed for document transformation. It has strong support for XML and can transform non-XML to XML and vice versa. Several packages exist to support bulk document translation, client-server situations, SOAP, and BizTalk.

9.8.2 Perl

There is a rich ensemble of XML-related modules (including SAX and DOM APIs) in the public Perl libraries (CPAN). Several modules deal with document transformation. Some are for specific transformations; others provide generic transformations similar to XSLT:

- GXML (Generic XML Transformation Tool) is one. According to the author, Josh Carter, "GXML is a perl module for transforming XML. It may be put to a variety of tasks; in scope it is similar to XSL, but less ambitious." The good thing is that this processor provides an extension mechanism via a callback mechanism, allowing the execution of Perl expressions at the start and end of each XML tag.
- An XSLT processor (XML::XSLT) has been implemented in Perl by Geert Josten, Egon Willighagen, and Mark A. Hershberger.
- Other options (with a better performance) are Perl wrappers for C++ transformation engines such as XML::Sablotron and XML::Informix.
- XML::Pyx is a simple event-oriented parser (i.e., similar to SAX). The client is informed about tags and the content of elements and can react accordingly.

- XML::Simple works in a similar way as DOM. It parses the entire XML file and loads it into a tree structure in memory. It does not work well for complex document-centric XML, but it works well for simple data-centric XML.
- XML::XPath is a Perl module for parsing and evaluating XPath expressions that conform to the W3C's XPath recommendation.

9.8.3 XDuce

Some functional languages such as Clean, Haskell (HaXML), ML, O'Caml, and XMLambda support XML. As one example from this group, we will briefly discuss XDuce (pronounced "transduce"), a research project at the University of Pennsylvania (Hosoya and Pierce 2000). It is a functional language based on the principles of ML but extended with the ability to utilize regular expressions for pattern matching and to recognize XML elements as datatypes. As regular expressions closely resemble structures that can be defined with a DTD, it is quite easy to formulate complex document transformations in XDuce.

Given the DTD

```
<!ELEMENT addrbook (name,addr,tel?)*>

<!ELEMENT name #PCDATA>

<!ELEMENT addr #PCDATA>

<!ELEMENT tel #PCDATA>
```

the following XDuce program converts an address book document into a phone list document:

```
fun mkTelList : (Name,Addr,Tel?)* -> (Name,Tel)* =
    name[n:String], addr[a:String], tel[t:String],
                                    rest:(Name,Addr,Tel?)*
       -> name[n], tel[t], mkTelList(rest)
  | name[n:String], addr[a:String], rest:(Name,Addr,Tel?)*
       -> mkTelList(rest)
  | ()
       -> ()
```

Strongly typed languages   Functional languages are usually strongly typed, and so is XDuce. Any document node establishes its own datatype (this is in fact very close to the concept of complex types in XML Schema). Types are carried across function definitions, and consequently the function `mkTelList` has the type of "Function mapping address book to phone list," which is declared in the first line of the program.

The processing is recursive: the whole address book is matched against a regular expression. While the left arguments of that expression match the constituents of one address book entry, the rest of the address book is matched against the `rest:(Name,Addr,Tel?)*` expression and is processed subsequently. There are three alternatives: one for address book entries with a phone number, one for entries without a phone number, and one for the empty list. The respective results are assembled on the right side of the arrow operator.

There are three advantages to this approach:

Advantages

- The functional paradigm seems to be better suited for document transformation than the rule-based (and sometimes surprising) mechanism in XSLT.
- Functional languages are strongly typed and use static type checking at compile time. This prevents many nasty surprises at runtime.
- The integration of XML transformations into a computationally complete language makes an extra extension mechanism obsolete.

Statically typed languages such as XDuce and others with type systems that can support the XML information set seem to be a very promising approach. However, this area is still very much a research topic.

9.9 GENERATING WEB PAGES

XSLT is not the only way to present XML data as HTML. There are several other techniques that are based on HTML and that can pull XML content into Web pages.

Sun Microsystem's Java Server Pages (*java.sun.com/products/jsp*) allows the embedding of Java directives into HTML pages. These directives are executed when a page is requested. XML data can be accessed from these directives using a Java API such as DOM or SAX.

Java Server Pages

Anakia is a similar technology in the context of Apache's Jakarta project (*jakarta.apache.org*). Anakia uses JDOM and Velocity to embed XML content into Web pages.

Anakia

XSP (eXtensible Server Pages) combines dynamic generation and transformation with XSLT style sheets. XSP is Cocoon's (also an Apache

XSP

project; see Section 11.5.1) technology for dynamically generated XML. Similar to Java Server Pages, XSP includes directives that are executed when an XSP page is requested. This results in a rendered XML document. This document can then be processed further with an XSLT style sheet.

Infrastructure

"Web services" has been the latest catch phrase out of the marketing departments of the IT industry. Despite the hype, Web services are important building blocks for Internet applications. Architectures such as Hewlett-Packard's e-speak, Sun Microsystem's ONE, Microsoft's .NET, or ebXML all rely on Web services. In Section 10.2, we take a closer look at this technology.

In Section 10.3, we move the discussion to ebXML. This standard, authored by UN/CEFACT and OASIS and adopted by major industry associations such as OTA or Covisint, combines the experience of the EDI community with the flexibility of XML. This leads to new and innovative solutions, such as the negotiation of shared business processes or the treatment of context, from which we can learn a lot. It will be interesting comparing ebXML with BizTalk, which is discussed in Chapter 11.

Finally, we list some of the most important XML industry vocabularies, such as SyncML, DocBook, FpML, HL7, and many more.

10.1 BUSINESS REQUIREMENTS

Business-to-business communication requires infrastructure and intermediaries. Intermediaries like marketplaces, exchanges, auctions, and so on provide transparency in an otherwise chaotic world. Just as in the real world, where markets, real estate agents, and other intermediaries provide transparency, Internet B2B intermediaries provide transparency regarding price, product features, availability, and supplier characteristics (Anant and Pandya 2001).

Intermediaries   In the current stage of the Internet such intermediaries take the form of online exchanges, markets, portals, auctions, reverse auctions, and so on. They simply bring buyer and supplier together and assist in the process of matching request and offer. They support the search for products or product requests and help in the configuration of products. For buyers, such intermediaries offer the chance to find a supplier with a better price or product. Suppliers benefit from a larger group of potential buyers. Typical examples of intermediaries are companies such as VerticalNet, Chemdex (now Ventro), Commerce One, and Ariba. Some marketplaces were founded by interested industry sectors such as the automotive industry and retail sectors. Both of these sectors have a long-standing experience with one-to-one data exchange via EDI but have moved into many-to-many Internet-based marketplaces. For example, the Global Net Exchange is an initiative by Sears, Carrefour, Sainsbury, and others; the competing Worldwide Retail Exchange is an initiative by Kmart, Target, Walgreens, Tesco, Auchan, Casino, and others; and the Grocery Manufacturers' Association's eCPG is an initiative by P&G, Unilever, Kraft Foods, and others.

EDI   Traditionally, online interchange between trading partners has been a bilateral affair. EDI (Electronic Data Interchange) requires each trade partnership to be negotiated separately. Within the next few years B2B trade will move quickly from a one-to-one model to a many-to-many relationship. According to Forrester Research:

> Online, bilateral trade—between two companies—will more than triple by 2004 to nearly $1.3 trillion, but the volume of trade through the marketplaces will surge from a tiny fraction of that number today to over half of online trade by 2004.

Many of the current online exchanges are the result of interested in-   Marketplaces
dustry groups. The result is that several similar exchanges operate within
the same market sector as competitors. In the next few years we will see
these exchanges grow together. Marketplaces will acquire the ability to
link with other marketplaces. These metamarkets will provide even better
transparency.

10.2 WEB SERVICES

An online exchange or marketplace is, however, just a special form of
Web service. Other intermediaries specialize in services such as credit card
checks, financing, and fulfillment. Nearly every day, we see additional
Web services come into existence—Web services that not only support
the buying/selling process but that support other business processes, too.
Even manufacturing could be offered as a Web service (and this is almost
the case in virtual enterprises).

In the end, shrink-wrapped software packages could become an endan-   An extinct
gered species (at least in the standard office environment)—or rather an   species?
augmented species.

Standard software will increasingly integrate Web services. Web services can range from very simple services to rather complex ones. Here
are a few examples of basic Web services: stock quotes, currency conversion, fetching articles from an archive, email sender, language translation, generating a UUID, real-time flight information, storage system for
XML documents, conversion between XML vocabularies, checking HTML
pages for accessibility, shared address book, FedEx tracker, eBay price
watcher, and registering and finding a Web service in a directory. (A list of
such services and their descriptions is found at *www.xmethods.com.*) It
seems that such Web services can add substantial value to existing standard software packages.

All of the big players in the industry have announced their own Web   The big players
service strategy. The merit of being the first goes to Hewlett-Packard,
which formulated a quite complete, albeit proprietary, solution with
e-speak. They were followed by IBM with its Web service strategy. Sun
Microsystems followed suit with Sun ONE. Then Microsoft added a substantial push to Web services with its .NET initiative, and recently with its
project Hailstorm.

With SOAP (see Section 6.5.2), WSDL (Section 6.6.3), and UDDI (Sec-   SOAP, WSDL,
tion 7.3), there is now a framework for message transport, protocol defi-   UDDI
nition, and service registration and recovery in place. This allows the

wide-scale application of Web services, just as TCP/IP, HTTP, and HTML were the prerequisites for the expansion of the World Wide Web. The integration of SOAP into Microsoft's Windows operating systems, the support of SOAP by Apache.org, and the support of XML, SOAP, WSDL, and UDDI by Sun Microsystem's Java programming language will facilitate this.

10.2.1 Orchestration

The inclusion of Web services into a business process can be achieved with varying degrees of automation:

- Manual invocation of Web services via a generic Web service client (similar to a Web browser).
- Invocation of Web services in the context of a traditional application. For example, a spreadsheet package could fetch stock quotes via a Web service and could then invoke another Web service to convert the quote into another currency.

BizTalk
- Invocation in the context of a custom-designed business process. Microsoft's BizTalk Orchestration is an example of this (see Section 11.3.3).

ebXML
- (Semi-)automatic localization of Web services and (semi-)automatic negotiation of business processes. ebXML is an example (see Section 10.3).

In the first two cases business processes are driven by the human operator. In the last two cases, business processes run autonomously in a workflow-like fashion, with human assistance becoming just another service.

10.2.2 Availability

As Web services are accessed via the Web, they are subject to intermittent availability. A service may not be available for a period of time due to downtime of the server or system overload.

Finding
alternatives
Business processes that use Web services have to decide what to do in such cases: wait until the service becomes available again, try to locate another equivalent service, or report a failure of service. This requires business rules that are able to describe alternatives and that are able to compromise on less-than-optimal solutions.

10.2.3 Collaboration Instead of Integration

Web services can be business processes, too. In some cases (especially in most of the services mentioned earlier), these processes are just simple stateless request/response type services. In other cases a Web service can offer a more complex interface involving several requests and responses depending on the current state of the service process. Therefore we speak of "business process collaboration."

Conceptually, these processes are communicating sequential processes (Hoare 1985). They require not only the definition of the format for requests and responses but also the definition of the process behavior. This is usually done in the form of a state transition table or a Petri net (but see Chapters 5 and 6 for a discussion).

Communicating sequential processes

10.2.4 Transactions

For business processes that consist of several services, process integrity becomes an issue. When one service fails, what should we do with the other services?

To run such a process properly, a transactional concept (see also Section 6.6) is required. This transaction concept differs from the classical database transaction concept (ACID). A suitable transaction concept for Web services is the concept of long-running (or long-lived) transactions. Transactional Web services are required to offer compensating actions (that can semantically undo a previous action) in order to support this transaction concept.

Long-running transactions

A business process that includes several Web services can be offered as a Web service itself and can thus be embedded into a larger business process. This technique allows for a high degree of modularity and specialization, and at the same time for arbitrarily large and complex processes. ebXML (see Section 10.3), for example, explicitly uses nested business processes to construct processes that involve more than two partners. For example, a process to make a reservation for a trip to Venice involves several subprocesses: one subprocess to book the flight, one to arrange for a hotel, and one to charter a gondola. If one of these processes fails, additional processes are needed to roll back (or compensate) the others.

Nested Web services

10.2.5 Software Engineering

Especially for supply chain integration, Web services can be combined into processes that span the complete life cycle process of a product and its parts. The resulting network from interrelated and collaborating business processes will exceed the complexity of traditional enterprise IT infrastructures. This requires software engineering techniques for the management, scalability, security, and auditing of business process collaborations—techniques that are, today, still in their infancy.

Complexity

10.2.6 Service Localization

When we look at the different parties involved in Web services, we can identify three roles:

- *Web service provider:* The service provider has to decide what to offer as a Web service, how to describe these services, and where to publish these descriptions. In Section 6.6.3 we discussed WSDL, a standard to describe Web services.
- *Web service consumer:* Service consumers first have to formulate their requirements, then have to try to discover a service that satisfies these requirements. In order to do so, they must understand the description of the service and negotiate a communication protocol with the service.
- *Web service broker:* Service brokers help the providers and the consumers get together. They provide repositories that contain the service descriptions. These repositories contain white and yellow pages that list services by name and by service type. In Section 7.3, we discussed UDDI, a standard that defines the registration of Web services in repositories.

Semantic maps   However, just a list of addresses and descriptions will only be of limited help. Crucial for service brokers is to provide sound taxonomies for Web services. A good taxonomy will help service consumers to understand the semantics of a service. Semantic navigation in the form of a semantic map (for instance, a topic map; see Section 7.2) will help to locate the right service.

Added value   In addition, Web brokers can offer auxiliary services, too. For example, they can gather statistics (which services are wanted most, and by whom). They can arrange for payment of services. They can even forward requests to other brokers. Thus Web service brokers provide Web services themselves.

Web services thus dissolve the classical client-server architecture into individual services that are scattered across the Web. They will rely heavily on peer-to-peer communication and on sophisticated semantic navigation techniques that allow consumers to find the right service. Or will the services begin to hunt the Web for possible consumers?

10.3 ebXML

ebXML may well be the most important development for electronic business in a long time. Started as an initiative of UN/CEFACT and OASIS, ebXML combines the industry's rich experience with EDI, the flexibility of XML, the reusability of component-oriented systems, and ground-breaking work in the treatment of context. According to Carol Geyer of Oasis:

> Members of the Global Commerce Initiative (GCI) announced plans to use ebXML as the backbone of their new data exchange standard for business-to-business trade in the consumer goods industry. . . . GCI members include 40 major manufacturers and retailers as well as eight trade associations, which in total represent 850,000 companies around the world. Exchanges such as Transora, the WorldWide Retail Exchange, GlobalNetXchange, and CPGmarket.com are taking active roles in the GCI development.

In early 2002, other industry alliances, such as the Open Travel Alliance (OTA) and Covisint, joined the ebXML initiative. For the business world, ebXML is probably the most important standard since XML. ebXML not only defines a global nonproprietary standard to exchange data between businesses, but it also introduces an infrastructure that supports collaborative business processes. This infrastructure enables ebXML to automate much of the process of locating and establishing business partnerships, in particular, where companies previously have not done business with each other.

In the first phase, ebXML will not replace existing EDI/EDIFACT solu- *EDI will stay* tions. Large corporations already have EDI/EDIFACT solutions in place, and according to the rule "if it ain't broke, don't fix it," these solutions will hardly be replaced at first sight. Thus, ebXML will initially exist in areas where EDI/EDIFACT is not in place (such as small businesses), but also where EDI/EDIFACT solutions must be integrated with other solutions.

10.3.1 Basic Concepts

From Oasis (2002):

> ebXML . . . is built on three basic concepts: provide an infrastructure that ensures data communication interoperability; provide a semantics framework that ensures commercial interoperability; and provide a mechanism that allows enterprises to find each other, agree to become trading partners and conduct business with each other.

The infrastructure is provided through a standard message transport *Message* mechanism, a well-defined interface, packaging rules, and a predictable *transport* delivery and security model. The specification allows any application-level protocol to be used for message transport, including common protocols such as SMTP, HTTP, FTP, and SOAP. An interface for business services handles messages at either end of the transport.

Semantic
framework

The semantic framework includes a metamodel for defining business process and information models, reusable core components that reflect common business processes and XML vocabularies, and a process for defining actual message structures and definitions as they relate to the activities in the business process model.

Shared
repositories

The mechanism for discovery, agreement, and collaboration is provided through shared repositories (OASIS 2001f) where enterprises can register and discover each other's business services via *collaborative partner profiles* (CPP), a process for defining and agreeing to a formal *collaboration protocol agreement* (CPA), and a shared repository for company profiles, business process models, and related message structures. ebXML can make use of UDDI to locate registries and repositories (OASIS 2001e).

10.3.2 Shared Repositories

The heart of
ebXML

The shared repositories (ebXML registry) for company profiles, business process models, and related message structures are the pivot points within the ebXML architecture.

Registration

When a company—let's call it Nuts & Bolts—plans to build its own ebXML-compliant application, it first reviews existing ebXML repositories (step 1 in Figure 10.1). (However, the use of repositories is optional. ebXML relationships can also be negotiated between two parties directly.) Utilizing the reusable components stored in the repositories, Nuts & Bolts will set up its own ebXML-compliant application (step 2). The company will then register the implementation details and its own company business profile in an ebXML registry (step 3). This profile describes Nuts & Bolts' ebXML capabilities and constraints, and the supported business scenarios. The registry then checks if format and usage of the business scenarios are correct and sends an acknowledgment to Nuts & Bolts.

Discovery

Now a company called Doors & Windows is looking for a supplier of hardware. Doors & Windows discovers Nuts & Bolts in the ebXML registry (step 4). They find that the business scenarios supported by Nuts & Bolts satisfy their requirements. Doors & Windows decides not to implement its own ebXML application but to buy an ebXML-compliant shrink-wrapped application. After installation of that package, they download the CPP of Nuts & Bolts (step 5) and construct a CPA by computing an intersection of the downloaded CPP and their own CPP (step 6). This can be done manually or automatically.

Negotiation

The resulting CPA is then proposed directly to Nuts & Bolts' ebXML-compliant software interface for further negotiation (step 7). The CPA outlines which business scenarios both companies agree on plus some

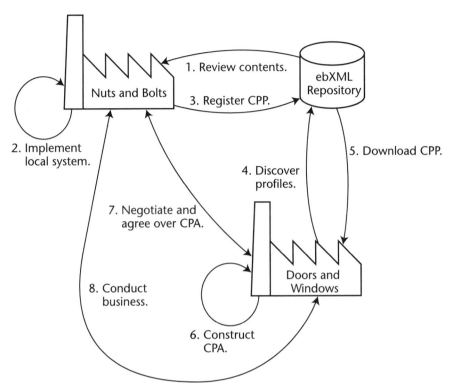

Figure 10.1 Registration, discovery, and negotiation in ebXML.

specific agreement. It is then used to configure the runtime systems of both companies. In particular, the CPA contains information about messaging requirements for transactions, the *conversations* that take place in a collaborative business process, contingency plans, and security-related requirements. After Nuts & Bolts accepts the business agreement, both companies are ready to engage in e-business using ebXML (step 8).

The ebXML architecture is in part influenced by the Open-edi Refer- Open-edi ence Model, ISO/IEC 14662. The Open-edi reference model (ISO/IEC 1997) was released by the International Organization for Standardization (ISO) and the International Electrotechnical Commission (IEC) in 1997. The Open-edi model is generic—it does not define an operational standard but serves as the basis for the work between the different agencies involved in EDI standardization.

Open-edi makes a clear distinction between the business operational view (business rules) and the functional service view (interoperability rules). Business scenarios can be defined and registered by business communities. Users can thus reuse existing scenarios instead of negotiating all the details from scratch. Each scenario consists of the following:

- *Roles:* A role defines a partner involved in a business scenario.
- *Information bundles:* Information bundles describe formally the semantics of the information exchanged between the parties involved in a business scenario.
- *Semantic components:* Information bundles are constructed using semantic components. A semantic component is a unit of unambiguously defined information in the context of the business goal of the business transaction.
- *Scenario attributes:* Scenario attributes describe information independent of roles or information bundles.

The dynamic aspects of scenarios are defined using existing formal methods such as state transition diagrams or Petri nets.

CPP in detail   The CPP is part of the *trading partners profile* (TPP) (OASIS 2001a). It defines the capabilities of a single partner in terms of becoming engaged in business with other partners. The specifications of the CPP form a layered architecture:

- *Process specification:* This is the top layer of the specifications and defines the services (business transactions) offered to other partners, as well as the transition rules that determine the valid sequence of service requests. These definitions are made in the separate process specification document (see below). This document is referenced by both CPP and CPA.
- *Delivery channels:* This layer describes the message-receiving characteristics of a party. One CPP can contain several delivery channels. Each channel consists of one document exchange definition and one transport definition.
- *Document exchange layer:* This layer processes business documents accepted from the process specification layer at one party. If specified, the documents are encrypted and digital signatures are added (see Section 6.8). The document is then passed to the transport layer for transmission to the other party. When documents are received from the other party, the inverse steps are performed. The document exchange layer complements the services offered by the transport layer. If, for example, the selected transport protocol does not provide encryption, but message security is required, then encryption must be specified at the document exchange layer.

The protocol for exchanging messages is defined by the ebXML messaging service specification or other similar messaging services.
- *Transport layer:* This layer is responsible for message delivery. The transport protocol can be specified—the choice may affect the choices selected for the document exchange layer. For example, some protocols may provide authentication and encryption, while others don't.

Here is a CPP example:

```
<CollaborationProtocolProfile
  xmlns="http://www.ebxml.org/namespaces/tradePartner"
  xmlns:bpm="http://www.ebxml.org/namespaces/businessProcess"
  xmlns:ds="http://www.w3.org/2000/09/xmldsig#"
  xmlns:xlink="http://www.w3.org/1999/xlink">

  <PartyInfo>
    <PartyId> … </PartyId>
    <PartyRef> … </PartyRef>
    <CollaborationRole>
      <CertificateRef certId = "…"/>
      <ProcessSpecification name="…" … />
      <Role name="…" … />
      <ServiceBinding name="…" channelId="…">
        <Override action="…" channelId="…" … />
      </ServiceBinding>
    </CollaborationRole>

    <Certificate> … </Certificate>

    <DeliveryChannel channelId="…" transportId="…"
                                      docExchangeId="…">
      <Characteristics
            nonrepudiationOfOrigin = "true"
            nonrepudiationOfReceipt = "true"
            secureTransport = "true"
            confidentiality = "true"
            authenticated = "true"
            authorized = "true"/>
    </DeliveryChannel>

    <Transport transportId = "…">
      <Protocol>…</Protocol>
      <Endpoint uri="…" type = "…"/>
      <TransportSecurity>
```

```
        <Protocol>…</Protocol>
        <CertificateRef certId = "…"/>
      </TransportSecurity>
    </Transport>

    <DocExchange docExchangeId = "…">
      <ebXMLBinding>
        <MessageEncoding> … </MessageEncoding>
        <ReliableMessaging deliverySemantics="…"
             idempotency="false"
             persistDuration="…">
          <Retries> … </Retries>
          <RetryInterval> … </RetryInterval>
        </ReliableMessaging>
        <NonRepudiation>
          <Protocol> … </Protocol>
          <HashFunction> … </HashFunction>
          <SignatureAlgorithm> … </SignatureAlgorithm>
          <CertificateRef certId = "…"/>
        </NonRepudiation>
        <DigitalEnvelope>
          <Protocol> … </Protocol>
          <EncryptionAlgorithm> … </EncryptionAlgorithm>
          <CertificateRef certId = "…"/>
        </DigitalEnvelope>
        <NamespaceSupported> … </NamespaceSupported>
      </ebXMLBinding>
    </DocExchange>

  </PartyInfo>

  <ds:Signature>

  …

  </ds:Signature>

  <Comment>text</Comment>

</CollaborationProtocolProfile>
```

CPP elements   Besides the namespace definitions for trade partners, business processes, signatures, and XLink, and optional elements for signature specification and comments, a CPP document contains at least one PartyInfo
element. Each of these contains the following:

- At least one `PartyId` element defining a logical identifier for the party, for example, a URI.
- At least one `PartyRef` element specifying a link (URI) to additional information about the party, for example, a URL pointing to the party's Web site, a UDDI or ebXML repository, or an LDAP directory.
- At least one `CollaborationRole` element defining the role of the party within a business process. Child elements identify the certificate to be used for this role, the business process to which the role belongs, and the role the party plays within this process (for example, buyer or seller). Each `CollaborationRole` contains `ServiceBinding` elements to bind the role to main and alternative delivery channels. `Override` elements can specify different channels for specific actions, for example, for acknowledgments or express messages.
- At least one `Certificate` element identifying the certificate to be used in this CPP.
- At least one `DeliveryChannel` element. Each delivery channel identifies one `Transport` element and one `DocExchange` element and contains a `Characteristics` element that specifies several channel attributes.
- At least one `Transport` element. Each of these contains child elements to specify the protocol used (HTTP, SMTP, FTP, SOAP), the channel end points, and security settings (protocol, certificate). There are different types of channel end points: login, request, response, error, allPurpose.

In addition, each `PartyInfo` element also contains at least one `Doc-Exchange` element. Each of these defines the properties of a messaging service to be used. Each `DocExchange` element contains an `ebXMLBinding` element that describes properties specific to the ebXML Message Service:

- `MessageEncoding` specifies the encoding standard used for the transmission, such as BASE64.
- `ReliableMessaging` describes the properties for reliable ebXML message exchange. The `deliverySemantics` attribute can take the values "Once-AndOnlyOnce" or "BestEffort" (no reliable messaging). The `idempotency` attribute can take the values "true" and "false". If set to "true", all messages are subject to an idempotency test ensuring that message duplicates are discarded. (Messages could be duplicated when message transmission is retried or restarted after an exception has happened.) The value of the `persistDuration` attribute is the minimum length of time a message should be kept in persistent storage. The `Retries` and `RetryInterval` child elements specify how often and in which intervals message transmissions should be repeated after a timeout.

- The NonRepudiation element allows the proof of who sent a message and prevents later repudiation. Nonrepudiation is based on the XML digital signature (see Section 6.8). The Protocol child element identifies the technology used to digitally sign a message, such as XMLDSIG. The HashFunction child element identifies the algorithm used for message digest. The SignatureAlgorithm child element identifies the digital signature algorithm. The CertificateRef child element refers to one of the Certificate elements elsewhere within the CPP.
- The DigitalEnvelope element specifies a symmetric encryption procedure. (The shared secret key is sent to the message recipient encrypted with the recipient's public key.) The Protocol child element identifies the security protocol to be used, for example, S/MIME. The EncryptionAlgorithm child element identifies the encryption algorithm to be used. The CertificateRef child element refers to one of the Certificate elements elsewhere within the CPP or CPA.
- The NamespaceSupported element lists any namespace extensions supported by the implementation, such as Security Services Markup Language or Transaction Authority Markup Language.

10.3.3 Contracts in ebXML

CPA in detail

The CPA is part of the trading partners agreement (TPA) (OASIS 2001a). A CPA describes on which capabilities two parties have agreed to conduct business. This includes technical capabilities such as communication and messaging protocols but also business capabilities (i.e., which business processes are shared in the context of a CPA).

Here is a CPA example:

```
<CollaborationProtocolAgreement id = "…"
    xmlns="http://www.ebxml.org/namespaces/tradePartner"
    xmlns:bpm="http://www.ebxml.org/namespaces/businessProcess"
    xmlns:ds = "http://www.w3.org/2000/09/xmldsig#"
    xmlns:xlink = "http://www.w3.org/1999/xlink">

  <CPAType>
    <Protocol> … </Protocol>
    <Type> … </Type>
  </CPAType>
  <Status value = "…"/>
  <Start> … </Start>
  <End> … </End>
  <ConversationConstraints invocationLimit = "…"
```

```
                concurrentConversations = "…"/>
  <PartyInfo> … </PartyInfo>
  <PartyInfo> … </PartyInfo>
  <ds:Signature> … </ds:Signature>
  <Comment> … </Comment>
</CollaborationProtocolAgreement>
```

Because a CPA is constructed from an intersection of the CPPs of the two parties, most elements of a CPA are the same in a CPP. We explain here only the additional elements.

- The optional CPAType element contains information about the general nature of the CPA. A Protocol child element identifies the business-level protocol, for example, PIP3A4, a RosettaNet Partner Interface Process. A Type child element specifies additional information regarding the business protocol. The specific values depend on the particular protocol. An example is RNIF (RosettaNet Implementation Framework).

- The required Status element identifies the state of the process that creates the CPA. Two values are possible in its value attribute: "proposed" when the agreement is still negotiated and "signed" if the agreement is closed.

- The required Start and End elements specify the date and time when the CPA takes effect and when the CPA must be renegotiated by the parties (i.e., the lifetime of the CPA).

- The optional ConversationConstraints element documents certain agreements about conversation processing. The invocationLimit attribute defines the maximum number of conversations that can be performed under this CPA. The concurrentConversations attribute defines the maximum number of conversations that can be processed under this CPA simultaneously.

- Two required PartyInfo elements, one for each party. These elements describe the terms under which each party has agreed to this CPA. For a detailed description of the PartyInfo element, see the earlier CPP section.

- At least one ds:Signature element that provides signing of the CPA using the XML Digital Signature standard.

- Optional Comment elements.

10.3.4 The ebXML Process Model

The ebXML Business Process Specification Schema (OASIS 2001b) defines the orchestration of business transactions into collaborative business processes. The specification is based on a subset of prior UN/CEFACT work, namely, the metamodel behind the UN/CEFACT Unified Modeling Methodology (UMM), which is based on UML. Thus ebXML process models can be represented in both XML and UML.

Binary
collaborations

The current specifications support only binary collaborations—business processes with more than two participating partners are not yet covered. However, in most cases, multiparty business processes can be synthesized from several binary business processes.

UML

Typically, an ebXML specification schema starts with the definition of a UML specification schema. The UML specification schema used in ebXML is a subset of the UMM.

An ebXML schema (DTD) can be generated from the UML specification with the help of production rules. This is possible without information loss, because the UML specification schema and the XML specification schema are isomorphic.

Web service
collaboration

ebXML Web services collaborate with other services via ebXML business service interfaces. These interfaces execute the business processes as configured with the specification schema. They do so by exchanging ebXML messages and business signals. (Business signals are application-level documents that signal the current state of a business transaction. Business signals, however, do not transport application data; they merely indicate the current state of a process.)

Business
process
collaboration

An ebXML business process collaboration is constituted from a number of elements. Let's take each in turn.

Partners

Two or more partners take part in a business process. Each partner plays one or several roles within a business process.

Business Document Flow

Document flows carry business documents between participating roles of a business transaction. Each document flow can carry one primary business document. There is always one requesting document flow, but there can be none, one, or many responding document flows, depending on the type of transaction.

```
<DocumentFlow
        isSuccess="true"
        documentType="Card validation acknowledgment"/>
</DocumentFlow>
```

```
<DocumentFlow
        isSuccess="false"
        documentType="Card validation rejection"/>
</DocumentFlow>
```

This example shows two responding document flows, one when the transaction was successful, the other when the transaction failed.

Business Transactions

A business transaction is an atomic unit of work in a business relationship between two roles, with one role in the position of a service requester, the other role in the position of a responder. Because in ebXML business transactions are atomic, they cannot be subdivided. A business transaction either succeeds or fails. If it succeeds, its outcome may be legally binding for both partners; if it fails, it must be treated as if it has never happened (rollback). Each business transaction contains one requesting document flow and zero, one, or many responding document flows.

Atomic transactions

```
<BusinessTransaction name="Card validation">
   <RequestingBusinessActivity
        name=""
        isNonRepudiationRequired="true"
        timeToAcknowledgeReceipt="P1M"
        timeToAcknowledgeAcceptance="P2M">
     <DocumentFlow
           isSuccess="true"
           documentType="Credit card slip"/>
   </RequestingBusinessActivity>
   <RespondingBusinessActivity
        name=""
        isNonRepudiationRequired="true"
        timeToAcknowledgeReceipt="P4M">
     <DocumentFlow
        isSuccess="true"
        documentType="Card validation acknowledgment"/>
     </DocumentFlow>
     <DocumentFlow
           isSuccess="false"
           documentType="Card validation rejection"/>
     </DocumentFlow>
   </RespondingBusinessActivity>
</BusinessTransaction>
```

In this business transaction two documents are exchanged: the request message contains a business card slip that needs to be validated. The respective response document contains the positive or negative answer. There are three additional business signals: the first acknowledges that the request has been received; the second acknowledges that the request has been accepted for processing; and the third is given by the requesting party to acknowledge that the response document has been received. The time periods specified are given in the format used in XML Schema ("P4M" means "period of 4 minutes") and are counted from the initial request on.

Collaborations

Two or more roles collaborate in a business process. Collaborations between more than two roles are always synthesized from binary collaborations (i.e., with two participating roles). A binary collaboration can be seen as a protocol between two roles.

Business
activities

Each collaboration consists of a set of business activities. A business activity might be atomic (a business transaction), or it may be complex (another binary collaboration). This allows the definition of nested and multiparty collaborations.

```
<BinaryCollaboration
        name="Credit Card Validation"
        timeToPerform="P5M">
  <AuthorizedRole name="merchant"/>
  <AuthorizedRole name="card-service"/>
  <BusinessTransactionActivity
        name="Card validation activity"
        businessTransaction="Card validation"
        fromAuthorizedRole="merchant"
        toAuthorizedRole="card-service"/>
</BinaryCollaboration>
```

Multiparty
collaboration

This example shows a simple binary collaboration constituted from the business transaction defined earlier. The following example shows a multiparty collaboration for a typical credit card purchase over the Internet:

```
<MultiPartyCollaboration name="Credit card purchase">
  <BusinessPartnerRole name="Customer">
    <Performs
        binaryCollaboration="e-Order"
```

```
            authorizedRole="buyer"/>
    </BusinessPartnerRole>
    <BusinessPartnerRole name="Retailer">
        <Performs
            binaryCollaboration="e-Order"
            authorizedRole="seller"/>
        <Performs
            binaryCollaboration="Credit Card Validation"
            authorizedRole="merchant"/>
    </BusinessPartnerRole>
    <BusinessPartnerRole name="Card Agency">
        <Performs
            binaryCollaboration="Credit Card Validation"
            authorizedRole="card-service"/>
    </BusinessPartnerRole>
</MultiPartyCollaboration>
```

This collaboration takes place between three parties (customer, retailer, and card agency) and involves two binary collaborations (e-order and credit card validation from the previous example).

Choreography

The ebXML business transaction choreography describes how the business activities (collaboration activities and business transaction activities) within a collaboration are ordered and sequenced. When using UML, this can be specified using a UML activity diagram.

The business activities define the business states within a choreography. In addition, there are auxiliary states such as `Start` state, `Terminal` state (which comes in a `Success` or `Failure` flavor), `Fork` state, and `Join` state. `Fork` splits a sequence of business activities into several concurrent sequences, while `Join` reunites several concurrent sequences.

Business states

The choreography defines the transitions between the business states. Each transition can be gated by *guards*—criteria such as the status of the document flow that caused the transition, the type of document sent, the content of the document, or postconditions on the prior state.

Transitions

Transitions are defined as child elements of a `BinaryCollaboration` element, or in the case of a `MultiPartyCollaboration` as child elements of `BusinessPartnerRole` elements.

```
<BusinessPartnerRole name="Retailer">
    ...
```

```
<Transition
        fromBinaryCollaboration="e-Order"
        fromBusinessState="Accept Order"
        toBinaryCollaboration="Credit Card Validation"
        toBusinessState="Accept Order"/>
</BusinessPartnerRole>
```

This is a simple transition definition for the MultiPartyCollaboration example shown earlier, arranging the sequential execution of both binary collaborations defined for the role "Retailer". There is only a single business state (Accept Order).

Patterns

The ebXML specification schema provides a set of predefined patterns that can be used to construct transactions and collaborations. This reuse mechanism leads to faster and more standardized work products.

Catalog   The ebXML Catalog of Common Business Processes (OASIS 2001c) specifies an initial list of various common business process names. This includes business processes defined by other common industry standards such as RosettaNet, X12, EDIFACT, JiPDEC/CII, OAG BOD, or xCBL. It is planned to create ebXML collaboration patterns on the basis of each of these business processes. These patterns can be stored in public or shared ebXML repositories. ebXML design tools will link into these repositories, support the discovery of predefined collaboration patterns, and help in the construction of customized business processes.

10.3.5 How Context Is Handled

Imagine the following situation: A printing house based in the United States wants to order spare parts for their printing press from a manufacturer based in Germany. Both partners in this transaction operate in different contexts. First, they are in different locations, one in the United States, one in Germany. Second, they belong to different industries, one to the printing industry, the other to the manufacturing industry. It is very likely that the formats of business documents (such as purchase orders or invoices) used by these partners are different. For example, the address element of such a business document would show differences: in the United States, the address contains a "state" element; in Germany it does not. The ZIP in a U.S. address is positioned after the state element; the German "Postleitzahl" is positioned before the town element.

Such differences are usually not a problem when transactions are handled by humans. But when a transaction is handled by a computer, it becomes a problem. Let's see how ebXML solves that problem.

First, ebXML subdivides contexts into context categories. In particular, for the purpose of doing business over the Internet, it identifies the following context categories (or context drivers):

Context categories

- *Region:* The geopolitical region, such as country or state.
- *Industry:* The industry domain to which a partner belongs.
- *Process:* The current business process. Different business processes may require specific formats in business documents.
- *Product:* Product categories may also influence the format of business documents.
- *Legislative:* The legislative context used for this document.
- *Role:* The current role of a partner. In our previous example, we had two roles: buyer and seller. Buyer and seller operated in different regional and industry contexts.
- And so on.

The value of each context category is a simple string, for instance, "US" or "Germany" for the region. It is possible to constrain the possible values for context categories by defining a reference to an established taxonomy such as ISO3166 for regional contexts.

Second, ebXML does not define specialized business documents for each purpose and each context. This would make it practically impossible for partners to agree on a document format. Instead, ebXML defines a set of generic *core components*. Business documents are assembled from these core components with the help of assembly rules and are further customized with the help of context rules. This sounds difficult, but it solves a problem that lingered in the EDI world for about 25 years: the inability of business partners to refer to a common business terminology. This is no easy task: different industries use different names for the same concepts, and the same concepts can look very different in different contexts. OASIS (2001d) defines how business documents are composed from a library of core components.

Core components

The initial catalogue of core components lists nearly 100 core components, including postal address, street building identifier, post office box identifier, party type, language, language usage, date, time, birth date and time, organization incorporation date and time, account identifier, and many more.

Domain components

Core components are complemented by user-defined *domain components*. Domain components should be specified in the same detail as core components, complete with the relevant contexts. Domain components and additional context categories should be registered with an ebXML repository, too, to allow reuse of these components and context categories.

Document assembly

Assembly rules compose a document schema from core components. This is done with the following operations:

- CreateGroup creates a model group consisting of several elements or other model groups.
- CreateElement creates a new simple type or complex type element.
- UseElement imports a core component.
- Rename can change the name (and even the path) of previously composed elements.
- Condition can specify context criteria under which the above operations are executed.

Here is an example of document assembly:

```
<?xml version="1.0"?>
<!DOCTYPE Assembly SYSTEM "assembly.dtd">
<Assembly version="1.0">
  <Assemble name="PurchaseOrder">
    <CreateGroup>
      <CreateElement
           type="PartyType" location="GUID" id="Buyer">
        <Name>Buyer</Name>
        <CreateGroup>
          <UseElement name="Name"/>
          <UseElement name="Address">
            <CreateGroup id="adr">
              <Condition test="Region='United States'">
                <UseElement name="BuildingNumber"/>
                <UseElement name="StreetName"/>
              </Condition>
              <Condition test="Region='Germany'">
                <UseElement name="StreetName"/>
                <UseElement name="BuildingNumber"/>
                <UseElement name="ZIP"/>
              </Condition>
              <UseElement name="City"/>
              <Condition test="Region='United States'">
```

```
                    <UseElement name="State"/>
                    <UseElement name="ZIP"/>
                  </Condition>
                  <UseElement name="Country"/>
                </CreateGroup>
              </UseElement>
            </CreateGroup>
            <Condition test="Region='Germany'">
              <Rename from="address" to="addressDE"/>
            </Condition>
          </CreateElement>
          <CreateElement
                type="PartyType" id="Seller" location="GUID">
            <Name>Seller</Name>
          </CreateElement>
        </CreateGroup>
        <CreateElement
              minOccurs="1" maxOccurs="unbounded"
              type="ItemType" location="GUID" id="Item">
          <Name>Item</Name>
        </CreateElement>
      </Assemble>
</Assembly>
```

Context rules can further modify a document. Each rule specifies a matching algorithm. Rules can match exactly; that is, the specified value in the Condition element must match the value of the context category exactly.

Alternatively, rules can match hierarchically, according to the definitions given in the referenced taxonomy. For example, the regional context would have a taxonomy that is structured according to the following hierarchy:

- Global
- Continent
- Economic region
- Country (ISO 3166.1)
- Region (ISO 3166.2)

If, for example, we would specify "North America" as regional context in a Condition, it would match concrete context values such as "United States", "Canada", "Mississippi", "Ontario", and so on, because these values are members of the "North America" hierarchy.

Actions   If the test specified in `Condition` succeeds, several actions can be performed:

- *Add:* This action includes new elements in a document.
- *Occurs:* This action specifies the number of occurrences in terms of `minOccurs` and `maxOccurs`. If nothing is specified, `minOccurs` and `maxOccurs` default to 1 (i.e., a single required element).
- *Subtract:* This action removes elements from a document.
- *Condition:* Apply another condition. Conditions can be nested.
- *Comment:* A comment block.
- *Rename:* Elements can be renamed (see above).

However, there is one problem: Context rules may conflict. For example, a context rule for the context "Region" could conflict with a context rule for the context "Industry". These conflicts must be resolved:

- Context rules are executed in the order they are specified in the context rule document.
- Context rules may be equipped with an explicit `order` attribute that can be used to force a given order on a set of rules.

Here is an example of context rules:

```xml
<?xml version="1.0"?>
<!DOCTYPE ContextRules SYSTEM "contextrules.dtd">
<ContextRules>
  <Rule apply="hierarchical" order="1">
    <Taxonomy context="Region"
        ref="http://ebxml.org/classification/ISO3166"/>
    <Condition test="Region='United States'">
      <Action applyTo="Buyer/Address">
        <Occurs>
          <Field name="State">
          </Field>
        </Occurs>
        <Add after="@id='adr'">
          <CreateGroup type="choice">
            <Field name="Floor" type="string">
            </Field>
            <Field name="Suite" type="string">
            </Field>
          </CreateGroup>
        </Add>
      </Action>
```

```
      </Condition>
    </Rule>
</ContextRules>
```

Third, ebXML defines a *semantic interoperability document* format, that   Pivot format
is, a syntax-neutral format for the exchange of documents between partners who use different formats for business documents. An ebXML
processor would translate a business document into the syntax-neutral
format before transmitting it to the receiver. At the receiver side the document is translated from the syntax-neutral format into the specific syntax used by the receiver. Using such a "pivot" format reduces the number
of required conversion procedures. UUIDs and globally unique URIs are
used to identify document elements in a syntax-neutral way.

10.3.6 Future

The ebXML specifications were released in May 2001. At the same time,
UN/CEFACT and OASIS demonstrated the first "proof of concept" applications. By mid-2001 the very first tools for ebXML appeared on the
market (see Chapter 11). However, it will still be a while before the first
all-in-one shrink-wrapped packages are available and the first ebXML repositories are in operation. Work continues in the OASIS Universal Business Language (UBL) Technical Committee to develop a standard XML
business library.

Also, we should not expect a fully automated negotiation process between business partners with the first products. The first products will
support manual or semiautomatic negotiation.

10.4 INDUSTRY VOCABULARIES

In this section we give a short overview of some relevant horizontal and
vertical XML-based industry vocabularies. The list is by no means repre-
sentative or comprehensive. The Web sites *www.xml.org* and *www.oasis-
open.org/cover/* should offer a much wider panorama.

10.4.1 Technical Vocabularies

- Bean Markup Language (BML): An XML-based component configuration or wiring language customized for the JavaBean component
  model (*www.alphaworks.ibm.com*).

10.4.2 Scientific Vocabularies

- Chemical Markup Language (CMLTM): An XML vocabulary for the management of chemical information (*www.xml-cml.org*).
- Mathematical Markup Language (MathML): An XML application for describing mathematical notation and capturing both its structure and its content (*www.w3.org*).

10.4.3 Horizontal Industry Vocabularies

- Call Processing Language (CPL): A language that can be used to describe and control Internet telephony services (*www.ietf.org*).
- Internet Open Trading Protocol (IOTP): An interoperable framework for Internet commerce (*www.ietf.org*).
- Information and Content Exchange (ICE): Facilitates the controlled exchange and management of electronic assets between networked partners and affiliates (*www.icestandard.org*).
- MatML: Addresses the problems of interpretation and interoperability for materials data that will permit the storage, transmission, and processing of materials property data (*www.ceramics.nist.gov/matml/matml.htm*).
- Product Definition Exchange (PDX): Standard for the e-supply chain. It is focused on the problem of communicating product content information between OEMs, EMS providers, and component suppliers (*www.pdxstandard.org*).
- Product Data Markup Language (PDML): An XML vocabulary designed to support the interchange of product information among commercial systems or government systems (*www.pdml.org*).
- SyncML: Synchronizes the exchange of data with and between mobile devices (*www.syncml.org*).
- Tutorial Markup Language (TML): An interchange format designed to separate the semantic content of a question from its screen layout or formatting (*www.ilrt.bris.ac.uk/mru/netquest/tml/*).

10.4.4 Vertical Industry Vocabularies

- aecXML: An XML-based language used to represent information in the architecture, engineering, and construction (AEC) industry (*www.iai-na.org*).

- DocBook: A DTD for computer documentation. It is suitable to be used for both books and papers, and for both computer software and hardware. This DTD was certified as an OASIS Standard on February 2, 2001, after a vote of the OASIS membership (*www.oasis-open.org*).
- Extensible Financial Reporting Markup Language (XFRML): An XML vocabulary for the preparation and exchange of business reports and data (*www.xbrl.org*).
- eXtensible Media Commerce Language (XMCL): An open XML-based language designed to establish industrywide standards for Internet media commerce (*www.xmcl.org*).
- Financial Product Markup Language (FpML): A business information exchange standard for electronic dealing and processing of financial derivatives instruments (*www.fpml.org*).
- HL7 (Health Level Seven): An XML-based framework for the health industry (*www.hl7.org*).
- Marine Trading Markup Language (MTML): A standard to help a broad base of small, medium, and large buyers and suppliers in the marine trading industry conduct their fundamental trading transactions electronically via the Internet (*www.mtml.org*).
- News Industry Text Format (NITF): A format that allows publishers to adapt the look, feel, and interactivity of their documents to the bandwidth, devices, and personalized needs of their subscribers. These documents can be translated into HTML, WML (for wireless devices), RTF (for printing), or any other format the publisher wishes (*www.nitf.org*).
- ONIX International: The international standard for representing and communicating book industry product information in electronic form (*www.editeur.org/onix.html*).
- swiftML: Aims at the interoperability issue of different financial XML implementations through the use of SWIFT Standards Modeling (*www.swift.com*).
- Translation Memory Exchange (TMX): Allows easier exchange of translation memory data between tools and/or translation vendors with little or no loss of critical data during the process (*www.lisa.org*).

Solutions

In this chapter we discuss selected XML technologies from the areas of design, data storage, middleware, authoring, and content management where practical solutions are already in place.

In Section 11.1, we present tools that support XML authors and architects in the design process. This includes tools for conceptual design such as UML tools, and also tools for the design of workflows such as Microsoft's BizTalk or the various RosettaNet-related design tools. Designing XML schemata has become easier as good visual editors for DTDs and XML Schema such as Tibco's XML Authority and Altova's XML Spy have gone on the market.

In Section 11.2, we browse the market for XML-enabled database management systems. We first discuss the requirements for such systems, and then we investigate some of the

DBMSs, such as Oracle and IBM's DB2, that provide XML support via an additional XML layer (mapped systems). Then we take a close look at native XML database management systems such as Software AG's Tamino. Finally, we recommend best practices on how to select an appropriate database management system.

In Section 11.3, we go into the details of three sample Web-enabled middleware systems: Hewlett-Packard's e-speak, RosettaNet, and Microsoft's BizTalk. Especially BizTalk is of interest here, as it is the first major application relying on the SOAP communications protocol.

In Section 11.4, we briefly list XML-enabled application servers. Basically all manufacturers of application servers provide support for XML and Web services related standards such as SOAP, WSDL, and UDDI.

In Section 11.5, we discuss tools for the authoring of presentation objects. This includes tools for the authoring of HTML, WML, SVG, SMIL, and VoiceXML, but also tools for the definition of transformation scripts such as XSLT scripts.

Finally, in Section 11.6, we briefly discuss the architecture of content management systems as an example of an architecture integrating various techniques presented throughout this book.

11.1 DESIGN TOOLS

Although sometimes paper and pencil are the best design tools, there are cases where the help of computer-based tools is appreciated. In this section, we discuss tools for conceptual design, process design, and schema design.

11.1.1 Conceptual Design

Good design tools for XML-centric conceptual design are still as rare as hen's teeth. Among general design methods and design tools, UML is the obvious choice, since UML has been proposed to become an ISO standard and other electronic business standards such as ebXML or UDDI rely on the UML design method.

UML tools
Commercial systems such as Rational Rose (*www.rational.com*) and TogetherSoft (*www.togethersoft.com*) also support the design of XML schemata. This integration covers only the possibility of modeling XML implementation structures within UML. You can, for example, model a particular document class in terms of specific UML stereotypes (see Sec-

tion 3.4.1) and then export these definitions as a DTD or schema. You can also import DTDs and schemata. However, UML and XML Schema have only a common subset of features. Advanced XML Schema features require proprietary extensions to the UML model that can make round-trip engineering difficult.

Directly generating XML from a conceptual model defined in UML is still an open problem. Starting with a conceptual model such as an entity relationship model and then arriving by automatic means at some XML Schema definitions is not covered by these systems. The user is required either to write explicit production rules (to generate XML schemata as code) or to export the definitions into the XMI format (see Section 3.4.1) and then transform this XMI serialization into an XML Schema definition with the help of XSLT style sheets, or into DTDs with software such as the XMI toolkit from IBM's alphaworks. If you want to play around a bit with UML and XMI, ArgoUML and Poseidon for UML are nice (and free) UML tools that can generate XMI. They can even export the graphics into SVG format. A design tool for AOM (see Section 3.2.2) is available at *www.aomodeling.org.*

11.1.2 Process Design

Processes can be defined with UML in the form of activity diagrams as well. Once again, to translate these diagrams into an XML process description language such as BPML or Microsoft's XLANG, you must transform the XMI output with the help of an XSLT style sheet.

Modeling processes for electronic business is usually not an isolated activity, so the modeling tools are usually integrated into the middleware product that supports a specific electronic business standard.

BizTalk, for example (see Section 11.3.3), uses a graphical design process based on Visio2000. A few VBA plug-ins then serialize the visual design into XLANG definitions.

For architectures such as RosettaNet or ebXML, design tools are required that are repository aware. Such design tools must allow you to browse directories, to discover existing partner profiles and building blocks for processes, to import and customize these building blocks, and to publish new building blocks within the repository.

At *www.rosettanet.org* you will find an impressive list of solution providers who offer appropriate tools to support that standard.

Since the ebXML specifications were only released in May 2001, the list of available tools is—at the time of writing—not very long. But the ink on the release documents was still wet when the first integrated solutions supporting ebXML appeared.

BizTalk

RosettaNet

ebXML

Sun Microsystems has released the Java API for XML Registries 1.0 (JAXR).

> JAXR provides an API for a set of distributed Registry Services that enables business-to-business integration between business enterprises, using the protocols being defined by ebXML.org, Oasis, ISO 11179 (*java.sun.com /aboutJava/communityprocess/jsr/jsr_093_jaxr.html*).

An open source development is on the way at *openebxml.sourceforge .net/*. This includes the definition of a binary markup language, an (optional) replacement for XML in the context of ebXML allowing a more compact message format and supporting binary attachments; a GUI workbench for editing process definitions; a business process server; an open implementation of an ebXML registry; and a high-performance message handler for ebXML messages.

Data Access Technologies (DAT) (*www.enterprise-component.com*) has released a "first-look" beta release of their Component-X for ebXML:

> Component-X provides visual and intuitive drag-and-drop assembly and configuration of Enterprise Business Components and Web Services. . . . Component-X provides a visual environment. . . . Components are "wired" together in the visual environment and configured for the local requirements.

BindSystems (*www.bindsys.com*) has released an early version of their BindPartner platform, which

> . . . provides a process-oriented approach to business collaboration. . . . These process models comply with the ebXML Business Process Specification Schema (or BPSS). . . . The process model can be imported as an ebXML compliant XML process schema document from an external location and possibly changed, or it can be created in the designer.

11.1.3 Schema Design

For XML schema, the use of visual design tools is highly recommended because they considerably shorten the learning curve for this complex standard.

There are quite a few editors to define XML schemata and DTDs:

- XML authority (*www.tibco.com*)
- XML Spy (*www.altova.com*)
- Envision XML (*www.popkin.com*)
- A number of free XML Schema validators available from Apache, IBM, Oracle, the University of Edinburgh, and topologi (see below)

The XML Schema section of the W3C Web site (*www.w3.org*) contains pointers to several XML Schema–related tools.

A Windows-based validator for Schematron (see Section 2.9.1) is available from *www.topologi.com*. The validator comes with popular XML schemata and Schematron scripts for languages such as RSS, RDF, SOAP, SMIL, WSDL, QAML, XTM, XLink, WAI, XHTML, RDDL XHTML, and CALS, but it also allows user-defined schemata (DTD and XML Schema) and Schematron scripts. In addition to producing validation reports, it can also harvest RDF descriptions and topic maps (XTM) from documents; in fact, it can be used as a front end for performing any XSLT translations.

Schema
validation

11.2 DATABASE SYSTEMS

The simplest way to store an XML file is in a native file system. This approach is, however, only feasible when the performance requirements are moderate, when the number of stored documents is small, when there are no stringent requirements for the integrity and safety of data, and when it can be excluded that several users want to update the same documents at the same time.

Database systems provide features that meet these requirements:

General
requirements

- Caching reduces the number of disk accesses and thus increases the performance.
- Indexing allows for fast searches against a large document base, instead of scanning documents in a linear fashion.
- A transaction concept makes sure that either all or none of the data involved in a logical transaction is written to the database.
- Backup and recovery procedures, logging, and auditing allow for high safety and traceability of the data.
- Locking mechanisms support the simultaneous updates from multiple users.
- In addition, modern database systems scale better. They support multiple hardware platforms and operating systems and multiprocessor architectures and allow several servers to cooperate in a distributed database.

In short, for enterprise solutions there is no other option than to store XML documents in a database management system. The problem, however, is that the current de facto standard, relational technology, is anything but adequate for storing and retrieving XML documents. SQL, for example, does not provide the means to drill down to a particular child element in a deeply nested hierarchical document. The relational world is flat, but XML is not. (This restriction has been mellowed with the definition of SQL:1999, which allows queries on object aggregations. However, the SQL:1999 object model differs from the XML information model.)

Let's briefly discuss the requirements for an XML-enabled database management system. Apart from the usual database features like performance, support for large document bases, transaction concept, data safety, concurrency control, and scalability, XML-enabled database management systems should provide

XML requirements

- a query language suitable for XML, such as XPath or XQuery
- a DOM API, allowing applications to navigate within documents and update parts of them
- the ability to check for the validity of documents against a supplied schema definition (DTD or XML Schema)
- the ability to store XML documents that do not have a schema definition (required behavior for all XML processors)

They could also provide, as additional features,

- the ability to update document parts
- the ability to access legacy data (i.e., relational data)
- the ability to store non-XML data (arbitrary text files and binary files such as images, audio clips, or executables)
- an integrated XSLT processor that allows document transformations when storing or retrieving documents
- communication methods, for instance, HTTP for the Web or COM+ for the back end

Integrity

We did not mention semantic integrity (including referential integrity between documents) because there is currently no standard for defining semantic integrity constraints. In this area, XML technology still falls short of relational technology. Also, we think that, due to the possibly distributed character of XML document sets, the validation of referential integrity constraints is more a task for XML middleware than for a database.

There are basically two strategies for implementing an XML database management system (XDBMS). We will discuss these strategies in the following two subsections and discuss some commercial implementations, too.

11.2.1 Mapped Systems

One solution is to equip an existing DBMS such as a relational database management system with an XML layer that converts incoming documents into the datatypes of the host DBMS, and converts outgoing documents back into the XML format. In addition, XML query expressions must be translated into the query language of the host system.

There are two ways to map an XML document onto a relational data structure. The first is the brute-force approach: store the whole document in a BLOB (binary large object). The second is to break the document into single elements and to construct a relational table for each nonterminal element. Both methods have their advantages and drawbacks:

- Reading and writing an XML document from and to a BLOB is relatively fast as long as documents are of a moderate size. However, updating document parts in large documents can cause severe performance penalties, since it requires physically rewriting the whole BLOB. Another problem with BLOBs is qualified searches. A search may require parsing the stored documents, which is especially slow when documents are large. Most systems offer text retrieval facilities (i.e., indexing of all relevant words within the document) to avoid the costly scanning of the document base. BLOBs
- Breaking documents apart into single elements and storing them in different relational tables improves the indexing capabilities. However, because documents must be reconstructed (via relational joins) when they are retrieved, retrieval operations can be slow. This approach works well for documents with a simple structure, but it can be slow for documents with a complex structure. Apart from the performance issues, the main disadvantage of this approach is that schema extensions require a redesign of the relational tables. It is not possible to use this approach to store XML documents that come without a schema definition. Breaking
documents apart

Oracle

Oracle 8i (*www.oracle.com*) supports both ways of storing an XML document:

- The document is broken down into an object tree and stored in relational tables. Mapping definitions define how this tree is mapped onto the relational tables. On retrieval the XML document is reassembled by applying the mapping inversely.

    Oracle 8i allows applications to retrieve the data in object form, too, and can thus avoid the reassembly process in many cases. Since Oracle 8i supports the SQL:1999 object view, it can maintain the hierarchical structure of the document in the object representation.

- The document is stored in a BLOB that can be searched using the Oracle Intermedia XML Search. The Oracle Intermedia XML Search is based on text retrieval technology and can analyze incoming documents and index the relevant words. This allows for efficient document searches based on the proximity of words, but it does not really recognize the element structure of an XML document.

Oracle 9i introduces a new datatype (XML Type) allowing the storage of an XML document within a column of a relational table. This datatype is basically a BLOB but "provides XPATH navigation capabilities."

IBM DB2 XML Extender

IBM's DB2 XML Extender (*www.ibm.com*) equips IBM's well-known DB2 database system with an XML layer. This layer translates XML documents into relational structures and vice versa. XML DTDs are mapped onto relational schemata using the proprietary Data Access Definition (DAD) language. A visual tool is supplied to define these mappings.

SQL Stored Procedures

DTDs and DAD documents are stored in their own relational tables in the database, too. Applications invoke the XML Extender via SQL Stored Procedures.

The XML Extender is complemented by the DB2 Text Extender, allowing text retrieval searches on larger text blocks—for example, when a whole XML document is stored in a single column (i.e., a BLOB).

Birdstep

Birdstep (*www.birdstep.com*) is the new kid on the block in terms of database technology. Their database engine features a novel design that goes even beyond the relational approach in atomizing complex data structures. Birdstep considers the content (and also the name) of each elementary data field as an atom. Each atom is only stored once in the whole database schema. Data structures are represented as pointers to these atoms (and to other data structures). If, for example, a database contains a manufacturer record containing the manufacturer name "Tulloch" and also contains a record describing a whiskey labeled "Tulloch," then both records point to the same physical storage location where the atom "Tulloch" is stored. This allows very small database sizes, since there is absolutely no redundancy within the database. Also, the database system itself is very small, and consequently Birdstep targets the market for mobile and embedded devices.

Because data structures are formed as a separate layer on top of the data atoms, the Birdstep database is able to allow hierarchical, relational, and object-oriented views on the same set of data. In particular, a layer for XML is available for the database that predefines the necessary access structures for storing and retrieving XML documents. This layer includes implementations of SAX, DOM, and XPath (which is used as a query language).

eXcelon

eXcelon's Portal Server features a Dynamic XML Engine (DXE) that accepts XML documents, breaks them apart into individual objects, and stores them in object form. The technology is probably based on eXcelon's ObjectStore, an object-oriented DBMS. The advantage when compared with a relational solution is that object-oriented databases display more flexibility when it comes to object aggregations. The DXE is flexible enough to allow for on-the-fly schema extensions. In addition to XML documents, the DXE can also store non-XML objects, including binary data such as images and executables.

Dynamic XML Engine

The DXE has a DOM API (Level 1 and Level 2 Core), uses XPath for queries, and has a built-in XSLT processor for document transformations. Both index-based searching and text-retrieval-based searching are supported.

Microsoft SQL Server 2000

Mighty Microsoft (*www.microsoft.com*) has also equipped its SQL Server product with an XML layer. In particular, SQL Server 2000 has an XML Rowset provider, which takes an XML document and returns the data in a relational fashion. Results are generated with the help of XQuery.

XML Rowset provider

Ozone

Ozone (*www.ozone-db.org*) is an open-source, object-oriented database system written in Java. In regard to XML, it acts as a persistent DOM implementation. An XML file is stored in the DOM format, that is, in the form of Java objects.

Persistent DOM

11.2.2 Native Systems

In native systems the core of the database system relies on the XML information model. Usually an incoming document is parsed, and the structural information is stored with the document content in order to allow efficient queries. These systems usually support some sort of XML query language and a DOM API. Examples of native XML database systems are Software AG's Tamino, Ipedo's XML Database (*www.ipedo.com*), IXIASOFT's TEXTML Server (*www.ixiasoft.com*), NeoCore's XMS (*www .neocore.com*), and the Open Source Development's dbXML (*www.dbxml*

.org) and eXist (*exist.sourceforge.net*). We will restrict our discussion to Tamino, which has the largest market share.

Tamino

Software AG (*www.softwareag.com*) has a long tradition as a maker of database systems. Their Adabas DBMS introduced table-based data structures long before relational technology became a topic. Adabas had always allowed a limited nesting of data structures within table fields, and consequently Adabas aficionados had always viewed relational technology with some suspicion when it came to performance. It was not a surprise that Software AG became active when XML—with its hierarchical data structures—appeared on the horizon. The result was Tamino, a database system that stores XML documents natively without conversion.

Access

Tamino supports a SAX and a DOM2 API. It also can hook up with popular Web servers, so that it is possible to store and retrieve documents through an HTTP client. There is also a WebDAV access layer allowing WebDAV-enabled applications (such as Microsoft Office products) to transparently access XML documents stored in Tamino. Incoming documents are analyzed and are indexed according to the definitions in the corresponding schema definition. Document schemata are defined with a subset of XML Schema, but Tamino is also able to store documents that do not have a schema definition, including non-XML documents such as word documents, images, or binaries.

Queries

Currently, subsets of XPath and XQuery are supported as query languages. It is possible to combine text retrieval and tag-related queries (based on indices) into a single query expression.

Schema support

DTDs and a subset of XML Schema are supported for schema definition. Tamino uses the `appinfo` section of XML Schema to store additional metainformation about the physical layout of the data. This includes information about indexing, but also information about mapping to other resource managers. Thus, documents that are written to and retrieved from Tamino are not necessarily stored in Tamino but can be stored in a remote relational database, a file system, a message service, and so on. This allows companies to leave existing enterprise data at the point of origin but still be able to integrate this data into XML scenarios.

11.2.3 Best Practices

We recommend the following practices:

• Select technology that stays close to the standards. Extensions are always nice to have, but they also lock you into a proprietary platform.

XML database technology is still young, so you will find that implementations differ vastly. The XML standard does define the document layout, but it does not define an interface and protocol for database access.

- Select technology that can scale well. What runs today on a PC or a Unix box may require a mainframe tomorrow.
- Do not use "exotic" XML features. In terms of databases, XML entities—and in particular external entities—are exotic features and are not supported by most database systems. Other database systems may support entities but "flatten" the document (i.e., resolving the entities) when it is stored. When you retrieve the document, it will definitely look different than when you stored it!
- A good test for portability is the "schema test": Can you take the DTDs or schemata of your XML application, load them into the database, and run the application without further work? Or is it necessary to set up SQL create commands, that is, repetitive work that you might have to do every time the schema changes?
- Some DBMSs generate internal object identifiers. Do not even consider storing these identifiers within your data structures! It is fine to use these identifiers in your programs and to store them in transient variables, but they should not be stored in persistent data structures. This type of identifier will almost certainly change when you rearrange your data or when you migrate to a different vendor. If you need to identify objects such as documents, create your own identifiers, either based on a unique domain name or by computing a UUID.

11.3 MIDDLEWARE

XML middleware is responsible for organizing message transport, orchestrating business processes, and much more. We will discuss a few important architectures.

11.3.1 e-speak

Hewlett-Packard's e-speak is the odd man out in this list of XML middleware for electronic business. e-speak is not really an XML technology, but it uses proprietary communication and storage formats. The reason why we discuss it here is that e-speak was the first fairly complete middleware architecture for enabling electronic business. It was probably the first architecture to introduce peer-to-peer communication.

In the meantime, e-speak has been opened up to the XML world. Hewlett-Packard has, for example, joined the UDDI bandwagon. e-speak Web services can thus be discovered via UDDI, and e-speak clients will be able to discover non–e-speak Web services.

Abstract resource layer

e-speak has been designed with the goal of making enterprise legacy IT infrastructures available as Web services. It does so by introducing an abstract layer of resources. A resource represents active and passive elements within the e-speak infrastructure, such as a service, a file, or a hardware device. All e-speak functionality is based on this abstract layer. The underlying physical entities are not accessed by e-speak directly. Instead, resource-specific handlers provide this access (Hewlett-Packard 2001):

> Every access to a resource through e-speak involves two different sets of manipulations:
> - The e-speak platform uses its resource descriptions to dynamically discover the most appropriate resource, transparent access to remote resources, and sending events to management tools.
> - The resource-specific handler directly accesses the resource such as reading the disk blocks for a file.

This technique allows e-speak to access existing and new infrastructures, while keeping the logical-level device and technology neutral. In particular, e-speak allows interoperation with component models such as Enterprise Java Beans, CORBA, and COM+.

Repository

Each e-speak platform constitutes a logical machine. Each logical machine has a repository that stores the resource descriptions. Service providers can register a service (i.e., store the resource metadata of the service) in such a repository. Clients in turn can look up a service in the repository and bind to it. Clients may then invoke an entry point on a service.

Peer-to-peer

This looks very much like an enterprise architecture. But what is different here is that multiple distributed e-speak machines can interoperate over the Internet. When, for example, a client issues a search for a specific service, he or she will ask the look-up service of the local e-speak machine. This machine will look in its local repository, but it will also propagate the request to other e-speak machines known to it. When an appropriate service description is found, the client is informed about its location and can then communicate with the foreign machine on a peer-to-peer basis.

Requirements for resources

This ability to interoperate with other machines requires some extra consideration when describing resources:

- Resources must be identified with a globally unique ID (URL).
- Resources must publish a public key, thus allowing secured communication with them.
- Resources must define a vocabulary.

In addition, resources possess all properties that are required in an enterprise environment as well, such as access control lists, descriptions, and so on. Descriptions consist of a set of attributes, each attribute consisting of a name/value pair. When a service provider registers a service, it provides an attribute-based description of the service. The attributes are later used to look up the service.

All attributes follow an agreed-upon vocabulary. Vocabularies define the name and type of attributes. They are implemented as first-class e-speak core services, thus enabling the registration of custom vocabularies and the discovery of vocabularies.

Vocabularies

e-speak's communication model follows a simple mailbox model. A client that wishes to send a message to a resource constructs a message consisting of a message header and payload and places the message into the client's outbox. The e-speak core reads the message header and forwards the message to the inbox of the receiver. The receiver's resource handler may then read the header information and the payload. e-speak supports pluggable transport protocols including TCP/IP, IrDA, WAP, and HTTP. Currently, there is no direct support for SOAP (Hewlett-Packard 2001).

Mailbox model

To allow the collaboration of applications the e-speak core implements an event service. Apart from core-generated events, resources can publish events and can subscribe to event distributors. However, e-speak does not directly support higher-level modeling of collaborating business processes. In particular, e-speak does not feature a process model.

Event service

11.3.2 RosettaNet

RosettaNet is named after the Rosetta Stone. This ancient document contained the same message in three languages and was the key to the modern deciphering of hieroglyphics. RosettaNet aims to break language barriers as well.

RosettaNet is a nonprofit consortium of more than 400 leading companies from the areas of information technologies, electronic components, and semiconductor manufacturing, representing more than $1 trillion in revenue. RosettaNet therefore does not address the requirements of the whole electronic business community but of only a certain sector of that community. However, because of its nonproprietary and international character and its foundation on XML, the influence of RosettaNet on electronic business as a whole cannot be underrated. RosettaNet is, for example, supported by Microsoft's BizTalk Server (see Section 11.3.3). RosettaNet also supports horizontal standards such as ebXML (in particular, the ebXML Messaging Service Specification for the secure transfer, routing, and packaging of electronic information—see Section 10.3) and UDDI (to simplify the registration and discovery of e-business processes across the supply chain—see Section 7.3).

Architecture   The principal foundation of the RosettaNet architecture (RosettaNet 2001) consists of dictionaries, implementation frameworks, and partner interface processes.

Dictionaries define a common vocabulary for trading partners, thus reducing the confusion due to each company's own terminology. Rosetta-Net business dictionaries contain the vocabulary for defining business transactions between trading partners, while RosettaNet technical dictionaries provide the vocabulary for defining products and services. Among the business dictionaries we find

- a dictionary with twelve *quantitative fundamental business data entities* ranging from

```
<QuantitativeFundamentalBusinessDataEntities>
  <NAME>Height Dimension</NAME>
  <DEFINITION>
    Vertical dimension of an object when object
    in the upright position.
  </DEFINITION>
  <Type>Real</Type>
  <Min>1</Min>
  <Max>15</Max>
  <Repr>9(13)V99</Repr>
</QuantitativeFundamentalBusinessDataEntities>
```

to

```
<QuantitativeFundamentalBusinessDataEntities>
  <NAME>Width Dimension</NAME>
  <DEFINITION>
    Shorter measurement of the two horizontal
    dimensions measured with object in the upright
    position.
  </DEFINITION>
  <Type>Real</Type>
  <Min>1</Min>
  <Max>15</Max>
  <Repr>9(13)V99</Repr>
</QuantitativeFundamentalBusinessDataEntities>
```

- a dictionary with 424 predefined *fundamental business data entities,* ranging from

```
<FundamentalBusinessDataEntities>
  <NAME>AccountNumber</NAME>
  <DEFINITION>
    Identification number of an account.
  </DEFINITION>
  <Type>String</Type>
  <Min>1</Min>
  <Max>35</Max>
  <Repr>X(35)</Repr>
</FundamentalBusinessDataEntities>
```

to

```
<FundamentalBusinessDataEntities>
  <NAME>WireTransferIdentifier</NAME>
  <DEFINITION>
    A unique identity of a wire transfer used for
    reference.
  </DEFINITION>
  <Type>String</Type>
  <Min>1</Min>
  <Max/>
  <Repr/>
</FundamentalBusinessDataEntities>
```

- a dictionary with 239 further *business data entities* ranging from

```
<BusinessDataEntity>
  <NAME>AcceptanceAcknowledgment</NAME>
  <DEFINITION>
    Business information returned to a
    requesting party to acknowledge the business
    acceptance of a request.
  </DEFINITION>
</BusinessDataEntity>
```

to

```
<BusinessDataEntity>
  <NAME>WorkInstructionsReadiness</NAME>
  <DEFINITION />
</BusinessDataEntity>
```

This all looks very much like a schema definition. Entities are defined with their name and several constraints such as datatype, minimum and maximum occurrences, and a representation. The description element defines further semantics in an informal way.

The *RosettaNet implementation framework* (RNIF) specification defines exchange protocols for the implementation of RosettaNet standards for the information exchange between trading partners. The RNIF covers the areas of transport, routing, and packaging; security; signals; and trading partner agreements.

PIPs

Partner interface processes (PIPs) are XML-based dialogs that define the business processes between trading partners. A PIP specification consists of a business document (with its vocabulary) and a business process (with the message dialog choreography). PIP specifications are not yet available in machine-readable format; however, it is expected that this will happen soon, so that the construction of business actions and signal messages can be automated.

A PIP specification comprises the following three views:

- *Business operational view* (BOV): This view describes the semantics of the business data entities (business documents) and how they are exchanged between the actors (roles) engaged in a business process.
- *Functional service view* (FSV): This view is derived from the BOV and describes the services within the network and the interactions between them that are necessary to execute a partner interface process. The description includes all transaction dialogs (i.e., requests, signals, and responses) within a PIP protocol.
- *Implementation framework view* (IFV): This view describes the network protocol formats and the communication requirements supported by the network services. The IFV allows multiple transport protocols for messages. Version 2.0 of RosettaNet implementation framework explicitly specifies SMTP and HTTP as transport protocols. S/MIME is used for message envelopes, and this might have been one reason why MIME was added as a message envelope format in version 2.0 of the BizTalk platform.

PIPs are specialized to the following core process areas: administration; partner, product, and service review; product information; order management; inventory management; marketing information management; service and support; and manufacturing. These areas are called *clusters* and are further subdivided into *segments* (Figure 11.1).

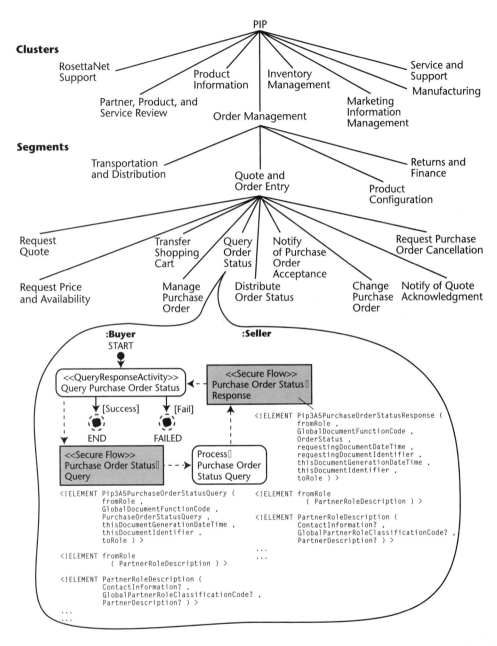

Figure 11.1 Hierarchy of predefined PIPs in RosettaNet (Version 2.0). Each PIP describes a specific collaborative process between partners. Here, we have drilled down into the business object view of the PIP QueryOrderStatus. We have also listed the beginnings of the DTDs for the two business documents exchanged in this process: PurchaseOrderStatusQuery and PurchaseOrderStatusResponse.

11.3.3 BizTalk

BizTalk is Microsoft's long-anticipated answer to ebXML. Just as the company had already done with COM in response to CORBA, it managed to provide a workable, XML-based solution for electronic business before the ebXML standard became finalized. But, in contrast to COM, which remained—in spite of some notable ports to other platforms by third parties—more or less a proprietary technology, Microsoft has vowed to keep BizTalk an open platform. Times have changed, and in the days of global business the market would not tolerate a narrow proprietary solution like COM. In fact, Microsoft's implementations of XML-related standards are very close to the specifications. By the time the ebXML specification was rolled out, Microsoft was able to present its functional and well-acclaimed BizTalk server.

But Microsoft's competitors have also learned from the past. Following the motto "If you can't beat them, join them," they have rallied to join the SOAP bandwagon (see Section 6.5.2). ebXML, for example, included SOAP as a transport method in its specifications.

The BizTalk Messaging Services

BizTalk's messaging services are an additional logical layer on top of the SOAP message layer. Both layers are implemented by a BizTalk framework 2.0 compliant server (or BFC server) such as—of course—the Microsoft BizTalk server (see Figure 11.2). The underlying transport layer can be HTTP or SMTP. From Microsoft (2000):

> The BizTalk Framework does not prescribe the content or structure (schema) of individual business documents. The details of the business document content and structure, or Schema, are defined and agreed upon by the business entities involved.

The business partners are free to publish their schemata of their business documents in the BizTalk Schemas Library, or somewhere else. The schema language of choice is XML Schema.

The Message Format

For packaging business documents into messages, BizTalk makes use of SOAP header and body elements.

BizTalk body
element

The SOAP body element can carry several business documents. XSL Schema is used to define the schemata of business documents. Each business document is a child element of the body element. Because there can also be elements that are shared between several business documents, and these elements must be stored on the root level, too, it is necessary to

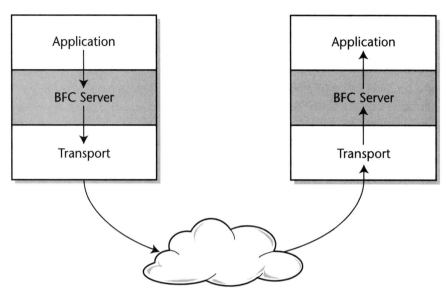

Figure 11.2 With the BizTalk compliant server, applications exchange business documents via the underlying transport service.

distinguish them from the business document elements. This is done through the SOAP-ENC:root attribute. This technique of wrapping several business documents and nondocument entities into a single message allows us to stay close to the conceptional model of our business case.

Here is an example of the BizTalk body element:

```
<SOAP-ENV:Body>
  <po:PurchaseOrder
        xmlns:po="http://hardware.org/purchase_order/">
    <po:item href="#productList"/>
        ...
  </po:PurchaseOrder>
  <ship:shippingInfo
        xmlns:ship="http://hardware.org/shippingInfo/">
    <ship:content href="#productList"/>
        ...
  </ship:shippingInfo>
  <productList xmlns="http://hardware.org/productList/"
      id="productList" SOAP-ENC:root="0">
    <Product>
```

```
            <Name>Nuts</Name>
            ...
         </Product>
         <Product>
            <Name>Bolts</Name>
            ...
         </Product>
         ...
      </productList>
</SOAP-ENV:Body>
```

This message body contains two business documents: `PurchaseOrder` and `ShippingInfo`. Both refer to the same `productList` element, thus reducing redundancy. The `productList` element is also a child element of `SOAP-ENV:Body` but is marked with `SOAP-ENC:root="0"` as a nondocument.

Header elements   A BizTalk message contains several SOAP header elements:

- The `<endpoints>` tag identifies the source and destination of a message. This tag is required.
- The `<properties>` tag defines additional properties of the message. It contains child elements specifying the identity of the message, sending date, expiration date, and a topic. The identity must be globally unique (for example, a UUID). The `<properties>` tag is always required.
- The `<services>` tag allows the specification of further options for the processing of the service request. It can ask the receiver to acknowledge the reception of the message or to signal the positive commitment to process the request. This tag is optional.
- The `<manifest>` tag specifies a document catalogue that lists all the documents and attachments belonging to a message. That may be business documents contained in the BizTalk messages itself, or non-XML attachments like binary data or images. These attachments may be carried within the same MIME envelope or be external resources. The `<manifest>` tag is optional.
- The `<process>` tag includes information about the business process that provides the processing context for the BizTalk Document. This information includes the type of business process, for example, *Query Purchase Order Status* or *Request Purchase Order Cancellation*. It also includes the identification (URI) of an individual instance of that particular business process type. Further included is implementation-dependent detail information such as a particular step or an entry point within the business process instance. The `<process>` tag is also optional.

The BizTalk Orchestration Services

BizTalk orchestration (i.e., the planning and running of business processes) is the proprietary part of the BizTalk architecture. The definition and execution of business processes is based on XLANG, an XML-based language developed by Microsoft. At present, Microsoft seems to have no intention of submitting this language to a standards body.

For the end user, anyway, this language is not visible. A business process is defined by visual means, using flowchartlike graphs. (Actually, Microsoft uses its Visio product for the visual interface and generates XLANG scripts from the drawings. Currently, there is no way to integrate this design step with UML design tools.) There seems to be no provision to construct a business process automatically by negotiation between partners. BizTalk supplies business process designers with a nice visual interface—but it still needs a business process designer. This may be a valid approach for the requirements of small businesses (and BizTalk is targeted at smaller businesses), but it is hardly feasible when hundreds or thousands of different business processes are involved.

Business processes are defined in terms of abstract tasks that can be executed in sequence and/or in parallel. At this stage, the designer need not be concerned with a particular implementation.

In a second step these abstract tasks are mapped to concrete implementations (called *ports* in BizTalk), COM+-based business object components that do the actual work. This mapping is dynamic—it can be changed at runtime, depending on the result of a previous task in the process. For example, if a customer makes a selection for a specific payment or shipment option, the mapping to the appropriate port can be changed on the fly as shown in Figure 11.3.

These ports implement the specific business logic for each task. Based on COM+ they can access data sources via the BizTalk Messaging services, SQL database access modules, or Web services access modules.

BizTalk orchestration allows modular business processes; that is, it is possible to construct complex processes from simple ones.

In addition, business processes can be transactional:

- BizTalk supports *short-lived* transactions like the classical ACID database transaction. This includes distributed transactions running under a transaction manager such as the Microsoft Transaction Server.
- BizTalk supports *long-lived* transactions. These transactions do not lock up resources but require programmers to define compensating actions in case a transaction must be rolled back. This ability to run long-lived

XLANG

Dynamic task
mapping

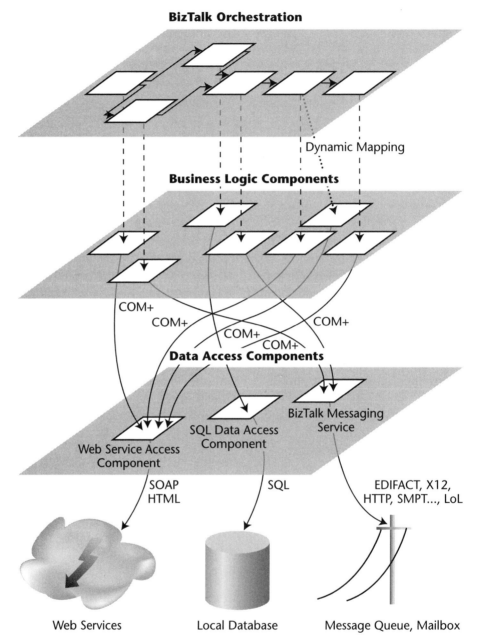

BizTalk Orchestration

Dynamic Mapping

Business Logic Components

COM+

COM+

COM+

COM+

COM+

Data Access Components

Web Service Access
Component

SQL Data Access
Component

BizTalk Messaging
Service

SOAP
HTML

SQL

EDIFACT, X12,
HTTP, SMPT..., LoL

Web Services

Local Database

Message Queue, Mailbox

Figure 11.3 The layered architecture of BizTalk. Orchestration is defined on an abstract level. The abstract tasks are dynamically mapped onto concrete implementations—business logic components. These make use of data access components to access Web services, databases, and messaging services.

transactions is essential in an electronic business world where transactions can span across hours, days, or even weeks.

* BizTalk supports *nested* transactions.

11.4 APPLICATION SERVERS

BizTalk is currently supported by Microsoft's BizTalk Server. Practically all other application servers from manufacturers such as BEA, Cape Clear, IBM, IONA, Fujitsu, Inprise, SilverStream, Webmethods, and others provide support for Web services with SOAP, WSDL, and UDDI. (Those that won't will probably not survive.) Some of these application servers have their own workflow engines to orchestrate Web services and business processes, but most manufacturers have opted to support ebXML, too.

11.5 AUTHORING

In the previous sections we gave an overview of tools that help the designer of software systems to define XML models and components on several architectural layers such as business middleware or data management.

In this section we will take the perspective of the designer building XML front-end applications as they are needed in Internet-based environments. He or she may need or prefer, for example, WYSIWYG editors that abstract from native XML code and allow the rapid composition of user interface applications. Of course, this intersects particularly with Section 11.1 on design tools because single tool components may be part of larger development environments (e.g., an XML editor in XML Spy). So we will focus on examples that have not been mentioned before.

WYSIWYG

11.5.1 Creating and Publishing Text-Based Content

We start our overview by considering "normal" Web publishing on the basis of XML, that is, bringing text-based information to the Internet. In doing so, we give just a limited number of examples. Further examples and additional information can be obtained from the following sites:

* *www.xmlsoftware.com/*
* *wdvl.com/Software/XML/editors.html*

- *www2.software.ibm.com/developer/tools.nsf/dw/xml-editing-byname*
- *xmlpitstop.com/xmlTools.htm*

XMetaL

Customization and integration

XMetaL (*www.softquad.com*) is the follow-up to the HTML editor Hot-Metal Pro. It is an XML/SGML word-processor-like editing tool that provides a source view as well as a tag view. It works with SGML or XML DTDs, offers context-sensitive lists of allowed elements and attributes, and supports CALS tables, DOM, CSS, and HTML. XMetaL has an integrated browser preview for XML documents.

The authoring environment can be customized to any DTD without programming. It may be integrated into publishing infrastructures due to its COM architecture/Windows scripting features. So the created content files can be integrated with the Web-based applications to be built.

In addition to the editing views a customizable structure view is provided to navigate documents. External data resources are connected via ODBC using the database import wizard. More advanced features include support for inline table editing (CALS, HTML) and XML constructs, that is, both valid and well-formed XML documents. They also include internal subsets, parsable and scriptable entities, the DOM, OASIS catalogues, and UTF-16 (Unicode) encoding.

UltraXML

Creation, workflow, and publishing

UltraXML (*www.webxsystems.com/UltraXML.htm*) is a WYSIWYG XML solution that allows document creation, workflow, and publishing. The necessary complementary tool is the WebXSystems PowerPublisher. Its features include the following:

- Native XML and XSL support
- Easy and quick XML text markup and creation methods
- Visual XML tree for easy document navigation and XML editing
- Visual XML attributes editor
- Export XML utilizing the integrated parser to indent and pretty-print the XML data

UltraXML contains two main components: the integrated Visual DTD editor and integrated ActiveXSL.

The integrated VisualDTD editor allows the designing of a DTD and visual editing of its attributes and entities. DTDs may be presented as a tree view starting from any XML element. The design of DTDs is supported on the import of XML. Checking and validation mechanisms are provided for XML data. XML is context sensitive, as in XMetaL, based on the DTD grammar. Visual XML Schema support is promised for future versions.

Integrated ActiveXSL allows the use of XSL code snippets as real-time style definitions. A document may encompass different XSL scripts for several views on XML data, that is, layouts for different presentation purposes such as Web or WAP. On export, XSL text is combined with filters available for conversion to HTML, CSS2, and XSL:FO. XSL scripts suitable for Internet publishing are created visually. Selective XSL scripts can be created for a style using the hierarchy from a branch of the XML tree. In turn the tool properties can be customized according to an active style to always create the correct XSL code.

Cocoon

Cocoon is part of the Apache XML Project (*www.apache.org*). It is a Java-written framework for XML Web publishing (i.e., Web site creation and management based on the XML paradigm and related technologies).

In Cocoon, the content, style, and logic of Web information are separately regarded. Thus Cocoon allows the independent design, creation, and management of information on the Web. This is done by holding content, style, and logic in separate XML files to be merged via XSL transformation. Furthermore Cocoon supports client-dependent presentation by transformation or rendering to PDF via XSL:FO or WML.

Content, style, and logic

Web content in Cocoon is developed in three steps:

1. An XML file is created on the basis of a particular set of tags, normally given by a DTD.
2. The file is processed employing its logic given in the separated logic sheet.
3. The content is rendered for presentation by applying an XSL style sheet. Cocoon does not provide its own dedicated text or XML-aware editor for content creation.

11.5.2 WML Tools for Mobile Applications

WML, as we saw in Section 8.4, is the XML-based language for defining WAP applications for wireless devices such as palmtops and mobile phones. Although presenting information on such devices is subject to some limitations, the underlying mechanisms are similar to rendering into other output formats. Therefore appropriate tools to define wireless applications would be helpful. We will outline two examples here.

WAPPage

WAPPage 2.1 (*www.zyglobe.com/products.html*) allows a developer to edit, compile and integrate WML pages including the conversion of HTML to WML. Since WAPPage is a visual design tool, the creation and maintenance of files in WYSIWYG manner does not require any knowledge about WML tags. So users work with GUI components and drag-and-drop techniques. This type of design includes cards and decks, allowing the collection of multiple WMF files and managing them in a single project file. Of course you can work on the source code directly. A second type of WYSIWYG editor using an XML tree view supports navigation through WAP sites. Additionally, WBMP is supported.

Dynamic business applications for WAP-enabled devices can be developed using the WAPobjects framework. Dynamic content is normally created from databases. This is realized by integrating the framework with Apple's WebObjects IDE. Applications are developed on prebuilt WML components and are based on the WebObjects application server. So existing application logic and database resources built with WebObjects can be reused unmodified, while WAPobjects enables the user to develop the appropriate user interfaces. External information resources, such as relational databases or enterprise resource planning systems, are included, using WAPobjects' corresponding object-oriented interface. As with WAP-Page the tools are visual ones.

DotWap

A freeware tool, DotWap 2.0, is available from Inetis (*www.inetis.com/freeware.asp*). A collection of further links is given at *www.wmlscript.com/devtool/devtools.asp?type=Software+Development+Kit+%28SDK%29*.

11.5.3 Multimedia

In Section 8.5, we discussed XML-based multimedia formats. Here is a short overview of tools that support SVG, SMIL, and VoiceXML.

SVG

When considering editing tools for SVG, the first approach is adding appropriate import/export capabilities to existing graphic tools. Examples of such tools are Adobe Illustrator 9.0 (*www.adobe.com*) and CorelDraw 10.0 (*www.corel.com*). This approach is very comfortable because users are normally familiar with the tool of their choice and do not have to learn anything about SVG.

Dealing with native SVG code from scratch is another viable solution. You can use any text editor if you are familiar with the SVG tag set and features, so this is a choice for sophisticated developers rather than for Web designers rapidly creating Web graphics for their applications.

An overview of viewers, editors, and converters for SVG can be found at *www.w3.org/Graphics/SVG/SVG-Implementations.htm8*. A Java-written open-source toolkit for SVG can be obtained from *sis.cmis.csiro.au/svg/*.

SMIL

What has been outlined for SVG is basically also true for SMIL. You can either create source code via a traditional editor or find an appropriate tool to compose SMIL applications.

RealNetworks offers an additional product bundle for streaming services, Meta Creation Pro (*www.realnetworks.com/products/mediacreation/ index.html*). It includes the GRiNS Editor Pro for RealSystem G2. The GRiNS SMIL editor and player started as a public domain tool developed at the National Research Institute for Mathematics and Computer Science in the Netherlands (*www.cwi.nl*) and has a spin-off at Oratrix. The current version of GRiNS for SMIL2.0 can be obtained from *www.oratrix.com/ Products/G2R*.

It has now become a SMIL creation tool that allows the developer to orchestrate a presentation of images, text, video, and audio. It also supports merging presentation from fragments by cut/copy/paste from presentation building blocks. Projects then can be published to a RealSystem Server for playback over the Internet. Alternatively a variety of SMIL players are available elsewhere. For a current development, see a nice Japanese site of DoCoMo (*www.docomo-sys.co.jp/prod/soft/smil2.html*).

VoiceXML

Here the difference from other XML technologies is that the information is not visual. So one element of voice-based application environments is a text-to-voice converter. This is comparable to the rendering step in visual applications.

An example of development tools for Web-based VoiceXML applications is Tellme Studio (*studio.tellme.com*). It enables you to build, test, and publish the applications on the Tellme Network. Tellme supports the developer community with several libraries of code and more—newsgroups and newsletters, as well as direct building and testing of applications via the Tellme site if you have registered for a developer ID and PIN.

Several studio resources support development and testing and do not require special software installations. Scratchpad supports editing simple applications that are made available via mouse clicks. You may also develop a more complex site, place it on a Web server, and point Studio to that URL. Again you may preview the site via the available phone number and your ID and PIN. Any change leads to syntax checking against the VoiceXML DTD. Studio also provides debugging and trace functionality. Instead of testing via phone, the execution of the application can be simulated with the MyStudio Terminal.

VoiceXML technology is also included, for example, in the Voice Server for IBM's Websphere environment (*www-4.ibm.com/software/speech/enterprise/ep_11.html*), to mention just one other industry product.

11.5.4 Converters

For the sake of completeness, we do not want to leave unmentioned a class of tools that allow converting several document types into XML and/or exporting XML code into other document types.

These tools may be of interest in some specific contexts and encompass the following options:

- From SGML to XML or vice versa
- From XML to HTML, RTF (or vice versa), and plain text
- From XML to PDF or PostScript
- From publishing formats such as QuarkXPress to XML
- From XML to Flash
- From relational database content to XML
- And many more

We will not discuss these tools in further detail. Instead, an overview of such converters can be found at *www.xmlsoftware.com/convert/*.

11.6 CONTENT MANAGEMENT

Content management systems (CMSs) integrate various technologies such as authoring, database systems, workflow control, and format conversion to provide a holistic approach to content production (see Figure 11.4). Content management systems support the phases of text and media acquisition (often also text and media authoring), editing, transformation into a generic format (often XML or SGML), administration of cross references (often with topic maps), postprocessing, customization and personalization, and multitarget publishing to targets such as Web, WAP, SMS, or print. During the publishing process the CMS is responsible for processing, checkin/checkout, versioning, rollback to earlier versions, access control, workflow control, logging, and more.

In recent years, new content management systems have appeared like mushrooms after a warm rain. The necessary technologies are in place,

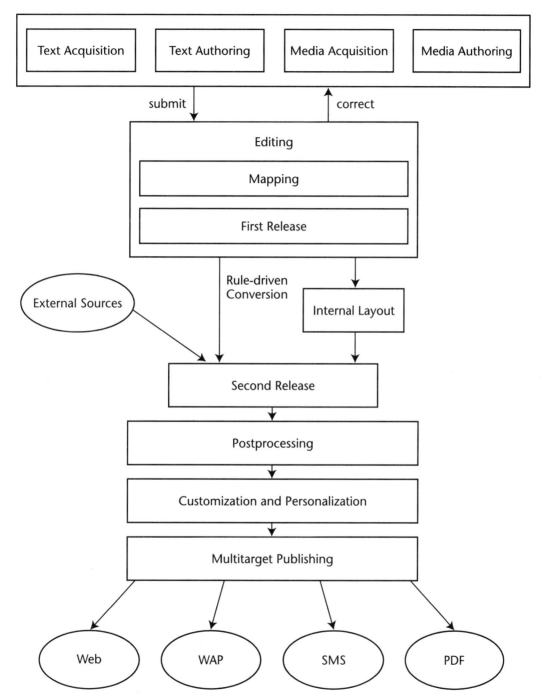

Figure 11.4 Workflow in a context management system.

and a viable market exists, not only in the traditional publishing industry but also in the field of corporate publishing. CMSs come in all flavors and price ranges, from open source systems to million- dollar proprietary systems. Popular systems include Allaire Spectra, Arbortext Epic, Broadvision, Interwoven TeamSite, UserLand Frontier, and Vignette StoryServer. Content management solutions are also found in portal servers such as the server from DataChannel.

Glossary

ACID transaction An acronym for the four primary attributes ensured to any database transaction: *atomicity, consistency, isolation, durability* (see also Section 6.6.1). The ACID concept is described in ISO/IEC 10026-1:1992, Section 4.

Activity A certain task within a process.

Activity diagram A method to describe the orchestration of activities in UML.

Actors Entities within a given scenario that are proactive; that is, they play a role. Actors can be end users, agents, and other systems.

Agent A software agent is an autonomous, somehow intelligent software component that performs tasks to achieve some goals, most likely on behalf of a human user. The term *agent* is also used in business process management. In modeling the business domain an agent denotes a human or machine entity performing a process step that adds some value to the overall business process.

Agent system The concept or implementation of agents that cooperate to perform tasks and achieve goals.

Aggregation A complex entity that has been composed from less complex entities.

AOM Asset-oriented modeling (see Section 3.2.2).

API Application Programming Interface.

Application server A Web server that can run applications for clients. Most application servers can offer application functionality in the form of Web services.

Asset In asset-oriented modeling, an abstract notion for any object or relationship between objects that we want to include in a model.

Association A relationship that somehow correlates entities with others.

Authoring Process of setting up a presentation, for example, on the Web, normally using an appropriate tool set.

Browser A user agent that can present HTML or XML pages on a computer screen and that supports navigation over the World Wide Web.

Business document Represents a "real world" document from the business problem domain.

Business object Represents a "real world" entity from the business problem domain.

Business process A networklike construct of business entities to describe a complex value creating (or servicing) business activity structured to whatever degree.

Business rule Business knowledge that describes policies and procedures for business transactions or work processes. Commonly based on event-condition-action triples.

Byte code A platform-independent and compact representation of a compiled computer program. The byte code needs an interpreter (or a runtime system) to execute on a concrete target machine.

Canonical form A preferred syntax for a given content. The canonical form allows the comparison of objects by their string representation: when their string representations are equal, then their content is equal, too.

CASE Computer aided software engineering. CASE tools support the design of software systems and can automatically generate certain parts of the implementation. Round-trip engineering allows the reflection of changes in the implementation back into the conceptual design.

Client-server The relationship between two computer programs where one program—the client—sends a request to the second program—the server—which in turn answers the client. In distributed computer networks the client-server model is the usual model for distributed applications, potentially including several distributed servers accessed by one or many distributed clients.

COM The Component Object Model is Microsoft's architecture for the development and deployment of software components. As an extension of OLE, COM is also responsible for services such as interface negotiation, version management, licensing, and event services. DCOM is an extension of COM to distributed environments, where distributed components can communicate via Remote Procedure Calls (RPC).

COMMIT The last step in a successful database transaction. In distributed database systems, a two-phase commit is necessary. The two-phase commit is a way of handling a transaction in a distributed environment, ensuring that the transaction is performed either on all participating units or on none.

Component An independent software module designed for plug & play reuse. Components contain an interface description, and most components can be configured according to the requirements of the container application. Examples of component models are JavaBeans, Enterprise Java Beans, CORBA, ActiveX/COM/DCOM.

Constraint A Boolean relation between the properties of one or more information items.

CORBA The Common Object Request Broker Architecture is the Object Management Group (OMG) component model. CORBA defines the creation, deployment, and management of distributed components in networks. CORBA requires object request brokers (ORBs) as container applications. An object request broker enables objects to transparently make and receive requests and responses in a distributed heterogeneous environment.

Design pattern A design technique that names, abstracts, and identifies aspects of a useful design structure for the purpose of reuse.

DOM The Document Object Model provides an API to describe, access, create, and modify SGML-based documents, like XML or HTML documents.

DTD A Document Type Definition defines the valid content of an XML document.

ebXML A nonproprietary XML-based standard for conducting business over the Internet. See Section 10.3.

EDI The Electronic Data Interchange standard describes the exchange of electronic documents between trading partners. EDI standards are ANSI X12 (United States) and EDIFACT (United Nations).

Encoding The code system used for a given text. Code systems define a supported character set and the mapping of the characters onto a range of integers (character codes).

Enterprise Application Integration (EAI) The integration of enterprise resource planning (ERP) systems, existing (legacy) applications, database and data warehouse systems, and front and back office into an automated business process.

Entity In XML, entities are used for text substitution, for single characters, and also for document parts. In conceptual modeling, an entity is an abstract notion of an object that we want to include in a model.

Facet In XML Schema, a specific constraint narrowing the domain of a datatype.

Formatting Process or result of defining the appearance of information objects, for example, font type and size, color, and many more.

HERM Higher Order Entity Relationship Model. A conceptual modeling method that allows structured attributes and relationships between relationships.

HTML Hypertext Markup Language. A hypertext document format used on the World Wide Web. HTML is an application of SGML. Tags embedded into the text describe certain properties of the text elements and can include other elements such as links to HTML pages or to other resources such as images. HTML is a recommendation of the W3C (World Wide Web Consortium).

HTTP Hypertext Transfer Protocol. The Internet protocol used for communication between clients and servers. HTTP messages consist of requests from client to server and responses from server to client.

HTTPS HTTP layered over the SSL protocol.

Instance An individual of a certain class or type.

Internet The largest network in the world. The Internet features a three-level hierarchy, consisting of backbone networks, midlevel networks, and stub networks. It spans many different physical networks around the world with various protocols, including the Internet Protocol TCP/IP.

Layer A set of components with the same degree of application specificity. Typically a higher layer is the client of a lower layer that serves the higher layer's requests (e.g., navigation layer, presentation layer).

Layout Process or result of (spatial) positioning of information objects according to an output device.

Legacy system A preexisting system that was created using other design methods and technologies.

Linkbase A separate document that defines the hyperlinks between a given set of Web resources. See Section 7.1.

Locking Mechanism within database management systems (DBMSs) to give a user exclusive access to a data object or a group of objects within an ACID transaction. Locking is an important concept to guarantee consistent data in multiuser databases.

Markup Syntactical means to make text more readable or to add metainformation to a text. In English prose, markup consists of punctuation, parentheses, dashes, footnotes, and so on. In XML, markup consists of tags.

Middleware Software systems that provide interoperability services for applications, such as distributed object computing, and conceal some aspects of hardware and operating system differences in a heterogeneous, distributed environment.

Mobility Feature of the π-calculus to describe the possibility of moving processes within a process system by creating new and deleting old communication links and thereby changing the neighborhood of the process.

Multitier In a multitier application the components of the application are distributed among several tiers, each located in a different computer in a network.

Namespace A concept to uniquely separate a set of identifiers from other identifiers. Namespaces are used to avoid name clashes. In XML, namespaces are identified by means of a unique URI.

Nil value/null value An artificial value indicating that a certain variable, element, and so on does not have a value.

Nondeterminism Feature of the π-calculus to describe the situation that the receiver of a communication cannot be predetermined when two or more processes "compete" for it. The process system evolves differently depending on who wins the race.

Object Constraint Language (OCL) A language defining constraints, pre- and postconditions, and navigation within UML diagrams.

Ontology An agreement about a shared conceptualization. Complete ontologies consist of vocabularies, thesauri, constraints, and axioms.

Parser A program that breaks a text string into a series of tokens, labeling each token with its grammatical role.

Pattern *See* Design pattern.

Persistence The property of objects to retain their states between independent requests or sessions.

π-calculus A set of formal elements and rules to represent, construct, and connect processes. Algebraic notation to describe process systems of all kinds.

Primary key A unique key (a field or combination of fields) that can be used to identify an information item.

Process *See* Business process.

Protocol A valid sequence of messages exchanged between partners.

Reification To make into a thing.

Relational algebra Used to model the data stored in relational databases and queries defined on the data. The main relational functions are the set functions like union, intersection, and Cartesian product, plus selection (keeping only some rows) and projection (keeping only some columns). Relational algebra was developed by E. F. Codd.

Relational database A database based on the relational data model. Queries in relational databases are formulated with SQL.

Repository A data store, typically based on a DBMS, where all development objects are stored.

Resource manager Provides access to a set of shared resources. A resource manager participates in transactions that are externally controlled and coordinated by a transaction manager. Database management systems are examples of resource managers.

Role Active entity in a business process abstracting from real-world allocations. Roles interact and perform work steps of a process.

ROLLBACK A rollback is the undoing of a partly completed transaction. *See also* COMMIT.

SAX Simple API for XML. Provides methods for parsing XML documents and for retrieving elements.

Scenario Describes the context in which a set of business processes takes place. Scenarios describe the prospective partners within these processes and their roles, and they can define a geographical, cultural, temporal, or technical context for these processes. A scenario does not describe how the partners interact nor does it describe the business processes.

Schema A definition that defines the layout of a certain class of information items.

Server A computer that provides some service for other computers connected to it via a network. *See also* Client-server.

SGML Standard Generalized Markup Language. A generic language for representing documents. SGML is defined in ISO 8879:1986.

Signature The signature of a method defines the parameters required when the operation is invoked. It consists of a method name and parameter types.

SOAP Simple Object Access Protocol. Used as a communication method in electronic business and to establish communication between heterogeneous component-oriented platforms and to access Web services.

SQL Structured Query Language. Used as an interface to relational database management systems (RDBMSs). A series of standards by ISO and ANSI culminated in SQL:1999 (SQL-3). While the original implementation of SQL in 1986 supported only flat tables, SQL:1999 strives to provide relational support for complex objects. The query constructs of SQL:1999 are almost fully compatible with OQL.

SSL Secure Socket Layer. A security protocol that provides privacy over the Internet.

States Used to represent a situation or condition of an object during which certain physical laws, rules, and policies apply. The state of an object is defined by the set of the values of attributes and relationships associated with that object. Associated with each state are one or more events that cause that state to change. Only states that are significant in determining the behavior of the object are modeled.

State transition A change in the state of an object caused by an event occurring to the object while it is in a given state.

Stereotype Used to extend the semantics of existing UML modeling elements.

Synchronization Specifying or controlling the temporal relationships between media elements incorporated in a presentation.

Tag A syntactical means to add metainformation to a piece of text. In XML, tags are enclosed in brackets.

TCP/IP Transmission Control Protocol over Internet Protocol. TCP/IP encompasses both network layer and transport layer protocols. telnet, FTP, UDP, RDP, and HTTP are based on TCP/IP.

Ternary association, ternary relationship A relationship where three roles take part.

Text retrieval The ability to effectively search across free, unformatted text.

Thesaurus A dictionary explaining a vocabulary, usually by relating notions to each other.

Topic map A separate document that describes and interrelates the themes of a set of Web resources in an abstract way and maps these themes to the actual resources. See Section 7.2.

Transaction A coherent unit of interaction between partners. *See also* ACID transaction.

Transaction manager Provides the services and management functions required to support transaction demarcation, transactional re-source management, synchronization, and transaction context propagation.

Transformation Process of reading an XML document that is based, for example, on a semantic vocabulary, and applying mapping rules defined, for example, by XSL to produce an output document that is based on another vocabulary, for example, for presentation purposes.

UDDI The Universal Description, Discovery, and Integration specification describes a standard way to register and discover Web services in shared repositories.

UML Unified Modeling Language. A set of semantics and notation for precisely describing system and business models.

Unicode A 16-bit character set standard. Unicode covers all major modern written languages.

URI Universal Resource Identifier. Identifies a resource (typically a resource on the Internet) uniquely with a short string. URIs are defined at *www.w3.org/hypertext/WWW/Addressing/ URL/URI_Overview.html*. The most common kind of URIs are URLs.

URL Uniform Resource Locator. Specifies the address of an Internet resource, such as a Web page, an image, a sound file, a script, and so on. URLs consist of a transfer protocol specification, such as http: or ftp:, a domain name, such as www.w3.org, and a path specification, such as http://www.w3.org/hypertext/WWW/ Addressing/URL/.

Web service A software application that provides a (specialized) service and can be invoked over the Internet.

White space Any character that does not ink the paper when printed; for example, blank, new line, tab.

Workflow Result of business process modeling with regard to implementation. Commonly a well-structured sequence of activities performed by processing stations (human and/or machine actors). Encompasses technical and human allocations, document and data flows. Activities are triggered and tools are launched via task lists for each actor.

Workflow management system   A WFMS allows the setup of workflow models and the creation of corresponding workflow instances. It has control over these instances as long as they are alive.

WSDL   Web Service Description Language. Describes the protocol to access Web services.

W3C   The World Wide Web Consortium is a nonprofit organization responsible for the development of World Wide Web standards (recommendations).

XML   Extensible Markup Language. As a "slimmed down" version of SGML, XML became a W3C recommendation in 1998.

XSL   Extensible Stylesheet Language. Consists of XPath for the selection of document nodes, XSLT for the transformation of documents, and XSL Formatting Objects for the description of document presentation.

Bibliography

Abiteboul, S., P. Buneman, and D. Suciu. 2000. *Data on the Web, From Relations to Semistructured Data and XML*. Morgan Kaufmann Publishers, San Francisco.

Ahmed, I. 2001. *A Case Study on the Use of XML Technologies for Automotive Standards Development*. Sun Microsystems, Developer Connection.

Allen, J. F. 1983. "Maintaining Knowledge about Temporal Intervals." *Communications of the ACM* 26(11): 832–843.

Anant, B., and D. Pandya. 2001. *Why We Need Extensible B2B Infrastructures*. TIBCO Software.

Austin, J. L. 1975. *How to Do Things with Words*. Harvard University Press, 2nd edition.

Back, A., and A. Seufert. 2000. "Computer Supported Cooperative Work (CSCW), State-of-the-Art und zukünftige Herausforderungen." *Praxis der Wirtschaftsinformatik,* HMD Heft 213.

Bayardo, R. J., Jr., W. Bohrer, R. Brice, A. Cichocki, J. Fowler, A. Helal, V. Kashyap, T. Ksiezyk, G. Martin, M. Nodine, M. Rashid, M. Rusinkiewicz, R. Shea, C. Unnikrishnan, A. Unruh, and D. Woelk. 1997. *InfoSleuth: Agent-Based Semantic Integration of Information in Open and Dynamic Environments*. Microelectronics and Computer Technology Corporation (MCC), Austin, TX.

Bechhofer, S., et al. 2000. *An Informal Description of Standard OIL and Instance OIL*. OIL Collaboration. November 28.

Beckett, D. (ed.). 2001. *Refactoring RDF/XML Syntax*. W3C Working Draft. September 6.

Behme, H., and S. Mintert. 2000. *XML in der Praxis*. Addison-Wesley.

Berners-Lee, T. 1998a. *Semantic Web Road Map*. World Wide Web Consortium.

Berners-Lee, T. 1998b. *Web Architecture from 50,000 Feet*. W3C.

Biezunski, M., M. Bryan, and S. Newcomb (eds.). 1999. ISO/IEC FCD 13250:1999– Topic Maps. ISO/IEC JTC 1/SC34.

Biezunski, M., and S. R. Newcomb (eds.). 2000. XML Topic Maps (XTM) Processing Model 1.0. TopicMaps.Org.

Biezunski, M., and S. R. Newcomb (eds.). 2001. XML Topic Maps (XTM) 1.0. TopicMaps .Org.

Biron, P. V., and A. Malhotra (eds.). 2001. *XML Schema Part 2: Datatypes*. W3C Recommendation. May 2.

Booch, G., M. Christerson, M. Fuchs, and J. Koistinen. 1999. *UML for XML Schema Mapping Specification*. Rational Software Corp. and CommerceOne Inc.

Booch, G., I. Jacobson, and J. Rumbaugh. 1997. *The Unified Modeling Language for Object Oriented Development*. Documentation set, version 1.0. Rational Software Corporation.

Boubez, T., M. Hondo, C. Kurt, J. Rodriguez, and D. Rogers. 2000. *UDDI Data Structure Reference*. V1.0UDDI Open Draft Specification. September 30. uddi.org.

Box, D., D. Ehnebuske, G. Kakivaya, A. Layman, N. Mendelsohn, H. F. Nielsen, S. Thatte, and D. Winer. 2000. *Simple Object Access Protocol (SOAP) 1.1*. Submission to the W3C.

Boyer, J. 2001. *Canonical XML, Version 1.0.* W3C Recommendation. March 15.

Bray, T., D. Hollander, and A. Layman (eds.). 1999. *Namespaces in XML.* World Wide Web Consortium. January 14.

Bray, T., J. Paoli, and C. M. Sperberg-McQueen (eds.). 1998. *Extensible Markup Language (XML) 1.0.* W3C Recommendation. February 10.

Buck, L. 1999. *Modeling Relational Data in XML.* Extensibility.

Buck, L., J. Robie, and S. Vorthmann. 2000. *The Schema Adjunct Framework.* Draft. November 30.

Buck, L., S. Vorthmann, and J. Robie. 2000. *The Schema Adjunct Framework.* Draft. November 30. TIBCO Software and Software AG.

Bush, V. 1945. "As We May Think." *The Atlantic Monthly.* July.

Butler, K. A., C. Esposito, and R. Hebron. 1999. "Connecting the Design of Software to the Design of Work." *Communications of the ACM* 42(1).

Carlson, D. 2001. *Modeling XML Applications with UML: Practical e-Business Applications.* Addison-Wesley.

Ceri, S., P. Fraternali, and A. Bongio. 2000. *Web Modeling Language (WebML): A Modeling Language for Designing Web Sites.* Dipartimento di Elettronica e Informazione, Politecnico di Milano, Italy.

Chamberlin, D., J. Clark, D. Florescu, J. Robie, J. Siméon, and M. Stefanescu. 2001. *XQuery: A Query Language for XML.* W3C Working Draft. June 7.

Chamberlin, D., P. Frankhauser, M. Marchiori, and J. Robie. *XML Query Use Cases.* W3C Working Draft. June 8.

Chang, W. W. 1998. *A Discussion of the Relationship Between RDF-Schema and UML.* W3C Note. August 4.

Chavez, A., and P. Maes. 1996. "Kasbah, An Agent Marketplace for Buying and Selling Goods." *Proc. of the 1st International Conf. on the Practical Application of Intelligent Agents and Multi-Agent Technology (PAAM'96).* London, April 22–24, pp. 75–90.

Chen, P. P. 1976. "The Entity-Relationship Model: Toward a Unified View of Data." *ACM Transactions on Database Systems* 1(1): 9–36.

Chen, P. P., B. Thalheim, and L. Y. Wong. 1999. *Future Directions of Conceptual Modeling.* Louisiana State University, Baton Rouge.

Christensen, E., F. Curbera, G. Meredith, and S. Weerawarana. 2001. *Web Services Description Language (WSDL) 1.1.* W3C Note. March 15.

Clark, J. (ed.). 1999a. *Associating Style Sheets with XML documents, Version 1.0.* W3C Recommendation. June 29.

Clark, J. (ed.). 1999b. *XSL Transformations (XSLT), Version 1.0.* W3C Recommendation. November 16.

Clark, J. (ed.). 2001. *XSL Transformations (XSLT), Version 1.1.* W3C Working Draft. August 24.

Clark, J., and S. DeRose (eds.). 1999. *XML Path Language (XPath), Version 1.0.* W3C Recommendation. November 16.

Clark, J., and M. Murata. *RELAX NG Tutorial.* Working Draft. June 12. OASIS.

Codd, E. F. 1970. "A Relational Model for Large Shared Data Banks." *Comm. ACM* 13(6): 377–387.

Codd, E. F. 1991. *The Relational Model for Database Management (Version 2).* Addison-Wesley, Reading, MA.

Conallen, J. 2000. *Working with XML Documents in UML.* rational.

Cowan, J., and R. Tobin (eds.). 2001. *XML Information Set.* W3C Recommendation. October 24.

CSS. 1996. *Cascading Style Sheets, Level 1.* W3C Recommendation. December 17. Revised January 11, 1999. *www.w3.org/TR/REC-CSS1.*

CSS. 1998. *Cascading Style Sheets, Level 2.* W3C Recommendation. May 12. *www.w3.org/TR/REC-CSS2.*

Daum, B. 2002. *The XML Schema Book.* Morgan Kaufmann Publishers, San Francisco.

Daum, B., and C. Horak. 2001. *The XML Shockwave, What Every CEO Needs to Know about the Key Technology for the Economy.* Software AG, Darmstadt, Germany.

Daum, B., and M. Scheller. 2000. *Success with Electronic Business.* Addison-Wesley, Harlow, England.

Davis, R., and R. G. Smith. 1983. "Negotiation as a Metaphor for Distributed Problem Solving." *Artificial Intelligence* 20: 63–109.

DCMI. 2000. *Dublin Core Qualifiers.* Dublin Core Metadata Initiative. July 11.

DeRose, S., E. Maler, and R. Daniel, Jr. 2001. *XML Pointer Language (XPointer), Version 1.0.* W3C Last Call Working Draft. January 8.

DeRose, S., E. Maler, and D. Orchard (eds.). 2001. *XML Linking Language (XLink) Version 1.0.* W3C Recommendation. June 27.

Dignum, F. P. M. 2000. *FLBC: From Messages to Protocols.* Dept. of Computer Science, Einhoven University of Technology.

Doerr, M. 1998. *Electronic Communication on Diverse Data—The Rose of the oo CIDOC Reference Model.* ICS FORTH, Crete, Greece.

Dubinko, M., J. Dietl, R. Merrick, D. Raggett, T. V. Raman, and L. B. Welsh. 2001. *XForms 1.0.* W3C Working Draft. August 28.

Eastlake, D., and J. Reagle (eds.). 2001. *XML Encryption Syntax and Processing.* W3C Working Draft. October 18.

Eastlake, D., J. Reagle, and D. Solo (eds.). 2001. *XML-Signature Syntax and Processing.* W3C Proposed Recommendation. August 20.

Eisenberg, J. D. 1991. "An Introduction to Scalable Vector Graphics." *www.xml.com/pub/a/ 2001/03/21/svg.html.*

Ellis, C. A., and K. Keddara. 2000. "A Workflow Change Is a Workflow." In W. van der Aalst, J. Desel, and A. Oberweis (eds.), *Business Process Management.* LNCS 1806. Springer, Berlin/Heidelberg.

Ennser, L., P. Leo, T. Meszaros, and E. Valade. 2000. "The XML Files: Using XML for B2B and B2C Applications." *IBM Redbook,* February. *www.redbooks.ibm.com/redpieces/pdfs/ sg246104.pdf.*

Fallside, D. C. (ed.). 2001. *XML Schema Part 0: Primer.* W3C Recommendation. May 2.

Finin, T., et al. 1993. *Specification of the KQML Agent-Communication Language.* Draft of the DARPA Knowledge Sharing Initiative. External Interfaces Workgroup. June 15.

Forsberg, K., and L. Dannstedt. 2000. *Extensible Use of RDF in a Business Context.* Viktoria Institute, Adera and Volvo Information Technology, Gothenburg, Sweden.

Fowler, M., and K. Scott. 1997. *UML Distilled.* Addison-Wesley.

Franklin, S., and A. Graesser. 1996. "Is It an Agent, or Just a Program? A Taxonomy for Autonomous Agents." In J. P. Müller and N. R. Jennings (eds.), *Intelligent Agents III, Proc. of the ECAI'96 Workshop ATAL.* Budapest/Hungary, August 12–13. Springer, Berlin/Heidelberg, pp. 21–35.

Gamma, E., R. Helm, R. Johnson, and J. Vlissides. 1995. *Design Patterns—Elements of Reusable Object-Oriented Software.* Addison-Wesley, Reading, MA.

Gardner, H. 1985. *The Mind's New Science. A History of the Cognitive Revolution.* Basic Books, New York.

Garzotto, F., P. Paolini, and D. Schwabe. 1993. "HDM—A Model-Based Approach to Hypertext Application Design." *TOIS* 11(1): 1–26.

Genesereth, M. R., and S. Ketchpel. 1994. "Software Agents." *Communications of the ACM* 37(7): 48–53.

Giga Information Group. 2001. "Giga Survey: XML Achieving Mainstream Usage." April 30.

Goldfarb, C. F., and P. Prescod. 2000. *The XML-Handbook, Second Edition.* Addison-Wesley, Harlow, England.

Gotthard, G. 1979. "Life as Poly-Contexturality." In *Beiträge zur Grundlegung einer operationsfähigen Dialektik.* Felix Meiner Verlag, Hamburg.

Guarino, N. 1997. *Understanding, Building, and Using Ontologies.* LADSEB-CNR, National Research Council, Padova, Italy.

Guarino, N. 1998. *Formal Ontology and Information Systems.* LADSEB-CNR, Padova.

Guarino, N., and C. Welty. 1998. *Conceptual Modeling and Ontological Analysis.* LADSEB-CNR, Padova.

Guha, R. V. 1995. *Contexts: A Formalization and Some Applications.* Ph.D. Thesis.

Guilfoyle, C. 1998. "Vendors of Intelligent Agent Technologies, A Market Overview." In N. R. Jennings and M. J. Wooldridge (eds.), *Agent Technology: Foundations, Applications, and Markets.* Springer, Berlin/Heidelberg, pp. 91–104.

Hailstone, R. 2000. *Yellowworld-Portal—The Hub of eBusiness in Switzerland.* IDC White Paper.

Halpin, T. 1999. "Entity Relationship Modeling from an ORM Perspective." *Journal of Conceptual Modeling,* December 1999–August 2000.

Harold, E. R. 2001. *The XML Bible, Second Edition.* IDG Books.

Heintz, J., and W. E. Kimber. 1999. *Using UML to Define XML Document Types.* DataChannel, Austin, TX.

Helio. 1999. "The SMIL Tutorial." *www.helio .org/products/smil/tutorial/chapter3/list_of_ media.html.*

Henderson, P. 1997. *Formal Models of Process Components.* Department of Electronics and Computer Science, University of Southhampton. August.

Hewlett-Packard. 2001. *e-speak, Architectural Specification.* Release A.0, Documentation Release A.03.11.00. January.

Hoare, C. 1985. *Communicating Sequential Processes.* Prentice-Hall International Ltd., Hemel Hempstead (UK).

Hosoya, H., and B. Pierce. 2000. "XDuce: A Typed XML Processing Language (Preliminary Report)." In *Proceedings of Third International Workshop on the Web and Databases (WebDB2000).*

HTML. 1999. *HTML 4.01 Specification.* W3C Recommendation. December 24. *www.w3 .org/TR/HTML401.*

IBM. 2000a. "B-to-B e-Commerce, Offering Suppliers New Opportunities to Connect with Buyers." *www-4.ibm.com/software/ webservers/commerce/community/resources/ btob_white.pdf.* September 13.

IBM. 2000b. "Business to Business Integration with Trading Partner Agreements." *www.ibm.com/developers/xml/tpaml/ b2b-integration-with-tpa.pdf.* September 13.

IBM. 2000c. "The XML Files, Using XML for B2B and B2C Applications." Red Book Draft. *www.redbooks.ibm.com/redpieces/pdfs/ sg246104.pdf.* September 13.

ISO/IEC. 1997. *Information Technologies— Open-edi Reference Model.* ISO/IEC14662.

JAXB. 2001. *The Java Architecture for XML Binding, User's Guide.* Early Access Draft. Sun Microsystems.

Jeffcoate, J., and A. Templeton. 1992. *Multimedia Strategies for the Business Market.* Ovum, London.

Jelliffe, R. 2001. *The Schematron, An XML Structure Validation Language Using Patterns in Trees.* Academia Sinica Computing Centre, Taibei.

Jennings, N. R., et al. 1996. Using Intelligent Agents to Manage Business Processes." In B. Crabtree and N. R. Jennings (eds.), *Proc. of the 1st International Conf. on Practical Applications of Intelligent Agents and Multi-Agent Technology (PAAM'96).* London, April 22–24, pp. 345–360.

Jennings, N. R., and M. J. Wooldridge. 1998. "Applications of Intelligent Agents." In N. R. Jennings and M. J. Wooldridge (eds.), *Agent Technology: Foundations, Applications, and Markets.* Springer, Berlin/Heidelberg, pp. 3–28.

Kamada, T. 1998. *Compact HTML for Small Information Appliances.* W3C Note. February 9. Available at *http://www.w3.org/TR/1998/ NOTE-compactHTML-19980209.*

Kamada, T., T. Asada, M. Ishikawa, and S. Matsui (eds.). 1999. *HTML 4.0 Guidelines for Mobile Access.* W3C Note. March 15.

Kay, M. 2001. *XSLT Programmer's Reference 2nd Edition.* wrox.

Kimber, W. E. 1998. *A Tutorial Introduction to SGML Architectures.* ISOGEN International.

Kimbrough, S. O., and S. A. Moore. 1994. "Message Management Systems at Work: Prototypes for Business Communication." *Journal of Organizational Computing* 5(2): 83–100.

Koegel, J. F. 1992. "On the Design of Multimedia Interchange Formats." In P. V. Rangan (ed.), *Proc. of the 3rd Int'l Workshop on Network and Operating System Support for*

Digital Audio and Video. November, pp. 262–271.

Kozierok, R., and P. Maes. 1993. "A Learning Interface Agent for Scheduling Meetings." In *Proc. of the ACM-SIGCHI International Workshop on Intelligent User Interface.* Florida, pp. 81–93.

Kretz, F., and F. Colaitis. 1992. "Standardizing Hypermedia Information Objects." *IEEE Comm. Magazine* (May): 60–70.

Kroenke, D. M. 1995. *Database Processing: Fundamentals, Design, and Implementation.* MacMillan.

Lee, R. 1999. "Distributed Electronic Trade Scenarios: Representation, Design, Prototyping." *IJEC* 3(2): 105–136.

Le Hors, A., G. Nicol, L. Wood, M. Champion, and S. Byrne. 2001. *Document Object Model (DOM) Level 3 Core Specification, Version 1.0.* W3C Working Draft. September 13.

Lenat, D. B. 2001. *From 2001 to 2001: Common Sense and the Mind of HAL.* CYCORP.

Leventhal, M. 1999. "XSL Is an Ugly, Difficult Language." *xml.com.* May 20.

List, B., et al. 2000. "The Process Warehouse Approach for Inter-Organisational e-Business Process Improvement. In H. Thoma et al. (eds.), *Proc. of the 6th International Conference on Re-Technologies for Information Systems Preparing to E-Business.* Österreichische Computer Gesellschaft.

Little, T. D. C. 1994. "Time-Based Representation and Delivery." In J. F. Koegel-Buford (ed.), *Multimedia Systems.* Addison-Wesley, pp. 175–200.

Lovett, C. 2000. "UDDI: An XML Web Service." XML Web Workshop, Microsoft Corporation.

Luttermann, H., and M. Grauer. 1999. "Using Interactive, Temporal Visualizations for WWW-based Presentation and Exploration of Spatio-Temporal Data." In *Workshop on Spatio-Temporal Database Management.* LNCS 1678. Springer, Berlin/Heidelberg, pp. 100–118.

Maes, P. 1994. "Agents That Reduce Work and Information Overload." *Communications of the ACM* 37(7): 31–40.

Malhotra, A., J. Robie, and M. Rys. 2001. *XML Syntax for XQuery 1.0 (XQueryX).* W3C Working Draft. June 7.

Marchiori, M., and J. Saarela. 2000. *Towards the Semantic Web: Metalog.* The World Wide Web Consortium.

Marsh, J. 2001. *XML Base.* W3C Recommendation. June 27.

Marsh, J., and D. Orchard. 2001. *XML Inclusions (XInclude) Version 1.0.* W3C Working Draft. May 16.

Martin, J. 1993. *Principles of Object Oriented Analysis and Design.* Prentice Hall, Englewood Cliffs, NJ.

Mayfield, J., Y. Labrou, and T. Finin. 1996. "Evaluation of KQML as an Agent Communication Language." In M. Wooldridge, J. P. Müller, and M. Tambe (eds.), *Intelligent Agents II, Proc. of the 1995 Workshop on Agent Theories, Architectures, and Languages.* Springer, Berlin/Heidelberg.

McCarron, S., S. Pemberton, and T. V. Roman. 2000. *XML Events.* W3C Working Draft. October 26.

McCarthy, J. 1998. *Notes on Formalizing Context.* Computer Science Department, Stanford University.

McCarthy, J. 1999. *The Common Business Communication Language.* Computer Science Department, Stanford University.

McCarthy, J. 2001. *The Robot and the Baby.* Computer Science Department, Stanford University.

Megginson, D. 1998a. *Structuring XML Documents.* Simon & Schuster.

Megginson, D. 1998b. *Using the XAF Package for Java.* Megginson Technologies.

Melnik, S. 2000. *Representing UML in RDF.* Stanford University.

Meyer, B. 1997. *Object-oriented Software Construction.* Prentice Hall, Upper Saddle River, NJ.

Meyer-Boudnik, T., and W. Effelsberg. 1995. "MHEG Explained." *IEEE Multimedia* 2(1): 26–38.

Microsoft. 2000. *Microsoft BizTalk Server, BizTalk Framework 2.0: Document and Message Specification.* December.

Milner, R. 1999. *Communicating and Mobile Systems, The π-Calculus.* Cambridge University Press.

Moore, S. A. 1996. *Categorizing Automated Messages.* Computer & Information Systems Department, University of Michigan Business School.

Müller, J. P., and N. R. Jennings (eds.). 1996. *Intelligent Agents III, Proc. of the ECAI'96 Workshop ATAL.* Budapest/Hungary, August 12–13. Springer, Berlin/Heidelberg.

Mylopoulos, J., L. Chung, and E. Yu. 1999. "From Object-Oriented to Goal-Oriented Requirements Analysis." *Communications of the ACM* 42(1).

Nelson, T. H. 1982. *Literary Machines.* Mindful Press.

Newcomb, S. R. 1995. "Multimedia Interchange Using SGML/HyTime, Part I: Structures." *IEEE Multimedia* (2): 86–89.

Newcomb, S. R., N. A. Kipp, and V. T. Newcomb. 1991. "HyTime." *Communications of the ACM* 34(11): 67–83.

Nielsen, H. F., and S. Thatte. 2001. *SOAP Routing Protocol.* Microsoft.

Nielsen, J. 1997. *Multimedia and Hypertext: The Internet and Beyond.* AP Professional, Boston.

Norman, T. J., et al. 1996. "Designing and Implementing a Multi-Agent Architecture for Business Process Management" In J. P. Müller and N. R. Jennings (eds.), *Intelligent Agents III, Proc. of the ECAI'96 Workshop ATAL.* Budapest/Hungary, August 12–13. Springer, Berlin/Heidelberg, pp. 261–275.

Nwana, H. S. 1996. "Software Agents: An Overview." *Knowledge Engineering Review* 11(3): 205–244.

OASIS. 2000. *Enabling Electronic Business with ebXML.* OASIS and UN/CEFACT.

OASIS. 2001a. *Collaboration-Protocol Profile and Agreement; Specification Version 1.0.* OASIS and UN/CEFACT.

OASIS. 2001b. *ebXML Business Process Specification Schema Version 1.01.* OASIS and UN/ CEFACT.

OASIS. 2001c. *ebXML Catalog of Common Business Processes, Document Version: 0.91.* OASIS and UN/CEFACT.

OASIS. 2001d. *ebXML Specification for the Application of XML Based Assembly and Context Rules, ebXML Core Components, Version 1.01.* OASIS and UN/CEFACT.

OASIS. 2001e. *Using UDDI to Find ebXML Reg/Reps.* OASIS and UN/CEFACT.

OASIS. 2001f. *ebXML Registry Information Model v1.0.* OASIS and UN/CEFACT.

O'Leary, D. E., and P. Selfridge. 1999. "Knowledge Management for Best Practices Intelligence." *ACM New Visions of AI in Practice* 10(4).

Olle, W. 1978. *The CODASYL Approach to Data Base Management.* Wiley, New York.

Park, D. 2000. *Minimal XML 1.0 Version: 2000-04-11.* Docuverse.

Partridge, C. 2000. *Business Objects: Re-engineering for Re-use.* Butterworth-Heinemann.

PDF. 2000. *PDF Reference, 2nd Edition.* Addison-Wesley. Available from *partners.adobe.com/asn/developer/technotes/acrobatpdf.html.*

Pepper, S. 1999. *Euler, Topic Maps, and Revolution.* STEP Infotek A.S, Oslo.

Pepper, S. 2000. *The TAO of Topic Maps.* STEP Infotek A.S, Oslo.

Portela, M. del Carmen. 1992. *Settlement Patterns in Unplanned Areas, Case Study San José de Chirica, Ciudad Guayana, Venezuela.* School of Architecture, McGill University, Montreal.

Porter, M. E. 1998. *Competitive Advantage, Creating and Sustaining Superior Performance.* Free Press, New York. Reprinted.

Raskin, J.-F., and Y.-H. Tan. 1996. *How to Model Normative Behavior in Petri Nets.* euridis, Erasmus University Rotterdam.

RDF. 1999. *Resource Description Framework Model and Syntax Specification.* W3C Recommendation. February 22.

RDF. 2000. *Resource Description Framework Schema Specification 1.0.* W3C Candidate Recommendation. March 27.

RosettaNet. 2001. *Several Documents and Specifications.www.rosettanet.org.*

Rossi, G., D. Schwabe, and F. Lyardet. 1999. "Web Application Models Are More Than Conceptual Models." In P. P. Chen, D. W. Embley, and S. W. Liddle (eds.), *Proc. Int. Workshop on the World Wide Web and Con-*

ceptual Modeling. Paris, October. Springer-Verlag.

Sachs, M., A. Dan, T. Nguyen, R. Kearney, S. Hidayatullah, and D. Dias. 2000. "Executable Trading-Partner Agreements in Electronic Commerce." IBM Corporation. *www.ibm.com/developer/xml/tpaml/tpapaper.pdf.* September 13.

Schaur, E. 1991. *Non-planned Settlements.* IL39. Institute for Lightweight Structures, University of Stuttgart, Germany.

Scheer, A. W., and M. Nüttgens. 2000. "ARIS Architecture and Reference Models for Business Process Management." In W. van der Aalst, J. Desel, and A. Oberweis (eds.), *Business Process Management.* LNCS 1806. Springer, Berlin/Heidelberg.

SMIL. 2000. *Synchronized Multimedia Integration Language (SMIL 2.0) Specification.* W3C Recommendation. August 7.

Smith, B. 1998. *Objects and Their Environments: From Aristotle to Ecological Ontology.* Department of Philosophy, Center for Cognitive Science and National Center for Geographic Information and Analysis, University of Buffalo.

Smith, B., and L. Zaibert. 1997. *The Metaphysics of Real Estate.* University of Buffalo.

Steinmetz, R., and K. Nahrstedt. 1995. *Multimedia: Computing, Communications and Applications.* Prentice Hall.

SVG. 2000. *Scalable Vector Graphics (1.0) Specification.* W3C Recommendation. September 4.

Thalheim, B. 1999. *Fundamentals of Entity-Relationship Modeling.* Springer-Verlag, Heidelberg.

Thalheim, B. 2000. Entity-Relationship Modeling. Springer-Verlag, Heidelberg.

Thompson, H. S., D. Beech, M. Maloney, and N. Mendelsohn (eds.). 2001. *XML Schema Part 1: Structures.* W3C Recommendation. May 2.

Thorpe, M. 2001. "Business Rule Exchange—The Next XML Wave." In *Proc. of the XMLeurope.* Berlin, May 21–25.

UDDI. 2000. *UDDI Technical White Paper.* uddi.org.

Uschold, M., and M. Gruninger. 1996. "Ontologies: Principles, Methods and Applica-tions." *The Knowledge Engineering Review* 11(2): 93–136.

Uschold, M., M. King, S. Moralee, and Y. Zorgios. 1997. *The Enterprise Ontology.* AIAI, The University of Edinburgh.

van der Aalst, W., J. Desel, and A. Oberweis (eds.). 2000. *Business Process Management.* LNCS 1806. Springer, Berlin/Heidelberg.

VXML. 2000. *Voice Extensible Markup Language (VoiceXML) Version 2.0.* W3C Working Draft. October 23.

WAE. 2000. *Wireless Application Protocol. Wireless Application Environment Overview, Version 1.3.* www1.wapforum.org/tech/documents/ WAP-195-WAEOverview-20000329-a.pdf. March 29.

W3C. 2000. "CSS & XSL. Which Should I Use?" *www.w3.org/Style/CSS-vs-XSL.* February 29.

W3C. 2001a. "What Are Style Sheets?" *www.w3.org/Style/#why.* February 1.

W3C. 2001b. "Voice Browser Activity." *www.w3.org/Voice.* March 24.

W3C 2001c. *W3C Semantic Web Activity Statement, Version 1.7.* World Wide Web Consortium. February.

Wahl, T., and K. Rothermehl. 1994. "Representing Time in Multimedia Systems." In *IEEE 1st International Conference on Multimedia Computing and Systems,* pp. 538–543.

WAP. 2000. *Wireless Application Protocol, White Paper.* WAP Forum. *www.wapforum.org/what/WAP_white_pages.pdf.* February 2.

WBXML. 2000. *WAP Binary XML Content Format, Version 1.3.* Approved May 15. *www1.wapforum.org/tech/documents/WAP-192-WBXML-20000306-a.pdf.*

Weigand, H., W.-J. van den Heuvel, and F. Dignum. 1998. *Modeling Electronic Commerce Transactions, A Layered Approach.* Tilburg University and Eindhoven University.

Williams, S., and M. Jones. 2001. *XML Protocol Abstract Model.* W3C Working Draft. July 9.

WML. 2000a. *Wireless Application Protocol. Wireless Markup Language Specification, Version 1.3.* www1.wapforum.org/tech/documents/WAP-191-WML-20000219-a.pdf. February 19.

WML. 2000b. *Wireless Application Protocol. WMLScript Standard Libraries Specification, Version 1.3. www1.wapforum.org/tech/documents/WAP-194-WMLScriptLibs-20000324-a.pdf.* June.

XHTML. 2000a. *XHTML 1.0: The Extensible HyperText Markup Language. A Reformulation of HTML 4 in XML 1.0.* W3C Recommendation. *www.w3.org/TR/xhtml1/.* January 26.

XHTML. 2000b. *XHTML Basic.* W3C Recommendation. *www.w3.org/TR/ xhtml-basic.* December 19.

XHTML. 2001a. *Modularization of XHTML.* W3C Recommendation. April 10.

XHTML. 2001b. *XHTML 1.1—Module Based XHTML.* W3C Recommendation. May 31.

XMI. 1999. *XML Metadata Interchange (XMI), Version 1.1.* Joint Submission. Object Management Group.

XML-RPC. 1999. *XML-RPC Specification.* UserLand.

XSL. 2001. *Extensible Stylesheet Language (XSL) Version 1.0.* W3C Recommendation. October 15.

Index

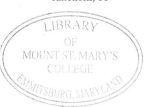